THE AGE OF CRISIS:
DEVIANCE, DISORGANIZATION,
AND SOCIETAL PROBLEMS

Harper & Row, Publishers

THE AGE OF CRISIS:

deviance, disorganization, and societal problems

ALFRED M. MIRANDE
University of California, Riverside

New York, Evanston, San Francisco, London

Sponsoring Editor: Ronald Taylor
Project Editor: Carol E. W. Edwards
Designer: Jared Pratt
Production Supervisor: Stefania J. Taflinska

THE AGE OF CRISIS: Deviance, Disorganization, and Societal Problems

Library of Congress Cataloging in Publication Data
Mirande, Alfred M   1940–
   The age of crisis: deviance, disorganization, and
societal problems.
   Includes bibliographical references.
   1. Social problems. 2. Deviant behavior.
3. United States—Social conditions. I. Title.
HN18.M56   362'.042   74–9326
ISBN 0–06–044557–2

The quotation on page 143 is reprinted from Dwight Macdonald, *Diogenes* (No. 3, Summer 1953, pp. 1–17) an international quarterly published under the auspices of Unesco.

The quotation on page 188 is reprinted by permission of The Society For The Study Of Social Problems from Alexander Liazas, "The Poverty of the Sociology of Deviance," in *Social Problems*, vol. 20, no. 1:119.

The quotation on page 235 is reprinted by permission of the *Harvard Law Review* from Roscoe Pound, "A Survey of Social Interests," *Harvard Law Review* 57 (October 1943): 1–39.

To Michele

Contents

Preface

My initial interest in writing this book developed from teaching courses in social problems and deviant behavior. The longer I taught, the more dissatisfied I became with both the available texts and the state of the field in general. I was particularly struck by the disparity that exists between advanced deviance texts, which are geared primarily to majors, advanced students, and professional sociologists; and introductory problems books, which are geared to nonmajors. Such introductory texts lack a theoretical or sociological perspective. *The Age of Crisis* is organized around three dominant approaches to the study of deviance and societal ills—Social Problems, Deviant Behavior, and Social Disorganization. While the approaches are obviously interrelated, each emerged from a distinctive historical tradition and is characterized by different assumptions and foci. By isolating the differences and similarities between the approaches, I hope to reduce some of the ambiguity that surrounds this area of study.

The field of social problems has been ridiculed and stigmatized by respectable sociologists. It has been viewed as dealing with interesting and topical issues, but not with serious sociology. A colleague, frustrated by the lack of sophistication among the "warm bodies" that we have in lower-division classes, recently asked in a tone of desperation, "But when do we teach the real meat of sociology?". My response was that I teach serious sociology at all levels. In fact, I know only one sociology and am lost when I am asked to differentiate between "serious" and "nonserious" sociology. Sociologists have long held to the mistaken notion that there are two sociologies—one for would-be sociologists and the other for nonmajors in service courses. This book is based on the premise that the sociological perspective and the sociological imagination are not the exclusive domain of professional sociologists, but rather are potentially available to all.

Sociology has also been characterized by a sense of dualism that divides ideas into two mutually exclusive categories—the theoretical and the practical. Many sociological theories are so abstract that they appear unrelated to the problems of everyday life. I subscribe to the belief that

xi

the most useful ideas are theoretical. That is, theories are useful because they help to make sense out of our daily problems and experiences. I have tried to follow C. Wright Mills in the tradition that he established of dedicating sociology to the task of bridging the gap between "private troubles and public issues." Thus, it is my hope that I have written a book that is both theoretical and practical. I hope, however, to avoid the pitfall of pushing practicality to the point that a work is dated and obsolete before it is published. Old ideas and questions are frequently as relevant as new ones. In fact, the most relevant issues are not those of the moment, but those that transcend society and time.

I have few persons to thank but my debt to them is substantial. Several colleagues and students made useful comments and suggestions on various parts of the manuscript; their most valuable contribution, however, was making their personal libraries accessible to me. I am also grateful to Karen Wangerud for diligently typing the manuscript. My greatest debt is to my wife, Mary, who read and commented on the entire book. Last, but certainly not least, I would like to thank my parents, Rosa Maria and Xavier, for making me possible and for giving me a rich legacy.

A.M.M.
University of California, Riverside

Introduction: the study of social problems

The study of social problems and social disorganization is almost as old as man, who since antiquity has been concerned with the problem of social order in society. Social philosophers throughout history have asked why individuals form societies and do not simply pursue their own selfish interests. The focus of these analyses has fluctuated between two polar extremes; one sees the lack of order as problematic, and the other sees overconformity and the lack of autonomy as the root of many evils. Hobbes exemplifies the first view, and Freud the second. Despite their differences, the two views share a common interest in the relation of the individual to the society.

Sociology had its genesis in the question of social order. It was only after social philosophers began to see social order as an empirical problem that sociology was recognized as a distinct science. Many of the early sociologists were committed to a philosophy of "social action," feeling that sociology had to justify its existence by solving social ills. A close link between sociology and social problems was thus established, but the link has, in retrospect, had both positive and negative consequences. On the positive side, some of the most important contributions to sociology have been made by men deeply interested in the problems of society (e.g., Durkheim's study of suicide). In addition, sociologists' concern with social problems has made sociology more relevant to the larger society. On the negative side, as a result of its ties to popular problems the field of social problems has become somewhat "marginal" to sociology. It has been viewed as a field that is interesting and provocative but that contributes little to the advancement of sociology as a science. These disparate views with respect to the role of social action in sociology have contributed to the emergence of three distinct approaches to the study of social problems and social disorganization: (1) social problems, (2) deviant behavior, and (3) social disorganization.

APPROACHES TO THE STUDY OF SOCIAL PROBLEMS

Social problems approach

This is undoubtedly the oldest and most common approach to the field. A typical definition of a social problem is a condition that is viewed as undesirable by a substantial segment of society. Some of the more typical problems studied are crime, delinquency, drug addiction, race and ethnic relations, prostitution, and the population explosion. At first glance it may appear that the problems facing American society are self-evident and that one could easily get consensus on what these major problems are. However, what is viewed as a problem by some may be viewed as desirable by others; for example, crime is defined as a problem by many citizens, but most racketeers and other members of organized crime do not agree with this definition. Prostitution is an excellent illustration of this point. It is usually included as a major problem in sociology texts, and many persons believe that it should be eliminated. Yet, sociologists contend that prostitution fulfills some important functions (Davis, 1937 and 1971:345–347). It provides an outlet for those who cannot get sexual gratification through legitimate channels. There are persons who are so physically or socially repulsive that they cannot effectively negotiate heterosexual relations. In addition, prostitution provides a fast and relatively inexpensive outlet without interpersonal obligations. One could argue that eliminating prostitution may create more problems than it solves. The elimination of prostitution without other basic changes in social institutions might, for example, lead to an increase in the prevalence of rape. My basic aim here is not to advocate the legalization of prostitution, but rather to point out that certain conditions may be undesirable when evaluated by moral or personal standards and desirable when evaluated by more objective criteria.

Two basic questions must be answered in defining a social problem. First, who is to define the problem? Second, what criteria are to be used in evaluating the problem? The most typical answers to these questions have been that members of society should define social problems and that they should use personal criteria (i.e., their own values or conceptions of the desirable). This view of social problems has contributed to the "marginality" of this field to sociology. To the extent that "problems" are defined by the members of a society rather than by scientists using scientific criteria the status of social problems as a subfield within a science is questionable. There is an additional assumption underlying the problems approach, sometimes implicit but usually explicit, which casts doubt on the scientific status of the field. This assumption is that the elimination of social problems is a major goal of sociology. As a result there has been much focus on solutions, or strategies for resolving social ills. This assumption has led to a confusion of sociology and social work about which more will be said later. For the moment, it should be noted that if scientists prescribe solutions to social problems, the assumption is that they "know what is best" for society. Science can certainly assess the probable outcomes of alternative courses of action, but to select the most desirable course requires the imposition of values, which is beyond the realm of science.

Deviant behavior approach

Before discussing this approach it will be necessary to distinguish between sociology and social psychology. While in practice sociology and social psychology are closely linked and many sociologists identify themselves as social psychologists, there are important analytical distinctions between the two fields. Sociology can be defined as the scientific study of the organization of human social behavior. It is concerned with the network of patterned social relations. Social psychology, on the other hand, is the study of the relationship of the individual to the society. It is concerned both with the effect of the society on the individual and that of the individual on the society. This distinction can be illustrated within the field of the family. The sociologist may be interested in the functions performed by the family institution for the society (e.g., reproduction and the training of new members), while the social psychologist may examine the consequences of certain child-rearing practices for the personality development of the child.

The founders of American sociology had a strong social-psychological, at times mainly a psychological, orientation. Many, like Mead, Cooley, Thomas, and Znaniecki, fall into the branch of social psychology that is commonly known as symbolic interactionism.[1] The symbolic interactionist school overlaps closely with the Chicago school (Manis and Meltzer, 1972:xi). During the first quarter of the century the University of Chicago and its brand of social psychology dominated much of sociology (Faris, 1967:88–99). The strong social-psychological focus of American sociolo-

---

[1] For discussion and review of symbolic interactionism see Manis and Meltzer (1972), Stone and Farberman (1970), and Cardwell (1971).

gists contrasts sharply with the more collectivist, and purely sociological, orientation of European sociologists such as Comte, Spencer, Durkheim, LeBon, and Tönnies.

The concern of pioneer American sociologists with social problems, coupled with their social-psychological emphasis, led to the development of the deviant behavior approach to social problems. Some of the most important contributions to the deviant behavior approach were made at the University of Chicago by its faculty and students, who spread their influence to other universities throughout the country. The deviant behavior approach will be discussed in greater detail in Part Two. Here, the primary characteristics of the approach will simply be outlined.

Deviant behavior is usually defined as behavior that fails to conform to certain specified standards or norms. The approach tends to be social-psychological because the basic question it seeks to answer is: Under what conditions are persons likely to conform to social norms? This approach has usually been more empirical and less value laden than the social problems approach, and consequently, more in the mainstream of American sociology.

Social disorganization approach

The social disorganization approach is primarily sociological in focus. Social organization has been defined as patterned and coordinated social relationships among interdependent persons or groups. It is the core of sociology. The sociologist's major concern is with patterned and predictable social behavior. Both the sociologist and the social psychologist are interested in the problem of order, or social organization, but they approach the problem from somewhat different perspectives. Generally speaking, the sociologist is interested in how the society, or group, functions as a relatively cohesive entity; the social psychologist is interested in why individuals organize collectively and submit to social control.

In contemporary sociology social disorganization is sometimes treated as a concept that is separate and distinct from social organization. Among sociologists there are experts in social organization as well as specialists in social disorganization, deviant behavior, and social problems. This distinction is, of course, extremely superficial because social organization and social disorganization are inseparable concepts; that is, they represent two ends of the same phenomenon. It makes little sense to talk about a society that is organized and another that is disorganized. In a totally organized society, socialization would be so effective that under all conditions every individual would want to do what the society expected him to do. Social relations would be perfectly coordinated, and deviant behavior would be nonexistent. Complete social organization is found only in fictional societies such as those of Plato's *Republic*, Sir Thomas More's *Utopia*, Huxley's *Brave New World*, and Orwell's *1984*. Similarly, a state of complete disorganization is never found. Hobbes contemplated the possibility of a "war of all against all," a society in which each man pursued his own selfish interests, but this "state of nature" has not been realized. In fact, in a state in which each man pursues his own interests and in which there is a complete absence of social organization, society, by definition, ceases to exist. On the other hand, it would appear that personality, as it is usually conceptualized, would cease to exist in a perfectly organized society. The idiosyncratic and relatively unique component of behavior would be eliminated. From this discussion it seems clear that the organization or disorganization of society is a matter of degree. The organization of any particular society is somewhere between the two polar extremes of a perfectly coordinated order and complete chaos.

As was mentioned previously, the social disorganization approach is more consistent with a purely sociological perspective than is the deviant behavior approach. The deviant behavior approach explores the conditions under which persons are likely to conform to social norms or standards, while the social disorganization approach is interested in the conditions that make for social cohesion in a society or group. The major unit of analysis in the first approach is behavior and its relation to social norms (i.e., the extent to which it deviates or conforms to norms). The unit of analysis in the second approach is the society or group. In other words, deviant behavior is assessed by comparing the correspondence between the standards of the group and the behavior of its members, and social disorganization is assessed by looking at the integration and coordination of the parts of the group or society. It should be noted that the distinction between deviant behavior and social disorganization is analytical—this does not mean that these two concepts are unrelated in the empirical world. Deviant behavior and social disorganization are intricately related. Persistent deviant behavior will usually, but not always, lead to social disorganization. In the United States there are many examples of deviant behavior that appear to have almost no impact on the organization of the society and there is much deviance that fulfills positive functions for the society. Prostitution, as was noted earlier, is defined as deviant behavior (on the part of both the prostitute and the client) and a social problem by the society at large, yet the oldest profession is found universally. The virtue of countless "nice" girls has undoubtedly been saved by prostitution. Despite the outrage of many citizens over the existence of prostitution, it seems clear that prostitution does little to bring about disorganization and may, in fact, promote organization in certain respects. More will be said about social disorganization later.

SOCIOLOGY AND SCIENCE

Nature of science

Sociology is sometimes defined as the science of human social behavior, or the scientific study of social organization. Although there are differences of opinion regarding what is the best or most desirable definition of sociology, there is general consensus that sociology is a science, or at least a would-be science. A discussion of the nature of science is therefore essential.[2] What is science? Probably everyone has an answer to this question. After all, we live in a society that places a strong value on science and courses in sciences are found throughout high school and college curricula. But unfortunately there are many misconceptions about science; for instance, science is frequently associated with a particular content, or subject. Some persons believe that a scientist is someone who studies atoms or molecules and wears a laboratory apron. It is even said that one is "scientific" if he is meticulous and precise in a particular undertaking. While this view is not completely wrong, it is limited, oversimplified, and somewhat misleading. Science is not a body of content but a general method of study that can be applied to any content. Science is a method of establishing empirically verifiable knowledge. Empirical knowledge is obtained directly or indirectly through the senses. Truth in science is established when competent observers agree that a particular phenomenon is empirically observable.

Science does not have a monopoly on the search for truth. Religion and philosophy, for example, also seek truth, but not empirical truth. Unlike religion and philosophy, truth in science is relative and always subject to modification in the light of new evidence. Contrary to popular belief, scientific knowledge is not absolute and unchangeable. The relative nature of science is evidenced by the form that scientific statements take. Scientific knowledge is always expressed through probabilistic statements: If certain conditions are met, then certain outcomes will follow. Science differs from other knowledge systems in that it "*combines* rational, empirical, and abstractive thought. . . . No system of knowledge is scientific unless it connects the observational and theoretic levels" (Willer, 1971:31).

The scientific status of sociology and other social sciences is questioned by many persons who have come to identify science with particular subject matter. Science has become identified for the most part with natural science. According to this view, the "sciences" (e.g., chemistry, physics, biology, and botany) study the natural world; other disciplines that study man or society are not regarded as true sciences because their subject matters are not natural phenomena and they are not subject therefore to prediction and control. The sociologist, on the other hand, takes the view that social phenomena are as much a part of the natural world as physical phenomena. He reasons that sociological data such as racial conflicts and prostitution are natural phenomena that can be studied with the same method used to study atoms and molecules. Sociological phenomena can be verified empirically; a race riot is as real as thunder or lightning. In short, sociology

[2] The reader interested in the nature of science and explanations in social science is referred to Cole (1972), Brown (1963), Greer (1969), Reynolds (1971), Meehan (1968), and Willer (1971).

rejects the view that man is a creature who is so unpredictable that his behavior cannot be studied scientifically. Thus no subject is inherently scientific or unscientific. The scientific method can be applied to any subject, and even the most traditionally scientific subjects may be studied nonscientifically. Astronomy, for example, is the scientific study of celestial bodies, and astrology is the nonscientific study of the same subject. The only similarity between the two fields is their concentration on celestial bodies. Man and society can also be studied from nonscientific perspectives. The study of man and his relation to society concerned men for many centuries before sociology came into existence. Philosophers, for example, have written thousands of volumes about utopian societies. As was mentioned earlier, their analyses of society have differed from the sociological in that philosophers prescribe how society should be ideally, whereas sociologists are interested in ascertaining how society is. Most religions also have well-developed conceptions about the basic nature of man and society. Man may be seen as basically evil, pursuing his own hedonistic ends, or as basically good, trustworthy and cooperating with other men. Another example of a nonscientific approach to society is the journalistic perspective. Journalists are very much concerned with society, especially its social problems. The journalist frequently employs empirical data, much of which is provided by social scientists, but his goals are quite different from those of the scientist. The journalist seeks to inform members of society and often to cure specific social ills. His major objective is not to analyze or understand societies in general, but rather to provide descriptive information. Finally, most members of society have their own personal conceptions of society. These views of society (philosophical, religious, journalistic, and personal) differ from the sociological perspective in that their primary goal is not to develop valid generalizations about the empirical world. The subject matter of sociology can, and frequently is, viewed from nonscientific perspectives. In fact, the sociologist as a person often sees society from these other perspectives.

Another common misconception about science is that it is always precise and quantitative. If something is quantifiable, it is assumed to be scientific, and if it is not, it is assumed to be out of the realm of science. This conclusion is a result of the emphasis on the peripheral, or secondary, characteristics of science. While quantification is desirable because it increases precision, it neither guarantees nor precludes science. One can be very scientific without mathematics, and very unscientific with mathematics. For many persons the link between mathematics and science is so strong that they regard mathematics as the epitome of science. Actually, mathematics per se is not a science (Willer, 1971:31). Mathematical concepts do not have empirical referents in the natural world, and the mathematician is not interested in developing generalizations about empirical phenomena. Mathematics is simply a tool that scientists, including sociologists, have found very useful for ordering their data and adding precision to their measurement of natural phenomena. In short, there is no necessary relationship between mathematics and science.

Goals of science

Science has two broad goals, prediction and explanation. Prediction is essential in science. An event can always be explained in an *ex post facto* manner, that is, after it occurs. A person who is prejudiced against Jews, for instance, might assert that they are extremely egocentric and will do anything to advance their own selfish interests. When he is told that Jews are the most generous minority group when it comes to supporting charities, he may assert that this demonstrates how Jews are always meddling in the affairs of others (Allport, 1958:13–14).

The prediction of events is an ultimate goal of science. However, prediction is not sufficient; science seeks to understand or explain specific empirical phenomena with more inclusive natural laws or theories. Prediction is a prerequisite to explanation, but one can certainly predict without understanding. A man vacationing in a high altitude, for instance, finds that his beard grows less rapidly during the day. He does not get a five-o'clock shadow until nine or ten in the evening. From this experience the man concludes that high altitude causes facial hair to grow less rapidly. Later he may discover that this causal inference was false and that the apparent slowdown in the growth of his beard was not due to the altitude but to the fact that while vacationing he was getting up later and shaving later in the morning. Another way of stating this same principle is that correlation does not prove cause and effect. From a simple correlation or association one does not know which of the factors is the cause of the other or if both factors are a consequence of a third factor. In order to establish causality between factors A and B one must demonstrate that A precedes B and that every time factor A is present factor B is also present. In the social sciences it is very difficult to establish causality, partly because there are so many uncontrolled factors. However, causal explanations are not essential in science (Hempel, 1959:274–275). "The objective of any science is not to formulate and verify theories of causation, but to construct an order among observables" (Quinney, 1970:5). Theory helps science move beyond correlation to explanation.

Fact and theory

In popular usage facts and theories are viewed as diametrically opposed. A fact is something that is "true," an empirically observable phenomenon. Theories, on the other hand, are wild hunches or predictions without a firm empirical basis. It is not unusual for persons to reject an explanation on the grounds that "it is just a theory." The scientific view of theory is very different; it assumes that facts and theories are inseparable (Goode and Hatt, 1952:7–8). Isolated facts are meaningless in science. The population of New York City, the altitude of Pikes Peak, the proportion of marriages that end in divorce, and the number of grains in a sand pile are facts, but, in and of themselves, they contribute little to an understanding of the empirical world. The collection of facts is essential in science, but it is not sufficient. The primary goal of science is to make sense of the millions of facts that surround us. Theories order and explain facts. More precisely, a theory is a general principle that accounts for, or explains, many specific facts. Theories are developed by combining empirical facts, or findings, with logic to produce general principles. An example is the theory of floating bodies (Archimedes' principle). The following deductive syllogism illustrates how this general theory can be used to explain specific facts:

1. A body will float in water when it displaces its own weight.
2. The *Queen Mary* displaces its own weight in the ocean.
3. Therefore the *Queen Mary* floats in the ocean.

Theories are derived by means of induction and deduction. Generally, theories are first arrived at inductively, as scientists discover a principle that underlies a number of empirical observations; for example, after Archimedes noticed the conditions under which boats, pieces of wood, and other objects float, he developed the theory of floating bodies. However, once the theory is formulated, through the use of deductive syllogisms one can derive hypotheses that provide specific tests of the theory. Hypotheses and theories have a very important relationship to one another. A hypothesis is a hunch or prediction about the empirical world that is deduced from theory. That is, it is a specific proposition that should be true if the general propositions from which it is derived are also true. Scientists are constantly evaluating theories through tests of specific hypotheses. If a hypothesis is supported, it enhances the validity of the theory. Failure to support a hypothesis may lead to the modification or rejection of a theory. Hypotheses are essential because theories are never ultimately proved; they are always subject to modification and revision. Hypotheses are the link between the empirical world and abstract theories.

Sociology uses the same method as the natural sciences in developing theories. It, however, has not yet generated theories that are as general or precise as those in the natural sciences. The task facing sociology is to develop general theories to explain such diverse facts as juvenile delinquency, crime, divorce, marriage, suicide, and child-rearing practices. In the area of delinquency a tenable explanation can be suggested, although it does not have the status of a "full-blown" theory:

1. The greater the amount of parental control the lower the delinquency.
2. The higher the social class standing the greater the parental control.
3. The higher the social class the lower the delinquency.

This theory does not claim to explain all, or perhaps even most, delinquency. The theory was selected for illustration because it possesses an important property, generality. The theory could potentially explain much delinquency that was previously viewed as unrelated. It provides at least a partial explanation for class differentials in delinquency rates, and seems to make some sense out of rural-urban, sex, and nativity differences in delinquency. The lower predisposition toward delinquency among the middleclass, rural residents, females, and the foreign-born may be due to greater parental control (see Chapters 5 and 6). A general theory is preferable to more limited explanations such as specific theories of social class, rural-urban, sex, and nativity differences in delinquency. The utility of a theory increases with its generality (Hempel, 1959:272–277). Science seeks to develop inclusive theories that explain many specific facts. The theory of relativity is useful and important because of its generality. Less inclusive theories such as Newton's theory of gravitation are subsumable under the theory of relativity. Some day sociology may be successful in subsuming most of its knowledge under a few general laws, but in the meantime sociologists must settle for more limited theories.

CONCEPTS IN SOCIOLOGY AND SCIENCE

The function of concepts

Man experiences his environment through the senses. He comes to know the physical world by touching, feeling, smelling, hearing, and seeing. Although this capacity for sensory experience is shared with other animals, man differs in that most of his experiences are not direct sensory contacts with the physical world but indirect symbolic experiences. The capacity for complex symbolic behavior is one of the most important characteristics that differentiates man from other animals. Symbols mediate between man and his environment, and they enable him to organize sensory experiences meaningfully.

Stated briefly, a symbol is something that stands for something else. The word "rose," for example, is a symbol that represents a particular flower, and the word "flower" in turn is a symbol for a class of objects in the empirical world. One should note Juliet's observation that "that which we call a rose by any other word would smell as sweet." In other words, symbols are arbitrarily selected, and there is no necessary connection between a symbol and its referent. Unfortunately, we frequently lose sight of the distinction between the symbol and its referent and behave toward the symbol as though it were the referent. The failure to distinguish between a symbol and its referent is called reification.

Since one does not experience phenomena directly, symbols are essential for ordering and understanding the empirical world. Consensus on the meaning of symbols is necessary for effective communication. In conventional usage there is considerable confusion about the meaning of many words. Some words have multiple meanings. "Fast" means to move rapidly, refrain from eating, and have loose morals. Furthermore, the same referent may be associated with several symbols. The feminine gender of the human species is known as a woman, female, broad, girl, chick, fox, dame, lady, babe, and tomato. In science it is necessary to gain greater precision over the use of symbols so that they will consistently convey the same meaning. The term "concept" is used in science to designate scientific symbols. Concepts interrelate symbols to form more complex and abstract descriptions of the empirical world. They are abstract in the sense that they do not describe all of empirical reality, but rather select significant segments of that reality. The development of a consistent conceptual framework is a major goal of science. A conceptual framework is a prerequisite to theory or explanation. One could say that concepts are the building blocks from which scientific explanations emerge. Sociology cannot hope to gain recognition as a complete science until it takes the important first step of developing a consistent conceptual framework that describes significant segments of empirical reality.

Basic concepts in sociology

Sociology is a mere neophyte among the sciences. For most of the twentieth century sociology has struggled to gain an identity, and sociologists have expended a great deal of energy in efforts to develop a conceptual framework. Perhaps it is a sign of progress that sociologists appear ready to move beyond this level to the development of sociological explanations. Today there is certainly no consensus on a conceptual framework, and yet there does appear to be general agreement on certain basic sociological concepts. The concepts that follow are not intended to be exhaustive, but they have gained some consistency in their usage and are essential building blocks in any sociology course. Before discussing these concepts an additional problem should be noted. Like other sciences, sociology must develop its own language. However, unlike other sciences, most concepts in sociology are already a part of a student's daily vocabulary. This is unfortunate because many students have to "unlearn" the meaning they attach to these concepts. It would probably be less confusing if they had to learn a completely new vocabulary.

1. **Status.** The concept status usually refers to a position or location in a group or collectivity. The position of father is meaningful relative to the positions of mother and child. It is the location of a position relative to other positions. A status has an existence that is independent of particular occupants of the position. The position elementary school teacher, for example, has a relatively consistent identity despite the fact that there is considerable turnover among the occupants of the position.

2. **Role.** Status and role are sister concepts. One can distinguish conceptually between them, but empirically they always appear together. Status and role are two dimensions of the same phenomenon; status refers to the

location of a position; role refers to the behavioral expectations that are associated with that position.[3] A role consists of the meanings shared by group members about the rights and duties of an incumbent in a position. Although someone cannot have a position without an attendant role, it is important to distinguish between them because the content of a particular role will vary among societies and within a society. The status of father is universal. Every society recognizes the position of adult male who is biologically responsible for the production of offspring, but the role of father is subject to considerable cross-cultural variation. Most societies define the father as the instrumental leader of the family; he is responsible for helping the family survive in its environment. In addition, societies usually delegate some of the responsibility for bringing up children to the father. However, Malinowski has pointed out that among the Trobriand Islanders much of the authority that is generally bestowed a father over a son is vested in the mother's brother over the sister's son (Homans, 1950: 256–259). Even within American society there is substantial variation in the role of father; for instance, in the lower class the father is frequently absent or only peripherally linked to the family, and the role of father is vested with less power and authority.

3. **Role performance.** Role is an ideational concept. It is the shared meanings or ideas among group members about the expectations of incumbents of a position. One should not confuse the expectations for occupants of a position with their behavior, or role performance. Role performance is used to designate the way persons actually carry out the demands of a particular role. In order for a role to attain a clear identity there must be some correspondence between role and role performance, but the amount of correspondence will vary considerably. While there is general consensus on the components of the father role in American society as a whole, there are vast differences in the way men actually perform this role. At one extreme is the man who is an ideal father and conforms to all of the expectations of the role. He is a good provider, loves his wife, serves as a leader for the family, spends many hours with his children, and is a source of emotional gratification for other family members. He is the fictional "father of the year." At the other extreme is the man who deserts his family and leaves them penniless, failing to meet even the most minimal requirements of the father role. Role and role performance are dynamically interrelated. Generally, roles guide the behavior of incumbents, but behavior also determines the nature of a role. Consistent deviation from the demands of a role may lead to modification of the role. Thus roles both guide behavior and arise out of behavior.

[3] A detailed analysis of the concepts of status and role is found in Yinger (1965: 98–138).

4. **Social norm.** Like role, social norm is an ideational concept. It refers to shared standards that apply to group members in general rather than to specific statuses. Norms are roles that define the appropriateness and inappropriateness of conduct under specified circumstances. The empirical locus of social norms is in the minds of men. They are ideas that are shared by group members. College students and professors, for instance, come into a classroom with shared meanings about the nature of college courses. They accept that the class will meet at a particular time on a given day of the week, that examinations and grades will be given, and that the instructor will set the direction for the class. Violations of norms are usually met with formal or informal punishments and conformity with rewards. It should be noted that norms are general rules or principles and not behavior. What is important in defining a particular act as normative or nonnormative is not the act per se but the conditions under which it occurs. The same act may be applauded under certain circumstances and condemned under other conditions. Killing is forbidden domestically if it is premeditated; but it is acceptable in self-defense and demanded and rewarded in time of war. Similarly, many persons would frown on a woman who engaged in sexual intercourse on the day before her wedding, but they would regard her with even greater disapproval if she refused to satisfy her husband after their wedding. The act of sexual intercourse is not inherently deviant or conforming; its appropriateness is determined by the conditions under which it occurs.

Generally, we can separate norms into two broad categories, folkways and mores. Folkways are procedural norms that facilitate social interaction. They are developed for convenience, and persons do not feel strongly about conformity to these norms. The phrase "first come, first served" provides an illustration of a norm that makes for smoother coordination of social relationships. Most of us have been struck by how readily Americans form lines to "wait their turn." This norm is so widely accepted that many people will go to the back of the line to enter a movie theater even in a rainstorm, but there are occasional deviants who insist on butting in line. This behavior is considered deviant, but it is neither immoral nor illegal. Folkways are developed for convenience, and violations are met with relatively mild sanctions.

In contrast to folkways, conformity to mores is considered essential for the survival or welfare of the group. Some mores, for example, specify that one should not have sexual relations with blood relatives (incest taboos), forbid murder, and require a man to support his family. Mores are so important to a group that they are usually formalized into laws. This ensures that violations will be met by official reaction and punishment. Violators of mores usually receive severe penalties that range from official prosecution to informal social ostracism.

Although the distinction has been made between folkways and mores, one should not assume that every norm can be classified into one or the other category. These concepts only get at the two extreme types of norms —those that are purely for convenience and those that are very important.

5. **Culture.** No other concept has been defined in so many different ways. It is therefore difficult, if not impossible, to develop a definition of culture that is acceptable to everyone. The term is well integrated into daily vocabulary. In popular usage culture designates the more refined aspects of life such as classical music, good books, the theater, and so on. If one is "cultured," he is refined and well educated. While music, art, and literature certainly are components of culture, the sociological usage of this concept is much broader. Culture is one of the most inclusive concepts in the social sciences. Culture is defined here as the complex system of shared beliefs, values, and norms among members of a human group or society. Like role and norm, culture is ideational. It is a system of ideas that is shared by group members and that organizes their actions relative to one another; without culture behavior is random and unpredictable.

Unfortunately, culture is sometimes defined behaviorally rather than ideationally. This definition neglects the fact that the behavior of persons is influenced not only by culture but also by biological and psychological factors. The ideational character of culture can be illustrated by an analogy between culture and the script of a play. The relationship between culture and behavior is similar to the relationship between the script and the performance of a play. Once the actors learn their parts, the empirical locus of the play is in the minds of the actors. The play serves as a blueprint for action, as does culture. It organizes the actions of all the actors relative to one another. A good performance results when the play is internalized by all of the players and their actions are coordinated into a meaningful and coherent whole. Similarly, culture organizes and guides the behavior of societal members.

Culture is both ideational and existential. It is ideational in the sense that it prescribes behavioral patterns for group members and existential because it provides collective definitions of the physical, social, and metaphysical world. One can say that culture defines both the ideal world and the real world for members of a society.

Having discussed the ideational dimension of culture, a consideration of its existential nature must be undertaken. Most Americans learn early in life that hallucinations and bizarre visions are abnormalities that are associated with mental illness. We approve of children having well-developed imaginations, but we become concerned when they are unable to distinguish between what they imagine and what is real. For the Sioux Indian, on the other hand, visions were not only tolerated but expected (Erikson, 1963:150). Every adolescent Sioux knew that he must go out into the prairie, exposing himself to danger and hunger, to seek a vision. Predictably, the vision came on the fourth day. and was evaluated by a committee of dream experts. This point can be illustrated further by the "romantic love" complex (Freeman, 1968; Goode, 1959). Most American girls define romantic love as a natural phenomenon that is found universally. Even before adolescence they learn that one day they will meet a young man, fall in love, and eventually marry. The idea of arranged marriages repels most American girls. Romantic love is equally unappealing to girls in societies in which arranged marriages are common. These two examples demonstrate the extent to which definitions of reality are culturally bound.

Several other characteristics of culture should be noted. Culture is *learned*. At birth, humans are the most malleable of all animals. Unlike most other animals the infant has few instincts; it is a bundle of predispositions that will not be realized without adequate care and training. Cultural characteristics are not developed inherently in the course of physiological maturation. They are acquired through continual interaction with adult members of society. The importance of culture cannot be overemphasized. It defines right and wrong, natural and unnatural, beautiful and ugly. Culture provides us with a set of lenses through which we see the world. Man experiences his environment through the senses, but his experiences are mediated by culture. The child must not only learn to distinguish between colors and shapes, but even more fundamentally he must learn to distinguish between himself and the environment and develop a consistent self-conception.

Culture is *transmitted from generation to generation.* Adults, especially parents, are responsible for transmitting the culture to new members. Culture exists in the minds of societal members. If culture were not transmitted intergenerationally, society as we know it would cease to exist. The behavior of persons would be unorganized (i.e., random and unpredictable). The importance of the transmission of culture is seen in the book *Fahrenheit 451* (Bradbury, 1953). In this story all knowledge was officially recorded by the government in a series of volumes, and all other books were outlawed. A number of persons formed a separate society called the "book people." They subverted the government by memorizing books and then destroying them. Each person was known by the name of the book he had committed to memory. Before death the contents of the book were transmitted to a child who would then assume the role of the book. In this way the culture of the "book people" was maintained, and knowledge was not lost even though books were forbidden. As the "book people," adults keep the knowledge of a society alive by transmitting it to new members.

The concept socialization is used in sociology to designate the process through which culture is transmitted to new members. Traditionally this concept was applied only to learning during childhood. It was assumed that socialization starts in infancy as the child is introduced to the ways of his society and ends in late childhood and early adolescence. More recently, sociologists have recognized that socialization is an ongoing process throughout the life cycle. Individuals are never fully socialized; they continue to learn the ways of new groups as adults. Furthermore, even within a particular group socialization is never final because the culture of a group is continually changing. Sociologists have tended to conceive of culture as a static phenomenon. Frequently culture is viewed as a constant mass of norms, roles, and values that is to be instilled in new members. This view is only partially correct. Culture is relatively stable. It is also useful to present a static view of culture in introducing students to the concept and its wide-ranging effects on behavior. However, this view can be misleading if it obscures the dynamic quality of culture. Culture is continually modified and redefined. It represents the collective solutions of group members to the problems that they face in their environment, but these solutions are never final. They are modified as the conditions that led to them also change. There is a dynamic interrelationship between culture and behavior. Culture gives direction to behavior and at the same time arises out of behavior.

The final characteristic of culture is that it is *shared*. As was mentioned previously, culture exists in the minds of men, but it is not a psychological phenomenon. Its distinctive characteristic is that it is not an isolated idea that one person holds independently of another. Culture is a shared idea which is held among members of a group. This point can be illustrated by an analogy to a symphony orchestra. Each member of the orchestra is well trained to play his part in the symphony. Although each member is essential to the total production, the music becomes meaningful only when all of the parts are integrated into a complete whole. Furthermore, the orchestra is more than the sum of the parts that go into it; that is, it is a separate and distinct reality. Culture is also more than the sum of its parts. It is a reality that comes about when members of a group develop a system of shared meanings that transcends them as individuals. Groups and societies maintain consistent identities and cultures, despite the fact that they have a rapid turnover in membership. In fact, culture can maintain its basic identity even though in a generation the membership of the society has changed.

6. **Subculture.** Subculture refers to a culture within a broader culture. The youth subculture in American society, for instance, is a part of the total culture and yet is somewhat distinct from it. American society can be conceived as a total entity by abstracting those cultural elements that are shared by members of the society as a whole. At the same time distinctive subunits can be identified within the society. On a lower level of abstraction one can see that American society is made up of thousands of overlapping subcultures. These subcultures are sometimes in conflict with one another or with the society at large.

A subculture is not a self-sufficient entity. "A subcultural system, by definition, is always incomplete. It furnishes normative guidelines for only part of the situations faced by those who hold it. It differentiates these people, in part, from other members of the society to which they belong" (Yinger, 1965:76). When a subculture becomes self-sufficient by meeting all of the social needs of its members, it is a culture and society. The Amish, a religious group in the United States, are so separated from the total society that they constitute a distinct society and culture, whereas Catholics are only a subculture.

7. **Social structure.** One can distinguish between culture and social structure analytically, but empirically they represent two dimensions of the same phenomenon. Culture is the shared system of ideas that guides and organizes the behavior of societal members; social structure is the organization of this behavior into patterned social relationships. Role is an element of culture, and status is an element of social structure. Another way of distinguishing between social structure and culture is to say that social structure refers to the form that social relationships take and culture refers to the content of these relationships. Within every society one can identify a family unit—a system of differentiated relationships among husband, wife, and children. However, the content of these relationships varies from society to society.

Durkheim was one of the first sociologists to clearly demonstrate social structural effects on behavior. In his classic study *Suicide* he postulated that the organization of a society has an effect on the propensity toward suicide of its members which is independent of culture and of personality characteristics. Durkheim presented three types of suicide: (1) egoistic— which results from a lack of integration of the individual into society, (2) altruistic—which results from overintegration of the individual into society, and (3) anomic—which results from a state of normlessness, a lack of regulation of the individual by the society. In the egoistic type the society is not cohesive, and the individual is thrown onto his own resources: ". . . the bond attaching man to life relaxes because that attaching him to society is itself slack" (Durkheim, 1966:214–215). Generally, the suicide rate is lower for Catholics than Protestants, married than single persons, and societies experiencing external threat (e.g., war) than those that are stable. These groups have a lower propensity to suicide not because of their distinctive cultural characteristics but because they are well integrated. "So we reach the general conclusion: suicide varies inversely with the degree of integration of the social groups of which the individual forms a part" (Durkheim, 1966:209).

In his analysis of anomic suicide, Durkheim examined both cultural and social structural effects. Durkheim used divorce as an example of conjugal anomie. The divorced are more prone to suicide because marital society no longer exercises its regulative influence upon the individual. The individual's needs have been regulated by the society; he has internalized the collective conscience, common beliefs, and practices. In other words, the individual has been regulated by the culture of the group. "When this regulation of the individual is upset so that his horizon is broadened beyond what he can endure . . . conditions for anomic suicide tend toward a maximum" (Durkheim, 1966:15). At this point it appears that Durkheim is primarily concerned with cultural effects; anomic suicide results from the lack of normative regulation of the individual. However, further analysis of his work reveals that anomic suicide also entails structural effects; for instance, Durkheim observed that in societies where divorce is high, suicides are also high even among persons who are *not* divorced.

8. **Society.** Society is defined as "an aggregate of people that is self-sustaining, that has a definite location and a long duration, and that shares a way of life" (Berelson and Steiner, 1964:587). As defined here, the concept society is even more inclusive than culture or social structure. Culture and social structure are subsumable under society. Society refers to the totality of a group of persons, both their ideational system and their patterned social relationships. Cultures and social structures cannot exist in a vacuum; they are found within human societies.

9. **Social control.** Social control is the ability of a group to bring about conformity to its expectations or demands. The term is similar to socialization, which was discussed earlier. The distinction between the two is that socialization is the process, or mechanism, through which control is brought about and social control is the product of this process. In other words, social control is the product of effective socialization. There are, of course, other mechanisms for inducing control such as the use or threat of force.

SOCIOLOGY AS A HUMANIZING ENTERPRISE

Before concluding this chapter it is necessary to discuss the relationship between science and existentialism, lest the reader assume that the sociological enterprise is irrelevant to the issue of freedom and human choice.[4] Science is deterministic. It takes events that have occurred and tries to explain or understand why they have occurred. In a sense then, predictions in social science are ex post facto reconstructions of events that have already taken place. Questions of choice and freedom are irrelevant, since one can hardly undo past events (Cuzzort, 1969:211).

The deterministic character of science has led many sociologists to assume a "value free" position. They argue that sociologists, as scientists, are not concerned with moral or political issues. Science according to this view is a tool that can be used to advance any end. While this view of

[4] This discussion is based in part on an excellent discussion of sociology and freedom found in Berger (1963:164–176).

science is technically correct in its assertion that science cannot prescribe values, carried to its logical extreme it is a form of "bad faith" or moral bankruptcy. Bad faith occurs when the sociologist uses the deterministic character of science as a personal shield in order to avoid stands on moral issues. The sociologist becomes a dispassionate observer who stands mute in the face of atrocities and injustices; he becomes an apologist for the status quo.

Existentialism, on the other hand, is concerned with human freedom and choice (Collins, 1952:1–3). Before an event occurs, individuals have choices as to the direction of their actions (Cuzzort, 1969:211). If man adopts an existential perspective, he can frustrate the scientist by deviating from scientific theories or predictions. There is then no necessary conflict between science and existentialism. Scientific knowledge can be used to change the future and for the betterment of man. Sociology becomes a humanizing enterprise whose ultimate value lies in its potential for improving humanity.

REFERENCES

Allport, Gordon W.
1958 The Nature of Prejudice. Garden City, N.Y.: Anchor Books.
Berelson, Bernard, and Gary A. Steiner
1964 Human Behavior: An Inventory of Scientific Findings. New York: Harcourt.
Berger, Peter
1963 Invitation to Sociology. Garden City, N.Y.: Anchor Books.
Bradbury, Ray
1953 Fahrenheit 451. New York: Ballantine.
Brown, Robert
1963 Explanation in Social Science. Chicago: Aldine.
Cardwell, Jerry D.
1971 Social Psychology: A Symbolic Interaction Perspective. Philadelphia: F. A. Davis.
Cole, Stephen
1972 The Sociological Method. Chicago: Markham.
Collins, James
1952 The Existentialists. Chicago: Gateway.
Cuzzort, R. P.
1969 Humanity and Modern Sociological Thought. New York: Holt, Rinehart & Winston.
Davis, Kingsley
1937 "The Sociology of Prostitution." American Sociological Review 2 (October):744–755.
1971 "Sexual Behavior." Pp. 313–360 in Robert K. Merton and Robert Nisbet (eds.), Contemporary Social Problems. Third ed. New York: Harcourt.

Durkheim, Emile
  1966 Suicide. (Translated by John A. Spaulding and George Simpson). New
       York: Free Press.
Erikson, Erik H.
  1963 Childhood and Society. Second ed. New York: Norton.
Faris, Robert E. L.
  1967 Chicago Sociology, 1920–1932. San Francisco: Chandler.
Freeman, Linton C.
  1968 "Marriage Without Love: Mate-Selection in Non-Western Societies."
       Pp. 456–469 in Robert F. Winch and Louis Wolf Goodman (eds.),
       Selected Studies in Marriage and the Family. New York: Holt, Rine-
       hart & Winston.
Goode, William J., and Paul K. Hatt
  1952 Methods in Social Research. New York: McGraw-Hill.
Goode, William J.
  1959 "The Theoretical Importance of Love." American Sociological Review
       24 (February):38–47.
Greer, Scott
  1969 The Logic of Social Inquiry. Chicago: Aldine.
Hempel, Carl G.
  1959 "The Logic of Functional Analysis." Pp. 271–307 in Llewellyn Gross
       (ed.), Symposium on Sociological Theory. New York: Harper & Row.
Homans, George C.
  1950 The Human Group. New York: Harcourt.
Manis, Jerome G., and Bernard N. Meltzer
  1972 Symbolic Interaction: A Reader in Social Psychology. Second ed. Bos-
       ton: Allyn & Bacon.
Meehan, Eugene J.
  1968 Explanation in Social Science: A System Paradigm. Homewood, Ill.:
       Dorsey.
Quinney, Richard
  1970 The Social Reality of Crime. Boston: Little, Brown.
Reynolds, Paul Davidson
  1971 A Primer in Theory Construction. New York: Bobbs-Merrill.
Stone, Gregory P., and Harvey A. Farberman
  1970 Social Psychology Through Symbolic Interaction. Waltham, Mass.:
       Ginn/Blaisdell.
Willer, Judith
  1971 The Social Determination of Knowledge. Englewood Cliffs, N.J.:
       Prentice-Hall.
Yinger, J. Milton
  1965 Toward a Field Theory of Behavior: Personality and Social Structure.
       New York: McGraw-Hill.

PART ONE

Social problems approach

INTRODUCTION

Social problems have traditionally been viewed as conditions that are seen as undesirable by members of the society. People, however, do not agree on what is undesirable in a society, and an individual's views in this regard will vary according to his values and position in the society. Government welfare is a social problem for many middle-class persons whose taxes are increased and spending power is lowered, but others, especially those who benefit from such programs, define societal opposition to welfare as a problem. The discrepancy in the definition of social problems becomes important when one considers that the opinions of all persons have not carried equal weight in determining which conditions are selected as social problems for study by sociologists. Sociologists have been more sensitive to the views of those who command power and control resources in the society. The federal government and other funding agencies, for example, have had a tremendous impact on the direction of social science research. Much of the substance of the social problems area consequently reflects a concern with violations of the values and norms of dominant members of society. There is some credence to the accusation that sociology has tended to serve as a tool used by the Establishment to maintain its position of power and control subordinates. Many social and natural scientists have engaged in war research in which the ultimate aim is the development of specific techniques for injuring or annihilating others rather than the development of science. In the social sciences Project Camelot (Horowitz, 1965) has stirred a great deal of controversy. This top-secret project, sponsored by the U.S. Army, was designed to measure and predict the causes of revolutions and insurrections in underdeveloped areas of the world, including several Latin American nations. It represented a reactionary mentality that viewed revolution and change as inherently undesirable and threatening to the security of the United States. The project raised important ethical questions about the uses and misuses of applied social science and revealed the dangers inherent in projects in which social scientists are defined as employees of a higher agency that places its own goals above those of science.

The tendency of the powerful to define and control the study of social problems has impeded the development of social problems as a subarea within a scientific field. Even though sociologists can be objective in re-searching a particular problem once it has been selected, the very selection of some problems for study and the neglect of others reflects a bias. Problems are frequently selected not according to their theoretical impor-tance but according to the importance given to them by the dominant society or particular clients. The emphasis given to crime and delinquency illustrates this tendency. Most persons see crime and delinquency as pressing social problems, and it is difficult to argue otherwise. While a great deal of money has been invested in the study of crime, such research has been extremely selective, focusing on lower-class crime and neglecting violations by the middle class. Researchers have also defined delinquency as a lower-class phenomenon, and there are only a few studies of delin-quency in the middle class. Sutherland's work on white-collar crime is probably more important for turning attention toward crime among respect-able members of society than for its substantive contribution. A number of issues, such as war, police brutality, and poverty, have been relatively neglected because they were not defined as problematic by the dominant society.

The preceding discussion suggests that sociologists have often not acted as objective and impartial observers in their investigations of social prob-lems but rather as representatives of the dominant society and specific interest groups. This bias is reflected not only in the selection of social problems but also in their research. Research is a selective process. The answers obtained are dependent on the questions asked, and there are always limits on the number of questions that can be asked. All too fre-quently sociological research is designed to obtain justification for moral precepts rather than to gain knowledge and test theoretical propositions. After examining the leading social problems texts of the time, C. Wright Mills (1943) concluded that they were based on an ideology that defines violations of middle-class, rural values as a social pathology. While sociolo-gists are becoming more sensitive to this bias, much research and writing still has a "moralistic" quality; for example, research (sponsored by the National Institute of Mental Health and other agencies) on marijuana and other drugs is usually labeled as the study of "drug abuse" rather than "drug use." Studies are designed to uncover the negative aspects of marijuana smoking rather than to investigate both positive and negative effects. The use of the term "hallucinogens" to refer to marijuana and LSD is revealing in and of itself. Government agencies and the society as a whole are primarily interested in controlling social problems and social deviants. When sociologists act as agents of the society, they are implicated in the process of social control, lose sight of their ultimate goal as scientists, to understand or explain social phenomena, and become overwhelmed by the immediate problem of control.

SOCIAL PROBLEMS AND SOCIAL ACTION

The social problems approach, as noted in the Introduction to the book, has been tied closely to social action. Because of its action orientation many sociologists wanting to establish sociology as a pure science were reluctant to accept social problems as a legitimate area of study. They argued that sociology had to be value free if it was to evolve into a respectable science. Although the controversy is far from settled, there seems to be some agreement today that there is a place for social problems in sociology; the study of their origin, distribution, and solution is as legitimate as the study of any other area. It is also legitimate, perhaps essential, for the sociologist to be concerned with solutions to problems. Most sociologists recognize that the ultimate value of science lies in its ability to improve man's conditions, and the prestige and influence accrued to natural science result from its demonstrated utility. While the application of social science knowledge is a worthy goal, as long as persons in power define the problems and determine which are worthy of investigation, sociology will contain a conservative bias. Only those areas that members of the dominant society define as problematic will be studied; more controversial areas that threaten the status quo will go unnoticed.

A second problem surrounding the application of knowledge concerns the confusion of application with prescription of social values. It is sometimes assumed that the scientist should prescribe solutions to social problems. The sociologist can certainly assess the relative merits of alternative courses of action for resolving social ills, but his capacity as a scientist does not enable him to determine which solutions are ultimately better or morally correct. Since there is much confusion surrounding this issue, it is essential to clarify the position taken here. The author does not advocate that the sociologist shrink from moral responsibility and hide behind the value-free ethic. The sociologist has a moral responsibility to take a stand on important issues as an informed and responsible citizen. He should oppose poverty, war, overpopulation, and other problems facing American society. However, it should be clear that this is a value position that is no better, or worse, than the value position of others in the society who are not sociologists. Expertise in an area does not legitimize prescribing values to others, although it is usually done. As an illustration, physicians have an obligation to take a position on moral issues such as abortion, but their position is no more sacred than that of lay persons. Similarly, the physicist does not have the right to prescribe whether or not nuclear weapons should be used. There is a danger that the application of science could lead to a kind of elitism in which the goals and values of societal members are relegated to secondary importance to those of scientists and other experts. Science is, after all, only a tool designed by man to improve his lot on earth. Science can certainly help solve social problems, but it can only determine which means are most desirable, not which ends.

SOCIAL PROBLEMS AND SOCIETAL PROBLEMS

One of the major drawbacks to the social problems approach lies in the definition of a social problem.[1] Since a particular condition may be viewed as problematic by one segment of society and as desirable by another, consensus on the major problems facing American society is not possible. If members could agree on the major problems, it is still questionable whether sociologists would want to confine themselves to studying these conditions. Certain conditions are problematic for the society even though its members are not aware of them, and they may in fact be especially problematic simply because they are subterranean.

The concept societal problem will be introduced in an attempt to overcome some of the difficulties inherent in the social problems approach. A societal problem is a condition that can be defined by objective criteria as disruptive to the society. The issue of racial prejudice in American society is an example of a societal problem. Of course, racial prejudice is also recognized as a social problem, but what is important is that it is a problem even if some persons do not perceive it as such. In South Africa and some parts of the United States racial prejudice is not viewed as a social problem by the dominant group, and yet it is a societal problem by any objective criteria. When a society contains subgroups having conflicting values and goals, the conditions for a societal problem are present even if members of the society do not define such conditions as problematic. Population is another societal problem, but its importance as a societal problem is much greater than the importance given to it as a social problem. Most Americans probably do not see overpopulation as a major social problem. List 1, for example, shows that overpopulation is not ranked among the most important problems facing this country. The objective data on population projections, overcrowding, and limited food supply speak for themselves, and few sociologists would deny that overpopulation is a pressing social issue. Many members of the society are also oblivious to poverty, believing that poverty in the United States has been eliminated. But approximately 30 million people in this country live in poverty. It is also clear that since poverty involves relative deprivation, it becomes a greater societal problem

[1] For additional discussion of the problems inherent in defining social problems see, Kitsuse and Spector (1973), Westhues (1973), and Ross and Staines (1972).

in an affluent society. Those who are poverty-stricken are less likely to accept their subordinate position when they are surrounded by affluence. Consequently, poverty qualifies as an important societal problem even though it may not be viewed as a major social problem by the society. On the other hand, certain conditions that are defined as social problems do not qualify as important societal problems. It is doubtful that inflation, busing of schoolchildren, and drug use are as disruptive to the society by objective standards as they are by the personal standards of societal members.

LIST 1
Public's list of most important problems

1. State of economy	41%
2. International problems	
Vietnam	15
Other	8
3. Drug use and abuse	8
4. Racial problems	6
5. Crime, lawlessness	6
6. Pollution, ecology	5
7. Unrest in nation	4
8. Lack of religion, moral decay	4
Other problems	14
No opinion	4
	*115%

* Total adds to more than 100 percent since some persons gave more than one answer.
Source: George Gallup, "A Decade of Problems." *Grand Forks Herald*, Grand Forks, N.D., December 19, 1971:52.

It appears that the concept of societal problem avoids some of the pitfalls inherent in the social problems perspective. With this conceptualization the sociologist is not limited to studying those problems that members of the society define as problematic, and the influence of powerful persons and agencies who control resources is reduced. The sociologist studies conditions that are disruptive to the society. Identifying such conditions is not an easy task, of course. In many cases social problems and societal problems coincide; some conditions that are perceived as undesirable are in fact disruptive.[2] The concept of societal problems should help the sociologist in restricting his study to those problems that are problematic for the society as a whole and to ignore social problems that simply represent violation of the norms of special interest groups in society.

[2] For a discussion of the relationship between the societal members' and the sociologist's definition of social problems see Kitsuse and Spector (1973).

REFERENCES

Horowitz, Irving Louis
1965 "The Life and Death of Project Camelot." Trans-action 3 (November):3–7.
Kitsuse, John I., and Malcolm Spector
1973 "Toward a Sociology of Social Problems: Social Conditions, Value-Judgments, and Social Problems." Social Problems 20 (Spring):407–419.
Mills, C. Wright
1943 "The Professional Ideology of Social Pathologists." The American Journal of Sociology, 49 (September):165–180.
Ross, Robert, and Graham L. Staines
1972 "The Politics of Analyzing Social Problems." Social Problems 20 (Summer):18–40.
Westhues, Kenneth
1973 "Social Problems as Systemic Costs." Social Problems 20 (Spring):419–431.

Population

1

THE NATURE OF THE PROBLEM

Population growth is one of the most pressing problems facing people throughout the world. The population explosion has become especially apparent during the present century. For most of man's history population grew at a relatively slow pace compared to the increases in the past sixty or seventy years and the projected increases for the future. The increase in population between 1920 and 1970 was greater than the total population of the earth in 1920 (Davis, 1971:365). Moreover, if population continues to increase at its current rate, the present world population of 3.7 billion will double every thirty-seven years so that in two hundred years the earth's population will be 157 billion (Davis, 1971:363). Within nine hundred years 4550 people would live on each square foot of land (Nuveen, 1966:983). These figures stagger the imagination. It is, of course, inconceivable that population will actually continue to increase at its current rate. Undoubtedly, certain controls will come into effect before population reaches such density.

Thomas Malthus (1964:19–35) an early eighteenth-century economist, suggested two major types of controls, positive and preventive checks. Positive checks refer to means that result in the taking of human life and include war, disease, and famine. Preventive checks reduce population by preventing births. Malthus opposed contraception and instead advocated moral restraint through delaying the time of marriage as a control. Today, contraception is the major type of preventive check. It is impossible to determine the extent to which positive or preventive checks will come into play in controlling population. What is clear is that population growth must be stabilized through some means. From a humanitarian standpoint preventive checks are preferable to positive checks, but if the former are not instituted, the latter will certainly go into effect.

Many Americans see overpopulation as a distant problem found only in less "developed" nations in Asia and Latin America and associate it with extreme poverty, famine, malnutrition, and overcrowding. The population problem is also de-emphasized because people tend to attribute it to large families. Most women who have three or four children do not see how they are contributing to overpopulation; in their view, the problem is created by still larger families. In order for the American population to stabilize, each couple in the United States must produce an average of about 2.1 children. There is reason to believe that the ideal family size is considerably greater than the replacement level of 2.1 children. Although the specific figure obtained varies according to a number of factors, including the wording of the question (e.g., "ideal," "desired," or "expected" number) and the sex, age, religion, and educational level of the respondent, parental desires seem to fall within a range of two to four children (Blake, 1966:163; Revelle, 1971:14). One national survey reported that women typically felt that three or four children were the ideal number for the average American family (Whelpton, Campbell, and Patterson, 1966:34). If women achieved the goal of 3.5 children during their lifetime, the population of the United States would double by the end of the current century, and after another generation at this rate of increase the population would approach 1 billion (Population Reference Bureau, 1966:61). More recent evidence, however, indicates that "the proportion of Americans who favor large families has declined dramatically . . ." (Gallup, 1973). Most couples presently plan to have between two and three children (The Commission on Population Growth and the American Future, 1972:97).

The desire for large families is tied, in part, to the agricultural heritage of the United States, which has been an agrarian nation for much of its history. In 1790 only about 5 percent of the population lived in urban areas (i.e., over 2500 persons). Although the urban population has been increasing steadily since this time, it did not exceed the rural population until 1920 (U.S. Bureau of the Census, 1950:12). Today almost 80 percent of American residents live in urban areas, and yet many Americans continue to adhere to values that evolved in an agrarian society. Children in agricultural societies are highly valued because they are economic assets, providing free labor and helping parents to maintain the farm. In such societies a man with many offspring, especially sons, is considered to be very fortunate. These values persist despite the fact that in our society children have become economic liabilities, and with more of them attending college and professional schools their economic dependency is prolonged. It is not uncommon for young adults to remain at least partially dependent on parents until the age of twenty-five or thirty. Spiraling costs of education have also helped to increase the economic burden of children. Any economic rewards that parents might reap from their investment in the education of their children will come late in life, if they come at all.

POPULATION GROWTH AND DISTRIBUTION IN THE UNITED STATES

Population qualifies as a major societal problem in that it is a condition that is potentially disruptive to the society. We can no longer continue to ignore the consequences for the society of uncontrolled population growth. To ignore the problem will lead to its intensification rather than its elimination.

Since 1790 when there were approximately 4 million persons in the United States, the population has grown steadily in excess of 200 million. This increase was attained even though the rate of growth has been declining. The population increased by about one-third during each of the seven decades between 1790 and 1860. The decennial rate of increase was about 25 percent for the period 1860 to 1890, 20 percent for 1890 to 1910, and 15 percent for 1910 to 1930. Between 1930 and 1940 the rate of increase hit its lowest point (U.S. Bureau of the Census, 1950:8–9). Thus, with the exception of the Depression years of the 1930s when the rate declined rapidly, the rate of growth has demonstrated a **consistent** downward trend. The rate of growth, 13.3 percent, during the past decade (1960–1970) is the second lowest in our history (Population Reference Bureau, 1970:7).

We are faced with the paradoxical situation—the population is increasing at a rapid pace at the same time that the rate of increase and the birth rate are declining (U.S. Department of Health, Education, and Welfare, 1974b:1). There are at least three reasons for this paradox. First, is the cumulative nature of population growth. We tend to forget that population may continue to grow even when the rate of growth is stabilized. A population of 10 million, for instance, growing at a decennial rate of 20 percent will increase by 2 million, whereas a population of 200 million increasing at the same rate will add 40 million to its population base. A population increasing at a rate of 4 percent per year will double in only eighteen years (Hardin, 1969:17). The cumulative effects of population growth are illustrated further by List 2. A family with 11 children would propagate into a population of over 25 billion if their descendants continue to reproduce at the same rate over ten generations.

LIST 2
The cumulative effects of population growth

(1)	11
	11
	——
(2)	121
	11
	——
(3)	1331
	11
	——
(4)	14,641
	11
	——
(5)	161,051
	11
	——
(6)	1,771,561
	11
	——
(7)	19,487,171
	11
	——
(8)	214,358,881
	11
	——
(9)	2,357,947,691
	11
	——
(10)	25,937,424,601

Source: Zero Population Growth, 1346 Connecticut Avenue, N. W., Washington, D. C. 20036

Mr. and Mrs. Lennon had 11 children. If their descendants continue the same rate of propagation for only 10 generations, there will be *25 billion* of them—more than 8 times the population of the earth today.

"Thou shalt go forth and multiply and replenish the earth. . . ."

A second factor contributing to population growth is the number of women of childbearing age. Age-specific fertility (the number of children per 1000 women in each age cohort) in the United States declined gradually up to the Depression when it reached an all-time low. After World War II the rate started to climb and continued at a high level until 1957. Since then there has again been a steady decline both in the fertility rate and in the birth rate (U.S. Department of Health, Education, and Welfare, 1974b:1). The drop in fertility might, however, be offset by a sharp increase in the proportion of women in the prime reproductive ages of twenty to twenty-nine, women born during the postwar "baby boom." In 1960 there were only 11 million women in this age group, but by 1980 there should be 20 million (Population Reference Bureau, 1970:12). In short, women are on the average having fewer babies, but the proportion of women in the reproductive years is increasing.

The last, and probably most important, contributing factor to increasing population is the declining rate of mortality. Advancements in medical technology and improvements in the quality of life have markedly reduced the death rate, not only in the United States but in countries throughout the world. Mortality control has been especially effective in reducing infant mortality and deaths resulting from diseases of childhood and adolescence (U.S. Department of Health, Education, and Welfare, 1974a:1). Thus decreases in the death rate not only allow persons to have a longer life expectancy, but also those persons who are born are more likely to survive and reproduce.

The increase in the size of the population is not the only, nor necessarily the most important, population problem facing American society. It appears unlikely that the population of the United States will grow in the foreseeable future to the point predicted by doomsday writers at which there will be massive starvation and a shoulder-to-shoulder, sardinelike existence. A more immediate problem is the effect of population growth on the quality of life. Since optimum population size and density are socially defined, increased population may be viewed as a social problem long before it reaches its maximum physical limits. Americans are becoming increasingly concerned with preserving the environment, improving the quality of life, and redistributing wealth throughout the society. Population has a direct bearing on the use of natural resources and improvement of the quality of life. One of the more obvious examples of this is housing, which not only occupies valuable space but also drains scarce natural resources such as forests. We may be able to feed and house 400 or 500 million people in the continental United States but not at a desirable level, and the cost may virtually exhaust our natural resources and open spaces. Such effects are felt in the current energy and food crisis. Some of the other effects of increased population would be overcrowding of schools, recreational areas, and transportation facilities. As it is today, millions of persons are living in poverty and many of our public facilities are severely taxed.

A problem closely related to the quality of life is the distribution of the population. The population of the United States is unevenly distributed, with the heaviest concentration found along the Eastern seaboard and the Pacific coast, and the lowest in more economically depressed areas, "especially those in the South and in a belt running due North from Texas to North Dakota" (Population Reference Bureau, 1970:7). In addition to regional variation in the distribution of the population, within regions the population is unevenly distributed between urban and rural areas. Throughout our history there has been a steady movement of persons from rural to urban areas. Between 1960 and 1970 more than half of the counties in the

United States lost population (Population Reference Bureau, 1970:7). Residents of these areas generally migrate to metropolitan centers to seek employment. Heavy outmigration not only helps to create overcrowding in metropolitan areas but is also costly to rural counties, since it is generally the younger and more able-bodied residents who migrate. The recent exodus from the inner city to the outlying suburbs is viewed by some as a reversal of this trend. Suburbs, however, have intensified urban problems by creating sprawling metropolitan areas.

The concentration of people in urban areas has produced a number of disruptive conditions that are generally not identified as part of the population problem. Traffic congestion and air and noise pollution are probably the most obvious of these conditions. Less obvious but equally important are problems of interdependence and coordination of services in metropolitan areas. This complex interdependence is generally taken for granted until crises such as garbage and transportation strikes demonstrate how easily large cities can virtually be paralyzed. In summary, we face two population problems of immediate concern: (1) to stabilize the population at an optimum level that is well under the physical limits of society in order to improve the quality of life, and (2) to redistribute the population more evenly throughout the society. The problem of population density could be alleviated substantially if the population could be more evenly distributed. While some states are characterized by wide open spaces, others are very densely populated. In Rhode Island there are 923 persons per square mile, whereas in Alaska there is only 1 person per square mile (U.S. Bureau of the Census, 1973:13). Although many believe that the movement toward heavily industrialized urban areas is irreversible, there are mechanisms that could be used to counter this trend. Especially promising are proposed state and federal programs to stimulate the economic development of rural areas with declining populations and encourage outmigration from densely populated centers.

FAMILY PLANNING IN THE UNITED STATES

Family planning, a movement that sees the production and distribution of effective methods of contraception as the key to population control, has gained wide support among political and religious leaders and population experts throughout the world (Davis, 1967:730–731). Massive programs have been initiated in underdeveloped nations to curve rapid rates of growth. Such societies are characterized by declining mortality rates and high birth rates and, according to proponents of family planning, population control will come only by educating the poor and uneducated masses to accept family planning.

Although the United States has a relatively low birth rate, the dominant approach to population control in this country has also been family planning. Attempts have been made to disseminate birth-control information and provide contraceptives, especially to the lower class, whose birth rate is high. The emphasis on fertility in the lower class has obscured the role played by the middle class in population growth. The middle class has a lower birth rate, but since it is much larger in numbers than the lower class, it contributes more children to the population. Furthermore, since infant mortality is lower and life expectancy is higher in the middle class, the chances are greater that a child born in this class will live to have children and to see his children reproduce. Many middle-class couples who have three or four children do not realize that they are contributing to over-population, since, in their view, overpopulation is a problem of the lower class. While most middle-income Americans accept the desirability of family planning, they are usually guided in such planning by economic and personal considerations. The belief that parents have a moral right to have as many children as they want and can afford is widely accepted. This poses a knotty problem in that it is probably more difficult to resocialize people to limit family size voluntarily when they can afford to have children than when they cannot. If family planning is to be effective, many persons must accept the idea that they will be able to have fewer children than they can afford.

POPULATION CONTROL: BEYOND FAMILY PLANNING

Considerable confusion has been generated by the tendency to equate family planning and population control. The two terms are far from syn-onymous. In part the confusion has been perpetuated by proponents of the family-planning movement who see birth control as the key to population control throughout the world. The United Nations Declaration, for example, states that "the opportunity to decide the number and spacing of children is a basic human right."

Family planning refers to decisions on the number and spacing of chil-dren by individual couples. It maintains that national interests are auto-matically served by individual couples pursuing their own interests (Davis, 1967:732). This approach to population control is technical and medical; it attempts to curb population growth by educating the public and making contraceptives available.

The family-planning movement makes a dubious assumption, that women will be motivated to limit their families to two children. Available evidence indicates that women in developed countries have *fewer* children than they want, while the reverse is true in less developed nations (Revelle, 1971:14). It was noted earlier that if American women were able to have their desired number of children, the United States would experience a very rapid rate of growth. While women in less developed nations generally have more children than they desire, they also want to have more children than is required for stabilizing the population. "If women in the cities of underdeveloped countries used birth-control measures with 100-percent efficiency, they would have enough babies to expand city populations sense-lessly, quite apart from the added contribution of rural-urban migration" (Davis, 1967:736).

It is clear that birth control is not adequate for controlling population growth, but this is not to suggest that contraception is without benefits. Family planning is necessary but not sufficient for achieving a stable population. The birth rate is only one of several factors that determine population growth. The rate of increase is also influenced by mortality, migration, fertility, and the spacing of generations.

Ironically, family planning has in some respects worked against popu-lation control. Moderate reductions in the birth rate have been taken as a sign that the problem is under control. However, the reduction in births may not compensate for decreased mortality, so that more infants live to reproduce. Another important factor that is frequently neglected is the spacing of generations. Early marriage coupled with a reduced mortality rate can rapidly accelerate population growth (see the selection by Glenn D. Everett at the end of the chapter). Under such conditions the popu-lation increases because more generations survive.

One of the most unfortunate consequences of the family-planning move-ment is that it reaffirms the "right" of couples to have as many children as they desire. Couples are led to believe that the population problem stems from poor planning and ignorance. The problem is to be resolved by couples' planning the number and spacing of their children.

Since the time of Malthus and Godwin there has been a recurrent debate over population control. "The neo-Malthusians paint horrendous pictures of a future in which, if present population growth rates continue, people will be packed together shoulder to shoulder covering every square foot of space on earth . . . neo-Godwinians, are likely to counter alarmism over the world population explosion with glowing estimates of the purely technical possibilities of increasing world agricultural output" (Wrong, 1967:108–109). One need not be a neo-Malthusian to see flaws in the neo-Godwinian argument. If one assumes that the world is finite, then popula-tion cannot continue to grow infinitely. We may devise means of feeding billions, but at some point a shortage of space will be encountered. This is the principal argument against interplanetary colonization as a solution to the population problem. Even if we find a planet where human life can be sustained and are able to relocate millions, the need to control population will simply be postponed.

Another method of controlling population is to increase the death rate. A national plan to increase mortality would be bitterly opposed as an inhumane alternative. Yet those who oppose other means of population control must realize that they are indirectly supporting higher mortality (Wrong, 1967:111). If preventive methods of control are not introduced, natural controls over the death rate will undoubtedly come into play. Mass famine and nuclear war, for example, would do much to stabilize the world's population. Paul Ehrlich, a vocal spokesman for population control, believes that overpopulation has already led to the starvation of millions and that the world is well on its way toward mass famine unless controls are instituted immediately (1968:17).

It appears that the more traditional methods of controlling population are not likely to solve the problem. How, then, are we to stabilize the population? Obviously, there is no single, simple solution to this complex and thorny problem (Berelson, 1969:539–541). In fact, the major obstacle to population control may be that proposed solutions have generally been simple and direct, focusing on the mechanics of control and ignoring basic social structural arrangements that perpetuate population growth. Structural changes that encourage marriage at a later age, for example, would help to slow the rate of increase. Women could be encouraged to further their education and to acquire interests outside of the family. Delay of marriage is related to two broader conditions in society, the emphasis on family life and the emancipation of women. Although replacement is not a problem in our society, we continue to adhere to an ideology that directly and indirectly encourages family life. There is subtle, and sometimes not so subtle, social and economic discrimination against persons who do not marry. The single person is not only viewed as odd or deviant, he is also discriminated against in housing and employment. The tax structure works against both single individuals and childless couples, although this situation has been improved in recent years. Instead of penalizing persons who choose not to have children, we need to make nonfamilial roles more attractive. Among the policies that would encourage family limitation are cash stipends for voluntary sterilization, free abortions on demand, and a reversal of the tax structure so that within a given income level greater benefits accrue to single individuals and childless couples (for a discussion of these alternatives see Berelson, 1969). Such policies should of course not be retroactive, so that those who already have children are not penalized.

Despite a substantial improvement in the status of women, the primary sources of emotional gratification and self-esteem for most women are probably marriage and motherhood. Although many women are employed, their employment is frequently viewed as secondary to their familial role. Nonfamilial roles must be made more rewarding for women so that they will compete with the childbearing role. If women received equal compensation with men for the same work and were permitted to assume socially important positions, they would be more motivated to pursue nonfamilial roles and to postpone, or perhaps even avoid, marriage.

While changes in the law and in economic policies may help to control population, they are probably not, in and of themselves, adequate solutions to the problem. What is needed in the long run to stabilize the population is a basic change in the social structure and in the values of societal members. One of the reasons why the family-planning movement has been widely acclaimed by politicians and other leaders throughout the world is that it does not require restructuring society. "By implying that the only need is the invention and distribution of effective contraceptive devices, they allay fears, on the part of religious and governmental officials, that fundamental changes in social organization are contemplated" (Davis, 1967:734). Population control will require changes in the family, the status of women, and sexual norms, changes that will not be popular with certain segments of the society. Population control is unlikely to be achieved as long as family planning is recognized as a private decision of individual families. We must instead bring about alterations in the social structure so that familial roles are de-emphasized and parenthood is recognized as a privilege granted and controlled by society rather than as a God-given right of each individual.

REFERENCES

Berelson, Bernard
  1969 "Beyond Family Planning." Science 163 (February 7):533–543.
Blake, Judith
  1966 "Ideal Family Size Among White Americans: A Quarter of a Century's Evidence." Demography 3 (Number 1):154–173.
The Commission on Population Growth and the American Future
  1972 Population and the American Future. Washington, D.C.: GPO.
Davis, Kingsley
  1967 "Population Policy: Will Current Programs Succeed?" Science 158 (November 10):730–739.
  1971 "The World's Population Crisis." Pp. 363–405 in Robert K. Merton and Robert Nisbet (eds.), Contemporary Social Problems. Third ed. New York: Harcourt.
Ehrlich, Paul R.
  1968 The Population Bomb. New York: Ballantine.
Gallup, George
  1973 "Acceptance of Large Families Falls in Favor." Grand Forks Herald, Grand Forks, N.Dak. (February 4):8.
Hardin, Garrett
  1969 Population, Evolution, and Birth Control. Second ed. San Francisco: Freeman.
Malthus, Thomas
  1964 First Essay on Population, 1798. Ann Arbor, Mich.: University of Michigan Press.
Nuveen, John
  1966 "The Facts of Life." Christian Century 83, Pt. 2 (August 10):983–986.
Population Reference Bureau
  1966 " 'Boom Babies' Come of Age: The American Family at the Crossroads." Population Bulletin 22 (August):61–79.
  1970 "Population Activities in the United States." Population Bulletin 26 (December):7–25.

Revelle, Roger
  1971 "Population." Pp. 4–15 in Roger Revelle, Ashok Khosla, and Maris
       Vinovskis (eds.), The Survival Equation: Man, Resources, and His
       Environment. Boston: Houghton Mifflin.
U.S. Bureau of the Census
  1950 Census of Population: 1950. United States Summary, Vol. II. Wash-
       ington, D.C.
  1973 Statistical Abstract of the United States. Ninety-fourth ed. Washing-
       ton, D.C.
U.S. Department of Health, Education, and Welfare
  1974a "Final Infant, Fetal, and Maternal Mortality, 1969." Monthly Vital
        Statistics Report 22, no. 10 (January 17):1–4.
  1974b "Births, Marriages, Divorces, and Deaths for 1973." Monthly Vital
        Statistics Report 22, no. 12 (February 28):1–8.
Whelpton, Pascal K., Arthur A. Campbell, and John E. Patterson
  1966 Fertility and Family Planning in the United States. Princeton, N.J.:
       Princeton University Press.
Wrong, Dennis H.
  1967 "People and Resources: The Malthusian Problem." Population and
       Society. Third ed. New York: Random House. Pp. 100–117.

INTRODUCTION TO THE READINGS

The readings illustrate some of the major issues raised in this chapter. The short selection by Everett dramatizes the importance of generational spacing and the cumulative effects of population growth. "One Man's Family" is a microcosm of the overpopulation problem in the larger society. Although John Miller only had seven children, his children and their children lived to reproduce so that at the time of his death he was survived by 410 descendants.

Hardin's essay focuses on the perennial conflict between individual interests and collective interests. We have characteristically searched for technical solutions to population and other societal problems and ignored structural and value impediments to change. These problems are not likely to be resolved until men learn to cope with "The Tragedy of the Commons."

One man's family

GLENN D. EVERETT

Recently, on the eve of his 95th birthday, John Eli Miller died in a rambling farmhouse near Middlefield, Ohio, 40 miles southeast of Cleveland, leaving to mourn his passing perhaps the largest number of living descendants any American has ever had.

He was survived by five of his seven children, 61 grandchildren, 338 great-grandchildren and six great-great grandchildren, a grand total of 410 descendants.

Shortly before his death, which came unexpectedly from a stroke, I had the privilege of two long visits with John E. Miller, during which I learned the feeling of one man who had personally watched the population explosion of the 20th century. A national magazine had determined that the venerable Ohio farmer was head of what almost certainly was the largest family in the United States.

A Swedish newspaper in 1958 ran a competition for the largest family in that country and when a family named Hellander turned up with 265 members, headed by a 92-year-old great-grandmother, it asserted a claim to the Swedish and to the world championship.

Soon reports of even larger families were streaming in to editors, with an elderly Mormon couple in Utah claiming 334 living descendants taking the lead. However, I was certain that among the Old Order Amish Mennonites, a sect in which families of more than 100 are commonplace, a family larger than this could be found. Through the medium of the Sugarcreek, Ohio, *Budget*, a unique weekly newspaper that is read by the Old Order Amish in all their communities throughout the Nation, it was soon ascertained that John Eli Miller, with his clan of more than 400, had the largest family among them. So far as could be learned, this family was the largest in America and probably the world's largest among monogamous peoples.

When John Miller and his family refused to pose for photographs because of their religious opposition to "graven images," the magazine gave up the idea of a story about this "largest family" but the interviews disclosed a number of facts about the impact of extremely rapid population growth on this family and the cultural group of which it is a part. These facts merit the serious attention of all students of population problems.

John Miller actually had seen with his own eyes a population explosion in his own lifetime. His data were not statistics on a graph or chart, but the scores of children at every family gathering who ran up to kiss Grandpa, so many that it confused a poor old man. His confusion can be forgiven for there were among them no less than 15 John Millers, all named in his honor. And what young man, much less an old one, could remember the names of 61 grandchildren and 338 great-grandchildren and keep straight just who their parents were?

The remarkable thing about this great clan of his was that it started with a family of just seven children.

From Glenn D. Everett, "One Man's Family," *Population Bulletin*, vol. 17, no. 8, December 1961, pp. 153–157, 169. Reprinted with the permission of the Population Reference Bureau, Inc.

This was actually a little smaller than the typical family among the Amish, who have been found by one researcher to average 8.4 children per completed family. Two of his children died in early life: Samuel Miller, who left six children when he died at 40, and Lizzie (Mrs. Jacob Farnwald), who left four when she died at 28.

During most of his long life, therefore, John Miller's family was not unusually large. It is just that he lived long enough to find out what simple multiplication can do.

One of his daughters, Mary (Mrs. Jacob Mast), had only five children. But all four of his sons had quite large families. His son, John, Jr., with whom he lived at the family homestead, had six children by his first wife, who died in an accident, and nine more by his present wife, a total of 15. Andrew Miller had 12, Eli Miller, 11, of whom ten are living, and Joseph Miller, ten, of whom nine are living.

Of the 63 grandchildren born to John Miller's family, 61 lived to survive him, all but six now grown and married. And of 341 great-grandchildren born to the families of his 55 married grandchildren, only three had died, two in infancy, and one in an accident. All six of his great-grandchildren were born during the last year of his life and were healthy infants.

Thus, a major factor in the world-wide population crisis was vividly evident in John Miller's family: the fact that nearly all children born in the 20th century, who enjoy the benefits of modern medicine, are growing up to become adults and to have families of their own. A century ago, the ravages of smallpox, typhoid fever, tuberculosis, diphtheria and the many fatalities that occurred at childbirth would have left a far different picture in a large rural family. Even though the Amish live in rural areas, they avail themselves of the benefits of medical care. Now most Amish children are born in hospital delivery rooms.

While the sharp reduction in infant mortality and childhood disease is a happy development of science, it inevitably means that population grows with extraordinary rapidity. The Miller family offers a cogent example. John Miller had seven children; his children averaged nine offspring; and his married grandchildren had averaged six each when he passed away. Six married great-grandchildren had one apiece. These were not unusually large families among the Amish nor among the rural families of other Americans in the past century. Yet this clan numbered 410 when John Miller died.

Moreover, at the end of his life, the postman was bringing John Miller word of the birth of a new descendant on the average of once every ten days. This rate, we calculated, would have accelerated to one every other day as his more than 300 great-grandchildren reached marriageable age. Only eight were married when he died and six had had children by their first wedding anniversaries.

So great is the rate of progression of population growth that had John Miller lived one more decade he would have seen more descendants born to him than in all his 95 years of life and would in ten more years have counted at least 1,000 living descendants!

The rate at which population increases is almost unbelievable—even when a man is watching it happen within his own family. John Miller found it difficult to comprehend what was happening. When I told him that all available evidence indicated that he had the largest family in the United States, the kindly old man passed a gnarled hand before his failing eyes and shook his head in amazement. . . .

What did John Miller think about his family? Did it worry him to see it growing so large? Indeed it did. Significantly, his concerns were the very ones that the demographers, the economists, the sociologists, and other serious students of world population problems have been voicing. He was not an educated man, for the Amish still believe eight grades of education in a one-room country school is sufficient, but John Miller summarized it in one simple question he constantly repeated, "Where will they all find good farms?" . . .

Some day, at some point, John Miller's plaintive question, "Where will they all find farms?" will have to be answered in the bleak negative. They can continue now only by buying farms others will sell them. Some day no more farms anywhere will be for sale. A finite world is of limited size. So, ultimately, at some point, is the population it can hold.

The tragedy of the commons

The population problem has no technical solution; it requires a fundamental extension in morality.

GARRETT HARDIN

At the end of a thoughtful article on the future of nuclear war, Wiesner and York (1) concluded that: "Both sides in the arms race are . . . confronted by the dilemma of steadily increasing military power and steadily decreasing national security. *It is our considered professional judgment that this dilemma has no technical solution.* If the great powers continue to look for solutions in the area of science and technology only, the result will be to worsen the situation."

I would like to focus your attention not on the subject of the article (national security in a nuclear world) but on the kind of conclusion they reached, namely that there is no technical solution to the problem. An implicit and almost universal assumption of discussions published in professional and semipopular scientific journals is that the problem under discussion has a technical solution. A technical solution may be defined as one that requires a change only in the techniques of the natural sciences, demanding little or nothing in the way of change in human values or ideas of morality.

In our day (though not in earlier times) technical solutions are always welcome. Because of previous failures in prophecy, it takes courage to assert that a desired technical solution is not possible. Wiesner and York exhibited this courage; publishing in a science journal, they insisted that the solution to the problem was not to be found in the natural sciences. They cautiously qualified their statement with the phrase, "It is our considered professional judgment. . . ." Whether they were right or not is not the concern of the present article. Rather, the concern here is with the important concept of a class of human problems which can be called "no technical solution problems," and, more specifically, with the identification and discussion of one of these.

It is easy to show that the class is not a null class. Recall the game of tick-tack-toe. Consider the problem, "How can I win the game of tick-tack-toe?" It is well known that I cannot, if I assume (in keeping with the conventions of game theory) that my opponent understands the game perfectly. Put another way, there is no "technical solution" to the problem. I can win only by giving a radical meaning to the word "win." I can hit my opponent over the head; or I can drug him; or I can falsify the records. Every way in which I "win" involves, in some sense, an abandonment of the game, as we intuitively understand it. (I can also, of course, openly abandon the game—refuse to play it. This is what most adults do.)

The author is professor of biology, University of California, Santa Barbara. This article is based on a presidential address presented before the meeting of the Pacific Division of the American Association for the Advancement of Science at Utah State University, Logan, 25 June 1968.

From Garrett Hardin, "The Tragedy of the Commons," *Science*, Vol. 162, 13 December 1968, pp. 1243–1248. Copyright 1968 by the American Association for the Advancement of Science. Reprinted with the permission of *Science* and the author.

The class of "No technical solution problems" has members. My thesis is that the "population problem," as conventionally conceived, is a member of this class. How it is conventionally conceived needs some comment. It is fair to say that most people who anguish over the population problem are trying to find a way to avoid the evils of overpopulation without relinquishing any of the privileges they now enjoy. They think that farming the seas or developing new strains of wheat will solve the problem—technologically. I try to show here that the solution they seek cannot be found. The population problem cannot be solved in a technical way, any more than can the problem of winning the game of tick-tack-toe.

WHAT SHALL WE MAXIMIZE?

Population, as Malthus said, naturally tends to grow "geometrically," or, as we would now say, exponentially. In a finite world this means that the per capita share of the world's goods must steadily decrease. Is ours a finite world?

A fair defense can be put forward for the view that the world is infinite; or that we do not know that it is not. But, in terms of the practical problems that we must face in the next few generations with the foreseeable technology, it is clear that we will greatly increase human misery if we do not, during the immediate future, assume that the world available to the terrestrial human population is finite. "Space" is no escape (2).

A finite world can support only a finite population; therefore, population growth must eventually equal zero. (The case of perpetual wide fluctuations above and below zero is a trivial variant that need not be discussed.) When this condition is met, what will be the situation of mankind? Specifically, can Bentham's goal of "the greatest good for the greatest number" be realized?

No—for two reasons, each sufficient by itself. The first is a theoretical one. It is not mathematically possible to maximize for two (or more) variables at the same time. This was clearly stated by von Neumann and Morgenstern (3), but the principle is implicit in the theory of partial differential equations, dating back at least to D'Alembert (1717–1783).

The second reason springs directly from biological facts. To live, any organism must have a source of energy (for example, food). This energy is utilized for two purposes: mere maintenance and work. For man, maintenance of life requires about 1600 kilocalories a day ("maintenance calories"). Anything that he does over and above merely staying alive will be defined as work, and is supported by "work calories" which he takes in. Work calories are used not only for what we call work in common speech; they are also required for all forms of enjoyment, from swimming and automobile racing to playing music and writing poetry. If our goal is to maximize population it is obvious what we must do: We must make the work calories per person approach as close to zero as possible. No gourmet meals, no vacations, no sports, no music, no literature, no art. . . . I think that everyone will grant, without argument or proof, that maximizing population does not maximize goods. Bentham's goal is impossible.

In reaching this conclusion I have made the usual assumption that it is the acquisition of energy that is the problem. The appearance of atomic energy has led some to question this assumption. However, given an infinite source of energy, population growth still produces an inescapable problem. The problem of the acquisition of energy is replaced by the problem of its dissipation, as J. H. Fremlin has so wittily shown (4). The arithmetic signs in the analysis are, as it were, reversed; but Bentham's goal is still unobtainable.

The optimum population is, then, less than the maximum. The difficulty of defining the optimum is enormous; so far as I know, no one has seriously tackled this problem. Reaching an acceptable and stable solution will surely require more than one generation of hard analytical work—and much persuasion.

We want the maximum good per person; but what is good? To one person it is wilderness, to another it is ski lodges for thousands. To one it is estuaries to nourish ducks for hunters to shoot; to another it is factory land. Comparing one good with another is, we usually say, impossible because goods are incommensurable. Incommensurables cannot be compared.

Theoretically this may be true; but in real life incommensurables *are* commensurable. Only a criterion of judgment and a system of weighting are needed. In nature the criterion is survival. Is it better for a species to be small and hideable, or large and powerful? Natural selection commensurates the incommensurables. The compromise achieved depends on a natural weighting of the values of the variables.

Man must imitate this process. There is no doubt that in fact he already does, but unconsciously. It is when the hidden decisions are made explicit that the arguments begin. The problem for the years ahead is to work out an acceptable theory of weighting. Synergistic effects, nonlinear variation, and difficulties in discounting the future make the intellectual problem difficult, but not (in principle) insoluble.

Has any cultural group solved this practical problem at the present time, even on an intuitive level? One simple fact proves that none has: there is no prosperous population in the world today that has, and has had for some time, a growth rate of zero. Any people that has intuitively identified its optimum point will soon reach it, after which its growth rate becomes and remains zero.

Of course, a positive growth rate might be taken as evidence that a population is below its optimum. However, by any reasonable standards, the most rapidly growing populations on earth today are (in general) the most miserable. This association (which need not be invariable) casts doubt on the optimistic assumption that the positive growth rate of a population is evidence that it has yet to reach its optimum.

We can make little progress in working toward optimum population size until we explicitly exorcize the spirit of Adam Smith in the field of practical demography. In economic affairs, *The Wealth of Nations* (1776) popularized the "invisible hand," the idea that an individual who "intends only his own gain," is, as it were, "led by an invisible hand to promote . . . the public interest" (5). Adam Smith did not assert that this was invariably true, and perhaps neither did any of his followers. But he contributed to a dominant tendency of thought that has ever since interfered with positive action based on rational analysis, namely, the tendency to assume that decisions reached individually will, in fact, be the best decisions for an entire society. If this assumption is correct it justifies the continuance of our present policy of laissez-faire in reproduction. If it is correct we can assume that men will control their individual fecundity so as to produce the optimum population. If the assumption is not correct, we need to reexamine our individual freedoms to see which ones are defensible.

TRAGEDY OF FREEDOM IN A COMMONS

The rebuttal to the invisible hand in population control is to be found in a scenario first sketched in a little-known pamphlet (6) in 1833 by a mathematical amateur named William Forster Lloyd (1794–1852). We may well call it "the tragedy of the commons," using the word "tragedy" as the philosopher Whitehead used it (7): "The essence of dramatic tragedy is not unhappiness. It resides in the solemnity of the remorseless working of things." He then goes on to say, "This inevitableness of destiny can only be illustrated in terms of human life by incidents which in fact involve unhappiness. For it is only by them that the futility of escape can be made evident in the drama."

The tragedy of the commons develops in this way. Picture a pasture open to all. It is to be expected that each herdsman will try to keep as many cattle as possible on the commons. Such an arrangement may work reasonably satisfactorily for centuries because tribal wars, poaching, and disease keep the numbers of both man and beast well below the carrying capacity of the land. Finally, however, comes the day of reckoning, that is, the day when the long-desired goal of social stability becomes a reality. At this point, the inherent logic of the commons remorselessly generates tragedy.

As a rational being, each herdsman seeks to maximize his gain. Explicitly or implicitly, more or less consciously, he asks, "What is the utility *to me* of adding one more animal to my herd?" This utility has one negative and one positive component.

1. The positive component is a function of the increment of one animal. Since the herdsman receives all the proceeds from the sale of the additional animal, the positive utility is nearly $+1$.
2. The negative component is a function of the additional overgrazing created by one more animal. Since, however, the effects of overgrazing are shared by all the herdsmen, the negative utility for any particular decision-making herdsman is only a fraction of -1.

Adding together the component partial utilities, the rational herdsman concludes that the only sensible course for him to pursue is to add another animal to his herd. And another; and another. . . . But this is the conclusion reached by each and every rational herdsman sharing a commons. Therein is the tragedy. Each man is locked into a system that compels him to increase his herd without limit—in a world that is limited. Ruin is the destination toward which all men rush, each pursuing his own best interest in a society that believes in the freedom of the commons. Freedom in a commons brings ruin to all.

Some would say that this is a platitude. Would that it were! In a sense, it was learned thousands of years ago, but natural selection favors the forces of psychological denial (8). The individual benefits as an individual from his ability to deny the truth even though society as a whole, of which he is a part, suffers. Education can counteract the natural tendency to do the wrong thing, but the inexorable succession of generations requires that the basis for this knowledge be constantly refreshed.

A simple incident that occurred a few years ago in Leominster, Massachusetts, shows how perishable the knowledge is. During the Christmas shopping season the parking meters downtown were covered with plastic bags that bore tags reading: "Do not open until after Christmas. Free parking courtesy of the mayor and city council." In other words, facing the prospect of an increased demand for already scarce space, the city fathers reinstituted the system of the commons. (Cynically, we suspect that they gained more votes than they lost by this retrogressive act.)

In an approximate way, the logic of the commons has been understood for a long time, perhaps since the discovery of agriculture or the invention of private property in real estate. But it is understood mostly only in special cases which are not sufficiently generalized. Even at this late date, cattlemen leasing national land on the western ranges demonstrate no more than an ambivalent understanding, in constantly pressuring federal authorities to increase the head count to the point where overgrazing produces erosion and weed-dominance. Likewise, the oceans of the world continue to suffer from the survival of the philosophy of the commons. Maritime nations still respond automatically to the shibboleth of the "freedom of the seas." Professing to believe in the "inexhaustible resources of the oceans," they bring species after species of fish and whales closer to extinction (9).

The National Parks present another instance of the working out of the tragedy of the commons. At present, they are open to all, without limit. The parks themselves are limited in extent —there is only one Yosemite Valley—

whereas population seems to grow without limit. The values that visitors seek in the parks are steadily eroded. Plainly, we must soon cease to treat the parks as commons or they will be of no value to anyone.

What shall we do? We have several options. We might sell them off as private property. We might keep them as public property, but allocate the right to enter them. The allocation might be on the basis of wealth, by the use of an auction system. It might be on the basis of merit, as defined by some agreed-upon standards. It might be by lottery. Or it might be on a first-come, first-served basis, administered to long queues. These, I think, are all the reasonable possibilities. They are all objectionable. But we must choose—or acquiesce in the destruction of the commons that we call our National Parks.

POLLUTION

In a reverse way, the tragedy of the commons reappears in problems of pollution. Here it is not a question of taking something out of the commons, but of putting something in—sewage, or chemical, radioactive, and heat wastes into water; noxious and dangerous fumes into the air; and distracting and unpleasant advertising signs into the line of sight. The calculations of utility are much the same as before. The rational man finds that his share of the cost of the wastes he discharges into the commons is less than the cost of purifying his wastes before releasing them. Since this is true for everyone, we are locked into a system of "fouling our own nest," so long as we behave only as independent, rational, free-enterprisers.

The tragedy of the commons as a food basket is averted by private property, or something formally like it. But the air and waters surrounding us cannot readily be fenced, and so the tragedy of the commons as a cesspool must be prevented by different means, by coercive laws or taxing devices that make it cheaper for the polluter to treat his pollutants than to discharge them untreated. We have not progressed as far with the solution of this problem as we have with the first. Indeed, our particular concept of private property, which deters us from exhausting the positive resources of the earth, favors pollution. The owner of a factory on the bank of a stream —whose property extends to the middle of the stream—often has difficulty seeing why it is not his natural right to muddy the waters flowing past his door. The law, always behind the times, requires elaborate stitching and fitting to adapt it to this newly perceived aspect of the commons.

The pollution problem is a consequence of population. It did not much matter how a lonely American frontiersman disposed of his waste. "Flowing water purifies itself every 10 miles," my grandfather used to say, and the myth was near enough to the truth when he was a boy, for there were not too many people. But as population became denser, the natural chemical and biological recycling processes became overloaded, calling for a redefinition of property rights.

HOW TO LEGISLATE TEMPERANCE?

Analysis of the pollution problem as a function of population density uncovers a not generally recognized principle of morality, namely: *the morality of an act is a function of the state of the system at the time it is performed* (*10*). Using the commons as a cesspool does not harm the general public under frontier conditions, because there is no public; the same behavior

in a metropolis is unbearable. A hundred and fifty years ago a plainsman could kill an American bison, cut out only the tongue for his dinner, and discard the rest of the animal. He was not in any important sense being wasteful. Today, with only a few thousand bison left, we would be appalled at such behavior.

In passing, it is worth noting that the morality of an act cannot be determined from a photograph. One does not know whether a man killing an elephant or setting fire to the grassland is harming others until one knows the total system in which his act appears. "One picture is worth a thousand words," said an ancient Chinese; but it may take 10,000 words to validate it. It is as tempting to ecologists as it is to reformers in general to try to persuade others by way of the photographic shortcut. But the essense of an argument cannot be photographed: it must be presented rationally—in words.

That morality is system-sensitive escaped the attention of most codifiers of ethics in the past. "Thou shalt not . . . " is the form of traditional ethical directives which make no allowance for particular circumstances. The laws of our society follow the pattern of ancient ethics, and therefore are poorly suited to governing a complex, crowded, changeable world. Our epicyclic solution is to augment statutory law with administrative law. Since it is practically impossible to spell out all the conditions under which it is safe to burn trash in the back yard or to run an automobile without smog-control, by law we delegate the details to bureaus. The result is administrative law, which is rightly feared for an ancient reason—*Quis custodiet ipsos custodes?*—"Who shall watch the watchers themselves?" John Adams said that we must have "a government of laws and not men." Bureau administrators, trying to evaluate the morality of acts in the total system, are singularly liable to corruption, producing a government by men, not laws.

Prohibition is easy to legislate (though not necessarily to enforce); but how do we legislate temperance? Experience indicates that it can be accomplished best through the mediation of administrative law. We limit possibilities unnecessarily if we suppose that the sentiment of *Quis custodiet* denies us the use of administrative law. We should rather retain the phrase as a perpetual reminder of fearful dangers we cannot avoid. The great challenge facing us now is to invent the corrective feedbacks that are needed to keep custodians honest. We must find ways to legitimate the needed authority of both the custodians and the corrective feedbacks.

FREEDOM TO BREED IS INTOLERABLE

The tragedy of the commons is involved in population problems in another way. In a world governed solely by the principle of "dog eat dog"—if indeed there ever was such a world—how many children a family had would not be a matter of public concern. Parents who bred too exuberantly would leave fewer descendants, not more, because they would be unable to care adequately for their children. David Lack and others have found that such a negative feedback demonstrably controls the fecundity of birds (*11*). But men are not birds, and have not acted like them for millenniums, at least.

If each human family were dependent only on its own resources; *if* the children of improvident parents starved to death; *if*, thus, overbreeding brought its own "punishment" to the germ line—*then* there would be no

public interest in controlling the breeding of families. But our society is deeply committed to the welfare state (*12*), and hence is confronted with another aspect of the tragedy of the commons.

In a welfare state, how shall we deal with the family, the religion, the race, or the class (or indeed any distinguishable and cohesive group) that adopts overbreeding as a policy to secure its own aggrandizement (*13*)? To couple the concept of freedom to breed with the belief that everyone born has an equal right to the commons is to lock the world into a tragic course of action.

Unfortunately this is just the course of action that is being pursued by the United Nations. In late 1967, some 30 nations agreed to the following (*14*):

The Universal Declaration of Human Rights describes the family as the natural and fundamental unit of society. It follows that any choice and decision with regard to the size of the family must irrevocably rest with the family itself, and cannot be made by anyone else.

It is painful to have to deny categorically the validity of this right; denying it, one feels as uncomfortable as a resident of Salem, Massachusetts, who denied the reality of witches in the 17th century. At the present time, in liberal quarters, something like a taboo acts to inhibit criticism of the United Nations. There is a feeling that the United Nations is "our last and best hope," that we shouldn't find fault with it; we shouldn't play into the hands of the archconservatives. However, let us not forget what Robert Louis Stevenson said: "The truth that is suppressed by friends is the readiest weapon of the enemy." If we love the truth we must openly deny the validity of the Universal Declaration of Human Rights, even though it is promoted by the United Nations. We should also join with Kingsley Davis (15) in attempting to get Planned Parenthood-World Population to see the error of its ways in embracing the same tragic ideal.

CONSCIENCE IS SELF-ELIMINATING

It is a mistake to think that we can control the breeding of mankind in the long run by an appeal to conscience. Charles Galton Darwin made this point when he spoke on the centennial of the publication of his grandfather's great book. The argument is straightforward and Darwinian.

People vary. Confronted with appeals to limit breeding, some people will undoubtedly respond to the plea more than others. Those who have more children will produce a larger fraction of the next generation than those with more susceptible consciences. The difference will be accentuated, generation by generation.

In C. G. Darwin's words: "It may well be that it would take hundreds of generations for the progenitive instinct to develop in this way, but if it should do so, nature would have taken her revenge, and the variety *Homo contracipiens* would become extinct and would be replaced by the variety *Homo progenitivus*" (16).

The argument assumes that conscience or the desire for children (no matter which) is hereditary—but hereditary only in the most general formal sense. The result will be the same whether the attitude is transmitted through germ cells, or exosomatically, to use A. J. Lotka's term. (If one denies the latter possibility as well as the former, then what's the point of education?) The argument has here been stated in the context of the population problem, but it applies

equally well to any instance in which society appeals to an individual exploiting a commons to restrain himself for the general good—by means of his conscience. To make such an appeal is to set up a selective system that works toward the elimination of conscience from the race.

PATHOGENIC EFFECTS OF CONSCIENCE

The long-term disadvantage of an appeal to conscience should be enough to condemn it; but has serious short-term disadvantages as well. If we ask a man who is exploiting a commons to desist "in the name of conscience," what are we saying to him? What does he hear?—not only at the moment but also in the wee small hours of the night when, half asleep, he remembers not merely the words we used but also the nonverbal communication cues we gave him unawares? Sooner or later, consciously or subconsciously, he senses that he has received two communications, and that they are contradictory: (i) (intended communication) "If you don't do as we ask, we will openly condemn you for not acting like a responsible citizen"; (ii) (the unintended communication) "If you *do* behave as we ask, we will secretly condemn you for a simpleton who can be shamed into standing aside while the rest of us exploit the commons."

Every man then is caught in what Bateson has called a "double bind." Bateson and his co-workers have made a plausible case for viewing the double bind as an important causative factor in the genesis of schizophrenia (17). The double bind may not always be so damaging, but it always endangers the mental health of anyone to whom it is applied. "A bad conscience," said Nietzsche, "is a kind of illness."

To conjure up a conscience in others is tempting to anyone who wishes to extend his control beyond the legal limits. Leaders at the highest level succumb to this temptation. Has any President during the past generation failed to call on labor unions to moderate voluntarily their demands for higher wages, or to steel companies to honor voluntary guidelines on prices? I can recall none. The rhetoric used on such occasions is designed to produce feelings of guilt in noncooperators.

For centuries it was assumed without proof that guilt was a valuable, perhaps even an indispensable, ingredient of the civilized life. Now, in this post-Freudian world, we doubt it.

Paul Goodman speaks from the modern point of view when he says: "No good has ever come from feeling guilty, neither intelligence, policy, nor compassion. The guilty do not pay attention to the object but only to themselves, and not even to their own interests, which might make sense, but to their anxieties" (*18*).

One does not have to be a professional psychiatrist to see the consequences of anxiety. We in the Western world are just emerging from a dreadful two-centuries-long Dark Ages of Eros that was sustained partly by prohibition laws, but perhaps more effectively by the anxiety-generating mechanisms of education. Alex Comfort has told the story well in *The Anxiety Makers* (*19*); it is not a pretty one.

Since proof is difficult, we may even concede that the results of anxiety may sometimes, from certain points of view, be desirable. The larger question we should ask is whether, as a matter of policy, we should ever encourage the use of a technique the tendency (if not the intention) of which is psychologically pathogenic. We hear much talk these days of responsible parenthood; the coupled words are incorporated into the titles of some organizations devoted to birth control. Some people have proposed massive propaganda campaigns to instill responsibility into the nation's (or the world's) breeders. But what is the meaning of the word responsibility in this context? Is it not merely a synonym for the word conscience? When we use the word responsibility in the absence of substantial sanctions are we not trying to browbeat a free man in a commons into acting against his own interest? Responsibility is a verbal counterfeit for a substantial *quid pro quo*. It is an attempt to get something for nothing.

If the word responsibility is to be used at all, I suggest that it be in the sense Charles Frankel uses it (*20*). "Responsibility," says this philosopher, "is the product of definite social arrangements." Notice that Frankel calls for social arrangements—not propaganda.

MUTUAL COERCION MUTUALLY AGREED UPON

The social arrangements that produce responsibility are arrangements that create coercion, of some sort. Consider bank-robbing. The man who takes money from a bank acts as if the bank were a commons. How do we prevent such action? Certainly not by trying to control his behavior solely by a verbal appeal to his sense of responsibility. Rather than rely on propaganda we follow Frankel's lead and insist that a bank is not a commons; we seek the definite social arrangements that will keep it from becoming a commons. That we thereby infringe on the freedom of would-be robbers we neither deny nor regret.

The morality of bank-robbing is particularly easy to understand because we accept complete prohibition of this activity. We are willing to say "Thou shalt not rob banks," without providing for exceptions. But temperance also can be created by coercion. Taxing is a good coercive device. To keep downtown shoppers temperate in their use of parking space we introduce parking meters for short periods, and traffic fines for longer ones. We need not actually forbid a citizen to park as long as he wants to; we need merely make it increasingly expensive for him to do so. Not prohibition, but carefully biased options are what we offer him. A Madison Avenue man might call this persuasion; I prefer the greater candor of the word coercion.

Coercion is a dirty word to most liberals now, but it need not forever be so. As with the four-letter words, its dirtiness can be cleansed away by exposure to the light, by saying it over and over without apology or embarrassment. To many, the word coercion implies arbitrary decisions of distant and irresponsible bureaucrats; but this is not a necessary part of its meaning. The only kind of coercion I recommend is mutual coercion, mutually agreed upon by the majority of the people affected.

To say that we mutually agree to coercion is not to say that we are required to enjoy it, or even to pretend we enjoy it. Who enjoys taxes? We all grumble about them. But we accept compulsory taxes because we recognize that voluntary taxes would favor the conscienceless. We institute and (grumblingly) support taxes and other coercive devices to escape the horror of the commons.

An alternative to the commons need not be perfectly just to be preferable. With real estate and other material goods, the alternative we have chosen is the institution of private property coupled with legal inheritance. Is this system perfectly just? As a genetically trained biologist I deny that it is. It seems to me that, if there are to be differences in individual inheritance, legal possession should be perfectly correlated with biological inheritance—that those who are biologically more fit to be the custodians of property and power should legally inherit more. But genetic recombination continually makes a mockery of the doctrine of "like father, like son" implicit in our laws of legal inheritance. An idiot can inherit millions, and a trust fund can keep his estate intact. We must admit that our legal system of private property plus inheritance is unjust—but we put up with it because we are not convinced, at the moment, that anyone has invented a better system. The alternative of the commons is too horrifying to contemplate. Injustice is preferable to total ruin.

It is one of the peculiarities of the warfare between reform and the status quo that it is thoughtlessly governed by a double standard. Whenever a reform measure is proposed it is often defeated when its opponents triumphantly discover a flaw in it. As Kingsley Davis has pointed out (21), worshippers of the status quo sometimes imply that no reform is possible without unanimous agreement, an implication contrary to historical fact. As nearly as I can make out, automatic rejection of proposed reforms is based on one of two unconscious assumptions: (i) that the status quo is perfect; or (ii) that the choice we face is between reform and no action; if the proposed reform is imperfect, we presumably should take no action at all, while we wait for a perfect proposal.

But we can never do nothing. That which we have done for thousands of years is also action. It also produces evils. Once we are aware that the status quo is action, we can then compare its discoverable advantages and disadvantages with the predicted advantages and disadvantages of the proposed reform, discounting as best we can for our lack of experience. On the basis of such a comparison, we can make a rational decision which will not involve the unworkable assumption that only perfect systems are tolerable.

RECOGNITION OF NECESSITY

Perhaps the simplest summary of this analysis of man's population problems is this: the commons, if justifiable at all, is justifiable only under conditions of low-population density. As the human population has increased, the commons has had to be abandoned in one aspect after another.

First we abandoned the commons in food gathering, enclosing farm land and restricting pastures and hunting and fishing areas. These restrictions are still not complete throughout the world.

Somewhat later we saw that the commons as a place for waste disposal would also have to be abandoned. Restrictions on the disposal of domestic sewage are widely accepted in the Western world; we are still struggling to close the commons to pollution by automobiles, factories, insecticide sprayers, fertilizing operations, and atomic energy installations.

In a still more embryonic state is our recognition of the evils of the commons in matters of pleasure. There is almost no restriction on the propagation of sound waves in the public medium. The shopping public is assaulted with mindless music, without its consent. Our government is paying out billions of dollars to create supersonic transport which will disturb 50,-000 people for every one person who is whisked from coast to coast 3 hours faster. Advertisers muddy the airwaves of radio and television and pollute the view of travelers. We are a long way from outlawing the commons in matters of pleasure. Is this because our Puritan inheritance makes us view pleasure as something of a sin, and pain (that is, the pollution of advertising) as the sign of virtue?

Every new enclosure of the commons involves the infringement of somebody's personal liberty. Infringements made in the distant past are accepted because no contemporary complains of a loss. It is the newly proposed infringements that we vigorously oppose; cries of "rights" and "freedom" fill the air. But what does "freedom" mean? When men mutually agreed to pass laws against robbing, mankind became more free, not less so. Individuals locked into the logic of the commons are free only to bring on universal ruin; once they see the necessity of mutual coercion, they become free to pursue other goals. I believe it was Hegel who said, "Freedom is the recognition of necessity."

The most important aspect of necessity that we must now recognize, is the necessity of abandoning the commons in breeding. No technical solution can rescue us from the misery of overpopulation. Freedom to breed will bring ruin to all. At the moment, to avoid hard decisions many of us are tempted to propagandize for conscience and responsible parenthood. The temptation must be resisted, because an appeal to independently acting consciences selects for the disappearance of all conscience in the long run, and an increase in anxiety in the short.

The only way we can preserve and nurture other and more precious freedoms is by relinquishing the freedom to breed, and that very soon. "Freedom is the recognition of necessity"— and it is the role of education to reveal to all the necessity of abandoning the freedom to breed. Only so, can we put an end to this aspect of the tragedy of the commons.

REFERENCES

1. J. B. Wiesner and H. F. York, *Sci. Amer.* **211** (No. 4), 27 (1964).
2. G. Hardin, *J. Hered.* **50,** 68 (1959); S. von Hoernor, *Science* **137, 18** (1962).
3. J. von Neumann and O. Morgenstern, *Theory of Games and Economic Behavior* (Princeton Univ. Press, Princeton, N.J., 1947), p. 11.
4. J. H. Fremlin, *New Sci.,* No. 415 (1964), p. 285.
5. A. Smith, *The Wealth of Nations* (Modern Library, New York, 1937), p. 423.
6. W. F. Lloyd, *Two Lectures on the Checks to Population* (Oxford Univ. Press, Oxford, England, 1833), reprinted (in part) in *Population, Evolution, and Birth Control,* G. Hardin, Ed. (Freeman, San Francisco, 1964), p. 37.
7. A. N. Whitehead, *Science and the Modern World* (Mentor, New York, 1948), p. 17.
8. G. Hardin, Ed. *Population, Evolution, and Birth Control* (Freeman, San Francisco, 1964), p. 56.
9. S. McVay, *Sci. Amer.* **216** (No. 8), 13 (1966).
10. J. Fletcher, *Situation Ethics* (Westminster, Philadelphia, 1966).
11. D. Lack, *The Natural Regulation of Animal Numbers* (Clarendon Press, Oxford, 1954).
12. H. Girvetz, *From Wealth to Welfare* (Stanford Univ. Press, Stanford, Calif., 1950).
13. G. Hardin, *Perspec. Biol. Med.* **6,** 366 (1963).
14. U. Thant, *Int. Planned Parenthood News,* No. 168 (February 1968), p. 3.
15. K. Davis, *Science* **158,** 730 (1967).
16. S. Tax, Ed., *Evolution after Darwin* (Univ. of Chicago Press, Chicago, 1960), vol. 2, p. 469.
17. G. Bateson, D. D. Jackson, J. Haley, J. Weakland, *Behav. Sci.* **1,** 251 (1956).
18. P. Goodman, *New York Rev. Books* 10(8), 22 (23 May 1968).
19. A. Comfort, *The Anxiety Makers* (Nelson, London, 1967).
20. C. Frankel, *The Case for Modern Man* (Harper, New York, 1955), p. 203.
21. J. D. Roslansky, *Genetics and the Future of Man* (Appleton-Century-Crofts, New York, 1966), p. 177.

Poverty

2

POVERTY AS A SOCIAL PROBLEM

In studying the emergence of poverty as a social problem we are confronted with an interesting paradox —poverty is not generally recognized as a problem until society attains a certain level of affluence. Throughout much of history man facing a hostile environment has had to devote much of his energy to attaining subsistence; only recently has attention shifted from problems of subsistence to those of redistribution of wealth. While recognition and identification of poverty as a social problem is a relatively recent phenomenon, concern with poverty is not new. In the past, however, it was viewed as a problem of undesirable, or deviant, individuals rather than as a social condition. The focus was on providing deterrents through punishment so that people would not choose to be poor, not on identifying the social conditions that produce poverty. Under the English Public Relief Provisions of 1536, for example, pauperism was defined as a crime. Today we have developed a more humanitarian outlook, as evidenced by the elimination of debtors prisons and the emergence of less punitive attitudes toward the poor. Nonetheless, you will see later in the chapter that a more subtle pejorative orientation toward the poor has emerged.

The beginning of large-scale governmental efforts to eradicate poverty in the United States dates to the Depression era. While many social welfare programs were initiated during the Roosevelt administration, New Deal legislation was aimed largely at putting the economy back on its feet rather than eliminating, or even reducing, poverty. In every society there is a segment of the population, the "hard core" poor, that is relatively impervious to economic fluctuations; they remain poor even during periods of economic prosperity. New Deal legislation (as well as subsequent legislation) did little to help the permanent poor. It simply helped the temporary poor out of poverty and improved the overall status of the economy. The New Deal, however, was significant in that the need for governmental intervention to reduce economic inequities was recognized.

During World War II and the postwar era the United States enjoyed substantial economic prosperity, and the poor were virtually forgotten through the 1940s and 1950s. In the early 1960s many Americans were shocked to read about the *Other America* depicted by Michael Harrington. Throughout the past decade there has been increasing concern with poverty as a major social problem. There is a growing realization that, perhaps for the first time in history, we have the capacity to eliminate poverty and hunger.

POVERTY IN THE UNITED STATES

Despite greater awareness of poverty, there has been reluctance on the part of some to recognize poverty as a major social problem. Many Americans believe that poverty was a problem during the Depression but that today it is only a problem of less developed nations. They have been socialized to accept the idea that the United States is the wealthiest country in the world, as measured by gross statistics such as the gross national product and median income per family. Statistics based on averages are misleading in that they obscure poverty among the permanent poor. If one family has an income of $100,000 and another has an income of $2,000, their average income is $51,000, but one of the families is still poor. It is precisely because the condition of the "have-nots" is hidden by the overall wealth of the society that the problem of poverty is difficult to attack in an affluent society. In this sense, the poor in the United States are hidden or invisible.

For those who believe that the United States is the affluent society statistics on poverty are shocking and perhaps incredible. Although the median family income exceeds $11,000 annually, millions of persons live below the poverty line (U.S. Bureau of the Census, 1973a:1). The exact number of poor in this country is subject to debate and varies according to which definition of poverty is used. In 1964 the *Ad Hoc* Committee on "The Triple Revolution" suggested that some 38 million Americans live in poverty. More recent, but perhaps conservative, figures suggest that the number is about 25 million (Kershaw, 1970:16; U.S. Bureau of the Census, 1972a: 329, and 1973b:1). There is reason to believe, though, that the proportion of persons living in poverty has been declining. Between 1947 and 1967 the number of families who received incomes of less than $3000 (in 1967 prices) decreased from 10.2 million to 6.2 million (Sheppard, 1970:4). This represented a reduction from 27 percent of all American families in 1947 to 13 percent in 1967. Similarly, in 1959 there were approximately 38.7 million persons living in poverty, whereas in 1967 the figure was down to 25.9 million (Kershaw, 1970:21). It is interesting to note, however, that between the beginning of 1969 and the end of 1970 the number of persons living below the official poverty line increased (U.S. Bureau of the Census, 1972a:329). During the 1960s there had been an average annual decline of 4.9 percent, but between 1969 and 1970 the number increased by 5.1 percent (Chapman, 1971).[1]

The gains made in reducing the absolute level of poverty can lead to a misplaced optimism. Official government statistics on poverty are based on absolute, or objective, figures, and the problem of poverty is one of relative deprivation. The U.S. Bureau of the Census calculates the poverty line for various sized families on the basis of a constant level of minimal subsistence[2] (Kershaw, 1970:10–14). The index does not take into account the relative component of poverty. A more meaningful conception of poverty may be to compare the lot of the poor with the level of affluence of the society as a whole. Such a comparison suggests that the relative position of the poor is not improving. In 1959 the bottom 25 percent of American families received incomes of $4000 or less; the top 10 percent received a minimum of $13,500 (in 1967 prices). In other words, the range was $9500. In 1967 the figures were $4900 and $16,300. The range had increased to $11,400 (Sheppard, 1970:7).

These figures indicate that while the median income has been increasing and the proportion of persons living in poverty decreasing, the gap between persons who are poor and the rest of the society is probably widening. It is an irony that the concept of relative deprivation becomes especially meaningful in an affluent society. Since human desires are insatiable, definitions of poverty, and even minimal necessities, are subject to change and

[1] Between 1971 and 1972, however, the number appears to have declined again (U.S. Bureau of the Census, 1973b:1).

[2] Relative measures of poverty suggest that the proportion of American families who are poor has not changed (Madden, 1971:12).

revision. A person who is poor by absolute standards but not relative to other persons around him is less likely to define himself as poor than one who is better off by absolute standards but is surrounded by affluent people. Indeed, this is the plight of many Americans, particularly urban blacks, who define a television as a necessity and have their feeling of relative deprivation intensified via television.

WHO ARE THE POOR?

Poverty, like wealth, is unevenly distributed among different segments of the society. The three social categories that are most overrepresented among the poor are members of racial and ethnic minorities, the aged, and female heads of households (U.S. Bureau of the Census, 1973b:1–2).

Blacks, Mexican Americans, and American Indians are undoubtedly the most poverty-stricken racial and ethnic minorities. Throughout most of our history black Americans have occupied an unequal, subordinate position in society, but in recent years they have made many significant educational and economic improvements. Between 1960 and 1970 the median income for black families increased from $4000 to $6191 (Kotz, 1971:A1). During the same period, white income rose from $7252 to $9794. Thus, in effect after a decade the black family was $352 further behind. The number of persons living below the low-income or poverty level has declined steadily since 1967 both within the white and black populations. "However, within the last year, there is some evidence that the number of black poor increased, whereas the number of low-income whites declined substantially" (U.S. Bureau of the Census, 1973c:2). Blacks have also made important advances in education, but they receive fewer rewards than whites with comparable schooling. A white person who completed the eighth grade earned more in 1970 ($7018) than a black who had graduated from high school ($6192). The salary of a white high school graduate in the same year ($8829) was higher than the salary for a black college graduate ($8669) (Kotz, 1971:A8). In summary, the educational and economic position of black Americans has progressed substantially by absolute standards but not relative to whites.

Since blacks constitute about 11 percent of the population, much attention has been given to poverty among them, and other minorities have been relatively neglected. Mexican Americans are the second largest ethnic minority in the country, with numbers in excess of 5 million. While comparable statistics are difficult to obtain, poverty among Mexican Americans is probably at least as prevalent as among black Americans. Most Mexican Americans are concentrated in the Southwest, especially in the states of Arizona, California, Colorado, New Mexico, and Texas. Only 12.8 percent of all persons in these states are below the low-income level, whereas 30.5 percent of persons of Mexican origin are below this level (U.S. Bureau of the Census, 1972b:9).[3] Family income figures actually underestimate the amount of poverty among Mexican Americans, since their families tend to be larger than either white or other nonwhite families. In California (the most prosperous southwestern state) the median income per individual member was $1380 for Mexicans, $1437 for nonwhites, and $2108 for white Anglos (Moore, 1970:71). As with blacks, the absolute economic position of Mexican Americans is improving, but their relative position is not.

While Mexican Americans have in recent years made important educational advances, their educational level is still lower than that of Anglos or blacks. Among persons twenty-five years and older the median number of years of schooling completed is 7.1 for Mexican Americans, 12.1 for Anglos, and 9.0 for nonwhites (Moore, 1970:65). Similarly, only 3.7 percent of white adults, twenty-five and older, and 12.8 percent of black adults have completed less than five years of school, as compared to 26.7 percent of Mexican Americans (U.S. Bureau of the Census, 1973e:112). It is frequently asserted that the key to improving the economic position of minorities is education, yet the gap between Mexican Americans and the rest of society appears to widen with increasing education (Moore, 1970: 60).

The last racial and ethnic minority to be discussed, the American Indian, is undoubtedly the most disadvantaged. Stories of wealthy Indian oilmen not withstanding, most American Indians live in poverty. The isolation of Indians on reservations and their relatively small numbers have obscured their poverty from the American public. About one-half of employable Indians are out of work, and in some areas unemployment is as high as 90 percent (Steiner, 1968:137–138). Their median family income was $5832 (U.S. Bureau of the Census, 1973d:120), but it varies somewhat by tribe and among some it is under $1000. The Pine Ridge Sioux of the Dakotas, for instance, reported an annual median family income of $105 (Steiner, 1968:137). American Indians are characterized not only by low incomes and high unemployment but also by substandard housing, high infant mortality, high death rates, widespread disease, and unsanitary living conditions (Steiner, 1968). Since the poverty of blacks, Mexican Americans, and Indians results mostly from prejudice and discrimination, these problems are discussed more fully in the following chapter.

Although racial and ethnic minorities are disproportionately represented among the poor, not all poor people are members of minorities. In fact, about three-quarters of the poor in this country are white. White persons are proportionately underrepresented among the poor, but in absolute numbers they account for a majority of the poor. Some of the white poor

[3] Nationally, 12.5 percent of the total population and 28.9 percent of the Mexican-American population are below the low-income level (U.S. Bureau of the Census, 1972b:9).

are the forgotten mountain people of Appalachia; others are mothers without a husband; and still others are the aged. Specifically, the rate of poverty is high not only for nonwhite families but also for families headed by a person over sixty-five, those headed by a woman, and rural families (President's Commission on Rural Poverty, 1968). The sex of the head of the family is one of the most important factors in determining whether a family is poor. About one out of three low-income white families is headed by a woman, whereas almost two out of three low-income black families have female heads (U.S. Bureau of the Census, 1973b:1). Moreover, while the proportion of poor families headed by a male has decreased dramatically the proportion headed by a female has increased (U.S. Bureau of the Census, 1973b:1). The prototype poor family, then, is one headed by a young, nonwhite female with less than an eighth-grade education. Such a family is poor in about 94 out of 100 cases (Meissner, 1966:44).

While relative to their number in the population the aged are over-represented among the poor, there are important differences in the age composition of white and black poverty groups. Among blacks poverty is generally a phenomenon of the young, but among whites it is more often a phenomenon of the old. Persons sixty-five years and older constitute about 19 percent of all whites who are below the poverty line, but they make up only about 8 percent of the black poor (U.S. Bureau of the Census, 1973b:2).

The significance of poverty among persons who are not part of a racial or ethnic minority lies in the fact that many of them were not always poor. They are not part of the permanent poor but rather have become poor as a result of a change in their economic status (e.g., women left without a husband and persons who become poor after retirement). The problem of poverty among the aged is particularly interesting because many become poor only after leaving the labor force. Their poverty results from a combination of factors including inadequate retirement benefits, insufficient savings, and mounting medical expenses. The poverty of the aged is in a sense achieved. It seems both ironic and unfortunate that after forty or more years in the labor force many Americans find themselves poverty-stricken.

It is important to distinguish between permanent and temporary poverty; each is caused by different conditions and calls for different solutions. Temporary poverty is much more readily resolvable than permanent poverty. The temporary poor are composed of a fluctuating membership. The number of temporary poor is relatively stable, but the membership is variable as persons go in and out of the labor force. It would be erroneous therefore to conclude that all persons who are unemployed are permanently poor. For many, poverty is a temporary status. The incidence of temporary poverty is greatly affected by fluctuations in the economy. In recent years, for example, unemployment has been high both among space engineers and teachers as a result of a decreased demand for their skills, but their poverty and unemployment is temporary, since they have the requisite training and education to find some type of employment. Furthermore, future changes in the economy could improve their position very rapidly. Government welfare and public assistance programs generally benefit the temporary poor more than the permanent poor. The temporary poor have more political power and influence and are able to bring about legislation to improve their condition. New Deal legislation was aimed primarily at alleviating large-scale temporary poverty; it did little to help the permanent poor. The permanent poor are relatively impervious to changes in the economy, and they lack the skills and training to assume positions that might go unfilled. They are by-passed not only by economic prosperity but also by government welfare.

CONCEPTIONS OF POVERTY

The poor are immoral

This is perhaps the oldest and most recurrent view of poverty. For centuries the poor have been classified into a morally degenerate almost subhuman category. This conception of poverty parallels closely the classical school of crime (see the Introduction to Part Two). According to the classical view of crime, criminals were criminals because they deliberately chose to violate the law. The religious concept of free will served as the underlying justification for the classical school (Quinney, 1970:58–64). Contrary to the principle of predestination, free will assumes that men can control their own destinies on this earth; they have choices to make, and one may choose to be good or evil, criminal or noncriminal. A simple extension of this principle to poverty would lead one to the conclusion that those who are poor want to be poor. Poverty was explained not in terms of natural forces or structural conditions beyond the control of individuals but as volitional behavior. Why would some persons choose to be poor? One explanation given was that the poor were lacking in moral development. There was a need, therefore, to discourage persons from selecting poverty as an alternative. According to this view, if the poor are punished with severe penalties and criminal sanctions, it may be possible to eliminate, or at least, reduce poverty. Paupers then, in this view, should be treated like other criminals.

The poor deserve what they get

The classical view of poverty predominated until the latter part of the nineteenth century when a new conception arose. Darwin's *Origin of the Species* was published in 1859, and the concept of evolution had a strong impact not only on biological theories of man but also on sociological theories. The school of thought that applied evolutionary theory to societal change was termed "Social Darwinism" (Timasheff, 1963:59–71; Hofstadter, 1955). The concepts of evolution and survival of the fittest were used by Social Darwinists to explain, or more accurately justify, the subordination of some people to others. Those who were economically wealthy were the fittest to survive socially, and the poor or have-nots were the unfit. Social Darwinism condoned the massive accumulation of wealth by the "robber barons" of the nineteenth century and the exploitation of the poor. Late nineteenth-century sociological theory was permeated by biological analogies and evolutionary models (see the Introduction to Part Three). Many of the founders of sociology, such as Comte and Spencer, subscribed to an organismic view of society. William Graham Sumner, for example, was a staunch defender of the doctrine of laissez faire, and in the book *What Social Classes Owe to Each Other* he strongly opposed governmental efforts to help the poor. He felt that government did not have the right to take money from the middle class, whom he called the "forgotten man," to give the poor (Sumner, 1961:22). Similarly, Herbert Spencer (1851:324) maintained that social philanthropists who sought to eradicate poverty are "blind to the fact, that under the natural order of things society is constantly excreting its unhealthy, imbecile, slow, vacillating, faithless members, these unthinking, though well-meaning, men advocate an interference which not only stops the purifying process, but even increases the vitiation. . . ."

The poor will always be with us

A corollary to Social Darwinism is the view that the poor are ubiquitous to society. If structured inequality is the natural order of things, then society will always have its haves and have-nots. Men compete over scarce resources, some win and others lose. Thus, it is written in the Scriptures that "Yea have the poor with you always." This view of man and society has been prevalent throughout history and is still adhered to by many Americans. Philip Slater (1971:100–118), however, argues that the old cultural values of scarcity, competition, and conflict are being replaced by a new set of values in the "new culture," which emphasizes abundance, cooperation, and harmony among people. As these values take hold, the belief that the poor will always be with us should fall by the wayside.

The protestant ethic and the poor

Although few Americans openly accept the view that the poor are immoral, vestiges of this conception remain. Many Americans still subscribe to an individualistic and rational view of man and society that holds that individuals can and do control their own destinies. The poor are still seen as morally suspect, since it is difficult to envision any honest and moral person wanting to be poor and no one is poor in this country unless he wants to be. This view of the poor is buttressed not only by American individualistic values but also by the teachings of the Protestant Ethic. Max Weber (1958) advanced the thesis that the Protestant Ethic, particularly Calvinism, made the emergence of modern capitalism possible. The concept of predestination was an essential component of Calvinist thought. It was believed that if one was not among the chosen, there was nothing that could be done to enhance one's standing in the eyes of God. At first such a belief appears inconsistent with the requirements of capitalism. If people are predestined, why should one be motivated to do good works on earth? The key lies in the belief that although only God knows who is predestined, success on this earth may be interpreted as a sign that one is among the saved. If economic success is a sign of moral virtue, then economic failure must be a sign of moral decay. The Protestant Ethic provides a subtle and indirect condemnation of the poor.

The poor have their own culture

The view that the poor are shiftless and immoral has been rejected by most social scientists in favor of a more liberal view called the "culture of poverty." This perspective is presented as a sociocultural theory of life among the poor. Proponents of the culture of poverty argue that the problem of poverty cannot be eliminated by simply improving the economic position of the poor (Lewis, 1966a:xliii–xlviii, 1966b). Poverty, in other words, is a way of life or culture, and it is essentially a sociocultural problem rather than an economic one. People who live in poverty develop a system of values and beliefs as an adjustment to their conditions, and this system constitutes a culture that is transmitted from generation to generation. Although economic conditions produce the culture, once it emerges, the culture gains an impetus of its own and is self-perpetuating.

Daniel P. Moynihan (1965) is probably the primary spokesman for the culture of poverty perspective. As Assistant Secretary of Labor, Moynihan, in the controversial Moynihan Report to President Johnson, proposed a national policy to attack the "Negro" family and eliminate the "tangle of pathology" that perpetuates poverty. The culture-of-poverty perspective provided the ideological underpinning for the "war on poverty." This liberal view of the poor has met with substantial opposition, particularly from black leaders who argue that it represents a subtle racist ideology that blames poverty on the poor rather than on the society. Most critics of this perspective assume a structural view of poverty.

Society creates poverty

Although the structural view of poverty is not new, it has occupied a somewhat marginal position in writings on poverty. Marx saw structured inequality as a product of the class conflict that is characteristic of capitalistic society. Unlike Spencer and Sumner who equated the poor with the waste or undesirable element in society and poverty as a natural product of the evolutionary process, Marx sought to explain poverty through a structural analysis of the class struggle.

In sociology today there are two distinctive and conflicting models of society that parallel the culture of poverty and the structural views of poverty. The pluralistic model sees the society as a relatively cohesive and integrated unit. It relies on concepts like consensus, cooperation, and assimilation (Horton, 1966). Persons who adhere to this position see the society as having a common value system that integrates diverse segments. This tradition has its roots in the works of Durkheim and is expressed in the contemporary theories of Talcott Parsons (1951) and Robert Merton (1963). The second tradition, the conflict perspective, has its origins in the work of Marx. Conflict theorists see the society as composed of conflicting and competing interest groups. Power, competition, and social conflict are key elements. More recent exponents of this position are C. Wright Mills (1963) and Ralf Dahrendorf (1959). These two positions will be developed more fully in the next chapter. For now it is sufficient to point out that the structuralist view of poverty is consistent with the conflict model of society.

The structuralist view differs primarily from the culture of poverty in that it sees the problem of poverty as resulting from structural arrangements that lead to the subordination of a segment of society by persons in power. Critics of the culture of poverty maintain that this view is not so much wrong as misdirected. It shifts the focus from the society that produces structured inequality to the poor; in effect, it blames poverty on the poor (Valentine, 1968:33). In a critique of the Moynihan Report Laura Carper (1966:137, 140) succinctly summarizes the structural view of poverty:

The Negro family is not the source of the "tangle of pathology" which the report attributes to the Negro community. It is the pathological relationship between white social institutions and the Negro community which has bred the statistics the report cites. . . . What is destructive to the Negro man and woman is social impotence . . . what rehabilitates them is social power and the struggle for it. It is not new for a ruling elite to characterize its poor as incontinent and shiftless. It is the characteristic way in which those on top describe those on the bottom, even when sincerely trying to uplift them.

ALTERNATIVE SOLUTIONS

Public assistance programs

Welfare in this country is currently distributed through a maze of national, state, and local programs of public assistance. While it is not possible to discuss these programs in detail, it should be noted that they are inadequate for meeting the needs of the poor.

Most programs provide a *means* test (an index employed to determine whether or not one needs welfare) in order for prospective recipients to qualify for assistance. There is considerable latitude in enforcing such tests, and public assistance programs typically become mechanisms for political and social control. Thus in some areas welfare has been refused because the welfare agent does not approve of the applicant's hair length, morality, or overall demeanor. Current public assistance programs can be criticized on several levels: (1) They are not administered uniformally with the same criteria. (2) They place the burden on the applicant to demonstrate that he is worthy of assistance. Welfare is treated as a privilege rather than a right. (3) Welfare is administered politically. Since welfare is a privilege, recipients must meet the moral and political standards of those who administer the programs. (4) Welfare recipients must undergo investigations that represent an invasion of privacy and are demeaning to them as human beings. (5) They typically do not benefit the poor. It is estimated that current programs reach only about one-fourth of the poor (Green, 1970:198; Morgan, et al., 1962:216).

The war on poverty

During his administration President Johnson waged what was supposed to be an all-out war against poverty which to date has not been won. The war on poverty was heralded as the most comprehensive and systematic attack on the problem, yet poverty is still with us. Why? Probably the basic flaw of the war on poverty was that it was based on the culture-of-poverty ideology and is therefore subject to the misconceptions of this ideology. The war on poverty intended not only to improve the economic position of the poor but, more importantly, to break the vicious poverty cycle. The primary thrust of programs such as Head Start, Job Corps, the Neighborhood Youth Corps, and VISTA was to change the values of the poor so that they would be able to pull themselves out of poverty. The Job Corps, for instance, was intended to teach more than basic skills. "Health care, personal guidance and counseling, and the away-from-home residential atmosphere were intended to act beneficially on the social attitudes of the corpsmen" (Kershaw, 1970:26). The culture-of-poverty ideology is best illustrated by Kershaw, who commented on the high drop-out rate in the corps. "This," he suggested, "does not seem unduly high, given the raw material coming into the system" (1970:27). The basic flaw in the war on poverty was that it felt that the war could be won by changing the personal and social characteristics of the poor. This is akin to trying to eliminate slavery by rehabilitating slaves. It is, at best, only a short-range solution. The programs fail to recognize that poverty is a societal problem that will only be alleviated by changing the structure of the society.

Structural solutions

An approach to poverty that is at variance with the culture of poverty is expounded by the authors of "The Triple Revolution" (*Ad Hoc* Committee, 1964). They point out that the United States is faced with an interesting, but distressing, paradox—increasing societal affluence coupled with the emergence of a permanent impoverished and jobless class. Some ask, how can we have poverty amidst affluence? "The Triple Revolution" answers that we have poverty because we have affluence. The United States has been undergoing an automation and cybernation revolution. The consequence of this revolution is that a smaller proportion of the population is needed to support the rest of the population at a high standard of living. Stated simply, everyone in the society cannot work, and if the present trend continues, a larger proportion will not be able to work. "Promises of jobs are a cruel and dangerous hoax on hundreds of thousands of Negroes and whites alike . . ." (*Ad Hoc* Committee, 1964:10). The war on poverty was based on the naïve assumption that if the poor have the requisite skills and motivation, they will find jobs, but it did not suggest the source of these jobs. The widespread acceptance of this assumption is illustrated by one of the leading social problems texts, which states that "the most pervasive cause of poverty in the United States appears to be the lack of a high school education" (Horton and Leslie, 1970:329). Such a view of poverty is reminiscent of the traditional conception that the poor are immoral and are to blame for their poverty.

A proposed solution to the problem of poverty that is consistent with a structural view is a guaranteed income as a right for every citizen of the society. Proposals such as these are generally opposed on the grounds that they are socialistic and will destroy human initiative. Our values are still deeply rooted in a scarcity economy in which every man must be productive in order to ensure survival of the group. These values need to be realigned with the realities of our economic system—we have an abundance economy that is characterized by over- rather than under-production. The federal government has in the past paid farmers not to raise crops; and we frequently destroy or export excess food, at the same time that thousands die from starvation and malnutrition. "Americans continually find themselves in the position of having killed someone to avoid sharing a meal which turns out to be too large to eat alone" (Slater, 1971:103). Before a structural solution can be implemented we must recognize that our society has the capacity to provide a guaranteed income for everyone. The President's Council of Economic Advisers estimated that about $11 billion a year would bring all poor families up to a $3000 income (Reagan, 1970: 229). The guaranteed income will not destroy initiative as long as we continue to value and reward productive employment. The issue of motivation, moreover, is irrelevant. In the long run we do need to reduce human initiative, or at least, recognize that everyone in the society cannot be productive in the traditional sense. We must create positions that are socially important and yet are not necessarily productive economically. A man who devotes his time and energy to helping and counseling youth in the ghetto, for example, is performing a socially valuable function and should be recognized and rewarded for it. In a sense we have already started to move in this direction by creating positions such as teaching, psychiatry, and social work that are not productive in a strict economic sense.

One of the most critical problems that a guaranteed income will not resolve is relative deprivation. If poverty is a relative phenomenon, a person with a guaranteed minimum income will feel deprived relative to others. This problem will never be eliminated in a society with a money economy and differential rewards, but it can be diminished. One solution would be to continually adjust the minimum income of the poor so that their position does not deteriorate relative to the rest of the society. Another program that would help reduce relative deprivation is to try to narrow economic differentials among people. In a sense we are committed in principle, though not in practice, to such a system in our graduated income tax. In other words, the goal of a poverty program should be not only to provide a minimum income but also to reduce the gap between the haves and the have-nots. It is implicit in this proposal, of course, that the minimum income represents not an absolute minimum for subsistence but a relative social definition, for as the society becomes more affluent, luxuries become necessities.

Poverty, therefore, is a structural problem that can only be eliminated through basic alterations in the social structure. A structural solution will require substantial economic expenditures, but the benefits will certainly outweigh the costs. The problem of poverty is not isolated, being intertwined with many other societal problems. A full-scale effort to end poverty will do much to alleviate a number of related problems including overpopulation, crime, and racial-ethnic prejudice.

REFERENCES

Ad Hoc Committee
 1964 "The Triple Revolution." Liberation 9 (April):9–15.
Carper, Laura
 1966 "The Negro Family and the Moynihan Report." Dissent 13 (March–April):133–140.
Chapman, William
 1971 "Poverty Up 5% in 69–70, Census Finds." Washington Post (May 8): A1, A12.
Dahrendorf, Ralf
 1959 Class and Class Conflict in Industrial Society. Stanford, Calif.: Stanford University Press.
Green, Christopher
 1970 "Income Guarantee Alternatives." Pp. 197–203 in Robert E. Will and Harold G. Vatter (eds.), Poverty in Affluence. New York: Harcourt.
Harrington, Michael
 1962 The Other America. New York: Macmillan.
Hofstadter, Richard
 1955 Social Darwinism in American Thought. Revised ed. Boston: Beacon.

Horton, John
1966 "Order and Conflict Theories of Social Problems." American Journal
of Sociology 71 (May):701–713.
Horton, Paul B., and Gerald R. Leslie
1970 The Sociology of Social Problems. Fourth ed. New York: Appleton.
Kershaw, Joseph A.
1970 Government Against Poverty. Chicago: Markham.
Kotz, Nick
1971 "Whites Still Hold Big Edge." Washington Post (July 27):A1, A8.
Larson, Calvin J.
1973 Major Themes in Sociological Theory. New York: McKay.
Lewis, Oscar
1966a La Vida: A Puerto Rican Family in the Culture of Poverty—San
Juan and New York. New York: Random House.
1966b The Culture of Poverty. Scientific American, 215 (4):19–25.
Madden, J. Patrick
1971 "Poverty Measures as Indicators of Social Welfare." Paper prepared
for Social Welfare Research Institute, University of Kentucky.
Marx, Karl
1909 Capital. Vol. 1. Chicago: Charles H. Kerr and Company (first published 1867).
Meissner, Hanna H.
1966 Poverty in the Affluent Society. New York: Harper & Row.
Merton, Robert K.
1963 Social Theory and Social Structure. Revised ed. Glencoe, Ill.: Free
Press.
Mills, C. Wright
1963 "The Structure of Power in American Society." Pp. 23–38 in Irving
Louis Horowitz (ed.), Power, Politics and People: The Collected
Essays of C. Wright Mills. New York: Oxford University Press.
Moore, Joan W,
1970 Mexican Americans. Englewood Cliffs, N.J.: Prentice-Hall.
Morgan, James N., Martin H. David, Wilbur J. Cohen, and Harvey E. Brazer
1962 Income and Welfare in the United States. New York: McGraw-Hill.
Moynihan, Daniel P.
1965 The Negro Family: The Case For National Action. Washington, D.C.:
GPO.
Parsons, Talcott
1951 The Social System. Glencoe, Ill.: Free Press.
President's Advisory Commission on Rural Poverty
1968 "The People Left Behind." Employment Service Review (April):17–19.
Quinney, Richard
1970 The Problem of Crime. New York: Dodd, Mead.
Reagan, Michael
1970 "For a Guaranteed Income." Pp. 227–234 in Harold L. Sheppard
(ed.), Poverty and Wealth in America. Chicago: Quadrangle.
Sheppard, Harold L.
1970 Poverty and Wealth in America. Chicago: Quadrangle.

Slater, Philip
1971 The Pursuit of Loneliness. Boston: Beacon.
Spencer, Herbert
1851 Social Statics. London: John Chapman (Reprinted by Augustus M. Kelley Publishers, 1969).
Steiner, Stan
1968 "The American Indian—Ghettos in the Desert." Pp. 136–146 in Arthur I. Blaustein and Roger R. Woock (eds.), Man Against Poverty: World War III. New York: Vintage Books.
Sumner, William Graham
1906 Folkways. Boston: Ginn.
1961 What Social Classes Owe to Each Other. Caldwell, Idaho: Caxton.
Timasheff, Nicholas S.
1963 Sociological Theory: Its Nature and Growth. Revised ed. New York: Random House.
U.S. Bureau of the Census
1972a Statistical Abstract of the United States. Ninety-third ed. Washington, D.C.
1972b "Selected Characteristics of Persons and Families of Mexican, Puerto Rican, and Other Spanish Origin: March 1972." Current Population Reports, Series P-20, No. 238 (July). Washington, D.C.
1973a "Money Income in 1972 of Families and Persons in the United States." Current Population Reports, Series P-60, No. 87 (June). Washington, D.C.
1973b "Characteristics of the Low-Income Population: 1972." Current Population Reports, Series P-60, No. 88 (June). Washington, D.C.
1973c "The Social and Economic Status of the Black Population in the United States, 1972." Current Population Reports, Series P-23, No. 46 (July). Washington, D.C.
1973d Census of Population: 1970. Subject Reports, Final Report PC(2)-1F, American Indians. Washington, D.C.
1973e Statistical Abstract of the United States. Ninety-fourth ed. Washington, D.C.
Valentine, Charles
1968 Culture and Poverty: Critique and Counter-Proposals. Chicago: University of Chicago Press.
Weber, Max
1958 The Protestant Ethic and the Spirit of Capitalism. (Translated by Talcott Parsons). New York: Scribner.

INTRODUCTION TO THE READINGS

The two readings illustrate some of the conceptions of poverty discussed in this chapter. The excerpt by William Graham Sumner, a pioneering American sociologist, is based on Social Darwinism, a view that sees poverty as an outgrowth of evolutionary processes such as natural selection and survival of the fittest. While Sumner made important contributions to sociology, and *Folkways* is considered a classic statement on the origin and function of social norms, he was deeply immersed in evolutionary thought. Sumner was a champion of the principle of laissez faire (Timasheff, 1963:66), and he opposed attempts to reconstruct society rationally on the grounds that doing so interfered with the natural evolution of society. His reference to the "Forgotten Man" in this selection is reminiscent of recent political appeals to the "silent majority." Sumner's position, however, was rejected by some of his contemporaries, especially Lester Frank Ward, an advocate of the application of scientific knowledge to reduce social inequality and improve mankind. Ward was also influenced by evolutionary doctrine, but he believed that sociological knowledge could be used to plan change and restructure society. Thus Sumner's position on poverty is consonant with Social Darwinism, and Ward's position anticipates structural views. The controversy waged between Ward and Sumner (Larson, 1973: 70–90) over the use of science for social reform continues to the present day.

While the Ward-Sumner controversy has abated somewhat, we are still faced with conflicting views of poverty. The selection by Wellman reveals the tension and conflict between two contemporary perspectives. Although Wellman does not identify the culture of poverty and the structural view of poverty, the different implications of these perspectives for action programs are suggested by his article, "The *Wrong* Way to Find Jobs for Negroes." The underlying ideology of the TIDE program is all too prevalent in action programs, which typically seek to eradicate poverty by changing the value system and culture of the poor.

On a new philosophy: that poverty is the best policy

WILLIAM GRAHAM SUMNER

It is commonly asserted that there are in the United States no classes, and any allusion to classes is resented. On the other hand, we constantly read and hear discussions of social topics in which the existence of social classes is assumed as a simple fact. "The poor," "the weak," "the laborers," are expressions which are used as if they had exact and well-understood definition. Discussions are made to bear upon the assumed rights, wrongs, and misfortunes of certain social classes; and all public speaking and writing consists, in a large measure, of the discussion of general plans for meeting the wishes of classes of people who have not been able to satisfy their own desires. These classes are sometimes discontented, and sometimes not. Sometimes they do not know that anything is amiss with them until the "friends of humanity" come to them with offers of aid. Sometimes they are discontented and envious. They do not take their achievements as a fair measure of their rights. They do not blame themselves or their parents for their lot, as compared with that of other people. Sometimes they claim that they have a right to everything of which they feel the need for their happiness on earth. To make such a claim against God and Nature would, of course, be only to say that we claim a right to live on earth if we can. But God and Nature have ordained the chances and conditions of life on earth once for all. The case cannot be reopened. We cannot get a revision of the laws of human life. We are absolutely shut up to the need and duty, if we would learn how to live happily, of investigating the laws of Nature, and deducing the rules of right living in the world as it is. These are very wearisome and commonplace tasks. They consist in labor and self-denial repeated over and over again in learning and doing. When the people whose claims we are considering are told to apply themselves to these tasks they become irritated and feel almost insulted. They formulate their claims as rights against society—that is, against some other men. In their view they have a right, not only to *pursue* happiness, but to *get* it; and if they fail to get it, they think they have a claim to the aid of other men—that is, to the labor and self-denial of other men—to get it for them. They find orators and poets who tell them that they have grievances, so long as they have unsatisfied desires.

Now, if there are groups of people who have a claim to other people's labor and self-denial, and if there are other people whose labor and self-denial are liable to be claimed by the first groups, then there certainly are "classes," and classes of the oldest and most vicious type. For a man who can command another man's labor and self-denial for the support of his own existence is a privileged person of the highest species conceivable on earth. Princes and paupers meet on this plane, and no other men are on it all. On the other hand, a man whose labor and self-denial may be diverted from

From William Graham Sumner, *What Social Classes Owe to Each Other* (Caldwell, Idaho: Caxton, 1961. Chapter 1, pp. 13–24.

his maintenance to that of some other man is not a free man, and approaches more or less toward the position of a slave. Therefore we shall find that, in all the notions which we are to discuss, this elementary contradiction, that there are classes and that there are not classes, will produce repeated confusion and absurdity. We shall find that, in our efforts to eliminate the old vices of class government, we are impeded and defeated by new products of the worst class theory. We shall find that all the schemes for producing equality and obliterating the organization of society produce a new differentiation based on the worst possible distinction—the right to claim and the duty to give to one man's effort for another man's satisfaction. We shall find that every effort to realize equality necessitates a sacrifice of liberty.

It is very popular to pose as a "friend of humanity," or a "friend of the working classes." The character, however, is quite exotic in the United States. It is borrowed from England, where some men, otherwise of small account, have assumed it with great success and advantage. Anything which has a charitable sound and a kind-hearted tone generally passes without investigation, because it is disagreeable to assail it. Sermons, essays, and orations assume a conventional standpoint with regard to the poor, the weak, etc.; and it is allowed to pass as an unquestioned doctrine in regard to social classes that "the rich" ought to "care for the poor"; that Churches especially ought to collect capital from the rich and spend it for the poor; that parishes ought to be clusters of institutions by means of which one social class should perform its duties to another; and that clergymen, economists, and social philosophers have a technical and professional duty to devise schemes for "helping the poor." The preaching in England used all to be done to the poor—that they ought to be contented with their lot and respectful to their betters. Now, the greatest part of the preaching in America consists in injunctions to those who have taken care of themselves to perform their assumed duty to take care of others. Whatever may be one's private sentiments, the fear of appearing cold and hard-hearted causes these conventional theories of social duty and these assumptions of social fact to pass unchallenged.

Let us notice some distinctions which are of prime importance to a correct consideration of the subject which we intend to treat.

Certain ills belong to the hardships of human life. They are natural. They are part of the struggle with Nature for existence. We cannot blame our fellow-men for our share of these. My neighbor and I are both struggling to free ourselves from these ills. The fact that my neighbor has succeeded in this struggle better than I constitutes no grievance for me. Certain other ills are due to the malice of men, and to the imperfections or errors of civil institutions. These ills are an object of agitation, and a subject of discussion. The former class of ills is to be met only by manly effort and energy; the latter may be corrected by associated effort. The former class of ills is constantly grouped and generalized, and made the object of social schemes. We shall see, as we go on, what that means. The second class of ills may fall on certain social classes, and reform will take the form of interference by other classes in favor of that one. The last fact is, no doubt, the reason why people have been led, not noticing distinctions, to believe that the same method was applicable to the other class of ills. The distinction here made between the ills which belong to the struggle for existence and those which are due to the faults of human institutions is of prime importance.

It will also be important, in order to clear up our ideas about the notions which are in fashion, to note the relation of the economic to the political significance of assumed duties of one class to another. That is to say, we may discuss the question whether one class owes duties to another by reference to the economic effects which will be produced on the classes and society; or we may discuss the political expediency of formulating and enforcing rights and duties respectively between the parties. In the former case we might assume that the givers of aid were willing to give it, and we might discuss the benefit or mischief of their activity. In the other case we must assume that some at least of those who were forced to give aid did so unwillingly. Here, then, there would be a question of rights. The question whether voluntary charity is mischievous or not is one thing; the question whether legislation which forces one man to aid another is right and wise, as well as economically beneficial, is quite another question. Great confusion and consequent error is produced by allowing these two questions to become entangled in the discussion. Especially we shall need to notice the attempts to apply legislative methods of reform to the ills which belong to the order of Nature.

There is no possible definition of "a poor man." A pauper is a person who cannot earn his living; whose producing powers have fallen positively below his necessary consumption; who cannot, therefore, pay his way. A human society needs the active co-operation and productive energy of every person in it. A man who is present as a consumer, yet who does not contribute either by land, labor, or capital to the

work of society, is a burden. On no sound political theory ought such a person to share in the political power of the State. He drops out of the ranks of workers and producers. Society must support him. It accepts the burden, but he must be cancelled from the ranks of the rulers likewise. So much for the pauper. About him no more need be said. But he is not the "poor man." The "poor man" is an elastic term, under which any number of social fallacies may be hidden.

Neither is there any possible definition of "the weak." Some are weak in one way, and some in another; and those who are weak in one sense are strong in another. In general, however, it may be said that those whom humanitarians and philanthropists call the weak are the ones through whom the productive and conservative forces of society are wasted. They constantly neutralize and destroy the finest efforts of the wise and industrious, and are a dead-weight on the society in all its struggles to realize any better things. Whether the people who mean no harm, but are weak in the essential powers necessary to the performance of one's duties in life, or those who are malicious and vicious, do the more mischief, is a question not easy to answer.

Under the names of the poor and the weak, the negligent, shiftless, inefficient, silly, and imprudent are fastened upon the industrious and prudent as a responsibility and a duty. On the one side, the terms are extended to cover the idle, intemperate, and vicious, who, by the combination, gain credit which they do not deserve, and which they could not get if they stood alone. On the other hand, the terms are extended to include wage-receivers of the humblest rank, who are degraded by the combination. The reader who desires to guard himself against fallacies should always scrutinize the terms "poor" and "weak" as used, so as to see which or how many of these classes they are made to cover.

The humanitarians, philanthropists, and reformers, looking at the facts of life as they present themselves, find enough which is sad and unpromising in the condition of many members of society. They see wealth and poverty side by side. They note great inequality of social position and social chances. They eagerly set about the attempt to account for what they see, and to devise schemes for remedying what they do not like. In their eagerness to recommend the less fortunate classes to pity and consideration they forget all about the rights of other classes; they gloss over all the faults of the classes in question, and they exaggerate their misfortunes and their virtues. They invent new theories of property, distorting rights and perpetuating injustice, as anyone is sure to do who sets about the readjustment of social relations with the interests of one group distinctly before his mind, and the interests of all other groups thrown into the background. When I have read certain of these discussions I have thought that it must be quite disreputable to be respectable, quite dishonest to own property, quite unjust to go one's own way and earn one's own living, and that the only really admirable person was the good-for-nothing. The man who by his own effort raises himself above poverty appears, in these discussions, to be of no account. The man who has done nothing to raise himself above poverty finds that the social doctors flock about him, bringing the capital which they have collected from the other class, and promising him the aid of the State to give him what the other had to work for. In all these schemes and projects the organized intervention of society

through the State is either planned or hoped for, and the State is thus made to become the protector and guardian of certain classes. The agents who are to direct the State action are, of course, the reformers and philanthropists. Their schemes, therefore, may always be reduced to this type—that A and B decide what C shall do for D. It will be interesting to inquire, at a later period of our discussion, who C is, and what the effect is upon him of all these arrangements. In all the discussions attention is concentrated on A and B, the noble social reformers, and on D, the "poor man." I call C the Forgotten Man, because I have never seen that any notice was taken of him in any of the discussions. When we have disposed of A, B, and D we can better appreciate the case of C, and I think that we shall find that he deserves our attention, for the worth of his character and the magnitude of his unmerited burdens. Here it may suffice to observe that, on the theories of the social philosophers to whom I have referred, we should get a new maxim of judicious living: Poverty is the best policy. If you get wealth, you will have to support other people; if you do not·get wealth, it will be the duty of other people to support you.

No doubt one chief reason for the unclear and contradictory theories of class relations lies in the fact that our society, largely controlled in all its organization by one set of doctrines, still contains survivals of old social theories which are totally inconsistent with the former. In the Middle Ages men were united by custom and prescription into associations, ranks, guilds, and communities of various kinds. These ties endured as long as life lasted. Consequently society was dependent, throughout all its details, on status, and the tie, or bond, was sentimental. In our modern state, and in the United States more than any-where else, the social structure is based on contract, and status is of the least importance. Contract, however, is rational—even rationalistic. It is also realistic, cold, and matter-of-fact. A contract relation is based on a sufficient reason, not on custom or prescription. It is not permanent. It endures only so long as the reason for it endures. In a state based on contract sentiment is out of place in any public or common affairs. It is relegated to the sphere of private and personal relations, where it depends not at all on class types, but on personal acquaintance and personal estimates. The sentimentalists among us always seize upon the survivals of the old order. They want to save them and restore them. Much of the loose thinking also which troubles us in our social discussions arises from the fact that men do not distinguish the elements of status and of contract which may be found in our society.

Whether social philosophers think it desirable or not, it is out of the question to go back to status or to the sentimental relations which once united baron and retainer, master and servant, teacher and pupil, comrade and comrade. That we have lost some grace and elegance is undeniable. That life once held more poetry and ro-mance is true enough. But it seems impossible that any one who has studied the matter should doubt that we have gained immeasurably, and that our farther gains lie in going forward, not in going backward. The feudal ties can never be restored. If they could be restored they would bring back personal caprice, favoritism, sycophancy, and intrigue. A society based on contract is a society of free and independent men, who form ties without favor or obligation, and co-operate without cringing or intrigue. A society based on contract, therefore, gives the utmost room and chance for individual development, and for all the self-reliance and dignity of a free man. That a society of free men, co-operating under contract, is by far the strongest society which has ever yet existed; that no such society has ever yet developed the full measure of strength of which it is capable; and that the only social improvements which are now conceivable lie in the direction of more complete realization of a society of free men united by contract, are points which cannot be controverted. It follows, however, that one man, in a free state, cannot claim help from, and cannot be charged to give help to, another. To understand the full meaning of this assertion it will be worth while to see what a free democracy is.

The *wrong* way to find jobs for negroes

The case history of an employment program that turned into a fiasco

DAVID WELLMAN

In the summer of 1966 I studied a Federal government program designed to help lower-class youths find jobs. The program was known as TIDE. It was run by the California Department of Employment, and classes were held five days a week in the Youth Opportunities Center of West Oakland.

The TIDE program was anything but a success. "I guess these kids just don't want jobs," one of the teacher-counselors told me. "The clothes they wear are loud. They won't talk decent English. They're boisterous. And they constantly fool around. They refuse to take the program seriously."

"But isn't there a job shortage in Oakland?" I asked. "Does it really *matter* how the kids act?"

"There's plenty of jobs. They're just not interested."

The students were 25 young men and 25 young women selected by poverty-program workers in the Bay Area. Their ages ranged from 16 to 22, and most were Negroes. The government paid them $5 a day to participate. Men and women usually met separately. I sat in on the men's classes.

The young men who took part in TIDE had a distinctive style. They were "cool." Their hair was "processed." All sported sunglasses—very lightly tinted, with small frames. They called them "pimp's glasses." Their clothes, while usually inexpensive, were loud and ingeniously altered to express style and individuality. They spoke in a "hip" vernacular. Their vocabularies were small but very expressive. These young men, as part of the "cool world" of the ghetto, represent a distinctively black working-class culture.

To most liberals these young men are "culturally deprived" or "social dropouts." Most had flunked or been kicked out of school. Few had any intention of getting a high-school degree. They seemed uninterested in "making it." They had long and serious arrest and prison records. They were skeptical and critical of both the TIDE program and white society in general.

The TIDE workers were liberals. They assumed that if the young men would only act a little less "cool" and learn to smooth over some of their encounters with white authorities, they too could become full-fledged, working members of society. The aim of TIDE was not to train them for jobs, but to train them how to *apply* for jobs—how to take tests, how to make a good impression during a job interview, how to speak well, how to fill out an application form properly. They would play games, like dominoes, to ease the pain associated with numbers and arithmetic; they would conduct mock interviews, take mock tests, meet with management representatives, and tour places where jobs might be available. They were told to consider the TIDE program itself as a job—to be at the Youth Opportunities Center office on time, dressed as if they were at work. If they were late or made trouble, they would be docked. But if they took the program seriously and did well, they were told, they stood a pretty good chance of getting a job at the end of four weeks. The unexpressed aim of TIDE, then, was to prepare Negro youngsters for white society. The government would serve as an employment agency for white, private enterprise.

The program aimed to change the youngsters by making them more acceptable to employers. Their grammar and pronunciation were constantly corrected. They were indirectly told that, in order to get a job, their appearance would have to be altered: For example, "Don't you think you could shine your shoes?" Promptness, a virtue few of the youngsters possessed, was lauded. The penalty for tardiness was being put on a clean-up committee, or being docked.

For the TIDE workers, the program was a four-week exercise in futility. They felt they weren't asking very much of the youngsters—just that they learn to make a good impression on white society. And yet the young men were uncooperative. The only conclusion the TIDE workers could arrive at was: "They just don't want jobs."

Yet most of the youngsters took *actual* job possibilities very seriously. Every day they would pump the Youth Opportunities Center staff about job openings. When told there was a job at such-and-such a factory and that a particular test was required, the young men studied hard and applied for the job in earnest. The TIDE program *itself*, however, seemed to be viewed as only distantly related to getting a job. The youngsters wanted jobs, but to them their inability to take tests and fill out forms was *not* the problem. Instead, they talked about the shortage of jobs available to people without skills.

Their desire for work was not the problem. The real problem was what the program demanded of the young men. It asked that they change their manner of speech and dress, that they ignore their lack of skills and society's lack of jobs, and that they act as if their arrest records were of no consequence in obtaining a job. It asked, most important, that they pretend *they*, and not society, bore the responsibility for their being unemployed. TIDE didn't demand much of the men: Only that they become white.

PUTTING ON THE PROGRAM

What took place during the four week program was a daily struggle between white, middle-class ideals of conduct and behavior and the mores and folkways of the black community. The men handled TIDE the way the black community in America has always treated white threats to Negro self-respect. They used subtle forms of subversion and deception. Historians and sociologists have pointed to slave subversion, to the content and ritual of Negro spirituals, and to the blues as forms of covert black resistance to white mores.

Today, "putting someone on," "putting the hype on someone," or "running a game on a cat" seem to be important devices used by Negroes to maintain their integrity. "Putting someone on," which is used as much with black people as with whites, allows a person to maintain his integrity in a hostile or threatening situation. To put someone on is to publicly lead him to believe that you are going along with what he has to offer or say, while privately rejecting the offer and subtly subverting it. The tactic fails if the other person recognizes what is happening. For one aim of putting someone on is to take pride in feeling that you have put something over on him, often at his expense. (Putting someone on differs from "putting someone down," which means active defiance and public confrontation.)

TIDE was evidently interpreted by the men as a threat to their self-respect, and this was the way they responded to it. Sometimes TIDE was put on. Sometimes it was put down. It was taken seriously only when it met the men's own needs.

There was almost no open hostility toward those in charge of TIDE, but two things quickly led me to believe that if the men accepted the program, they did so only on their own terms.

First, all of them appeared to have a "tuning-out" mechanism. They just didn't hear certain things. One young man was a constant joker and talked incessantly, even if someone else was speaking or if the group was supposed to be working. When told to knock it off, he never heard the command. Yet when he was interested in a program, he could hear perfectly.

Tuning-out was often a collective phenomenon. For instance, there was a radio in the room where the youngsters worked, and they would play it during lunch and coffee breaks. When the instructor would enter and tell them to begin work, they would continue listening and dancing to the music as if there were no one else in the room. When *they* were finished listening, the radio went off and the session began. The youngsters were going along with the program—in a way. They weren't challenging it. But they were undermining its effectiveness.

A second way in which the young men undermined the program was by playing dumb. Much of the program consisted of teaching the youngsters how to fill out employment applications. They were given lengthy lectures on the importance of neatness and lettering. After having filled out such forms a number of times, however, some students suddenly didn't know their mother's name, the school they last attended, or their telephone number.

This "stupidity" was sometimes duplicated during the mock job interviews. Five or more of the students would interview their fellow trainees for an imaginary job. These interviewers usually took their job seriously. But after it became apparent that the interview was a game, many of the interviewees suddenly became incredibly incompetent. They didn't have social-security numbers, they couldn't remember their last job, they didn't know what school they went to, they didn't know if they really wanted the job—to the absolute frustration of interviewers and instructors alike. Interestingly enough, when an instructor told them one morning that *this* time those who did well on the interview would actually be sent out on a real job interview with a real firm, the stupid and incompetent were suddenly transformed into model job applicants.

The same thing happened when the youngsters were given job-preference tests, intelligence tests, aptitude tests, and tests for driver's licenses. The first few times the youngsters took these tests, most worked hard to master them. But after they had gotten the knack, and still found themselves without jobs and taking the same tests, their response changed. Some of them no longer knew how to do the test. Others found it necessary to cheat by looking over someone's shoulder. Still others flunked tests they had passed the day before. Yet when they were informed of actual job possibilities at the naval ship yard or with the post office, they insisted on giving and taking the tests themselves. In one instance, some of them read up on which tests were relevant for a particular job, then practiced that test for a couple of hours by themselves.

Tuning-out and playing stupid were only two of the many ways the TIDE program was "put-on." Still another way: Insisting on work "breaks." The young men "employed" by TIDE were well-acquainted with this ritual, and demanded that it be included as part of their job. Since they had been given a voice in deciding the content of the program, they insisted that breaks become part of their daily routine. And no matter what the activity, or who was addressing them, the young men religiously adhered to the breaks.

The program started at 9:30 A.M. The youngsters decided that their first break would be for coffee at 10:30. This break was to last until 11. And while work was never allowed to proceed a minute past 10:30, it was usually 11:15 or so before the young men actually got back to work. Lunch began exactly at 12. Theoretically, work resumed at 1. This usually meant 1:15, since they had to listen to "one more song" on the radio. The next break was to last from 2:30 to 3. However, because they were finished at 3:30 and because it took another 10 minutes to get them back to work, the fellows could often talk their way out of the remaining half hour. Considering they were being paid $5 a day for five hours' work, of which almost half were regularly devoted to breaks, they didn't have a bad hustle.

TRIPS AND GAMES

Games were another part of the TIDE program subverted by the put-on. Early in the program an instructor told the students that it might be helpful if they mastered arithmetic and language by playing games—dominoes, Scrabble, and various card games.

The students considered this a fine idea. But what their instructor had intended for a pastime during the breaks, involving at most an hour a day, they rapidly turned into a major part of the instruction. They set aside 45 minutes in the morning and 45 minutes in the afternoon for games. But they participated in these games during their breaks as well, so that the games soon became a stumbling block to getting sessions back in order after breaks. When the instructor would say, "Okay, let's get back to work," the men would sometimes reply, "But we're already working on our math—we're playing dominoes, and you said that would help us with our math."

To familiarize the students with the kinds of jobs potentially available, the TIDE instructors took them on excursions to various work situations. These excursions were another opportunity for a put-on. It hardly seemed to matter what kind of company they visited so long as the visit took all day. On a trip to the Oakland Supply Naval Station, the men spent most of their time putting the make on a cute young WAVE who was their guide. One thing this tour did produce, however, was a great deal of discussion about the war in Vietnam. Almost none of the men wanted to serve in the armed forces. Through the bus windows some of them would yell at passing sailors: "Vietnam, baby!" or "Have a good time in Vietnam, man!"

The men would agree to half-day trips only if there was no alternative, or if the company would give away samples. Although they knew that the Coca-Cola Company was not hiring, they wanted to go anyway, for the free Cokes. They also wanted to go to many candy and cookie factories. Yet they turned down a trip to a local steel mill that they knew was hiring. TIDE, after all, was not designed to get them an interview—its purpose was to show them what sorts of jobs might be available. Given the circumstances, they reasoned, why not see what was *enjoyable* as well?

When the men were not putting-on the TIDE program and staff, they might be putting them down. When someone is put-down, he knows it. The tactic's success *depends* on his knowing it, whereas a put-on is successful only when its victim is unaware of it.

THE INTERVIEW TECHNIQUE

Among the fiercest put-downs I witnessed were those aimed at jobs the students were learning to apply for. These jobs were usually for unskilled labor: post-office, assembly-line, warehouse, and longshore workers, truck drivers, chauffeurs, janitors, bus boys, and so on.

The reaction of most of the students was best expressed by a question I heard one young man ask an instructor: "How about some tests for I.B.M.?" The room broke into an uproar of hysterical laughter. The instructor's response was typically bureaucratic, yet disarming: "Say, that's a good suggestion. Why don't you put it in the suggestion box?" The students didn't seem able to cope with that retort, so things got back to normal.

Actual employers, usually those representing companies that hired people only for unskilled labor, came to TIDE to demonstrate to the men what a good interview would be like. They did *not* come to interview men for real jobs. It was sort of a helpful-hints-for-successful-interviews session. Usually one of the more socially mobile youths was chosen to play the role of job applicant. The entire interview situation was played through. Some employers even went so far as to have the "applicant" go outside and knock on the door to

begin the interview. The students thought this was both odd and funny, and one said to the employer: "Man, you've already *seen* the cat. How come you making him walk out and then walk back in?"

With a look of incredulity, the employer replied: "But that's how you get a job. You have to sell yourself from the moment you walk in that door."

The employer put on a real act, beginning the interview with the usual small talk.

"I see from your application that you played football in high school."

"Yeah."

"Did you like it?"

"Yeah."

"Football really makes men and teaches you teamwork."

"Yeah."

At this point, the men got impatient: "Man, the cat's here to get a job, not talk about football!"

A wisecracker chimed in: "Maybe he's interviewing for a job with the Oakland Raiders."

Usually the employer got the point. He would then ask about the "applicant's" job experience, draft status, school record, interests, skills, and so on. The young man being interviewed usually took the questions seriously and answered frankly. But after a while, the rest of the group would tire of the game and (unrecognized, from the floor) begin to ask about the specifics of a real job:

"Say man, how much does this job pay?"

"What kind of experience do you need?"

"What if you got a record?"

It didn't take long to completely rattle an interviewer. The instructor might intervene and tell the students that the gentleman was there to help them, but this would stifle revolt for only a short while. During one interview, several of the fellows began loudly playing dominoes. That got the response they were looking for.

"Look!" shouted the employer. "If you're not interested in learning how to sell yourself, why don't you just leave the room so that others who are interested can benefit from this?"

"Oh no!" responded the ringleaders. "We work here. If you don't dig us, then *you* leave!"

Not much later, he did.

Sometimes during these mock interviews, the very nature of the work being considered was put-down. During one mock interview for a truck-driving job, some of the men asked the employer about openings for salesmen. Others asked him about executive positions. At one point the employer himself was asked point-blank how much he was paid, and what his experience was. They had turned the tables and were enjoying the opportunity to interview the interviewer. Regardless of a potential employer's status, the young men treated him as they would their peers. On one tour of a factory, the students were escorted by the vice-president in charge of hiring. To the TIDE participants, he was just another guide. After he had informed the students of the large number of unskilled positions available, they asked him if he would hire some of them, on the spot. He replied that this was just a tour and that he was in no position to hire anyone immediately. One youth looked at him and said: "Then you're just wasting our time, aren't you?"

Although shaken, the executive persisted. Throughout his talk, however, he innocently referred to his audience as "boys," which obviously bothered the students. Finally one of the more articulate men spoke up firmly. "We are young *men*, not boys!"

The vice-president blushed and apologized. He made a brave attempt to avoid repeating the phrase. But habit was victorious, and the word slipped in again and again. Each time he said "you boys" he was corrected, loudly, and with increasing hostility.

The students treated State Assemblyman Byron Rumford, a Negro, the same way. The meeting with Rumford was an opportunity for them to speak with an elected official about the job situation in the state. The meeting was also meant to air differences and to propose solutions. At the time, in fact, the men were quite angry about their rate of pay at TIDE. An instructor had suggested that they take the matter up with Rumford.

The meeting was attended by both the young men and women in the TIDE program. The young women were very well-dressed and well-groomed. Their clothes were not expensive, but were well cared for and in "good taste." Their hair was done in high-fashion styles. They looked, in short, like aspiring career women. The young men wore their usual dungarees or tight trousers, brightly colored shirts and sweaters, pointed shoes, and sunglasses.

The women sat quietly and listened politely. The men spoke loudly whenever they felt like it, and constantly talked among themselves.

Rumford, instead of speaking about the job situation in the Bay Area, chose to talk about his own career. It was a Negro Horatio Alger story. The moral was that if you work hard, you too can put yourself through college, become a successful druggist, then run for public office.

The moment Rumford finished speaking and asked for questions, one of the men jumped up and asked, "Hey man, how do we get a raise?" A male chorus of "Yeah!" followed.

Before Rumford could complete a garbled answer (something like, "Well, I don't really know much about the procedures of a federally sponsored program"), the battle of the sexes had been joined. The women scolded the men for their "disrespectful behavior" toward an elected official. One said: "Here he is trying to help us and you-all acting a fool. You talking and laughing and carrying on while he talking, and then when he finishes you want to know about a raise. Damn!"

"Shit," was a male response. "You don't know what you talking about. We got a *right* to ask the cat about a raise. We elected him."

"We supposed to be talking about jobs," said another. "And we're talking about *our* job. If y'all like the pay, that's your business. We want more!"

The debate was heated. Neither group paid any attention to Rumford, who wisely slipped out of the room.

BATTLE OF SEXES— OR CLASS CONFLICT?

During the exchanges it became clear to me that the differences in clothing and style between the sexes reflected their different orientations toward the dominant society and its values. In the minds of the young women, respect and respectability seemed paramount. At one point, a young woman said to the men, "You acting just like a bunch of *niggers*." She seemed to identify herself as a Negro, not as a "nigger." For the men, on the other hand, becoming a Negro (as opposed to a "nigger") meant giving up much that they considered positive. As one young man said in answer to the above, "You just ain't got no soul, bitch."

The women's identification with the values of white society became even clearer when the debate moved from what constituted respect and respect-ability to a direct attack on a personal level: "Do you all expect to get a job looking the way you do?" "Shit, I wouldn't wear clothes like that if I was on welfare."

The direction of the female attack corresponded closely with the basic assumptions of the TIDE program: People are without jobs because of themselves. This barrage hit the young men pretty hard. Their response was typical of any outraged male whose manhood has been threatened. In fact, when one young woman gibed, "You ain't no kinda man," some of the fellows had to be physically restrained from hitting her.

One of the men explained that "maybe the reason cats dress the way they do is because they can't afford anything else. Did you ever think of that?"

The woman's response was one I had not heard since the third or fourth grade: "Well, it doesn't matter what you wear as long as it's clean, pressed, and tucked-in. But hell, you guys don't even shine your shoes."

The battle of the sexes in the black community seems to be almost a class conflict. Many observers have noted that the black woman succeeds more readily in school than the black man. Women are also favored by parents, especially mothers. Moreover, the black woman has been for some time the most stable force and the major breadwinner of the Negro family. All these things put Negro women in harmony with the major values attached to work and success in our society. Black men, however, have been estranged from society, and a culture has developed around this estrangement—a male Negro culture often antagonistic to the dominant white society. The black woman stands in much the same relation to black men as white society does.

Even including Rumford, no group of officials was put down quite so hard as the Oakland police. Police brutality was constantly on the youngsters' minds. A day didn't pass without at least one being absent because he was in jail, or one coming in with a story about mistreatment by the police. A meeting was arranged with a sergeant from the Community Relations Bureau of the Oakland police. The students seemed excited about meeting the officer on their own turf and with the protection provided by the program.

In anticipation of his arrival, the fellows rearranged the room, placing all the separate tables together. Then they sat down in a group at one end of the table, waiting for the officer.

PUTTING DOWN THE POLICE

Sergeant McCormack was an older man. And while obviously a cop, he could also pass for a middle-aged businessman or a young grandfather. "Hi boys," he said as he sat down. His first mistake. He began with the five-minute speech he must give to every community group. The talk was factual, uninteresting, and noncontroversial: how the department is run, what the qualifications for policemen are, and how difficult it is for police to do their work and still please everyone. His talk was greeted with complete silence.

"I understand you have some questions," McCormack finally said.

"What about police brutality?" asked one man.

"What is your definition of police brutality?" the sergeant countered.

"How long you been a cop?" someone shouted.

"Over 20 years."

"And you got the nerve to come on sounding like you don't know what

we talking about. Don't be jiving us. Shit, if you've been a cop *that* long, you *got* to know what we talking about."

"Righteous on that, brother!" someone chimed in.

"Well, I've been around a while, all right, but I've never seen any brutality. But what about it?"

"What *about* it?" There was a tone of disbelief mixed with anger in the young man's voice. "Shit man, we want to know why you cats always kicking other cats' asses."

The officer tried to draw a distinction between necessary and unnecessary police violence. The fellows weren't buying that. They claimed the police systematically beat the hell out of them for no reason. The officer asked for examples and the fellows obliged with long, involved, and detailed personal experiences with the Oakland Police Department. The sergeant listened patiently, periodically interrupting to check details and inconsistencies. He tried to offer a police interpretation of the incident. But the fellows were simply not in a mood to listen. In desperation the sergeant finally said, "Don't you want to hear *our* side of the story?"

"Hell no, motherfucker, we *see* your side of the story every night on 14th Street."

One young man stood up, his back to the officer, and addressed his contemporaries: "We *tired* of talking! We want some action! There's a new generation now. We ain't like the old folks who took all this shit off the cops." He turned to the sergeant and said, "You take that back to your goddamn Chief Preston and tell him."

McCormack had a silly smile on his face.

Another youngster jumped up and hollered, "You all ain't going to be smiling when we put dynamite in your police station!"

The officer said simply, "You guys don't want to talk."

"You see," someone yelled, "the cat's trying to be slick, trying to run a game on us. First he comes in here all nice-talking, all that shit about how they run the police and the police is to protect us. And then when we tell him how they treat us he wants to say we don't want to talk. Shit! We want to talk, he don't want to listen."

From this point on, they ran over him mercilessly. I, with all my biases against the police, could not help feeling compassion for the sergeant. If the police are an authority figure in the black community, then this episode must be viewed as a revolt against authority—*all* authority. There was nothing about the man's life, both private and public, that wasn't attacked.

"How much money you get paid?"

"About $12,000 a year."

"For being a cop? Wow!"

"What do you do?"

"I work in the Community Relations Department."

"Naw, stupid, what *kind* of work?"

"I answer the telephone, speak to groups, and try to see if the police treat the citizens wrong."

"Shit, we could do that and we don't even have a high-school education. Is that all you do? And get that much money for it?"

"Where do you live?"

"I'll bet he lives up in the hills."

"I live in the east side of Oakland. And I want you to know that my next-door neighbor is a colored man. I've got nothing against colored people."

"You got any kids?"

"Yeah, two boys and a girl."

"Shit, bet they all went to college and got good jobs. Any of your kids been in trouble?"

"No, not really."

"What do they do?"

"My oldest boy is a fighter pilot in Vietnam."

"What the hell is he doing over there? That's pretty stupid."

"Yeah man, what are we fighting in Vietnam for? Is that your way of getting rid of us?"

"Well, the government says we have to be there and it's the duty of every citizen to do what his country tells him to do."

"We don't want to hear all that old bullshit, man."

"Hey, how come you wear such funny clothes? You even look like a goddam cop."

"Yeah baby, and he smells like one too!"

The barrage continued for almost half an hour. The instructor finally called a halt: "Sergeant McCormack has to get back, fellows. Is there anything specific that you'd like to ask him?"

"Yeah. How come Chief Preston ain't here? He's always talking to other people all over the country about how good the Oakland cops are and how there ain't going to be no riot here. Why don't he come and tell us that? We want to talk with the chief."

The next day, Deputy Chief Gain came—accompanied by the captain of the Youth Division, the lieutenant of that division, and a Negro sergeant. It was a formidable display of police authority. The youngsters were noticeably taken aback.

Chief Gain is a no-nonsense, businesslike cop. He takes no static from anyone, vigorously defends what he thinks is correct, and makes no apologies for what he considers incorrect. He is an honest man in the sense that he makes no attempt to cover up or smooth over unpleasant things. He immediately got down to business: "All right now, I understand you guys have some beefs with the department. What's the story?"

The fellows started right in talking about the ways they had been mistreated by the police. The chief began asking specific questions: where it happened, when it happened, what the officer looked like, and so on. He never denied the existence of brutality. That almost seemed to be assumed. He did want details, however. He always asked whether the youth had filed a complaint with the department. The response was always No. He then lectured them about the need to file such complaints if the situation was to be changed.

He explained the situation as he saw it: "Look fellows, we run a police force of 654 men. Most of them are good men, but there's bound to be a few rotten apples in the basket. I know that there's a couple of men who mistreat people, but it's only a few and we're trying our best to change that."

"Shit, I know of a case where a cop killed a cat and now he's back on the beat."

"Now wait a minute—"

"No more waiting a minute!" someone interrupted. "You had two cops got caught taking bribes. One was black and the other Caucasian. The black cat was kicked off the force and the white cat is back on."

"Yeah, and what about that cat who killed somebody off-duty, what about him?"

"Hold on," Gain said firmly. "Let's take these things one at a time." He didn't get very far before he was back to the "few rotten apples" argument.

"If it's only a few cops, how come it happens all the time?"

The deputy chief told them that he thought it was the same few cops who were causing all the problems. "Unless you file complaints each time you feel you've been mistreated, we can't do anything about it. So it's up to you as much as it is up to us."

For the first time in weeks, I intruded into the discussion. I pointed out to Gain that he was asking citizens to police their own police force. He had argued that in most situations the department had a good deal of control over its own men—the same argument the police had used against a civilian-review board. Now he was saying the opposite: that it was up to the citizens. This seemed to break the impasse, and the students howled with delight.

"What happens if a cop beats my ass and I file a complaint?" demanded one. "Whose word does the judge take?"

"The judge takes the evidence and evaluates it objectively and comes to a decision."

"Yeah, but it's usually two cops against one of us, and if both testify against me, what happens? Do you think the judge is going to listen to me?"

"Bring some witnesses."

"That ain't going to do anything."

"That's your problem. If you don't like the legal system in this country, work to change it."

"Okay man," one fellow said to Gain, "You pretty smart. If I smack my buddy here upside the head and he files a complaint, what you gonna do?"

"Arrest you."

"Cool. Now let's say one of your ugly cops smacks *me* upside the head and I file a complaint—what you gonna do?"

"Investigate the complaint, and if there's anything to it, why we'll take action—probably suspend him."

"Why do *we* get arrested and *you* investigated?"

The deputy chief's response was that most private companies with internal difficulties don't want to be investigated by outside agencies. The fellows retorted: "Police are *not* a private business. You're supposed to work for the people!"

"And shit, you cats get to carry guns. No businessman carries guns. It's a different scene, man."

"How come you got all kinds of squad cars in this neighborhood every night? And have two and three cops in each of them?"

"The crime rate is high in this area," replied Gain, "and we get a lot of calls and complaints about it."

"Yeah, and you smart enough to know that when you come around here, you better be wearing helmets and carrying shotguns. If you that clever, you got to be smart enough to handle your own goddamn cops."

At this point the fellows all jumped on the deputy chief the same way they had jumped on the sergeant the day before:

"Why don't you just let us run our own damn community?"

"Yeah. There should be people on the force who've been in jail because they the only people who know what it means to be busted. People in West Oakland should be police because they know their community; you don't."

"Why do we get all the speeding tickets?"

"How come we got to fight in Vietnam?"

"Why the judges so hard on us? They don't treat white cats—I mean dudes—the way they do us."

The chief began assembling his papers and stood up. "You guys aren't interested in talking. You want to yell. When you want to talk, come down to my office and if I'm free we'll talk."

But the fellows had the last word. While he was leaving they peppered him with gibes about how *they* were tired of talking; promised to dynamite his office; and called the police chief a coward for not coming down to speak with them.

When the deputy chief had gone, the instructor asked the fellows why they insisted on ganging up on people like the police. The answer provides a lot of insight into the young men's actions toward the police, businessmen, and public officials:

"These people just trying to run a game on us. If we give them time to think about answers, they gonna put us in a trick. We've *got* to gang up on them because they gang up on us. Did you dig the way that cat brought three other cats with him? Besides, how else could we put them down?"

A SUBTLE FORM OF RACISM

In effect, the young men had inverted the meaning and aims of the TIDE program. It was supposed to be an opportunity for them to plan careers and prepare themselves for their life's work. The immediate goal was to help them get started by showing them how to get a job. The youngsters had a different view. The program was a way to play some games and take some outings—an interesting diversion from the boredom and frustration of ghetto life in the summer. In some respects it was also a means of confronting, on equal terms, high-status people normally unavailable to them—and of venting on them their anger and hostility. But primarily they saw it as a $5-a-day job.

The program simply did not meet the needs of these young men. In fact, it was not really meant to. The Great Society was trying to "run a game on" black youth. TIDE asked them to stop being what they are. It tried to lead them into white middle-class America by showing that America was interested in getting them jobs. But America does not provide many jobs—let alone attractive jobs—for those with police records, with few skills, with black skins. The youths knew that; TIDE workers knew that, too. They did not train youths for work, but tried to make them believe that if they knew *how* to get a job, they could. The young men saw through the sham.

Ironically, the view that Negro youths, rather than society, are responsible for the employment problem is very similar to the familiar line of white racism. Negroes will not work because they are lazy and shiftless, the old Southern bigot would say. The Northern liberal today would put it a little differently: Negroes cannot get jobs because of their psychological and cultural impediments; what they need is cultural improvement, a proper attitude, the ability to sell themselves. Both views suggest that inequities in the job and opportunity structure of America are minor compared to the deficiencies of Negroes themselves. In the end, Northern liberals and Southern racists agree: The problem is

mainly with Negroes, not with our society. This fallacy underlies much of the war on poverty's approach and is indicative of the subtle forms racism is taking in America today.

FURTHER READING SUGGESTED BY THE AUTHOR

Autobiography by Malcolm X (New York: Grove Press, 1965). Malcolm X argues that "gaming" and "put-ons" are an important part of Negro life.

Manchild in the Promised Land by Claude Brown (New York: Macmillan, 1965). Brown describes some of the games he ran on people as a youth.

Tally's Corner by Elliot Liebow (Boston: Little, Brown & Co., 1967). The author describes the attempts the men make at running games on their women, on one another, and on "the man."

Genetic Psychology Monographs, 1967, pages 23–93. In "The Leader and the Lost: A Case Study of Indigenous Leadership in a Poverty Program Community Action Committee," Louis A. Zurcher discusses the put-on and the ways in which American Indians dealt with the poverty program. It comes very close to the conclusions of this article.

Racial and ethnic problems

3

THE NATURE OF SOCIAL STRATIFICATION

Social differentiation and stratification

In order to carry out those activities that are necessary for survival and maintenance of the social system, societies have developed a division of labor, that is, differentiation among specialized status-roles. Social differentiation appears to be universal in human societies; all are differentiated at least along age and sex lines.

Although differentiation is universal in human societies, it is not peculiar to such societies. Many subhuman societies are also differentiated. Bees and ants have an intricate and complex division of labor. There is, however, an important difference between human and subhuman differentiation. Whereas the division of labor in subhuman societies is physiologically or genetically based, human differentiation is culturally acquired. Since social differentiation is not endowed genetically, it must be acquired or learned by members of the society. The society has the task of socializing its members to assume the various position-roles in the division of labor. Societal members are induced to assume positions through the selective use of punishment and rewards, but all positions are not rewarded equally. Those that are valued more by the society will generally receive greater rewards. Stratification therefore evolves from social differentiation as rewards are differentially distributed. When these rewards are accumulated and transmitted to offspring, we have structured social inequality. Social stratification refers to the ordering of societal members into a hierarchy of social strata or classes; it occurs when structured social inequality produces categories (classes) of persons who are relatively homogeneous with respect to the rewards and privileges they command from society.

A division of labor and differential rewards are necessary but not sufficient conditions for the emergence of stratification. An additional criterion is permanence. A stratification system has a hereditary basis so that wealth and privilege are accumulated and passed on to children. In order for structured social inequality to become institutionalized a society must develop an economic surplus. It seems doubtful that full-blown stratification systems are found among relatively simple societies that live at a subsistence level. Stratification emerges when there is an economic surplus that can be hoarded and passed on to the next generation. A minimal level of affluence then appears to be a prerequisite to the development of relatively permanent structured inequality (i.e., stratification).

Is stratification necessary?

The question of whether or not social stratification is an essential component of human societies has generated substantial conflict and discussion among sociologists. Some relatively simple societies, living at or near subsistence, have apparently been able to survive without establishing a clear-cut system of social stratification. But such societies have been few in number, and stratification is virtually universal.

A number of sociologists have attempted to explain the apparent universality of stratification through the functional theory of stratification. According to this theory, every society has certain activities and functions that are essential for its survival (Davis and Moore, 1945; Davis, 1953; Moore, 1953). The division of labor is used to distribute these activities among different positions and to induce members to fill them through rewards and privileges. Since some positions are more important than others, the society must be sure that these do not go unfilled. The functionally important positions generally require special skills that are relatively scarce. Through differential rewards society motivates those persons with unusual skills to undergo the training that is necessary to assume these important positions. The result is social stratification.

From the preceding discussion it is clear that the functional theory is based on an order rather than a conflict view of society (see Chapter 2). Critics of this position maintain that it provides a rationalization or justification for the status quo in that stratification is seen as a functional or normal phenomenon. In some respects the functional theory resembles Social Darwinism. Social Darwinists saw structured social inequality as "survival of the biologically fit," and the functionalists see it as "survival of the socially fit"—those who contribute most to the system. In both cases the rich and the poor deserve what they get, albeit for different reasons.

It is difficult to provide counterevidence to the functional theory of stratification, and to functionalism in general, because its arguments are teleological (for a general discussion of functionalism see the Introduction to Part Three). Teleological statements assume that phenomena contain a purpose or an end. Thus if something exists, it must exist for a reason or to fulfill some purpose. The argument starts with an end as a given and then works back to explain the end. Teleological predictions and explanations are almost foolproof in that they are made after the fact. Functionalism assumes that what is (or at least what has been) has to be; for example, because stratification is found in all but the most simple societies, it must be an inevitable component of society. Functional explanations tend to be conservative, ignoring alternate forms of social organization that may not have evolved in society but that are at least possible. As a response to the conservatism of sociological theory a new orientation has emerged called, for lack of a better name, the Sociology of the Possible (Ofshe, 1970). This orientation, as opposed to a theory or field, attempts to get sociologists to examine possible (though perhaps not probable) alternative systems of social organization. With respect to stratification, for example, Tumin (1953 a and b) points out that while societies have used differential rewards to motivate persons to assume positions, it would be possible to use other methods of inducement such as intrinsic work satisfaction, social duty, and social service. To state that it is impossible to institutionalize alternative systems is to go beyond our knowledge.

A related criticism of the functional position is that it does not distinguish between the factors that lead to the emergence of stratification and those that maintain or perpetuate it. While the initial emergence of stratification might be explained in functional terms (i.e., functionally important positions receiving greater rewards), once social classes emerge, they become special interest groups that seek through a variety of means to perpetuate their advantage. The latter interpretation is consistent with a conflict perspective. The conflict perspective is more concerned with explaining the maintenance of structured social inequality than with explaining its origin. Regardless of how or why some persons obtain positions of power, once power is obtained, attempts are made to maintain it. Power is an obvious correlate of social stratification. Persons who command greater rewards and privileges are able to exercise control over other members of society.

Let us examine a specific occupational group from both the functional (order) and the conflict perspective. The medical professional is an occupational group that is highly rewarded in American society. The position is considered to be prestigious, receives high monetary rewards, and its occupants command a great deal of power. According to the functional view, medicine is a functionally important position that requires special skills and an extensive program of training. The society must provide differential rewards in order to motivate some from the limited pool of persons with special skills to undergo the necessary training and to perform the demanding tasks required by the role. If unusual rewards are not provided, there will be little incentive for the talented few to become physicians and the position may go unfilled. The conflict position, on the other hand, sees medicine as a special interest group that has managed to retain its position of power and prestige through a variety of political techniques. The American Medical Association (AMA), for instance, has for many years controlled the output of M.D.s so that they would remain in high demand. There is an abundance of talented persons who wish to enter medicine, but they are not able to do so because of limitations on the number that may enter. The fact that the AMA is one of the most powerful lobbies in the country lends credence to the conflict perspective. The medical profession spends millions on the national and local level lobbying to protect its interests and to influence legislation. It has, for instance, strongly opposed socialized medicine, the licensing of chiropractors, and more recently, acupuncture.

Perhaps the two perspectives can be reconciled. There probably is some validity to the functional assertion that the emergence of stratification can be explained, at least in part, through the differential distribution of rewards according to functional importance. However, to explain the emergence of a system is not to explain its continuation. Once social strata emerge and certain positions receive differential rewards, they become special interest groups that seek to retain their advantageous positions vis-à-vis other groups. Thus in a given stratification system there are groups that command rewards and power not commensurate with their functional importance. Certain trade unions have been able to demand and receive high wages for their members, not because of their functional importance but because they have a monopoly on the services they provide, while other occupational groups that are ostensibly functionally important but politically inept (teachers) have not been highly rewarded. The teaching profession has not deliberately limited its numbers, and teachers have not acted as an effective political interest group.

Although the functional (order) and the conflict view of stratification have some fundamental differences, they are similar in certain respects. Both perspectives appear to define stratification as necessary or inevitable. For the functional theory stratification is essential for the maintenance of the society, while for the conflict perspective it is essential in order for persons in power to maintain their superordinate position. Thus both views come to essentially the same conclusion but for very different reasons. The utopian thinker cannot help but be discouraged by this rather pessimistic view of man and society. Both perspectives conclude that stratification is inevitable. For the functionalist this is good because the society could not function if it were not stratified; for the conflict theorist this is bad because it involves the exploitation of the have-nots. The task of those sociologists who are interested in creating a Sociology of the Possible is to begin to suggest alternatives to stratification systems. At present we have not moved beyond science-fiction utopias, but perhaps science fiction offers a good starting point in creating alternative social systems.

TYPES OF STRATIFICATION SYSTEMS

We can isolate three basic types of stratification systems. They range from the most to the least structured—caste, estate, and class. Each stratification system will, for the sake of clarity, be treated as an ideal type. Ideal types do not correspond to empirical entities, but rather are exaggerated or extreme constructs that are useful in comparing and understanding the real world. There has never been a society whose network of stratification corresponded exactly to the caste system, but the Indian castes come closer to the pure type than most. (The reader is cautioned against the tendency to reify ideal types, that is, to treat them as descriptions of actual systems.) Although no two stratification systems are identical, we can pinpoint certain characteristics that some systems have in common. The concepts of caste, estate, and class are useful in describing and understanding the clustering of these characteristics.

Caste

The caste system is the most structured of all stratification networks. In its pure form, there is no social mobility, and one acquires a social position at birth and retains this position until death. The system is ascribed in the sense that a person has no control over his status. It is predetermined at birth by factors over which he has no control.

The major organizational units of the system are the castes. Castes are ordered in a hierarchy of prestige, with each being clearly identifiable by its distinctive dress, symbols, customs, and rights and privileges relative to other castes. Three primary mechanisms are used to maintain and perpetuate caste differentials. First, caste positions are linked to occupational groups and differential economic rewards, with the upper castes occupying the most prestigious occupations and receiving the greatest rewards and the lower castes occupying the least prestigious occupations and receiving the fewest rewards. Second, social contact among castes is limited and controlled by custom and ritual. When contact occurs, it is only under certain specified conditions that maintain caste distinctions through an elaborate social protocol. Finally, and perhaps most importantly, intermarriage between different castes is prohibited.

One of the oldest systems of caste is found in India. Indian castes originated and are justified by a body of religious beliefs that have persisted for over three thousand years. At the top of the system are the priestly caste, or *Brahmans*. The *Kshatryias* form the military aristocracy whose major function is the protection of the social order. The third caste, the *Vaisyas*, is composed of peasants, craftsmen, and merchants. The *Sudras*, the fourth major caste, perform manual labor and other menial tasks (Mayer, 1964). The last group is a large residual category of persons without caste, or outcastes. Although these five groups provide the primary division, the Indian caste system is extremely complex and internally subdivided into hundreds of subcastes. Among persons without caste, the lowest, most depressed members are called untouchables (Nisbet, 1970: 211). Social relations as well as physical contact between Brahmans and untouchables are carefully regulated so that the former are not contaminated by the latter. If there is a breach of these rules, the upper-caste person must rid himself of his clothing, bathe and ritually purify himself.

In discussing caste in India it is important to distinguish between the ideal prescriptions of the system and its actual operation. According to the ideal description, there is no social mobility, but in reality there has always been mobility not only within castes but also by castes themselves (Lipset and Bendix, 1962:267). "The caste system is far from a rigid system in which the position of each component caste is fixed for all time. Movement has always been possible, and especially so in the middle regions of the hierarchy" (Srinivas, 1952:30). A caste can raise its position over a couple of generations if it alters its diet, customs, and way of life and successfully presses its claim to higher status (Srinivas, 1952:30).

The rules governing contact among castes suggest that one of the most important ways of maintaining caste distinctions is through rigid segregation. However, with urbanization, industrialization, and modernization it is becoming increasingly difficult to maintain the system. The greatest stronghold of the caste system today appears to be in rural, isolated areas. Urbanization and industrialization tend to break down traditional distinctions and separation of castes, as members of different castes come into daily contact in factories, schools, public transportation systems, and other settings.

Another reason why the caste system is inconsistent with the needs of an urban-industrial society is that it provides an inefficient utilization of the limited pool of talent available in the population. As noted in the earlier discussion of the functional theory, the primary function of social stratification is to motivate persons with scarce talents or unusual skills to assume important societal positions. The caste system, however, appears to impede the utilization of persons with special talents. If we assume that scarce talents tend to be randomly distributed in the population, then many talented persons in lower castes are excluded from important positions. The pool of talent is limited to persons who happen to be born in an upper caste. Since urban-industrial societies have many specialized roles that require scarce or unusual skills, they require a fairly high level of intergenerational social mobility.

Other castelike stratification networks are black-white relations in the United States, which will be discussed later in the chapter, and apartheid in South Africa. A small minority of whites in South Africa have been able to control the large black majority through a system that resembles the Indian system. Despite their similarities the two systems differ in at least one important respect. While the Indian system has a religious justification, the South African system has a racist basis (Legum, 1967). The Dutch, who settled South Africa in the eighteenth century, were able to develop a rigid stratification system based on racism, discrimination, and economic exploitation of the native population. This domination has been implemented through a comprehensive program of social segregation termed apartheid. Like the lower castes of India, blacks in South Africa are categorically excluded from positions of power and prestige and socially and physically isolated from the dominant minority.

Estate

The estate system is intermediate in rigidity between the caste and class system (Nisbet, 1970:210–211). The estate system flourished throughout most of Europe during the Middle Ages; today it is virtually obsolete. Prestige and power in the social structure was based on one's relation to the land. The society was composed of three relatively homogeneous strata, or estates: nobility, clergy, and peasantry (Mayer, 1964:16–21). At the top of the hierarchy was the nobility, which controlled large, landed estates. The land was worked by serfs who owed their allegiance to a noble lord or vassal. The nobility, a landed, military aristocracy, was charged with protection from foreign invasion and the administration of justice. The primary function of the clergy was to meet the spiritual needs of the population and serve as an intellectual elite. The clergy consisted of a complex and powerful hierarchy that controlled much of the land. The church, in effect, constituted a separate state that cut across national boundaries. The head of the church estate was the Pope, followed by archbishops, bishops, abbots, and parish priests. The clergy with its own authority structure, laws, and courts rivaled the state in many cases (Mayer, 1964:16–21).

Although the estate system had a relatively structured, hereditary basis, it was far from a closed system (Nisbet, 1970:210). The greatest opportunity for social mobility was offered by the clergy. The rule of celibacy made it necessary for it to go outside of its ranks to recruit new members. Most recruits came from the ranks of nobility, but there was a limited opportunity for the disadvantaged to become parish priests and, perhaps, move up the status hierarchy. Unlike the caste system, social mobility involved individuals rather than entire groups.

The estate system was able to function as long as European societies were predominantly agrarian. The rise of the town and the emergence of a bourgeoisie stratum, made up of merchants and artisans, had a profound effect on the estate system. As commercial towns arose, a third estate was recognized in the bourgeoisie. An especially important development in commercial towns was the recognition of freedom as a territorial privilege inherent in urban centers. Regardless of their origin men could acquire their freedom by residing in a town for over a year. Thus the commercial town opened many avenues to social mobility and served as a bridge between the estate and the class system by breaking up the link between land ownership and social status.

Class

Unlike the caste and estate systems, which have a hereditary basis, the class system, at least in its ideal form, is based on the accumulation of wealth. Caste and, to a lesser extent, estate are predominantly ascriptive systems; in the class system a person, regardless of class origin, may theoretically achieve a high status if he accumulates wealth and assumes a prestigious position. It is important, however, to distinguish between the ideal components of the system and its actual operation. While class distinctions are ideally based on achievement, in reality heredity plays an important role in the distribution of wealth. In even the most "open" stratification system the family functions in a manner that limits mobility within the society. Although in a class system one's ultimate position is not determined by heredity, a child assumes the position of his parents at birth, and their social status has an important effect on his life chances.

The United States has an equalitarian ideology that glorifies rags-to-riches stories and denies the existence of social classes. Nonetheless, social classes are present in American society, and the rate of social mobility is comparable to other complex urban-industrial societies (Lipset and Bendix, 1962:72). The equalitarian ideology has been perpetuated in part by the absence of a feudal past, our frontier tradition, and enough social mobility to reinforce the Horatio Alger's mythology[1] (Lipset and Bendix, 1962: 76–78).

An important issue that has been debated extensively is the degree to which social classes are discrete, organized social groups. Some sociologists, following the tradition established by Marx, have argued that social classes are relatively cohesive entities. Marx saw capitalistic societies as moving toward the establishment of two polar and antagonistic classes—the bourgeoisie, owners of the means of production, and the proletariat, the working class (Bottomore and Rubel, 1963:201). The concept of class consciousness (awareness and identification with one's economic position) was critical for Marx. Class awareness was the springboard to political action

---

[1] The discussion of class here pertains mostly to white Americans, for the United States is characterized by two distinctive networks: a class system for whites and a caste system separating whites and nonwhites.

and, ultimately, the catalyst to revolutionary change. More recently, Centers (1949) has attempted to develop and measure the concept of class consciousness. A number of other sociologists, however, maintain that collective class consciousness is not present in the United States and other modern nations. Cuber and Kenkel (1954: Chapters 2 and 13), for example, argue that social classes constitute continuous, rather than discrete, categories without clear-cut demarcations or boundaries.

Closely related to the issue of class consciousness is the relative emphasis given to economic considerations in the analysis of stratification. Marx felt that social classes and political activity could only be understood through analysis of economic forces. Values, ideology, and political orientation are a direct result of class, or economic position. The German sociologist Max Weber (Gerth and Mills, 1964:180–195), on the other hand, saw economic position as only one, and not necessarily the most important, dimension of social stratification. He felt it necessary to distinguish among class, honor, and power. Class refers to the economic dimension, honor to social status or prestige, and power to the ability to implement one's goals even in the face of opposition by others. For Weber the difference between classes and status groups was critical. A class consists of a number of persons in a comparable economic position. While class is an important determinant of life chances, it should not be confused with a status group. Classes are social aggregates, but they are not communities:

In contrast to classes, *status groups* are normally communities. . . . In contrast to the purely economically determined "class situation" we wish to designate as "status situation" every typical component of the life fate of men that is determined by a specific, positive or negative, social estimation of *honor*. . . . Status honor is normally expressed by the fact that above all else a specific *style of life* can be expected from all those who wish to belong to the circle. Linked with this expectation are restrictions on "social" intercourse . . . (Gerth and Mills, 1964:186–187).

Thus status groups function as communities based on status distinctions, with social contacts and marriage tending to be limited to the status circle. In its extreme form the status group evolves into a closed caste (Gerth and Mills, 1964:188). Another way of stating the distinction is "that 'classes' are stratified according to their relations to the production and acquisition of goods; whereas 'status groups' are stratified according to the principles of their *consumption* of goods as represented by special 'styles of life' " (Gerth and Mills, 1964:193).

Weber differed from Marx in that he did not believe that class consciousness (i.e., status groups) would necessarily follow class distinctions. The two concepts were related but independent. Another basic difference lies in the priority given to the economic dimension. For Marx economic class was paramount; for Weber it occupied a secondary role. Weber pointed out that social honor and political power do not necessarily result from economic power. In fact, social honor (prestige) was frequently the basis of political and economic power (Gerth and Mills, 1964:180). The third concept introduced by Weber in conjunction with class and honor, but not as well developed, is party. While class belongs to the economic order and honor to the social order, party lies within the sphere of power. Parties are oriented to the acquisition of political power. The concept of party is somewhat ambiguous, but it seems to resemble a political power or special interest group.

A final distinction of a class system is that classes are not officially acknowledged by the legal system. Their existence is therefore informal. Status groups may be relatively well crystalized, moving toward closure, but their rules and customs are enforced informally through social custom. In a class system interclass marriages may be discouraged, for instance, but the restriction is not enforced legally as in a caste system.

SOCIAL MINORITIES

Although class systems are theoretically based on achievement rather than ascription, they tend to develop castelike qualities. In most societies certain groups are subjected to differential or unequal treatment on the basis of ascriptive characteristics such as skin color, national origin, or religious affiliation. The term "social minority" refers to a group of persons who are the objects of prejudice and discrimination as a result of their membership in a socially despised group; members are relegated to a subordinate position regardless of individual accomplishments. The minority characteristic overrides other factors such as education, occupation, and income.

A social minority should not be confused with a numerical minority. A group may constitute a numerical majority and still receive the treatment of a social minority (e.g., blacks in South Africa). The essence of a social minority is that it lacks social power and its members are systematically and categorically denied basic rights and privileges granted other citizens. Kameny (1971:52–53) has isolated four basic characteristics that can be used to define and identify a social minority:

1. *The minority characteristic.* This is the characteristic or characteristics that is used by members of the society to define the minority (e.g., skin color, religion, and nationality).
2. *Prejudice and discrimination.* Persons with the minority characteristic are subjected to prejudice and discrimination. Prejudice is a negative or adverse attitude toward a group; discrimination involves the unequal treatment of minorities relative to other groups. The two concepts are related but not synonymous. Prejudice is an attitude or feeling, whereas discrimination is the implementation of such an attitude through dif-

ferential and unequal treatment. The two phenomena tend to appear together, but one can find prejudice without discrimination (a powerless bigot) and discrimination without prejudice (discrimination based on economic expedience rather than a strong antipathy toward a group).

3. *Depersonalization.* Minority group members are not treated and evaluated as individuals but rather in an impersonal, categorical, and derogatory manner. The society develops a stereotyped characterization of the group, and individuals are ascriptively assigned this evaluation. Although the stereotype applies to only a fraction of the minority, it is maintained and perpetuated through selective perception. If a member of a minority commits an offensive act (a homosexual molesting young children), the entire group is blamed, whereas if a member of the dominant group commits the same act, only he is held responsible.

4. *Internalization.* This last defining characteristic of a social minority is probably the most important. Before a group is defined as a social minority by the society, the minority characteristic is only of secondary importance as a source of identification for members. One's racial or ethnic background, for instance, is not inherently or inevitably the primary basis of identification. The more importance ascribed to minority status by the society, the more it becomes a primary basis of identification for minority group members. The stigma attached to minority status turns it into a salient characteristic. One sees himself first as a black or a homosexual and only then as a writer, comedian, or whatever.

One of the most interesting corollaries of internalization is that members of the minority tend to adopt the negative stereotypes that the society ascribes to them (internalization resembles the concept of secondary deviation discussed in the Introduction to Part Two). Societal stereotypes are so pervasive that minority groups come to develop a lower self-image and self-esteem. The result is a self-fulfilling prophecy and a vicious cycle, which is illustrated in the following figure (the diagram should be read starting at twelve o'clock and moving clockwise).

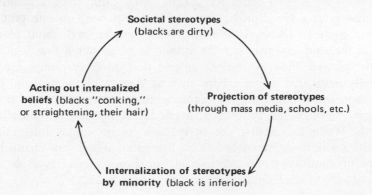

Societal stereotypes
(blacks are dirty)

Projection of stereotypes
(through mass media, schools, etc.)

Internalization of stereotypes
by minority (black is inferior)

Acting out internalized
beliefs (blacks "conking,"
or straightening, their hair)

The figure shows how societal stereotypes of minorities come full circle. The stereotypes are projected onto minorities who eventually internalize at least some of these stereotypes. When the minority group exhibits the characteristics, it further reinforces the initial stereotype. We will see in the remainder of the chapter that such a vicious cycle is difficult to break.

National and religious minorities

The term "minority" is believed to have originated in Europe with the emergence of national minorities (Rose, 1966:409). As a result of wars, migrations, and other factors, members of certain nationality groups frequently found themselves within the territorial boundaries of another nation. The displaced group was called a minority in relation to the dominant group, and it was "set apart" from the rest of the society by custom and law.

The concept of national minority has been less applicable to the United States than to European nations. The United States has, from its inception, contained a variety of nationalities with no one group holding a numerical majority (Rose, 1966:410). A number of groups did, however, become social minorities relative to the heterogeneous majority. While some groups were integrated into the society and gained political power, others (usually the newest arrivals) were the objects of prejudice and discrimination. Swedes and Germans, for example, were once members of minorities, but today they are well assimilated into the society. The Irish who occupied minority status during the nineteenth century and Italians during the twentieth are also fairly well integrated into the society.

The assimilation of minority groups into the mainstream of American society has been used to support the melting-pot view of the United States. The melting-pot, or pluralistic, view is consistent with the order perspective discussed earlier. According to pluralism, American society is composed of a heterogeneous mixture of national, religious, and racial groups, and the political representation of these diverse groups is assured by democratic processes. In time, all groups are assimilated into the vast melting pot. One of the leading authorities on minority relations has stated, for instance, that "since the United States has a democratic form of government, and since few groups are denied access to the ballot box, no one group has political control" (Rose, 1966:410). More will be said about pluralism later in the chapter—here it is important to point out a few fallacies of this perspective. First, we cannot assume that minority groups are automatically integrated. Some groups such as American Indians and blacks have been social minorities for centuries. Second, the belief in "peaceful progress" through the ballot box, a critical component of pluralism, is a myth. While the melting-pot perspective assumes that integration of minorities will be accomplished through regular, nonviolent channels, the history of minority group relations in American society is replete with cases of violent confrontation (Skolnick, 1969:3–23).

Another basis for ascribing minority status in the United States is religion. Many colonists came to this country to avoid religious persecution. Ironically, these same groups have persecuted Catholics and Jews throughout much of our history. Although Jews and, to a lesser extent, Catholics have been subjected to prejudice and discrimination, religion has played a less dominant role in assigning minority status in the United States than in many other countries (e.g., India and Northern Ireland). The negative treatment of American Catholics was probably based more on their membership in national minorities (e.g., Irish and Italians) than on religion per se. Despite the prejudice and discrimination against Jews, they have not been exploited economically. Compared to other minorities, Jews have a high-level economic and educational attainment. The minority status of Jews appears to be mostly in the area of honor. They are relatively well off economically (class) and have some political power but are excluded from status groups. The Jewish minority, however, is somewhat unique in that much of their isolation from the society is self-imposed. They are a highly cohesive, endogamous international community. Their rate of interfaith marriage is the lowest of any religious group in this country (Cavan, 1969: 213).

Racial minorities

Race is probably the most significant basis for minority status in the United States. The melting pot has not been equally accessible to all groups; those with a less visible minority characteristic were more readily assimilated into the society. Since religion and national origin are relatively unobtrusive factors, Caucasian members of such minorities have been integrated with relative ease. Race provides the majority with a number of physical characteristics that can be used to identify and control members of the minority.

The three groups that have been most consistently and systematically exploited in the United States are Mexican Americans, Indians, and blacks. Prejudice and discrimination have kept members of these groups in a subordinate position. The extensive poverty among Mexican Americans, Indians, and blacks was discussed at length in Chapter 2. In addition to their impoverished condition, minorities generally occupy low-status occupations and are without social and political power. One of the primary mechanisms for blocking the advancement of a minority group is to limit its educational opportunities.

The importance of Weber's distinction among class, honor, and power becomes apparent here. The concepts are related and yet independent. Of the three, changes in class probably come first for minorities and changes in honor last. Education enables some members of a minority to improve their economic position and to assume more political power, although less power than majority members of comparable class standing. The last and most difficult barrier for minorities to overcome is honor or prestige.

Because status groups form not only across class but also racial and ethnic lines, members of minorities are slow to be accepted into status groups. Even a lower-class white family is reluctant to accept an upper-class black family into its status group. Segregation in housing, schools, and social clubs, and a taboo against intermarriage are used to limit contact with the minority.

MEXICAN AMERICANS

Mexican Americans are a national minority from one perspective and a racial minority from another. Their minority status was created by the redefinition of political boundaries, which turned them into a national, or political, minority. Most of the territory that is today the American Southwest was under the jurisdiction of the Mexican government during the early part of the nineteenth century. "Between the Battle of San Jacinto in 1836 and the Gadsden Purchase of 1853, the United States acquired the present states of Texas and New Mexico and parts of Colorado, Arizona, Utah, Nevada, and California" (Moore, 1970:11). The majority became a minority (NEA, 1970:105). The minority status of Mexican Americans thus resulted from military and political domination rather than immigration, although it was perpetuated by immigration during the twentieth century.

With the exception of New Mexico, where Mexicans owned large tracts of land and were well represented in the territorial legislature, the nineteenth century witnessed the steady pauperization of Mexican Americans. Small sheep and cattle ranches were gradually displaced by large ranches, small farms by large-scale mechanized and intensive farming. The cotton industry created great demand for cheap, unskilled labor, and much of this labor was provided by Mexican *peones*. The expansion of the railroads also contributed to the minority status of Mexican Americans, who provided much of the cheap labor that built them. The railroads brought many Anglos into areas previously dominated by Mexican Americans. During the California gold rush, for example, thousands of Anglo residents rushed to the newly created mining towns (Moore, 1970:11–30).

The net effect of these events was to create an impoverished minority. Mexican Americans were mostly limited to lower-status, menial jobs. They were segregated into residential ghettos; in cities there were the *barrios*, and in rural areas migratory workers lived in squalid "Mextowns" near fields where they worked (Moore, 1970:21). Many Mexicans in the Southwest became laborers, working for substandard wages and living in dilapidated housing under unsanitary conditions. These conditions impaired health and produced much illness in the Mexican community:

. . . Mexican Americans show higher than average rates of tuberculosis, infant mortality, chronic disease, and illnesses associated with poverty and lack of adequate medical care. Studies of specific Mexican American communities show that over half the pre-school children did not receive immunization, that half the families had no family doctor, and about 85% did not own health insurance (Burma, 1970:327).

Given the economic position of Mexican Americans and conflict between them and Anglos, it is not surprising that a pattern of prejudice and discrimination emerged. The Mexican American came to be thought of as an inferior person, and a number of stereotypes were used to support this belief. Even today the word "Mexican" evokes images among Anglos of a man sleeping under a *sombrero* or of a bearded, greasy *bandido*. The conception of the Mexican American as lazy and shiftless served an important function for the Anglo community, legitimizing economic exploitation. According to this view, Mexican Americans are poor because they are too lazy to work. In effect, their cultural stereotype was the obverse of the image idealized by the Protestant Ethic. While the Protestant was ideally hard working, thrifty, and nonindulgent, the Mexican American was regarded as lazy, shiftless, and self-indulgent.

The history of relations between Mexican Americans and Anglos is marked by tension and conflict. From the early nineteenth century to the present Mexican Americans have been the victims of violence perpetrated not only by ordinary citizens but also law enforcement agencies. Incidents of police brutality were common during the early 1900s as Texas Rangers killed many innocent Mexican Americans (Morales, 1972:13). The Mexican-American police conflict has surfaced once again in the recent Los Angeles riots (Morales, 1972).

The negative image of the Mexican American is perpetuated by historical accounts, the mass media, and the schools (particularly in the Southwest). The Mexican American is taught that it is much better to call himself Spanish (which means white) or Latin (Salazar, 1971:395). The role of the Mexican American in American history has been grossly neglected. A state-approved textbook in Texas, for example, states: "The first comers to America were mainly Anglo-Saxons but soon came Dutchmen, Swedes, Germans, Frenchmen, Africans, then the great nineteenth-century period of immigration added to our already melting pot. Then later on, the Spaniards came" (quoted in Salazar, 1971:395). The text fails to mention that Spaniards settled Santa Fe, New Mexico in 1609, eleven years before the Pilgrims landed at Plymouth Rock (NEA, 1970:104).

Mexican-American children usually perform poorly in school. In addition to the obstacles faced by other poor children, Mexican-American children must overcome a language barrier, since for many English is a second language.

Guided by the melting pot theory, it has been an assumption among educators that instruction was for a basically homogeneous student population which was already English speaking. . . . The net effect of English language instruction is often destructive of the self-image and very ego of many Spanish-speaking children. Their individual needs have been submerged or suppressed in favor of a uniform curriculum established to make everyone speak and act like a typical American (Nava, 1970:126).

Mexicans are not a homogeneous racial group, most being of mixed Indian and Caucasian ancestry, but they have been defined as a racial group by members of the dominant majority. They therefore constitute a racial grouping in a social but not a biological sense.[2] The history of Mexican-Anglo relations points to the importance of societal definitions of physical characteristics. Since Mexican Americans were defined as a distinctive race, Mexican-Anglo relations took on a castelike quality. With the exception of New Mexico, where there has been considerable social mingling and inter-marriage, Mexican Americans in the Southwest were segregated socially and economically. Taboos against intermarriage were used to maintain the "purity of the races."

Despite the obvious similarities between the Mexican and black minori-ties, there are also important differences. First, it is obviously easier for many Mexican Americans to "pass" in the society because their physical characteristics are less distinctive than those of black Americans. Second, the castelike distinctions between Mexican Americans and Anglos are not as rigidly enforced. Finally, the subordination of Mexican Americans was for the most part de facto rather than de jure; that is, their subordination was enforced through informal custom rather than through legal restric-tions. The combined effect of these differences was to diminish the castelike quality of Mexican-Anglo relations. Prejudice toward Mexican Americans is probably less intense than is prejudice toward black Americans (Pinkney, 1970:79–80; Burma, 1970:55). Many Mexican Americans, especially outside the Southwest, who are light-complected are able to marry Anglos and become integrated into the dominant society.

NATIVE AMERICANS

American Indians are obviously the oldest minority in the United States. Since the coming of the white man, Indians have struggled to retain their land. The Battle of Wounded Knee in December of 1890 in which hun-dreds of Indian adults and children were slaughtered marked the end of the struggle for freedom and the military conquest of the Indian (Josephy, 1970:67).

The term "forgotten minority" is probably more applicable to Native Americans than to any other social minority in the United States. The Indian's role in shaping American history has been grossly neglected. There is a virtual blackout of information about Indians. The image that is por-trayed is one of "an inferior, or even subhuman species in intelligence and adaptability . . ." (Josephy, 1970:68). Since our history is biased, written

[2] The popularity of the term *La Raza* (The Race) as a reference to Mexican Americans suggests that many think of themselves as a distinctive racial group.

from the perspective of the conquering white man, until recently it was virtually impossible to obtain an accurate account of the American Indian, without either consulting original documents or statements written by Indians themselves (Josephy, 1970:71). Indians have long been aware of the negative image presented of them in history books. As early as 1928 a group of concerned Indians living in Chicago and calling themselves the Grand Council Fire of American Indians observed that Indians are portrayed in history as murderers:

. . . is it murder to fight in self-defense? Indians killed white men, because white men took their lands, ruined their hunting grounds, burned their forests, destroyed their buffalo. . . . White men who rise to protect their property are called patriots—Indians who do the same are called murderers (Josephy, 1970: 68).

The stereotype of Indians as wild, murdering savages is perpetuated today by novels, magazines, movies, and television. While other minorities have successfully challenged blatant stereotyping in the mass media, the subordination of the Indian is so deeply rooted in our historical heritage that Indian stereotypes go unquestioned. An analysis of stereotyping in magazine cartoons, for example, found that relative to their proportion in the population, blacks (especially American blacks) were greatly under-represented and Indians greatly overrepresented (Houts and Bahr, 1972: 112). Indians were typically depicted as warriors shooting arrows. Other studies have shown that elementary and high school texts both neglect and distort Indian history. The Indian's role in history is not only minimized, but when he is discussed, it is in a stereotyped and derogatory manner (Bowker, 1972). In short, while black Americans are being portrayed more favorably than in the past, both in history books and cartoons, the American Indian continues to be portrayed as a wild savage.

Perhaps the most distinctive characteristic of the American Indian today is his "transparency." To be an Indian in modern American society is in a very real sense to be unreal and ahistorical (Deloria, 1969:2). As a result of the many treaties, Indians were "given" land that was rightfully theirs. The effect of these treaties and of congressional legislation, however, was to place Indians in a dependent relationship relative to the United States government. Their land was held in "trust" by the Great White Fathers. Throughout much of our history then Indians have been separated from the dominant society both territorially and socially. Our treatment of the American Indian is reminiscent of Philip Slater's "Toilet Assumption." Americans believe that social problems and other undesirable conditions will disappear if they are out of our sight (Slater, 1971:15). We "solve" social problems by putting deviants and other undesirables away. Criminals are incarcerated, the mentally ill committed to institutions, and Indians are placed on reservations. Our approach to social problems is basically "out of sight, out of mind." We eliminate poverty with a bulldozer and call it urban renewal. When the problem rises to the surface again (a black riot or an Indian protest), we are shocked and angered and call in the emergency plumber (Slater, 1971:15). We set up a crash program such as the war on poverty or a special commission of experts to give us an instant solution to the problem. Vine Deloria, Jr., has summarized the Indian's plight: "Every two years some reporter causes a great uproar about how Indians are treated by the Bureau of Indian Affairs. This, in turn, causes great consternation among Senators and Congressmen. . . . So a TASK FORCE REPORT is demanded on Indian problems. . . . We are TASK FORCED to death" (1969:13, 27).

Just as task force reports are designed to advance the ends of congressmen and to relieve the collective white guilt, so has academic research done little, if anything, to improve the position of the Indian. Deloria has written a humorous, yet cutting critique of anthropologists, or "anthros":

. . . Indians have been cursed above all other people in history. Indians have anthropologists.

Every summer when school is out a veritable stream of immigrants heads into Indian country. . . . "They" are the anthropologists. . . . An anthropologist comes out to Indian reservations to make OBSERVATIONS. During the winter these observations will become books by which future anthropologists will be trained, so that they can come out to reservations years from now and verify the observations they have studied (1969:78–79).

Sociologists are not without bias in their treatment of Indians, but here we have more an error of omission rather than commission. While "anthros" have "milked" the study of Indians, sociologists have for the most part neglected the topic. Contemporary social problems texts contain a dearth of material on the Indian minority. An examination of the indices of three major texts revealed that American Indians were practically ignored. One book has a short paragraph about infant mortality among Indians (Becker, 1967:444–445). Another has three parenthetical sentences about Indians in the crime, race relations, and poverty sections and a three-page discussion of Indian suicide (Merton and Nisbet, 1971:109, 444, 610, 281–284). The third book contains a single sentence concerning medical care among blacks, Mexican Americans, and Indians (Horton and Leslie: 1970:537).

The invisibility, or transparency of the American Indian has some important implications. First, Native Americans do not have sufficient political power to bring the kind of pressure on the mass media, school boards, and other agencies that is necessary to eliminate negative stereotyping. Second, since the American Indian is a transparent figure, stereotyping of Indians is not perceived as prejudice against any living social group. Even liberals allow their children to watch movies and television programs that present Indians as murderers who slaughter innocent women and children. Whites are taken aback when an occasional Indian is offended by expressions such as "Indian giver" or "give it back to the Indians" and by the use of Indian figures as mascots for athletic teams. In effect, then, prejudice and discrimination against Indians is difficult to control because it is perceived as an innocent component of our cultural heritage. Finally, the invisibility of the Indian means that they appear to be a people without a history, with an antiquated image and no place in contemporary society.

Although there are obvious parallels between the red and black minorities, we have characteristically perceived and treated each differently. White society has typically thought of the black man as a draft animal and the Indian as a wild animal (Deloria, 1969:171–172). These views had a profound effect on our treatment of each group. Because the black man is viewed as an inferior animal, he is excluded from white institutions so that he will not "contaminate" the society. The Indian, on the other hand, is regarded as a wild animal that is worth taming or domesticating. "Indians were therefore subjected to the most intense pressure to become white" (Deloria, 1969:172). One need not accept the animal metaphor to realize that the treatment of Indians has been much more assimilative than the treatment of blacks. The federal government and religious missionaries consistently reflected a colonial ideology that saw Indian culture as inferior and attempted to convert the Indian to a civilized culture and religion. The dominant attitude towards blacks has traditionally been exclusionary. Recently, however, the culture of poverty ideology (see Chapter 2) proposed by white liberals as a solution to the "race problem" is reminiscent of colonialism.

The assimilative orientation toward the Indian may not have been motivated exclusively by altruistic motives. The fact that Indians owned large tracts of land provided some incentive for assimilating them. By converting the Indian to the American way of life, we could legitimize taking his land. This would be facilitated by introducing the Indian to the alien private-property system (MacMeekin, 1972:116). The ownership of land has also had an important effect on the development of Indians as a people. It has enabled them to retain their distinctive cultural heritage and to resist cultural encroachment by whites. Black Americans, on the other hand, have not had a land base around which to develop a culture. These differences must be taken into account in dealing with the problems faced by the two minorities.

BLACK AMERICANS

Black Americans are the largest racial and ethnic minority, comprising roughly 11 percent of the United States population. The term "race relations" immediately brings up the image of black Americans and their subordination by white society. White-black relations, especially in the South, approximated the ideal typical caste system. The races were separated in order to avoid contamination of the superior race by the inferior one, initially through slavery, then by de jure segregation, and most recently by de facto or extralegal exclusion of blacks.

No account of black Americans as a social minority would be complete without at least a brief discussion of *The Peculiar Institution* of slavery (Stampp, 1956). It is difficult to write objectively about slavery, since historical writing on the subject has been dominated by polemical works (Elkins, 1968:2). Since antebellum days writing on slavery has had a strong moral tone, intended to either defend or condemn slavery. Two of the primary exponents of these positions were Ulrich B. Phillips (1918), a spokesman for the Southern position, and James Ford Rhodes (1893), a New Englander who pointed out the evils of slavery. The racist position expounded by Phillips was widely accepted by scholars for most of the early part of the twentieth century until the 1930s and 1940s when antislavery writing came into vogue and racist positions were attacked by psychology, anthropology, and sociology. Today the antislavery position is still dominant, but we have not moved beyond the polemics. Unfortunately moral condemnations of slavery are frequently presented as objective analyses of the problem. The truth is probably somewhere between these polemics. Perhaps the future will bring a new synthesis of these polar and conflicting positions. Slavery was certainly not the virtuous, benevolent institution depicted by apologists for the South, but neither was it as ruthless as some would have us believe.

Slavery dates practically to the arrival of the colonists. The first Negro slaves were sold to settlers of Jamestown, Virginia, by Dutch traders (Pinkney, 1969:1), a significant fact when one realizes that it occurred one year before the arrival of the *Mayflower* at Plymouth Rock. Blacks initially occupied an ambiguous position. Since there was no precedent for slavery in English law, most were treated as indentured servants. Like white indentured servants, they were able to gain their freedom after working for a specified period of time (Pinkney, 1969:2). Eventually laws emerged that defined the status of the Negro as a member of a caste with few, if any, of the rights enjoyed by citizens. These laws were supported by a system of beliefs according to which the black man was an inferior person, in a sense a subhuman work animal unworthy of considerations given other persons. Slaves were property to be bought, traded, or given away at the discretion of the slaveowner. Slavery was a permanent caste status enforced by the legal system. A slave was to remain subordinate until his death, and his status was transmitted to his children and to his children's children.

There has been considerable controversy over the extent to which slaves accepted the institution of slavery. Defenders of the system painted an idyllic picture of happy, singing slaves who loved their masters, while opponents of slavery pointed to the atrocities of the system. Enough evidence has been gathered to dismiss the myth of the complacent, fully contented slave. Slavery was maintained only through extremely coercive measures; revolts occurred from the inception of slavery. At least 250 revolts or insurrections were reported throughout the history of black

American slavery (Pinkney, 1969:12). The revolts, however, were doomed to failure from the start. Slaves were in a minority, and slaveholders could rely on the militia or slave patrols to help put down uprisings. "A system of patrols, often more or less loosely connected with the militia, existed in every slave state" (Stampp, 1956:214). Virginia, for example, "empowered each county or corporation court to 'appoint, for a term not exceeding three months, one or more patrols' to visit 'all negro quarters and other places suspected of having therein unlawful assemblies,' and to arrest 'such slaves as may stroll from one plantation to another without permission' " (Stampp, 1956:214). Other less coercive methods were used to control slaves. Stampp (1956:149–150) has isolated six rules for controlling slaves that were generally agreed upon:

1. An overseer was not to be absent from the estate without his employer's consent.
2. A slave was not to be out of his cabin after "hornblow." . . .
3. A slave was not to leave the estate without a pass which gave his destination and the time he was to return.
4. Free Negroes or whites were not to work with slaves.
5. Slaves were not to marry free Negroes. . . .
6. A slave was not to sell anything without a permit, have whiskey in his cabin, quarrel or fight, or use abusive language.

The belief underlying these rules was that slaves were not to be trusted; they had to be watched continuously. The slaveowner, however, needed the cooperation and loyalty of some slaves:

Usually he found his allies among the domestics, skilled artisans, and foremen, all of whom he encouraged to feel superior to, and remain apart from, the field-hands. He gave them better clothes, more food, and special privileges as long as they remained true to his interests. He withdrew these favors and demoted them to field labor when they failed him (Stampp, 1956:151).

The division among slaves was so effective that some of the slave elite helped to capture runaway slaves. Poor whites also helped to catch fugitives. "Poor white men habitually kept their eyes open for strange Negroes without passes, for the apprehension of a fugitive was a financial windfall. Few southern white laborers showed much sympathy for the runaway slave" (Stampp, 1956:153). Thus slaveholders were able to keep slaves in a deprived and oppressed status not only by using force but also by maintaining division among slaves and between slaves and lower-class whites.

Despite the elaborate system of controls for maintaining the institution of slavery, many blacks did escape from bondage. The Underground Railroad was an organized effort by "free" blacks and white abolitionists to help slaves escape to the North and to Canada. It is estimated that between

1810 and 1850 perhaps as many as 100,000 slaves were led to freedom by the Underground Railroad (Franklin, 1947:255–256).

Even when slaves escaped they were never truly free. Free blacks, whether fugitive slaves or legally free, occupied an ambiguous legal and social status—neither free nor enslaved. His position was higher than the slave but much lower than the white man. Laws restricted freedom of movement, the right to vote, and the type of occupation entered (Pinkney, 1969:16–18). Perhaps the greatest problem faced by free blacks was to retain the little bit of freedom they did enjoy. Many feared being fraudulently returned to slave status. If a white man claimed that a black was a runaway slave, there was little that the black could do to retain his freedom (Franklin, 1947:215–216). It was not uncommon for free blacks to be kidnapped by gangs of slave stealers and sold as slaves (Stampp, 1956: 258).

Most slaves lived under extremely adverse conditions. Although owners were required by law to house and feed slaves, accommodations were generally substandard. They lived in small huts or cottages with dirt floors. The incidence of disease, illness, and infant mortality was very high. Slaves were frequently subjected to cruel punishment by slaveowners or overseers.

Under slavery the black family was not recognized as a functioning legal or social unit. Since slaves were property, they were disposed of at the will of the owner with little regard for the family unit (Elkins, 1968:53–55). Slaves were mated for economic gain, as animals are bred selectively. The father was neither the head of the household nor the breadwinner. Because slaves could not enter into contracts, marriages between them were not legal. The North Carolina Supreme Court ruled, for instance: " 'The relation between slaves is essentially different from that of man and wife joined in lawful wedlock . . . with slaves it may be dissolved at the pleasure of either party, or by the sale of one or both, depending upon the caprice or necessity of the owners' " (Stampp, 1956:198).

The dissolution of the slave family is but one example of the many attempts to strip the black man of his native African culture. Contrary to popular belief, slaves came from diverse cultural backgrounds. In America they were treated as a mass without regard to their cultural heritage or their native language (Pinkney, 1969:7). Slaves were forced to learn English in order to adjust to their new surroundings and to communicate with their masters. It was felt that blacks were an inferior people with an inferior culture, and attempts were made to resocialize the slave and introduce him to a "civilized" culture.

Religion became a primary mechanism for social control. Slaves were introduced to Christianity in the hope that religious beliefs would legitimize their subordinate position. Biblical scriptures were used to justify slavery. Slaves were taught to obey their masters and told of punishments awaiting the disobedient in the hereafter (Marx, 1967). The control of the slave's belief system may have proved more powerful than coercive methods.

Religion enabled many slaves to accept their lot as ordained by God.[3]

The conflict between supporters of abolition and the proslavery Southern states culminated in the Civil War. This confrontation had important implications for black Americans. "In the midst of the Civil War, on January 1, 1863, President Lincoln proclaimed that 'all persons held as slaves within any State, or designated part of the State, the people whereof shall be in rebellion against the United States, shall be then, thenceforward, and forever free'" (Pinkney, 1969:20). More than a hundred years after the Emancipation Proclamation black Americans are still not "free." While it is difficult to summarize the postslavery struggle for liberation, we can divide the black movement into four fairly distinct periods: **Radical Reconstruction, institutionalized white supremacy, civil rights,** and **black militancy.**

Radical reconstruction. This dates roughly from 1865 to 1876. Much was done during this period to guarantee equal rights for blacks and to increase their political participation (Pinkney, 1969:24–26). The passage of the Thirteenth, Fourteenth, and Fifteenth amendments was especially important for ending slavery as a legal status. The Thirteenth Amendment abolished slavery, the Fourteenth made blacks citizens and gave them equal protection of the law, and the Fifteenth guaranteed them the right to vote.

"Perhaps the most revolutionary aspect of the Reconstruction was the participation by blacks in the political arena" (Pinkney, 1969:24). In 1868 blacks constituted a majority of those registered to vote in the Confederate states. Blacks also had a majority at the South Carolina state convention and half of the delegates in Louisiana (Pinkney, 1969:25). Throughout the South many black Americans were elected to public office on the local, state, and national levels.

Institutionalized white supremacy. The disputed presidential election of 1877 marked the end of Radical Reconstruction and the beginning of institutionalized white supremacy. The steps taken toward implementing racial democracy were bitterly opposed by Southern conservatives, and by 1876 they had taken control of eight state governments (Pinkney, 1969: 26). The congressional compromise of 1877, which led to the selection of Rutherford B. Hayes as the winner, "signaled a return toward slavery which was to characterize the relations between blacks and whites in the South for decades to follow" (Pinkney, 1969:26). The net effect of the compromise was to end Reconstruction by withdrawing federal troops and returning home rule to the South. The Confederate states moved rapidly

---

[3] This is not to suggest that religion always functioned to maintain the status quo, for many religious leaders of both races were involved in the abolitionist movement. Religion has at different times served both as an opiate and an inspiration to civil rights militancy (Marx, 1967).

toward reinstituting the caste system that had prevailed before the Civil War. Although slavery was outlawed and civil rights were "guaranteed" by constitutional amendments, the Negro was kept in an inferior position. Separation of the races and subordination of blacks was enforced through both legal and extralegal means.

Between the end of Reconstruction and World War II blacks made some advancements in the courts, but their basic position was not improved. The National Association for the Advancement of Colored People (NAACP), established in 1909, sought to abolish segregation and discrimination and to implement the Fourteenth and Fifteenth amendments. It was to accomplish these goals by challenging discriminatory and segregationist policies in the courts. The NAACP achieved unusual success, winning a series of important court battles culminating in the landmark 1954 *Brown* v. *Board of Education* decision, which declared that the doctrine of "separate but equal" (established in the *Plessy* v. *Ferguson* decision of 1896) was discriminatory. The Court argued that separate facilities were inherently unequal. Despite the importance of these attempts to enforce the constitutional rights of blacks, they had little immediate impact on the status of black Americans.

Civil rights. Two dominant movements have emerged since World War II, civil rights and black militancy, each having roots in an earlier period but not flourishing until after the war. The civil rights phase of the black movement was dominant from 1945 until about 1965, although it originated with earlier efforts to gain equal protection of the law through the courts. In the later period the movement moved from legal battles to direct confrontation of discriminatory practices.

The civil rights movement is usually linked with Dr. Martin Luther King, Jr. King helped organize a long series of protests that challenged discrimination and segregation. His emphasis on "passive resistance," or *satagraha*, reflects the influence of Mahatma Gandhi (Bondurant, 1965: 1–40). On December 1, 1955, Mrs. Rosa Parks refused to yield her seat at the front of the bus to a white man in Montgomery, Alabama. The ensuing bus boycott, organized by King and other black leaders, was extremely successful and provided the impetus for future demonstrations. Among the more noteworthy of these were the use of federal troops to force the integration of Central High School in Little Rock (1957), the lunch-counter sit-in in Greensboro (1960), and numerous subsequent sit-ins in other cities throughout the South, the Battle of Selma (1963), a series of demonstrations and bombings in Birmingham, and the march on Washington (1963).

Although the civil rights movement was committed to passive resistance, it elicited much violence from white society. These violent confrontations helped to dramatize the plight of black Americans throughout the world.

The civil rights phase has a number of characteristics that differentiate it from black militancy. Its ultimate goal was equality for blacks and the integration of the races. The ideology of the movement was based on an orderly and pluralistic conception of society, committed to nonviolence and passive resistance. The movement was biracial; liberal whites and, to some extent, the federal government were allies in the struggle against bigotry and discrimination. Finally, the civil rights movement focused its attack on the South, although Martin Luther King later initiated protests in several northern cities including Chicago (Skolnick, 1969:125–175).

Black militancy. The black militancy phase of the black movement dates from 1965 and continues to the present. Prior to this, there were advocates of black nationalism and black power, but they played a secondary role to civil rights. As early as 1860 Martin R. Delaney sought to establish a black colony in Africa (Anderson, 1970:119). Perhaps the most influential of these early movements was the Universal Negro Improvement Association established by Marcus Garvey during the 1920s. Garvey's nationalist movement appealed particularly to poor blacks. It is estimated that the organization was able to gather over 6 million members. "Middle-class Negroes, especially the leadership of the NAACP, were his strongest critics, for they envisioned the complete integration of black people in American society" (Pinkney, 1969:33). More recently, the Nation of Islam (i.e., Black Muslims) has been able to establish a separatist organization. The Muslims have successfully implemented a system of black ownership and black capitalism. Elijah Muhammad, the founder of the Nation of Islam, teaches that the original man was black and that white men are devils (Stone, 1965:3). Ironically, although the Nation of Islam is separatist, it is not nationalist. Its members believe that they are Asians, not Africans, and that their original language is Arabic.

Malcolm X was one of the strongest and most influential spokesmen for Pan-Africanism. Initially he was converted to the Nation of Islam and became a follower of Elijah Muhammad, but at the time of his death he had become alienated from the Muslims and split with Muhammad (see Malcolm X, 1965; Breitman, 1965; Clarke, 1969). One source of conflict was the Muslims' rejection of their African heritage:

". . . hidden under the surface of the Black Nationalist creed to which he was won there lay a peculiar anti-Negroism. The true nationalist loves his people and their peculiarities; he wants to preserve them; he is filled with filial piety. But there is in Elijah Muhammad's Black Muslim creed none of the love for the Negro one finds in W. E. B. du Bois, or of that yearning for the ancestral Africa which obsessed Garvey (Stone, 1965:3).*

* Reprinted with permission from *The New York Review of Books.* Copyright © 1965, Nyrev, Inc.

Malcolm X taught not only black pride and dignity but also violence as a defense against white supremacy. He stated, "if he only understands the language of a rifle, get a rifle. If he only understands the language of a rope, get a rope. But don't waste time talking the wrong language to a man if you really want to communicate with him" (Stone, 1965:5). This ideology represented a complete reversal of the nonviolent, passive philosophy advocated by Martin Luther King.

Stokely Carmichael (1966 and 1967) is a transitional figure between the civil rights and black militancy movements. In the early 1960s he served as coordinator of the Student Nonviolent Coordinating Committee (SNCC), an arm of the civil rights movement. Eventually, partly as a result of white violence, he broke with the nonviolent tradition of civil rights and advocated black power. Carmichael (1966) felt that it was essential for blacks to gain power and establish a strong and independent community.

Perhaps the most highly publicized exponents of black power and black separatism are the Black Panthers. The Black Panther Party for Self-Defense was organized in 1966 to provide armed patrols that would protect ghetto residents in Oakland from harassment and abuse. The party grew from a small local group to a nationwide organization. Since their inception the Panthers have been the subject of police abuse (Skolnick, 1969:152). One of the most blatant of these attacks was the raid by the Cook Co. state attorney's office on December 4, 1968, which resulted in the murder of Fred Hampton and Mark Clark (Calhoun, 1971:34–47). While the Panthers have preached violence, they have done so primarily as a means of defense against attack by white society, especially the police. The negative publicity given the Panthers by the white press has tended to obscure the extent to which they have gained support in ghetto areas through breakfast programs and other attempts to instill black pride.

The reaction of white society to black militance provides an interesting cultural contradiction. Self-defense is considered a basic right by most Americans. "The picture of the armed American defending his home, his family, his possessions, and his person has its origins in frontier life. . . . In that picture, however, the armed American is always white" (Skolnick, 1969:150). Since we view blacks as docile animals incapable of aggression, we are resentful of the thought of a black man defending himself. In both the early slave codes and in the Southern caste system blacks were not permitted to strike whites, even in self-defense (Skolnick, 1969:150). It is therefore not surprising that militant rhetoric has struck a violent chord in white society. For the most part, however, black militancy has not moved beyond rhetoric. Black militant groups have generally been the victims rather than the perpetrators of violence. A task force report submitted to The National Commission on the Causes and Prevention of Violence concluded that, "The Black Panther Party has been repeatedly harassed by police" (Skolnick, 1969:152).

There are a number of important differences between the black militant movement and the civil rights movement. Whereas the civil rights movement is based on the order model of society, black militancy is based on a conflict view. The primary goal of civil rights is equality, while that of black militancy is liberation. Civil rights advocates the integration of the black into the mainstream of our pluralistic society; militancy advocates the development of black power and the retention of black identity and culture. Nonviolence and passive resistance have been replaced by self-defense. The militancy movement's call for black pride and self-determination has reduced the biracial quality of the movement. Most blacks realize that their identity can only emerge through movements and programs that are designed by blacks. A final difference in the two movements is that black militants have moved the battle for equality from the South to large urban centers throughout the country. Liberation for them is no longer exclusively a Southern problem.

The "other" minorities

Until recently the term "minority" referred only to racial and ethnic groups, not groups that were the objects of prejudice and discrimination on the basis of other characteristics. Among the groups that may be considered "other" minorities are homosexuals, women, the physically or mentally disabled, and, perhaps, even the young and the aged.

While these other minorities have long been subjected to differential and unequal treatment, they have not typically been viewed as minorities. The women's liberation movement, for example, has a long tradition that dates back to women's suffrage, but it is only in recent years that we have thought of women as a social minority. Women's rights were considered to be more a problem of providing legal rights for women than of pervasive prejudice and discrimination by a dominant group over a subordinate group (Millet, 1971:24–25).

In some ways it is misleading to speak of a women's liberation movement, since in effect there are at least two movements: sexual rights and female militancy. These two movements parallel the civil rights and black militancy movements discussed previously. The more moderate sexual rights movement is an extension of the earlier suffrage movement. It seeks equality before the law for women and the end of discriminatory practices in employment. Women should have equal opportunity to enter professions traditionally reserved for males and to receive equal compensation for the same work. Sexual rights appears to have more support both among men and women than the more radical female militancy movement. Female militancy accepts the goals of the sexual rights movement but seeks to go beyond them toward more radical and extensive goals. Adherents to this movement wish to liberate women from their traditional subordinate status and to end sexual and social exploitation. Women, according to this view, have never been recognized as human beings with needs and desires similar to those of men. From Biblical times women have been subordinate to men, viewed as property, owned and disposed of by man at his pleasure; theirs is a condition of servitude, more subtle but no less binding than slavery. The more militant members, like their black counterparts, advocate the use of self-defense against males:

Women are attacked, beaten, and raped every day. By men. Women are afraid to walk certain streets after dark, and even afraid to walk into buildings where they live. It's about time that we as women got strong in order to defend ourselves! . . . Women's liberation has a long, tough, political fight before it, and our oppression, which is ultimately maintained by force, can only be overcome by force (Pascalé, Moon, and Tanner, 1970:469, 477).

While there are parallels between the treatment of women and the treatment of other minorities (Hacker, 1951), there are also important differences. Women are discriminated against as individuals, but, unlike racial and ethnic minorities, they are not an impoverished group. Through marriage they acquire the social and economic status of their husbands. According to a norm enforced by custom and the legal codes, the male as the breadwinner must support his wife and children. Women are therefore dependent and subordinate but not deprived economically. Another important difference is that caste separation is not a prominent feature of male-female relations.

The discussion of differences between the female minority and racial and ethnic minorities is not intended to minimize the importance of women's liberation. The fact that women are not segregated and isolated from the dominant group makes it more difficult to attack the problem. Their minority status is in this sense invisible, for they appear to share the fruits of the affluent society equally with men: "Sex class is so deep as to be invisible. Or it may appear as a superficial inequality, one that can be solved by merely a few reforms, or perhaps by the full integration of women into the labor force" (Firestone, 1972:1). The sexual division of labor is basic to all human societies, having its origin in biological differences between the sexes. The emergence of a sex class (or caste), apparently a universal occurrence, can be traced to the biological family that makes females and children dependent on men (Firestone, 1972:9). From this perspective women's liberation, or more accurately sexual liberation, can only come about through revolutionary changes in the social structure that will free individuals from the tyranny of the biological family:

. . . the end goal of feminist revolution must be, . . . not just the elimination of male *privilege* but of the sex *distinction* itself: genital differences between human beings would no longer matter culturally. . . . The reproduction of the species by one sex for the benefit of both would be replaced by (at least the option of) artificial reproduction . . . (Firestone, 1972:11).

Like women's liberation, gay liberation has only come into prominence in recent years. Homosexuals have been subjected to prejudicial and discriminatory treatment for thousands of years, but homosexuality has generally been viewed as a personal malady or sickness, not a group phenomenon. With the emergence of other minority movements, gay liberation has developed into a full-fledge social movement in the past decade. The gay liberation movement, however, is not without precedent. For years the Mattachine Society has functioned as the NAACP of the gay world. The goals of this predominantly middle-class organization are consistent with those of the civil rights movement (and the sexual rights movement)— to obtain equal protection of the law and fair employment practices for homosexuals. The more recent and militant homosexual groups such as the Gay Liberation Front and The Gay Alliance have, like black militants, attempted to develop gay pride and integrity. They speak of oppression by the white sexist society and seek alliances with other oppressed groups, particularly women. The common elements between the gay movement and other minority movements is illustrated by the Gay Manifesto:

Male chauvinism, however, is not central to us. We can junk it much more easily than straight men can. For we understand oppression. We have largely opted out of a system which oppresses women daily—our egos are not built on putting women down and having them build us up. . . . Finally, we have a common enemy: the big male chauvinists are also the big anti-gays.

But we need to purge male chauvinist behavior and thought among us. Chick equals nigger equals queer. Think about it (Wittman, 1972:160).

Militant homosexuals feel that it is necessary to instill pride in homosexuals in order to undue thousands of years of negative stereotyping. Society has taught that homosexuals are diseased and that homosexuality is dirty. After being subjected to oppression and physical attack for centuries some homosexuals are starting to advocate violence as self-defense. A number of homophile organizations have adopted positions that reflect this increased militance:

We have been shoved around for some 3,000 years. We're fed up with it and we're starting to shove back. If we don't get our rights and the decent treatment as full human beings which we deserve, and get them NOW, there's going to be a lot more shoving back (Kameny, 1972:183).

There are some significant differences between the homosexual minority and other minorities. Because homosexuality, unlike skin color, is not an obvious malady, most are secret or semisecret deviants. Homosexuals as a group, therefore, are not oppressed economically, although individuals are discriminated against when their homosexuality is uncovered. This is the plight of the homosexual—he cannot openly admit his homosexuality. If he is a "closet queen," he can function without discrimination or prejudice; but if he openly admits his sexual preference, he is persecuted.

A NOTE ON SOLUTIONS TO MINORITY PROBLEMS

It is doubtful that social stratification will ever be completely eliminated from society, nor is it clear that its elimination would be desirable. If there is any validity at all to the functional position, a minimum of stratification may be not only desirable but essential. This is not to suggest that structured social inequality cannot be reduced substantially and the system made less rigid.

The distinction between a classless society and an open society is important here. While the prospects of a classless society are dim, the possibility of a more open society is very real. An open society would be one in which the social status of a person would not be affected by the status of his parents. The hereditary quality of stratification would be abolished, and a new system of stratification would emerge with each generation. This of course is the essence of minority group status—it is ascriptive. Regardless of a person's qualifications or achievements he is relegated to a lower status by virtue of minority group membership. Thus a more open stratification system coupled with a more equitable redistribution of rewards across the society would do much to diminish minority problems and to implement our basic democratic values.

We have isolated two dominant strategies for resolving minority group problems. The civil rights strategy, based on an order or pluralistic conception of society, seeks to end minority problems by implementing Constitutional guarantees and civil rights legislation. Its goals are basically assimilative and integrative. The militant strategy, on the other hand, adopts a conflict view of society; rejecting the assimilative orientation of the civil rights strategy on the grounds that it threatens the very existence of minority groups. To assimilate into the dominant society is to obliterate the cultural distinctiveness of the group. As Deloria says of the civil rights movement: "Equality became sameness. . . . In the minds of most people in 1963, legal equality and cultural conformity were identical" (1969:179–180). Deloria continues: "Peoplehood is impossible without cultural independence, which in turn is impossible without a land base" (1969:180).

The fact that Indians have a land base has important implications. They, more than other minorities, have a choice between integrating into the pluralistic society and developing their own independent cultural identity. The probability of establishing cultural independence and "peoplehood" is greater for Indians than other groups. It seems unlikely that a new black state or nation will be formed. Blacks must then either develop cultural integrity and "peoplehood" within the mass society or face integration into that society.

The problems of the so-called other minorities are obviously different from those of racial and ethnic minorities. The other minorities are generally not exploited economically as a group, although they have been the objects of prejudice and discrimination as individuals. Solutions to the problems of the other minorities are therefore not closely tied to programs that reduce poverty. Another important difference is that members of other minorities do not perpetuate their minority status to another generation. Women and homosexuals, for instance, obviously do not have offspring within their minority group. This means that relations between the other minorities and the larger society lack the castelike quality characteristic of minority status.

It is clear that minority group problems are complicated and diverse. Single, simple solutions to these problems are untenable. Programs that seek to reduce minority problems must take into account this internal diversity.

REFERENCES

Anderson, S. E.
1970 "Revolutionary Black Nationalism and the Pan-Africa Idea." Pp. 99–126 in Floyd B. Barbour (ed.), The Black Seventies. Boston: Porter Sargent.

Bahr, Howard M., Bruce A. Chadwick, and Robert C. Day (eds.)
1972 Native Americans Today: Sociological Perspectives. New York: Harper & Row.

Becker, Howard S.
1967 Social Problems: A Modern Approach. New York: Wiley.

Bondurant, Joan V.
1965 Conquest of Violence: The Gandhian Philosophy of Conflict. Revised ed. Berkeley, Calif.: University of California Press.

Bottomore, T. B., and Maximilien Rubel
1963 Karl Marx: Selected Writings in Sociology and Social Philosophy. London: Watts.

Bowker, Lee H.
1972 "Red and Black in Contemporary American History Texts: A Content Analysis." Pp. 101–110 in Bahr, Chadwick, and Day.

Breitman, George
1965 Malcolm X Speaks. New York: Merit.

Burma, John H.
1970 Mexican-Americans in the United States. Cambridge, Mass.: Schenkman.

Calhoun, Lilian S.
1971 "The Death of Fred Hampton." Pp. 34–47 in Theodore L. Becker and Vernon G. Murray (eds.), Government Lawlessness in America. New York: Oxford University Press.

Carmichael, Stokely
1966 "What We Want." The New York Review of Books 7 (September 22):5–8.

Carmichael, Stokely and Charles V. Hamilton
1967 Black Power: The Politics of Liberation in America. New York: Vintage Books.

Cavan, Ruth S.
1969 The American Family. Fourth ed. New York: Crowell.

Centers, Richard
1949 The Psychology of Social Classes. Princeton, N.J.: Princeton University Press.

Clarke, John Henrik
1969 Malcolm X: The Man and His Times. New York: Collier.

Cuber, John F., and William F. Kenkel
1954 Social Stratification in the United States. New York: Appleton.

Davis, Kingsley
1953 "Reply to Tumin." American Sociological Review 18 (August):394–397.

Davis, Kingsley, and Wilbert E. Moore
1945 "Some Principles of Stratification." American Sociological Review 10 (April):242–249.

Deloria, Vine, Jr.
1969 Custer Died for Your Sins. London: Macmillan.

Elkins, Stanley M.
1968 Slavery. Second ed. Chicago: University of Chicago Press.

Firestone, Shulamith
1972 The Dialectic of Sex. New York: Bantam.

Franklin, John Hope
1947 From Slavery to Freedom. New York: Knopf.

Gerth, Hans H., and C. Wright Mills
1964 From Max Weber: Essays in Sociology. New York: Oxford University Press.

Hacker, Helen Mayer
1951 "Women as a Minority Group." Social Forces 30 (October):60–69.

Horton, Paul B., and Gerald R. Leslie
1970 The Sociology of Social Problems. Fourth ed. New York: Appleton.

Houts, Kathleen C., and Rosemary S. Bahr
1972 "Stereotyping of Indians and Blacks in Magazine Cartoons." Pp. 110–114 in Bahr, Chadwick, and Day.

Huxley, Aldous
1960 Brave New World. New York: Harper & Row.

Josephy, Alvin M., Jr.
1970 "Indians in History." The Atlantic 225 (June):67–72.

Kameny, Franklin E.
1971 "Homosexuals as a Minority Group." Pp. 50–65 in Sagarin.
1972 "Gay Liberation and Psychiatry." Pp. 182–194 in Joseph A. McCaffrey (ed.), The Homosexual Dialectic. Englewood Cliffs, N.J.: Prentice-Hall.

King, Martin Luther, Jr.
1958 Stride Toward Freedom. New York: Harper & Row.

Legum, Colen
1967 "Color and Power in the South African Situation." Daedalus 96 (Spring):483–495.

Lipset, Seymour M., and Reinhard Bendix
1962 Social Mobility in Industrial Society. Berkeley, Calif.: University of California Press.

MacMeekin, Daniel H.
1972 "Red, White, and Gray: Equal Protection and the American Indian." Pp. 115–127 in Bahr, Chadwick, and Day.

Malcolm X (with the assistance of Alex Haley)
1965 The Autobiography of Malcolm X. New York: Grove.

Marx, Gary
1967 "Religion: Opiate or Inspiration of Civil Rights Militancy." American Sociological Review 32 (February):64–72.

Mayer, Kurt B.
1964 Class and Society. Revised ed. New York: Random House.

Merton, Robert K., and Robert Nisbet
1971 Contemporary Social Problems. Third ed. New York: Harcourt.

Millet, Kate
1971 Sexual Politics. New York: Avon Books.

Moore, Joan W.
1970 Mexican Americans. Englewood Cliffs, N.J.: Prentice-Hall.

Moore, Wilbert E.
1953 "Comment." American Sociological Review 18 (August):397.

Morales, Armando
1972 Ando Sangrando (I Am Bleeding): A Study of Mexican American-Police Conflict. La Puente, Calif.: Perspectiva Publications.

Nava, Julian
1970 "Cultural Backgrounds and Barriers That Affect Learning by Spanish-Speaking Children." Pp. 125–133 in Burma.

NEA-Tucson Survey on the Teaching of Spanish to the Spanish Speaking
1970 "The Invisible Minority." Pp. 103–118 in Burma.

Nisbet, Robert A.
1970 The Social Bond. New York: Knopf.

Ofshe, Richard
1970 The Sociology of the Possible. Englewood Cliffs, N.J.: Prentice-Hall.

Pascalé, Susan, Rachel Moon, and Leslie B. Tanner
1970 "Self-Defense for Women." Pp. 469–477 in Robin Morgan (ed.). Sisterhood Is Powerful. New York: Random House.

Phillips, Ulrich B.
1918 American Negro Slavery: A Survey of the Supply, Employment and Control of Negro Labor as Determined by the Plantation Regime. New York: Appleton.

Pinkney, Alphonso
1969 Black Americans. Englewood Cliffs, N.J.: Prentice-Hall.
1970 "Prejudice Toward Mexican and Negro Americans: A Comparison." Pp. 73–80 in Burma.

Rhodes, James Ford
1893 History of the United States From the Compromise of 1850 to the Final Restoration of Home Rule at the South in 1877. New York: Macmillan.

Rose, Arnold M.
1966 "Race and Ethnic Relations." Pp. 409–478 in Robert K. Merton and Robert A. Nisbet (eds.), Contemporary Social Problems. New York: Harcourt.

Sagarin, Edward
1971 The Other Minorities. Waltham, Mass.: Ginn/Blaisdell.
Salazar, Ruben
1971 "Stranger in One's Land." Pp. 390–415 in Robert Perrucci and Marc Pilisuk (eds.), The Triple Revolution. Boston: Little, Brown.
Skolnick, Jerome H.
1969 The Politics of Protest. New York: Simon & Schuster.
Slater, Philip
1971 The Pursuit of Loneliness. Boston: Beacon.
Srinivas, M. N.
1952 Religion and Society Among the Coorgs of South India. New York: Oxford University Press.
Stampp, Kenneth M.
1956 The Peculiar Institution. New York: Knopf.
Stone, I. F.
1965 "The Pilgrimage of Malcolm X." The New York Review of Books 5 (November 11):3–5.
Tumin, Melvin M.
1953a "Some Principles of Stratification: A Critical Analysis." American Sociological Review 18 (August):387–394.
1953b "Reply to Kingsley Davis." American Sociological Review 18 (December):672–673.
Wittman, Carl
1972 "Refugees from Amerika: A Gay Manifesto." Pp. 157–171 in Joseph A. McCaffrey (ed.), The Homosexual Dialectic. Englewood Cliffs, N.J.: Prentice-Hall.

INTRODUCTION TO THE READINGS

The readings included here are examples of the Sociology of the Possible. The two selections from the world of science fiction present very different solutions to the problems of social differentiation and social stratification.

The first is an excerpt from Aldous Huxley's story of an antiutopian society, *Brave New World.* In this fictional society the functional problem of stratification (motivating persons to assume those positions that are essential for the society) is resolved through total societal control over reproduction and socialization. Members of the society are literally created to fit the positions they are required to fill. Social minorities are nonexistent, since persons who occupy menial positions are equipped not only to assume such positions but to be satisfied with their lot. Huxley has created a stable system in which people are "happy" and there is little, if any, social change.

The second selection provides an equally revolutionary, though perhaps more palatable, solution to the problem of stratification. B. F. Skinner's utopian society, Walden Two, implements various principles of "psychological behaviorism." One of the underlying assumptions of the society is that rewards are both more effective and more desirable mechanisms of social control than punishment. Through scientific "social engineering" social problems and the "negative emotions" such as hate, fear, and jealousy are done away with. Walden Two is unique in that it is able to retain differentiation without developing a system of stratification. Persons who assume traditionally important societal positions do not receive differential rewards.

From Brave New World

ALDOUS HUXLEY

CHAPTER 1

A squat grey building of only thirty-four stories. Over the main entrance the words, CENTRAL LONDON HATCHERY AND CONDITIONING CENTRE, and, in a shield, the World State's motto, COMMUNITY, IDENTITY, STABILITY.

The enormous room on the ground floor faced towards the north. . . . Wintriness responded to wintriness. The overalls of the workers were white, their hands gloved with a pale corpse-coloured rubber. The light was frozen, dead, a ghost. Only from the yellow barrels of the microscopes did it borrow a certain rich and living substance, lying along the polished tubes like butter, streak after luscious streak in long recession down the work tables.

"And this," said the Director opening the door, "is the Fertilizing Room."

Bent over their instruments, three hundred Fertilizers were plunged, as the Director of Hatcheries and Conditioning entered the room, in the scarcely breathing silence, the absent-minded, soliloquizing hum or whistle, of absorbed concentration. A troop of newly arrived students, very young, pink and callow, followed nervously, rather abjectly, at the Director's heels. Each of them carried a notebook, in which, whenever the great man spoke, he desperately scribbled. Straight from the horse's mouth. It was a rare privilege. The D.H.C. for Central London always made a point of personally conducting his new students round the various departments.

"Just to give you a general idea," he would explain to them. For of course some sort of general idea they must have, if they were to do their work intelligently—though as little of one, if they were to be good and happy members of society, as possible. For particulars, as every one knows, make for virtue and happiness; generalities are intellectually necessary evils. Not philosophers but fret-sawyers and stamp collectors compose the backbone of society.

"To-morrow," he would add, smiling at them with a slightly menacing geniality, "you'll be settling down to serious work. You won't have time for generalities. Meanwhile . . ."

Meanwhile, it was a privilege. Straight from the horse's mouth into the notebook. The boys scribbled like mad.

Tall and rather thin but upright, the Director advanced into the room. He had a long chin and big, rather prominent teeth, just covered, when he was not talking, by his full, floridly curved lips. Old, young? Thirty? Fifty? Fifty-five? It was hard to say. And anyhow the question didn't arise; in this year of stability, A.F. 632, it didn't occur to you to ask it.

"I shall begin at the beginning," said the D.H.C. and the more zealous students recorded his intention in their notebooks: *Begin at the beginning.* "These," he waved his hand, "are the incubators." And opening an insulated door he showed them racks upon racks of numbered test-tubes. "The week's supply of ova. Kept," he explained, "at blood heat; whereas the male gametes," and here he opened another

---

door, "they have to be kept at thirty-five instead of thirty-seven. Full blood heat sterilizes." Rams wrapped in theremogene beget no lambs.

Still leaning against the incubators he gave them, while the pencils scurried illegibly across the pages, a brief description of the modern fertilizing process; spoke first, of course, of its surgical introduction—"the operation undergone voluntarily for the good of Society, not to mention the fact that it carries a bonus amounting to six months' salary"; continued with some account of the technique for preserving the excised ovary alive and actively developing; passed on to a consideration of optimum temperature, salinity, viscosity; referred to the liquor in which the detached and ripened eggs were kept; and, leading his charges to the work tables, actually showed them how this liquor was drawn off from the test-tubes; how it was let out drop by drop onto the specially warmed slides of the microscopes; how the eggs which it contained were inspected for abnormalities, counted and transferred to a porous receptable; how (and he now took them to watch the operation) this receptable was immersed in a warm bouillon containing free-swimming spermatozoa—at a minimum concentration of one hundred thousand per cubic centimetre, he insisted; and how, after ten minutes, the container was lifted out of the liquor and its contents re-examined; how, if any of the eggs remained unfertilized, it was again immersed, and, if necessary, yet again; how the fertilized ova went back to the incubators; where the Alphas and Betas remained until definitely bottled: while the Gammas, Deltas and Epsilons were brought out again, after only thirty-six hours, to undergo Bokanovsky's Process.

"Bokanovsky's Process," repeated the Director, and the students under-lined the words in their little note-books.

One egg, one embryo, one adult—normality. But a bokanovskified egg will bud, will proliferate, will divide. From eight to ninety-six buds, and every bud will grow into a perfectly formed embryo, and every embryo into a full-sized adult. Making ninety-six human beings grow where only one grew before. Progress.

"Essentially," the D.H.C. concluded, "bokanovskification consists of a series of arrests of development. We check the normal growth and, paradoxically enough, the egg responds by budding."

Responds by budding. The pencils were busy.

He pointed. On a very slowly moving band a rack-full of test-tubes was entering a large metal box, another rack-full was emerging. Machinery faintly purred. It took eight minutes for the tubes to go through, he told them. Eight minutes of hard X-rays being about as much as an egg can stand. A few died; of the rest, the least susceptible divided into two; most put out four buds; some eight; all were returned to the incubators, where the buds began to develop; then, after two days, were suddenly chilled, chilled and checked. Two, four, eight, the buds in their turn budded; and having budded were dosed almost to death with alcohol; consequently burgeoned again and having budded—bud out of bud out of bud—were thereafter—further arrest being generally fatal—left to develop in peace. By which time the original egg was in a fair way to becoming anything from eight to ninety-six embryos—a prodigious improvement, you will agree, on nature. Identical twins—but not in piddling twos and threes as in the old viviparous days, when an egg would sometimes accidentally divide; actually by dozens, by scores at a time.

"Scores," the Director repeated and flung out his arms, as though he were distributing largesse. "Scores."

But one of the students was fool enough to ask where the advantage lay.

"My good boy!" The Director wheeled sharply round on him. "Can't you see? Can't you *see*?" He raised a hand; his expression was solemn. "Bokanovsky's Process is one of the major instruments of social stability!"

Major instruments of social stability.

Standard men and women; in uniform batches. The whole of a small factory staffed with the products of a single bokanovskified egg.

"Ninety-six identical twins working ninety-six identical machines!" The voice was almost tremulous with enthusiasm. "You really know where you are. For the first time in history." He quoted the planetary motto. "Community, Identity, Stability." Grand words. "If we could bokanovskify indefinitely the whole problem would be solved."

Solved by standard Gammas, unvarying Deltas, uniform Epsilons. Millions of identical twins. The principle of mass production at last applied to biology.

"But, alas," the Director shook his head, "we *can't* bokanovskify indefinitely."

Ninety-six seemed to be the limit; seventy-two a good average. From the same ovary and with gametes of the same male to manufacture as many batches of identical twins as possible— that was the best (sadly a second best) that they could do. And even that was difficult.

"For in nature it takes thirty years for two hundred eggs to reach maturity. But our business is to stabilize the population at this moment, here and now. Dribbling out twins over a quarter of a century—what would be the use of that?"

Obviously, no use at all. But Podsnap's Technique had immensely accelerated the process of ripening. They could make sure of at least a hundred and fifty mature eggs within two years. Fertilize and bokanovskify—in other words, multiply by seventy-two—and you get an average of nearly eleven thousand brothers and sisters in a hundred and fifty batches of identical twins, all within two years of the same age.

"And in exceptional cases we can make one ovary yield us over fifteen thousand adult individuals."

Beckoning to a fair-haired, ruddy young man who happened to be passing at the moment, "Mr. Foster," he called. The ruddy young man approached. "Can you tell us the record for a single ovary, Mr. Foster?"

"Sixteen thousand and twelve in this Centre," Mr. Foster replied without hesitation. He spoke very quickly, had a vivacious blue eye, and took an evident pleasure in quoting figures. "Sixteen thousand and twelve; in one hundred and eighty-nine batches of identicals. But of course they've done much better," he rattled on, "in some of the tropical Centres. Singapore has often produced over sixteen thousand five hundred; and Mombasa has actually touched the seventeen thousand mark. But then they have unfair advantages. You should see the way a negro ovary responds to pituitary! It's quite astonishing, when you're used to working with European material. Still," he added, with a laugh (but the light of combat was in his eyes and the lift of his chin was challenging), "still, we mean to beat them if we can. I'm working on a wonderful Delta-Minus ovary at this moment. Only just eighteen months old. Over twelve thousand seven hundred children already, either decanted or in embryo. . . .

In the Bottling Room all was harmonious bustle and ordered activity. Flaps of fresh sow's peritoneum ready cut to the proper size came shooting up in little lifts from the Organ Store in the sub-basement. Whizz and then, click! the lift-hatches flew open; the bottle-liner had only to reach out a hand, take the flap, insert, smooth-down, and before the lined bottle had had time to travel out of reach along the endless band, whizz, click! another flap of peritoneum had shot up from the depths, ready to be slipped into yet another bottle, the next of that slow interminable procession on the band.

Next to the Liners stood the Matriculators. The procession advanced; one by one the eggs were transferred from their test-tubes to the larger containers; deftly the peritoneal lining was slit, the morula dropped into place, the saline solution poured in . . . and already the bottle had passed, and it was the turn of the labellers. Heredity, date of fertilization, membership of Bokanovsky Group—details were transferred from test-tube to bottle. No longer anonymous, but named, identified, the procession marched slowly on; on through an opening in the wall, slowly on into the Social Predestination Room.

"Eighty-eight cubic metres of card-index," said Mr. Foster with relish, as they entered.

"Containing *all* the relevant information," added the Director.

"Brought up to date every morning."

"And co-ordinated every afternoon."

"On the basis of which they make their calculations."

"So many individuals, of such and such quality," said Mr. Foster.

"Distributed in such and such quantities."

"The optimum Decanting Rate at any given moment."

"Unforeseen wastages promptly made good."

"Promptly," repeated Mr. Foster. "If you knew the amount of overtime I had to put in after the last Japanese earthquake!" He laughed good-humouredly and shook his head.

"The Predestinators send in their figures to the Fertilizers."

"Who give them the embryos they ask for."

"And the bottles come in here to be predestinated in detail."

"After which they are sent down to the Embryo Store."

"Where we now proceed ourselves."

And opening a door Mr. Foster led the way down a staircase into the basement.

The temperature was still tropical. They descended into a thickening twilight. Two doors and a passage with a double turn insured the cellar against any possible infiltration of the day.

"Embryos are like photograph film," said Mr. Foster waggishly, as he pushed open the second door. "They can only stand red light."

And in effect the sultry darkness into which the students now followed him was visible and crimson, like the darkness of closed eyes on a summer's afternoon. The bulging flanks of row on receding row and tier above tier of bottles glinted with innumerable rubies, and among the rubies moved the dim red spectres of men and women with purple eyes and all the symptoms of lupus. The hum and rattle of machinery faintly stirred the air.

. . .

Showed them the simple mechanism by means of which, during the last two metres out of every eight, all the embryos were simultaneously shaken into familiarity with movement. Hinted at the gravity of the so-called "trauma of decanting," and enumerated the precautions taken to minimize, by a suitable training of the bottled embryo, that dangerous shock. Told them of the tests for sex carried out in the neighbourhood of metre 200. Explained the system of labelling—a T for the males, a circle for the females and for those who were destined to become freemartins a question mark, black on a white ground.

"For of course," said Mr. Foster, "in the vast majority of cases, fertility is merely a nuisance. One fertile ovary in twelve hundred—that would really be quite sufficient for our purposes. But we want to have a good choice. And of course one must always leave an enormous margin of safety. So we allow as many as thirty percent of the female embryos to develop normally. The others get a dose of male sex-hormone every twenty-four metres for the rest of the course. Result: they're decanted as freemartins—structurally quite normal (except," he had to admit, "that they *do* have just the slightest tendency to grow beards), but sterile. Guaranteed sterile. Which brings us at last," continued Mr. Foster, "out of the realm of mere slavish imitation of nature into the much more interesting world of human invention."

He rubbed his hands. For of course, they didn't content themselves with merely hatching out embryos: any cow could do that.

"We also predestine and condition. We decant our babies as socialized human beings, as Alphas or Epsilons, as future sewage workers or future . . ." He was going to say "future World controllers," but correcting himself, said "future Directors of Hatcheries," instead.

The D.H.C. acknowledged the compliment with a smile.

They were passing Metre 320 on rack 11. A young Beta-Minus mechanic was busy with screwdriver and spanner on the blood-surrogate pump of a passing bottle. The hum of the electric motor deepened by fractions of a tone as he turned the nuts. Down, down . . . A final twist, a glance at the revolution counter, and he was done. He moved two paces down the line and began the same process on the next pump.

"Reducing the number of revolutions per minute," Mr. Foster explained. "The surrogate goes round slower; therefore passes through the lung at longer intervals; therefore gives the embryo less oxygen. Nothing like oxygen-shortage for keeping an embryo below par." Again he rubbed his hands.

"But why do you want to keep the embryo below par?" asked an ingenuous student.

"Ass!" said the Director, breaking a long silence. "Hasn't it occurred to you that an Epsilon embryo must have an Epsilon environment as well as an Epsilon heredity?"

It evidently hadn't occurred to him. He was covered with confusion.

"The lower the caste," said Mr. Foster, "the shorter the oxygen." The first organ affected was the brain. After that the skeleton. At seventy percent of normal oxygen you got dwarfs. At less than seventy eyeless monsters.

"Who are no use at all," concluded Mr. Foster.

Whereas (his voice became confidential and eager), if they could discover a technique for shortening the period of maturation what a triumph, what a benefaction to Society!

"Consider the horse."

They considered it.

Mature at six: the elephant at ten. While at thirteen a man is not yet sexually mature; and is only full-grown at twenty. Hence, of course, that fruit of delayed development, the human intelligence.

"But in Epsilons," said Mr. Foster very justly, "we don't need human intelligence."

Didn't need and didn't get it. But though the Epsilon mind was mature at ten, the Epsilon body was not fit to work till eighteen. Long years of superfluous and wasted immaturity. If the physical development could be speeded up till it was as quick, say, as a cow's, what an enormous saving to the Community!

"Enormous!" murmured the students. Mr. Foster's enthusiasm was infectious.

He became rather technical; spoke of the abnormal endocrine co-ordination which made men grow so slowly; postulated a germinal mutation to account for it. Could the effects of this germinal mutation be undone? Could the individual Epsilon embryo be made a revert, by a suitable technique, to the normality of dogs and cows? That was the problem. And it was all but solved.

Pilkington, at Mombasa, had produced individuals who were sexually mature at four and full-grown at six and a half. A scientific triumph. But socially useless. Six-year-old men and women were too stupid to do even Epsilon work. And the process was an all-or-nothing one; either you failed to modify at all, or else you modified the whole way. They were still trying to find the ideal compromise between adults of twenty and adults of six. So far without success. Mr. Foster sighed and shook his head.

Their wanderings through the crimson twilight had brought them to the neighbourhood of Metre 170 on Rack 9. From this point onwards Rack 9 was enclosed and the bottles performed the remainder of their journey in a kind of tunnel, interrupted here and there by openings two or three metres wide.

"Heat conditioning," said Mr. Foster.

Hot tunnels alternated with cool tunnels. Coolness was wedded to discomfort in the form of hard X-rays. By the time they were decanted the embryos had a horror of cold. They were predestined to emigrate to the tropics, to be miners and acetate silk spinners and steel workers. Later on their minds would be made to endorse the judgment of their bodies. "We condition them to thrive on heat," concluded Mr. Foster. "Our colleagues upstairs will teach them to love it."

"And that," put in the Director sententiously, "that is the secret of happiness and virtue—liking what you've *got* to do. All conditioning aims at that: making people like their unescapable social destiny."

. . .

CHAPTER 2

Mr. Foster was left in the Decanting Room. The D.H.C. and his students stepped into the nearest lift and were carried up to the fifth floor.

INFANT NURSERIES. NEO-PAVLOVIAN CONDITIONING ROOMS, announced the notice board.

The Director opened a door. They were in a large bare room, very bright and sunny; for the whole of the southern wall was a single window. Half a dozen nurses, trousered and jacketed in the regulation white viscose-linen uniform, their hair aseptically hidden under white caps, were engaged in setting out bowls of roses in a long row across the floor. Big bowls, packed tight with blossom. Thousands of petals, ripe-blown and silkily smooth, like the cheeks of innumerable little cherubs, but of cherubs, in that bright light, not exclusively pink and Aryan, but also luminously Chinese, also Mexican, also apoplectic with too much blowing of celestial trumpets, also pale as death, pale with the posthumous whiteness of marble.

The nurses stiffened to attention as the D.H.C. came in.

"Set out the books," he said curtly.

In silence the nurses obeyed his command. Between the rose bowls the books were duly set out—a row of nursery quartos opened invitingly each at some gaily coloured image of beast or fish or bird.

"Now bring in the children."

They hurried out of the room and returned in a minute or two, each pushing a kind of tall dumb-waiter laden, on all its four wire-netted shelves, with eight-month-old babies, all exactly alike (a Bokanovsky Group, it was evident) and all (since their caste was Delta) dressed in khaki.

"Put them down on the floor."

The infants were unloaded.

"Now turn them so that they can see the flowers and books."

Turned, the babies at once fell silent, then began to crawl towards those clusters of sleek colours, those shapes so gay and brilliant on the white pages. As they approached, the sun came out of a momentary eclipse behind a cloud. The roses flamed up as though with a sudden passion from within; a new and profound significance seemed to suffuse the shining pages of the books. From the ranks of the crawling babies came little squeals of excitement, gurgles and twitterings of pleasure.

The Director rubbed his hands. "Excellent!" he said. "It might almost have been done on purpose."

The swiftest crawlers were already at their goal. Small hands reached out uncertainly, touched, grasped, unpetaling the transfigured roses, crumpling the illuminated pages of the books. The Director waited until all were happily busy. Then, "Watch carefully," he said. And, lifting his hand, he gave the signal.

The Head Nurse, who was standing by a switchboard at the other end of the room, pressed down a little lever.

There was a violent explosion. Shriller and ever shriller, a siren shrieked. Alarm bells maddeningly sounded.

The children started, screamed; their faces were distorted with terror.

"And now," the Director shouted (for the noise was deafening), "now we proceed to rub in the lesson with a mild electric shock."

He waved his hand again, and the Head Nurse pressed a second lever. The screaming of the babies suddenly changed its tone. There was something desperate, almost insane, about the sharp spasmodic yelps to which they now gave utterance. Their little bodies twitched and stiffened; their limbs moved jerkily as if to the tug of unseen wires.

"We can electrify that whole strip of floor," bawled the Director in explanation. "But that's enough," he signalled to the nurse.

The explosions ceased, the bells stopped ringing, the shriek of the siren died down from tone to tone into silence. The stiffly twitching bodies relaxed, and what had become the sob and yelp of infant maniacs broadened out once more into a normal howl of ordinary terror.

"Offer them the flowers and the books again."

The nurses obeyed; but at the approach of the roses, at the mere sight of those gaily-coloured images of pussy and cock-a-doodle-doo and baa-baa black sheep, the infants shrank away in horror; the volume of their howling suddenly increased.

"Observe," said the Director triumphantly, "observe."

Books and loud noises, flowers and electric shocks—already in the infant mind these couples were compromisingly linked; and after two hundred repetitions of the same or a similar lesson would be wedded indissolubly. What man has joined, nature is powerless to put asunder.

"They'll grow up with what the psychologists used to call an 'instinctive' hatred of books and flowers. Reflexes unalterably conditioned. They'll be safe from books and botany all their lives." The Director turned to his nurses. "Take them away again."

Still yelling, the khaki babies were loaded on to their dumb-waiters and wheeled out, leaving behind them the smell of sour milk and a most welcome silence.

One of the students held up his hand; and though he could see quite well why you couldn't have lower-caste people wasting the Community's time over books, and that there was always the risk of their reading something which might undesirably decondition one of their reflexes, yet . . . well, he couldn't understand about the flowers. Why go to the trouble of making it psychologically impossible for Deltas to like flowers?

Patiently the D.H.C. explained. If the children were made to scream at the sight of a rose, that was on grounds of high economic policy. Not so very long ago (a century or thereabouts), Gammas, Deltas, even Epsilons, had been conditioned to like flowers—flowers in particular and wild nature in general. The idea was to make them want to be going out into the country at every available opportunity, and so compel them to consume transport.

"And didn't they consume transport?" asked the student.

"Quite a lot," the D.H.C. replied. "But nothing else."

Primroses and landscapes, he pointed out, have one grave defect: they are gratuitous. A love of nature keeps no factories busy. It was decided to abolish the love of nature, at any rate among the lower classes; to abolish the love of nature, but *not* the tendency to consume transport. For of course it was essential that they should keep on going to the country, even though they hated it. The problem was to find an economically sounder reason for consuming transport than a mere affection for primroses and landscapes. It was duly found.

"We condition the masses to hate the country," concluded the Director. "But simultaneously we condition them to love all country sports. At the same time, we see to it that all country sports shall entail the use of elaborate apparatus. So that they consume manufactured articles as well as transport. Hence those electric shocks."

"I see," said the student, and was silent, lost in admiration.

.   .   .

From Walden Two

B. F. SKINNER

We found space near the windows of a small lounge and drew up chairs so that we could look out over the slowly darkening landscape. Frazier seemed to have no particular discussion prepared and he had begun to look a little tired. Castle must have been full of things to say, but he apparently felt that I should open the conversation.

"We are grateful for your kindness," I said to Frazier, "not only in asking us to visit Walden Two but in giving us so much of your time. I'm afraid it's something of an imposition."

"On the contrary," said Frazier, "I'm fully paid for talking with you. Two labor-credits are allowed each day for taking charge of guests of Walden Two. I can use only one of them, but it's a bargain even so, because I'm more than fairly paid by your company."

"Labor-credits?" I said.

"I'm sorry. I had forgotten. Labor-credits are a sort of money. But they're not coins or bills—just entries in a ledger. All goods and services are free, as you saw in the dining room this evening. Each of us pays for what he uses with twelve hundred labor-credits each year—say, four credits for each workday. We change the value according to the needs of the community. At two hours of work per credit—an eight-hour day—we could operate at a handsome profit. We're satisfied to keep just a shade beyond breaking even. The profit system is bad even when the worker gets the profits, be-cause the strain of overwork isn't re-lieved by even a large reward. All we ask is to make expenses, with a slight margin of safety; we adjust the value of the labor-credit accordingly. At present it's about one hour of work per credit."

"Your members work only four hours a day?" I said. There was an overtone of outraged virtue in my voice, as if I had asked if they were all adulterous.

"On the average," Frazier replied casually. In spite of our obvious in-terest he went on at once to another point. "A credit system also makes it possible to evaluate a job in terms of the willingness of the members to un-dertake it. After all, a man isn't doing more or less than his share because of the time he puts in; it's what he's do-ing that counts. So we simply assign different credit values to different kinds of work, and adjust them from time to time on the basis of demand. Bellamy suggested the principle in *Looking Backward*."

"An unpleasant job like cleaning sewers has a high value, I suppose," I said.

"Exactly. Somewhere around one and a half credits per hour. The sewer man works a little over two hours a day. Pleasanter jobs have lower values —say point seven or point eight. That means five hours a day, or even more. Working in the flower gardens has a very low value—point one. No one makes a living at it, but many people like to spend a little time that way, and we give them credit. In the long run, when the values have been adjusted, all kinds of work are equally desir-able. If they weren't, there would be a demand for the more desirable, and the credit value would be changed. Once in a while we manipulate a preference, if some job seems to be avoided without cause."

"I suppose you put phonographs in your dormitories which repeat 'I like to work in sewers. Sewers are lots of fun,' " said Castle.

"No, Walden Two isn't that kind of brave new world," said Frazier. "We don't *propagandize*. That's a basic principle. I don't deny that it would be possible. We could make the heaviest work appear most honorable and desirable. Something of the sort has always been done by well-organized governments—to facilitate the recruiting of armies, for example. But not here. You may say that we propagandize *all* labor, if you like, but I see no objection to that. If we can make work pleasanter by proper training why shouldn't we? But I digress."

"What about the knowledge and skill required in many jobs?" said Castle. "Doesn't that interfere with free bidding? Certainly you can't allow just anyone to work as a doctor."

"No, of course not. The principle has to be modified where long training is needed. Still, the preferences of the community as a whole determine the final value. If our doctors were conspicuously overworked *according to our standards*, it would be hard to get young people to choose that profession. We must see to it that there are enough doctors to bring the average schedule within range of the Walden Two standard."

"What if nobody wanted to be a doctor?" I said.

"Our trouble is the other way round."

"I thought as much," said Castle. "Too many of your young members will want to go into interesting lines

in spite of the work load. What do you do, then?"

"Let them know how many places will be available, and let them decide. We're glad to have more than enough doctors, of course, and could always find some sort of work for them, but we can't offer more of a strictly medical practice than our disgustingly good health affords."

"Then you don't offer complete personal freedom, do you?" said Castle, with ill-concealed excitement. "You haven't really resolved the conflict between a *laissez-faire* and a planned society."

"I think we have. Yes. But you must know more about our educational system before I can show you how. The fact is, it's very unlikely that anyone at Walden Two will set his heart on a course of action so firmly that he'll be unhappy if it isn't open to him. That's as true of the choice of a girl as of a profession. Personal jealously is almost unknown among us, and for a simple reason: we provide a broad experience and many attractive alternatives. The tender sentiment of the 'one and only' has less to do with constancy of heart than with singleness of opportunity. The chances are that our superfluous young premedic will find other courses open to him which will very soon prove equally attractive."

"There's another case, too," I said. "You must have some sort of government. I don't see how you can permit a free choice of jobs there."

"Our only government is a Board of Planners," said Frazier, with a change of tone which suggested that I had set off another standard harangue. "The name goes back to the days when Walden Two existed only on paper. There are six Planners, usually three men and three women. The sexes are on such equal terms here that no one guards equality very jealously. They may serve for ten years, but no longer. Three of us who've been on the Board since the beginning retire this year.

"The Planners are charged with the success of the community. They make policies, review the work of the Managers, keep an eye on the state of the nation in general. They also have certain judicial functions. They're allowed six hundred credits a year for their services, which leaves two credits still due each day. At least one must be worked out in straight physical labor. That's why I can claim only one credit for acting as your Virgil through *il paradiso.*"

"It was Beatrice," I corrected.

"How do you choose your Planners?" said Rodge.

"The Board selects a replacement from a pair of names supplied by the Managers."

"The members don't vote for them?" said Castle.

"*No,*" said Frazier emphatically.

"What are Managers?" I said hastily.

"What the name implies: specialists in charge of the divisions and services of Walden Two. There are Managers of Food, Health, Play, Arts, Dentistry, Dairy, various industries, Supply, Labor, Nursery School, Advanced Education, and dozens of others. They requisition labor according to their needs, and their job is the managerial function which survives after they've assigned as much as possible to others. They're the hardest workers among us. It's an exceptional person who seeks and finds a place as Manager. He must have ability and a real concern for the welfare of the community."

"*They* are elected by the members, I suppose?" said Castle, but it was obvious that he hoped for nothing of the sort.

"The Managers aren't honorific per-

sonages, but carefully trained and tested specialists. How could the members gauge their ability? No, these are very much like Civil Service jobs. You work up to be a Manager—through intermediate positions which carry a good deal of responsibility and provide the necessary apprenticeship."

"Then the members have no voice whatsoever," said Castle in a carefully controlled voice, as if he were filing the point away for future use.

"Nor do they wish to have," said Frazier flatly.

"Do you count your professional people as Managers?" I said, again hastily.

"Some of them. The Manager of Health is one of our doctors—Mr. Meyerson. But the word 'profession' has little meaning here. All professional training is paid for by the community and is looked upon as part of our common capital, exactly like any other tool." . . .

"Why should everyone engage in menial work?" I asked. "Isn't that really a misuse of manpower if a man has special talents or abilities?"

"There's no misuse. Some of us would be smart enough to get along without doing physical work, but we're also smart enough to know that in the long run it would mean trouble. A leisure class would grow like a cancer until the strain upon the rest of the community became intolerable. We might escape the consequences in our own lifetime, but we couldn't visualize a permanent society on such a plan. The really intelligent man doesn't want to feel that his work is being done by anyone else. He's sensitive enough to be disturbed by slight resentments which, multiplied a millionfold, mean his downfall. Perhaps he remembers his own reactions when others have imposed on him; perhaps he has had a more severe ethical training. Call it conscience, if you like." . . .

We fell silent. Our reflections in the windows mingled confusingly with the last traces of daylight in the southern sky. Finally Castle roused himself.

"But four hours a day!" he said. "I can't take that seriously. Think of the struggle to get a forty-hour week! What would our industrialists not give for your secret. Or our politicians! Mr. Frazier, we're all compelled to admire the life you are showing us, but I feel somehow as if you were exhibiting a lovely lady floating in mid-air. You've even passed a hoop about her to emphasize your wizardry. Now, when you pretend to tell us how the trick is done, we're told that the lady is supported by a slender thread. The explanation is as hard to accept as the illusion. Where's your proof?"

. . .

"Very well, then," said Frazier quickly, as if he had actually been spurred on by Castle's remark. "First of all we have the obvious fact that four is more than half of eight. We work more skillfully and faster during the first four hours of the day. The eventual effect of a four-hour day is enormous, provided the rest of a man's time isn't spent too strenuously. Let's take a conservative estimate, to allow for tasks which can't be speeded up, and say that our four hours are the equivalent of five out of the usual eight. Do you agree?"

"I should be contentious if I didn't," said Castle. "But you're a long way from eight."

"Secondly," said Frazier, with a satisfied smile which promised that eight would be reached in due time, "we have the extra motivation that comes when a man is working for himself instead of for a profit-taking boss. That's

a true 'incentive wage' and the effect is prodigious. Waste is avoided, workmanship is better, deliberate slow-downs unheard of. Shall we say that four hours for oneself are worth six out of eight for the other fellow?"

"And I hope you will point out," I said, "that the four are no harder than the six. Loafing doesn't really make a job easier. Boredom's more exhausting than heavy work. But what about the other two?"

"Let me remind you that not all Americans capable of working are now employed," said Frazier. "We're really comparing eight hours a day on the part of *some* with four hours on the part of practically *all*. In Walden Two we have no leisure class, no prematurely aged or occupationally disabled, no drunkenness, no criminals, far fewer sick. We have no unemployment due to bad planning. No one is paid to sit idle for the sake of maintaining labor standards. Our children work at an early age—moderately, but happily. What will you settle for, Mr. Castle? May I add another hour to my six?"

"I'm afraid I should let you add more than that," said Castle, laughing with surprising good nature.

"But let's be conservative," said Frazier, obviously pleased, "and say that when every potential worker puts in four hours for himself we have the equivalent of perhaps two-thirds of all available workers putting in seven out of eight hours for somebody else. Now, what about those who are actually at work? Are they working to the best advantage? Have they been carefully selected for the work they are doing? Are they making the best use of labor-saving machines and methods? What percentage of the farms in America are mechanized as we are here? Do the workers welcome and improve upon labor-saving devices and methods? How many good workers are free to move on to more productive levels? How much education do workers receive to make them as efficient as possible?"

"I can't let you claim much credit for a better use of manpower," said Castle, "if you give your members a free choice of jobs."

"It's an extravagance, you're right," said Frazier. "In another generation we shall do better; our educational system will see to that. I agree. Add nothing for the waste due to misplaced talents." He was silent a moment, as if calculating whether he could afford to make this concession.

"You still have an hour to account for," I reminded him.

"I know, I know," he said. "Well, how much of the machinery of distribution have we eliminated—with the release of how many men? How many jobs have we simply eliminated? Walk down any city street. How often will you find people really usefully engaged? There's a bank. And beyond it a loan company. And an advertising agency. And over there an insurance office. And another." It was not effective showmanship, but Frazier seemed content to make his point at the cost of some personal dignity. "We have a hard time explaining insurance to our children. Insurance against what? And there's a funeral home—a crematory disposes of our ashes as it sees fit." He threw off this subject with a shake of the head. "And there and there the ubiquitous bars and taverns, equally useless. Drinking isn't prohibited in Walden Two, but we all give it up as soon as we gratify the needs which are responsible for the habit in the world at large."

"If I may be permitted to interrupt this little tour," I said, "what are those needs?"

"Well, why do you drink?" said Frazier.

"I don't—a great deal. But I like a cocktail before dinner. In fact, my company isn't worth much until I've had one."

"On the contrary, I find it delightful," said Frazier.

"It's different here," I said, falling into his trap. Frazier and Castle laughed raucously.

"Of course it's different here!" Frazier shouted. "You need your cocktail to counteract the fatigue and boredom of a mismanaged society. Here we need no antidotes. No opiates. But why else do you drink? Or why does anyone?—since I can see you're not a typical case."

"Why—to forget one's troubles—" I stammered. "Of course, I see what you will say to that. But to get away, let's say, or to get a change—to lower one's inhibitions. You do have inhibitions, don't you? Perhaps someone else can help me out." I turned tactlessly to Barbara, who looked away.

Frazier chuckled quietly for a moment, and struck out again.

"Let me point out a few businesses which we haven't eliminated, but certainly streamlined with respect to manpower," he said. "The big department stores, the meat markets, the corner drugstores, the groceries, the automobile display rooms, the furniture stores, the shoe stores, the candy stores, all staffed with unnecessary people doing unnecessary things. Half the restaurants can be closed for good. And there's a beauty parlor and there a movie palace. And over there a dance hall, and there a bowling alley. And all the time busses and streetcars are whizzing by, carrying people to and fro from one useless spot to another."

It was a bad show but a devastating argument.

"Take your last hour and welcome," said Castle when he saw that Frazier was resting from his labors. "I should have taken your word for it. After all, as you say, it's an accomplished fact."

"Would you like to see me make it *ten* hours?" said Frazier. He smiled boyishly and we all laughed. "I haven't mentioned our most dramatic saving in manpower."

"Then you still have a chance to get away from the book," I said. "I must confess that I'm not quite so impressed as Mr. Castle. Most of what you have said so far is fairly standard criticism of our economic system. You've been pretty close to the professors."

"Of course I have. Even the professors know all this. The economics of a community are child's play."

"What about those two extra hours?" I said, deciding to let the insinuation pass.

Frazier waited a moment, looking from one of us to another.

"*Cherchez la femme!*" he said at last. He stopped to enjoy our puzzlement. "The women! The women! What do you suppose they've been doing all this time? There's our great-est achievement! We have industrialized housewifery!" He pronounced it "huzzifry" again, and this time I got the reference. "Some of our women are still engaged in activities which would have been part of their jobs as housewives, but they work more efficiently and happily. And at least half of them are available for other work."

Frazier sat back with evident satisfaction. Castle roused himself.

"I'm worried," he said bluntly. "You've made a four-hour day seem convincing by pointing to a large part of the population not gainfully employed. But many of those people don't live as well as you. Our present average production may need only four hours per day per man—but that won't do. It must be something more than the average. You'd better leave the unproductive sharecropper out of it. He neither produces *nor consumes* —poor devil."

"It's true, we enjoy a high standard of living," said Frazier. "But our personal wealth is actually very small. The goods we consume don't come to much in dollars and cents. We practice the Thoreauvian principle of avoiding unnecessary possessions." . . .

Mass society and alienation

4

If a society is to persist over time, it must motivate its members to perform those tasks that are essential for its survival and maintenance. It must, in short, have the allegiance of its members. Massive alienation and withdrawal therefore have dire consequences for society. Humanistic literary figures have long been concerned with the adverse effects of a technological society. More recently, social scientists have joined in the debate over the consequences of mass society. Yet most Americans do not perceive mass society and alienation as a major social problem. Why? The problem of mass society is abstract and diffuse. There may be widespread alienation in the society, but people generally attribute their frustration and dissatisfaction to more specific issues such as busing, crime in the streets, and a decay in morals and religion. It is as though Americans have an uneasy feeling that something is amiss but are unable to pinpoint the source of the problem. This results in a displacement of goals so that attempts to reduce anxiety and tension are focused on the effects rather than the source of the problem—mass society. Although not all contemporary problems can be traced to mass society, this chapter will examine the extent to which mass society as such is a societal problem.

THE RISE OF MASS SOCIETY

Mass society is a relatively recent phenomenon, dating to the Industrial Revolution and the development of a complex technology. One of the first sociologists to study the effects of mass society was Emile Durkheim, who during the nineteenth century described various changes that accompany the division of labor in society. He outlined two primary bases of social organization, "mechanical" and "organic." Simpler, preindustrial societies are characterized by a mechanical solidarity, based on consensus of values and similarity of individuals. As the society becomes more complex and differentiated, the basis of solidarity (organic) is interdependence among internally differentiated parts. A complex division of labor requires interdependence and cooperation among the many diverse units in society. The primary cause of this trend has been the increased size and density of the population (Merton, 1965:106). For Durkheim the movement from mechanical to organic solidarity represented a natural evolutionary trend.

Two distinctive traditions to the study of mass society and alienation have emerged. One originates with Durkheim and is continued by various order theorists, the other with Marx and the conflict perspective. The concept anomie is associated with the Durkheimian tradition and alienation with the Marxist perspective.

Although Durkheim did not discuss mass society as such, he did introduce a related concept—anomie. Durkheim (1966:247–249) felt that since most of man's needs, unlike those of other animals, have no natural point of satisfaction, they are in need of regulation by society. "It alone has the power necessary to stipulate law and to set the point beyond which the passions must not go" (1966:249). Under normal conditions these are regulated by society, but in times of crisis or during periods of rapid social change the individual is thrown onto his own resources. Durkheim used the term "anomie" to refer to a state of normlessness in which individuals pursue individual interests without societal regulation. More recently, the concept anomie has been developed by Robert K. Merton (1963:131–160) in his typology of deviant behavior (see the Introduction to Part Two), Talcott Parsons (1951:301–306), and Richard Cloward (1959).

For Durkheim anomie occurred when the society was in a state of disequilibrium; for Marx alienation was ubiquitous to capitalistic society. Marx, like Durkheim, was concerned with the division of labor, but he approached it from a very different perspective.

The division of labour implies from the outset the division of the *prerequisites of labour*, tools and materials, and thus the partitioning of accumulated capital among different owners. This also involves the separation of capital and labour and the different forms of property itself. The more the division of labour develops and accumulation increases, the more sharply this differentiation emerges (Bottomore and Rubel, 1963:174).

Alienation is the result of two basic forces. "First, that the work is *external* to the worker, that it is not a part of his nature, that consequently he does not fulfil himself in his work but denies himself. . . . The worker therefore feels himself at home only during his leisure, whereas at work he feels homeless" (Bottomore and Rubel, 1963:169). Second, the work does not belong to him but to someone else (Bottomore and Rubel, 1963:170).

Although Marx was primarily concerned with economic alienation, he also spoke of religious and political alienation (Israel, 1971:31–36). The basis of alienation in all three spheres appears to be the substitution of "reified" intermediaries for man in interpersonal relations. The intermediary is the world of objects and money in the economic area, God in religion, and the state in politics. "Through this *alien intermediary*—whereas man himself should be the intermediary between men—man sees his will, his activity and his relation to others as a power which is independent of him and of them" (Bottomore and Rubel, 1963:172). The projection of the best human qualities to God produces alienation and conceals secular misery (Israel, 1971:36). Similarly, Marx opposed the reification of the state on the grounds that submission to a totalitarian state can be used to hide existing social evils. He saw the state as starting with man. "The solution to the existing division and the ensuing alienation cannot be a totalitarian state, but a democratic order. . . . Marx speaks of democracy, but democracy without a state, for in a true democracy the state will vanish" (Israel, 1971:35).

The concepts of anomie and alienation thus reveal the conflicting political philosophies of Durkheim and Marx. Anomie refers to a state of society. A society is anomic when it is in disequilibrium, or disorganized. Alienation, on the other hand, is the response of an individual to a set of societal conditions. Durkheim represents a positivistic, conservative tradition that seeks to apply objectively the methods of natural science to social phenomena. "Durkheim witnessed a major phase of what many observers have since called moral anarchy as it enveloped large sectors of the French Republic" (Coser and Rosenberg, 1965:520). His work reveals a moral concern over a society in a state of flux as an aftermath of the French Revolution and the Industrial Revolution (Nisbet, 1965:19–28). While Durkheim was collectivistic in orientation, Marx was individualistic and humanistic. Marx was influenced by Hegel, but he identified with the more politically left followers called the Young Hegelians, and much of his work was critical of Hegel's conservative and collectivist political philosophy (Israel, 1971:30–36).

THE NATURE OF MASS SOCIETY

The term "mass society" has been used in a variety of ways with numerous and, at times, conflicting meanings. Mass society is defined here as a heterogeneous aggregate of individuals who do not engage in direct interaction with one another, are largely anonymous, and are bound together by their exposure to common stimuli that are transmitted through impersonal media.

The concept mass society is an ideal type that does not correspond to any concrete empirical society (Mills, 1956b:302). This ideal type is usually contrasted, explicitly or implicitly, with another ideal but polar type— "folk society" (Redfield, 1941). In part these concepts parallel Tönnies (1963) distinction between community (Gemeinschaft) and society (Gesellschaft) and Durkheim's typology of mechanical and organic solidarity. In the ideal typical folk society, or "community," persons are homogeneous, engage in face-to-face interaction, and are bound together by common interests and intimate association. Societies should not be categorized then, as either mass societies or communities. These logical constructs should be used rather as standards for comparing actual societies; for example, the United States is not totally a mass society, but relative to most other past and present societies it is closer to the ideal type.

One of the most significant features of mass society is that it allegedly produces sameness or uniformity in its members. As society becomes larger and more complex, there is an increasing division of labor and heterogeneity among differentiated parts. Societal relations in mass society become attenuated, impersonal, and transitory. Much of the communication among persons takes place through mass media and other impersonal agencies. The advent of mass communication, mass advertising, and rapid transportation reduces the importance of geographical proximity for the emergence of culture. The result is a mass culture that is shared by diverse segments of the population. Mass society then reverts back to the homogeneity characteristic of community. This is the paradox of mass society— sameness among heterogeneity.

In discussing folk societies and mass societies one should distinguish between two patterns, "conformity" and "uniformity":

Our society gives far more leeway to the individual to pursue his own ends, but, since *it* defines what is worthy and desirable, everyone tends, independently but monotonously, to pursue the same things in the same way. The first pattern combines cooperation, conformity, and variety; the second, competition, individualism, and uniformity (Slater, 1971:9).

Through television and other media sources millions of diverse individuals, not only in the United States but throughout the world, share common experiences. Mass advertising is able to exploit the needs of consumers, consciously and subliminally, and also to create new needs. One of the major criticisms of mass society is that it is based on the lowest common denominator (Bensman and Rosenberg, 1963:339). Mass media, especially television, tend to appeal to the broadest possible audience rather than to the educated, or intellectual, segments of the population. Thus in the mass society many persons are exposed to the same advertising, entertainment, music, and literature. Book clubs and advertisements promote exposure to a limited number of best sellers. Mott (1960) suggests that there may be a "best seller formula" that does not guarantee success but certainly improves the chances of a work becoming a best seller. A number of themes such as sensationalism, self-improvement, personal adventure, and juveniles have been associated with successful books. The best-seller formula was employed by a number of persons who came together and independently wrote chapters for a sex novel—to their surprise it became a best seller (Ashe, 1969).

Another important feature of mass society is mass production of consumer goods. Through mass production a large segment of the population has access to consumer goods that may differ in quality but appear comparable. Copies of expensive fashions and reproductions of artistic masterpieces are available to most members of the society. For as little as $4.95 one can get a collection of some of the "World's Most Beautiful Paintings." Two areas in which mass production is most conspicuous are in clothing and fashion and in housing. There is substantial uniformity in clothing, in part because copies of new fashions are successfully promoted and marketed but also because the range of alternatives is limited for persons who desire to deviate from the norm. Housing is similarly produced. Few architectural options are open to all but the wealthy. The worst of mass society is illustrated by the endless rows of identical boxlike houses in many suburban areas. The housing shortage and mounting building costs have produced a market for condominiums, in which land is owned jointly and the buyer chooses from two or three basic designs.

Mass culture

During the past twenty years or so there has been a heated controversy over the effects of mass culture and a wide range of opinions concerning it.[1] Supporters of mass society see mass culture as a boon to modern man, providing culture for the millions. Critics, on the other hand, maintain that "mass," or popular, culture is a threat to traditional "high" culture. The latter is defined as classical music, the arts, and literature.[2]

[1] The intensity of the controversy is, perhaps best reflected in a classic volume on mass culture (Rosenberg and White, 1960 and 1971) in which the editors take polar positions on mass culture. Rosenberg is critical of mass culture, while White presents a more favorable view.

[2] It should be noted that the use of the term "culture" here is more focused than is the traditional sociological use. For a discussion of the broader sociological view of culture, see the Introduction to the book.

In most societies high culture has been almost the exclusive domain of the aristocracy. Literature, of course, was available only to the literate. Except for folk art and folk music, "high culture was confined to an elite, an aristocracy made up of those who could commission works of art, cultivate their tastes, and school themselves" (Bensman and Rosenberg, 1963:328).

One of the most significant events in the development of mass culture was the invention of the printing press (Bensman and Rosenberg, 1963: 324). Previously, most books were hand copied, and the distribution of literature was extremely limited, but with the advent of the printing press and movable type, books, pamphlets, and newspapers could be widely distributed at a reasonable cost. In the twentieth century the introduction of the paperback reduced the cost of publishing and made possible the distribution of literature to the masses. In addition to the printing press, a number of other factors have contributed to the emergence of mass culture. "Political democracy and popular education broke down the old upper-class monopoly of culture" (Macdonald, 1953:2). With a more literate and affluent population there was a ready market for mass culture. Technological innovations made possible the cheap reproduction and distribution of literature, pictures, and furniture. New media such as movies and television emerged to facilitate further the mass distribution of popular culture (Macdonald, 1953:2).

We are faced with the paradoxical situation today in which "culture" has been made available to a large proportion of the population but at the cost of reducing the quality of this "culture." Those who are critical of mass culture argue that mass culture and high culture cannot coexist. When the two appear together, mass culture tends to absorb high culture.

Whereas Folk Art had its own special quality, Mass Culture is at best a vulgarized reflection of High Culture. And whereas High Culture could formerly ignore the mob and seek to please only the *cognoscenti*, it must now compete with Mass Culture or be merged into it. . . . There seems to be a Gresham's Law in cultural as well as monetary circulation: bad stuff drives out the good, since it is more easily understood and enjoyed (Macdonald, 1953:4).

Since popular culture is digested by a broad segment of the population, its quality is necessarily lowered to the lowest common denominator. Popular books exploit themes such as sex and violence, which appeal to a large cross-section of the population. Too many magazines present a maximum of sensory and visual stimuli and a minimum of intellectual content. Art is similarly mass produced and mass consumed. The person who has little or no knowledge or appreciation of art can readily obtain mass-produced prints of glossy pictures at discount department stores. Sometimes it appears that such pictures are priced by the foot. *Kitsch* (the German word for popular and commercial culture) "pre-digests art for the spectator and spares him effort, provides him with a short cut to the pleasure of art that detours what is necessarily difficult in genuine art" (Greenberg, 1960:105).

Even our universities are not immune to mass culture. They have for the most part abandoned the dialectic approach to learning and substituted a system of mass instruction, whereby lecturers present neatly packaged information that is to be digested as "knowledge" by the students and regurgitated on exams. If education seeks to bring out the best qualities in an individual, the concept of mass education is self-contradictory (de Grazia, 1971:47). Universities have adapted to the mass media by using numerous mechanisms such as taped lectures, recordings, films, and video tapes. Increasingly, the professor's role is shifting from a source of knowledge or information to entertainer.

Quite often the most "popular" teachers in our universities are those who simplify their material, make it look simple, and thereby foster the illusion that a challenging body of knowledge can be easily assimilated. This is catchphrase pedagogy: Plato was an Idealist, Aristotle a Realist, Kant a Dialectician. All you need is a label, and every field has its Will Durant who will retail it for you (Rosenberg, 1960:9).

While most of the writing on mass culture has been critical, a number of sociologists have argued that mass culture is not necessarily detrimental to society and may, in fact, contain some very positive qualities. One of the most questionable assumptions made by critics of mass culture is that in the past a large proportion of the population was exposed to high culture. "The mass culture critic always insinuates that in some previous era the bulk of men were rational, pacific, and learned. . . . Each age, each people, each culture has its own brand of coarseness, vulgarity, and stupidity, and always enough to suffice unto itself" (White, 1971:13 and 15). Contemporary mass culture is evaluated relative to an idealized, nonexistent standard of the past. In a nutshell, the issue of mass culture seems to boil down to whether a diluted culture that reaches the masses is preferable to a purer high culture that is available only to an elite. Bernard Rosenberg is more optimistic, however, believing that high culture is potentially accessible to the masses. He argues that any person who has not experienced severe brain damage is capable of enjoying art and learning (Rosenberg, 1971:9). While this is a commendable, humanistic position, unfortunately Rosenberg does not reveal how high culture is to be made available to the millions.

A second, major criticism of mass culture critics is that they frequently mistake cause for effect. Mass culture is turned into a powerful, amorphous ogre that controls modern man mercilessly. It becomes a scapegoat responsible for all of the ills of contemporary society. "It's like blaming John Wayne for creating the Green Berets and the Vietnam war. . . . if we make the mass media the scapegoat for the miasmic lives we have given ourselves during this century, we may be insulating ourselves from more basic problems" (White, 1971:14). There is much truth to the adage that, in the last analysis, a society gets the kind of art, music, literature, and entertainment that it deserves.

Mass advertising

One cannot talk about mass culture without also talking about mass advertising; in the United States they are closely intertwined. Mass audiences provide an important economic incentive for advertising. In fact, the economic success of the mass media can be traced directly to these two factors: mass audiences and advertising (Bensman and Rosenberg, 1963: 337). The paradox, however, is that while the cost of supporting mass media is high, the cost of a single message is very low. Through exposure to millions of persons advertisers gain a substantial return on their initial outlay. Television is presented "free," and the cost to the consumer is hidden.

The fact that the mass media are subsidized by advertising has important implications for the content of the media. Profits can be maximized by enlarging the audience. The broadcast appeal is attained by ignoring differentiation (Bensman and Rosenberg, 1963:339). The media generally exploit themes that are simple and broad and that appeal to the widest audience. "The themes and characters they present must be broadened and thickened and coarsened. Uniqueness of theme, character, or appeal would only stand in the way of mass acceptance" (Bensman and Rosenberg, 1963:339).

The importance given to profits both by the mass-communication and the advertising industry has led to numerous criticisms of such industries (see, for example, the confessions of an ex-Madison Avenue ad man in Baker, 1971). Of special concern has been the exploitation of existing needs and the creation of new needs. Jules Henry (1963:45–49) has coined the term "pecuniary philosophy" to refer to the system of values and beliefs that pervades the advertising industry and is used to stimulate spending and create false needs. "Pecuniary philosophy" is supported by "pecuniary pseudo-truth," "a false statement made as if it were true, but not intended to be believed. . . ." (Henry, 1963:47). Henry states further that the essence of truth in pecuniary philosophy is summed up by these three postulates:

Truth is what sells.
Truth is what you want people to believe.
Truth is that which is not legally false. (Henry, 1963:47, 50).

Pecuniary truth is therefore self-validating. The proof of the argument is that it sells. If advertising does not sell, it is assumed to be false (Henry, 1963:47).

Although mass advertising has been made into a villain by many of its critics, the direction of cause and effect between advertising and mass culture is not clear. To some extent the argument is of the "chicken-and-egg" variety. Advertising can create new needs, but to a great extent it simply exploits existing values and needs. Pecuniary philosophy would not be successful without a mass pecuniary mentality. C. Wright Mills characterized American society as the Great Salesroom in which "the salesman's world has now become everybody's world and, in some part, everybody has become a salesman" (Mills, 1951:161). The salesman is largely a product of mass society. In the past when demand exceeded production, the salesman took orders or provided information. "But when the pressure from the producer to sell became much greater than the capacity of the consumer to buy, the role of the salesman shifted into high gear. . . . high-pressure selling is a substitute stimulator of demand, not by lowering prices but by creating new wants and more urgent desires" (Mills, 1951: 162). Mills (unlike Marx, who was concerned with the alienation of labor from work) focused on the alienation of the middle-class worker. He argued that the conditions of modern work are as alienating to the white-collar worker as to the laborer (Mills, 1951:224–228). In large bureaucratic organizations the white-collar worker is separated from the product of his labor. He also does not own the product of his labor.

The capacity to manipulate others is an important commodity in mass society. The distinction between a salesman and others is blurred, since in some ways we are all salesmen. In a sense American society is a Great Salesroom within which individuals compete for status in the "personality market." "The employer of manual services buys the workers' labor, energy, and skill; the employer of many white-collar services, especially salesmanship, also buys the employees' social personalities" (Mills, 1951:182).

With the growing importance of selling in mass society there has been a concerted effort to standardize salesmanship. The dominant goal has been to make selling more efficient and to lower the cost of selling per person (Mills, 1951:178–179). A new field has emerged, interpersonal management, which aims to perfect techniques for manipulating customers and creating false needs. The philosophy underlying interpersonal management is illustrated by Dale Carnegie's *How to Win Friends and Influence People*. Carnegie (1964:39) states:

I go fishing up in Maine every summer. Personally I am very fond of strawberries and cream; but I find that for some strange reason fish prefer worms. So when I go fishing, I don't think about what I want. I think about what they want. I don't bait the hook with strawberries and cream. Rather, I dangle a worm or a grasshopper in front of the fish and say: "Wouldn't you like to have that?"

Man becomes a fish to be baited and manipulated. The salesman sacrifices his own preference in order to control the behavior of the customer (victim?).

Mass politics

A number of political analysts have been concerned with the effects of mass society on political behavior. Those who adhere to the theory of mass politics argue that as democratic societies become mass societies, they are increasingly susceptible to political extremism and antidemocratic ideologies (Arendt, 1954; Fromm, 1945; Kornhauser, 1959; Nisbet, 1953; Selznick, 1960). In its extreme form mass society becomes vulnerable to totalitarian control.

William Kornhauser has done much to develop the theory of mass politics. He distinguishes between elites and nonelites. Elites are expected to provide leadership and maintain the basic values of the society, while nonelites are expected to follow their leadership. With the emergence of mass society relations between elites and nonelites change. Ties to primary groups, the family, and community weaken. As the society becomes increasingly bureaucratized and impersonal, elites are viewed as more distant and less accessible. Members of the mass feel powerless and alienated. The leadership and authority of elites is eroded. This void provides an opportunity for counter-elites to challenge the traditional authority of elites and to assume power. Under these conditions the masses may be mobilized to reject liberal democratic values and to accept antidemocratic ideologies such as fascism and communism. According to Kornhauser:

Thus it is that popular mobilization generally is the work of counter-elites, since they are not inhibited by commitments to the social order, nor by constraints resulting from participation in a balance of power. These counter-elites are pushed towards making allies among the masses, since this is the only way to gain total power in mass society. . . . A rising totalitarian movement finds its prey not only in an exposed mass but also in an exposed elite. The penetration of an existing elite by a successful totalitarian movement (as the Nazis penetrated the Weimar government) is *prima facie* evidence of its accessibility (1959:36–37).

Theories of mass politics share a common concern that previously democratic mass societies may be transformed into totalitarian societies. Once in power counter-elites can retain their position through effective manipulation and control of the mass media. Erich Fromm in *Escape from Freedom* (1945) maintains that the rise of Hitler and Nazism in Germany constituted an escape from freedom for modern man. Similarly, Eric Hoffer in *The True Believer* (1966) depicts the follower of mass movements as one who is compelled to follow any cause with blind fanaticism. "When people are ripe for a mass movement, they are usually ripe for any effective movement, and not solely for one with a particular doctrine or program. In pre-Hitlerian Germany it was often a tossup whether a restless youth would join the Communists or the Nazis" (Hoffer, 1966:25).

While the theory of mass politics has had wide appeal not only among academicians but also among critics of contemporary mass society, it has not been accepted by all scholars. One of the most persuasive critics of the theory of mass politics is Joseph Gusfield who argues that the theory is based on a pluralistic (order) model. Extremist politics in mass society are compared to an earlier period when "political democracy functioned relatively unimpeded under non-mass conditions. . . . pluralistic structure is implicitly posited as an essential condition for democratic politics" (Gusfield, 1962:22).

Gusfield maintains that mass society is less susceptible to extremist politics than is assumed by the theory of mass politics. A certain level of cultural cohesion is necessary to maintain democratic politics. Conditions in mass society actually support democratic norms. The mass media increase cohesion by intensifying ties among individuals and strengthening their attachment to institutions. "Conditions of mass society develop a homogeneous set of cultural experiences for members. . . . The consequences of such homogenizing forces are the development of a national mass culture and a national society" (Gusfield, 1962:28).

In a more recent critique and reformulation of the theory of mass politics, Pinard has made some interesting observations. ". . . the main proposition of mass theory states that a society with mass tendencies, because it lacks restraining mechanisms, cannot prevent its members from turning to mass behavior and to mass movements" (1968:683). It erroneously assumes that under nonmass conditions primary and secondary groups necessarily act as restraining forces to political action. The theory does not recognize that under certain conditions primary and secondary groupings may act as neutral or mobilizing forces. In short, "the intermediate structure can limit or foster the rise of political movements, but it is not, in itself, a sufficient condition for their appearance. In particular, the presence of strain is a crucial condition" (Pinard, 1968:687).

Although there is disagreement over whether mass society leads to extremist politics, there is unanimity on one point—mass society significantly alters political processes. Mass society virtually precludes direct contact between the mass and elites or political leaders. Local communities and local issues are superseded in importance by national politics and national issues. Persons geographically dispersed throughout the country are linked together through mass communication and rapid transportation systems. The emergence of mass political movements is greatly facilitated. Political leaders can appeal to millions of persons through television and other media. A charismatic political leader can circumvent the political machinery and appeal directly to the mass. The popular support elicited by Huey Long during the 1930s and George Wallace in the 1970s illustrates the effectiveness of mass politics.

Mass politics places a premium on political organization and on sophistication in the manipulation of public opinion. Recent political campaigns have borrowed a variety of techniques from mass advertising. The successful politician is one who manipulates impressions and creates a favorable

public image. *The Selling of the President: 1968* (McGinniss, 1969) provides a fascinating, though frightening, account of the effective use of television to sell a new image of Richard Nixon to the American public. A
small group of ad men and political advisers were extremely successful
in applying techniques of mass advertising to the 1968 presidential campaign. The candidate, like a new product on the market, was packaged,
exposed, promoted, and, eventually, "sold" to the public.

Mass leisure

Leisure is ubiquitous to mass society. Technological advancements, automation, and cybernation have combined to produce a more efficient division
of labor. The end result is increased leisure for most members of the
society. In the past, leisure was available only to an elite leisure class. It is
only in the twentieth century that leisure has been made available to the
masses (Mills, 1951:235).

Leisure and time released from productive work are generally used
interchangeably. While there has been a decrease in the length of the work-
week, it is doubtful if members of mass society have more "leisure" in the
classical sense of the word. True leisure is separated from both work and
time (de Grazia, 1971:38). "The man of leisure . . . is always at play
or (as Plato would say) on the hunt, in the exercise of the mind" (de
Grazia, 1971:57). One cannot have leisure unless he is free to work or
not work depending on his mood. Released time from work may, in fact,
decrease (or even preclude) leisure. "By saying that free time is time off
the job, one may forget momentarily that the job comes first, and that
unless one has a job he has no free time: he is unemployed" (de Grazia,
1971:27). Free time in modern society is linked to leisure equipment,
commodities, and goods. Mass advertising promotes the sale of leisure
items. Man in modern society is locked into a vicious circle in which he
works hard so that he eventually increases his free time and purchases an
unlimited quantity of goods that are "needed" in order to have fun. However, in the process he destroys his leisure.

Another important characteristic of mass leisure is routinization. Because leisure is defined as time released from work, it occurs at about the
same time for most members of society. The crowding that takes place
on weekends, holidays, and peak summer vacation periods illustrates the
extent to which leisure, like work, has been standardized. Philip Slater
attempts to place the problem of leisure within the broader context of the
continuous attempt by Americans to deny their interdependence. We seek
privacy and escape to the crowded suburbs. However, the more privacy
we get the more alienated we feel:

. . . our encounters with others tend increasingly to be competitive as a result
of the search for privacy. We less and less often meet our fellow man to share
and exchange, and more and more often encounter him as an impediment or a
nuisance: making the highway crowded when we are rushing somewhere,

cluttering and littering the beach or park or wood, pushing in front of us at the supermarket, taking the last parking place, polluting our air and water. . . . We are continually surprised to find, when we want something, that thousands or millions of others want it, too—that other human beings get hot in summer and cold in winter. The worst traffic jams occur when a mass of vacationing tourists departs for home early to "beat the traffic" (Slater, 1971: 7–8).

Americans are engaged in a never-ending "pursuit of loneliness," behaving individually and independently, yet producing uniformity.

The phrase "mass leisure" connotes that free-time activities are standardized. Not only do persons share the same leisure time, but they are likely to engage in the same activities. ". . . the techniques of mass production were applied to amusement as they had been to the sphere of work" (Mills, 1951:236). Mass society means organized society. Leisure activities are organized, first, in the sense that they are planned rather than spontaneous and, second, in that they involve collective participation. It is not sufficient to bowl, for example—one must participate in a league, compete with others, and demonstrate proficiency. But by collectively attacking free time, we avoid leisure. "In no case can leisure be collective or organized. It does not depend on other people" (de Grazia, 1971:38).

We have approached leisure with a seriousness of purpose that has led to its professionalization. Standards of work such as competition and excellence are applied to recreational activities. Leisure is too important to be wasted by playing in idleness. Individuals are even embarrassed when they simply "play at something" and are not too good at it. One must master leisure and excel at whatever activity is undertaken.

Thus Americans face the paradoxical situation in which they apparently have more time released from work but actually less leisure. The importance placed on work leads to the use of work-related standards to evaluate leisure. The line between work and leisure is blurred, and leisure is organized and collective. We do not heed the old Mexican saying *Hay mas tiempo que vida*—there is more time than life (de Grazia, 1971:38).

THE OLD CULTURE AND THE NEW

A common pitfall in sociological analysis is that abstract conceptualizations tend to be reified and treated as the complex phenomena that they represent. In this chapter the United States has been depicted as a mass society. American society is in actuality extremely complex and constantly in a state of flux. Sociologists are interested in ascertaining not only where the society has been but also where it is going, although this is admittedly a difficult task. In this section an attempt will be made to isolate some of the major changes that the United States has undergone by tracing the movement from an agricultural to a mass society. We will also speculate about the emergence of a new culture following that of the mass society.

Sociologists have long been concerned with societal changes that accompany industrialization and urbanization. Over the years a number of typologies have been generated that seek to explain, or at least describe, the movement from simpler to more complex societies. In the nineteenth century Durkheim (1933) distinguished between simpler societies characterized by mechanical solidarity and modern societies characterized by organic solidarity, and Tönnies, as was mentioned earlier, saw a movement from community (Gemeinschaft) to society (Gesellschaft). These nineteenth-century writers believed that the Industrial Revolution and urbanization had a profound effect on the organization of society. The two parts of each typology correspond to a preindustrial and a postindustrial society.

The tradition established by Durkheim and Tönnies has been continued by several twentieth-century sociologists. One of the best known of these works is *The Lonely Crowd* by David Riesman (1955). Riesman is interested in the interrelationship between the individual and the society. His work centers on the effect that society has on the development of national character. One of the guiding propositions is that different types of societies, by placing different demands on the individual, tend to produce modal personality types.

The first type of society discussed by Riesman, "tradition-directed" society, and its corresponding character type closely resemble Durkheim's mechanical society and Tönnies' Gemeinschaft. It is a simple, preindustrial, folk society. Tradition-directed societies generally have stable social relations, the relative absence of social change, and the uncritical acceptance of time-honored traditions. Such societies develop a character type that is tradition directed, that is, conforming to tradition and resisting innovation.

In the transitional period between traditional and modern societies there emerges a society dominated by "inner direction." A society undergoing industrialization, urbanization, and rapid change cannot rely on tradition to resolve emergent problems. Its demands require that individuals be capable of dealing with novel situations. Children in inner-directed societies are inculcated with certain basic values that enable them to cope with societal expansion and rapidly changing conditions. One way of dealing with unexpected contingencies is to develop a set of stable values that persons carry with them across different situations. A premium is placed on individual resourcefulness and initiative. Control shifts from the extended family to the nuclear family. There is an emphasis on achievement and competition. The inner-directed personality in many respects parallels the Protestant Ethic.

The inner-directed personality was prevalent during the nineteenth century in the United States, but today it has been replaced by the "other-directed" personality. The demands placed on individuals by a stable, industrial society are drastically different from those of a young, expanding and transitional society. In an other-directed society emphasis is placed on cooperation and getting along well with others. The entrepreneurial middle class is replaced by a new middle class as individuals are increasingly employed by large, bureaucratic organizations. The achievement ethic and competitive spirit gives way to a group ethic that values cooperation and getting along well with others. Parents become more interested in the adjustment of their children than in their achievement. The peer group becomes paramount in the other-directed society. Conformity is enforced through sensitivity to the expectations of contemporaries. The other-directed ethic is epitomized by Dale Carnegie's philosophy. *How to Win Friends and Influence People* (1964), an anti-individualistic work that lauds the virtues of the group and deprecates the worth of the individual, sets down a formula for developing an other-directed personality. Ironically, one is able to manipulate others effectively by superficially, or outwardly, subordinating one's needs.

The character type depicted by William H. Whyte, Jr., in *The Organization Man* (1956) closely resembles Riesman's other-directed personality. Following the tradition established by Max Weber, Whyte analyzes the replacement in American society of the Protestant Ethic with the values of the organization man. The modern version of the Protestant Ethic is a secular value system that extols the virtues of hard work, thrift, competition, and achievement. Many still adhere to the American "dream" and pay lip service to individualism and the Protestant Ethic. These values are, however, inconsistent with the realities of a complex society dominated by large bureaucratic organizations (Whyte, 1956:4–7). Although we cling to individualistic values, the Protestant Ethic has been supplanted by a collectivistic, bureaucratic value system which Whyte labels the "Social Ethic." This ethic is a

contemporary body of thought which makes morally legitimate the pressures of society against the individual. Its major propositions are three: a belief in the group as the source of creativity; a belief in "belongingness" as the ultimate need of the individual; and a belief in the application of science to achieve the belongingness (Whyte, 1956:7).

While the other-directed character type and the organization man appear to be adequate conceptualizations of the demands placed on individuals by a mass bureaucratic society, they seem inadequate for understanding recent societal trends and predicting new directions in society. A new ethic appears to be emerging, particularly among the young college-educated segments of society. Although different labels have been used to describe this ethic, there seems to be general agreement on a core set of values. Simmons and Winograd (1968) call it the "hang-loose" ethic; Reich (1970) speaks of "consciousness III," and for Slater (1971) it is the "new culture."

Simmons and Winograd maintain that since the 1960s the hang-loose ethic has been supplanting the social, or as they term it, the "sociable" ethic. One of the basic tenets of the sociable ethic was moderation:

Moderate in politics, moderate in work—not too much because it doesn't really pay, not too little because you might get dropped. . . . moderately attached to your spouse and children and moderately concerned with their welfare and you were moderately unfaithful and moderately blasphemous. But you also gave a moderate allegiance to your family and your company and your country.

This was not a picture window nightmare. Most of those involved were probably moderately comfortable and moderately happy (Simmons and Winograd, 1968:386).

The hang-loose ethic, on the other hand, is characteristically irreverent. It challenges traditional values, institutions, and authority. Traditional values are replaced by a number of other values including humanism, the pursuit of experience, spontaneity, tolerance, and the elimination of restrictions. A person who is "cool" and "hangs loose" follows the dictates of his own conscience without imposing his values on others (Simmons and Winograd, 1968).

One of the difficulties in evaluating the emergent new culture is that social analysts such as Simmons and Winograd are simultaneously observers, social critics, and participants in the new culture. They are part of the phenomenon that they describe. Even if one grants that the seeds of a new culture have been planted and one is sympathetic to the emerging ethic, it is obvious that descriptions of the new culture are idealized. Portrayals of the two cultures contain an implicit assumption that the old culture was bad, tainted, and immoral and that the new culture is good, pure, and moral. Descriptions of the new culture are, at a minimum, idealistic conceptions of the way many of us would like the culture to be. In a very real sense then, those who write about the new culture are not only social analysts of an emerging trend but more importantly architects of change.

REFERENCES

Arendt, Hannah
 1954 The Origins of Totalitarianism. New York: Harcourt.
Ashe, Penelope
 1969 Naked Came the Stranger. New York: Dell.
Baker, Samm Sinclair
 1971 "Advertising: The Permissible Lie." Pp. 359–376 in Rosenberg and White.
Bensman, Joseph, and Bernard Rosenberg
 1963 Mass, Class, and Bureaucracy. Englewood Cliffs, N.J.: Prentice-Hall.
Bottomore, T. B., and Maximilien Rubel
 1963 Karl Marx: Selected Writings in Sociology and Social Philosophy. London: Watts.
Carnegie, Dale
 1964 How to Win Friends and Influence People. New York: Simon & Schuster.

Cloward, Richard A.
1959 "Illegitimate Means, Anomie, and Deviant Behavior." American Sociological Review 24 (April):164–176.
Coser, Lewis A., and Bernard Rosenberg
1965 Sociological Theory: A Book of Readings. Second ed. New York:
Macmillan.
de Grazia, Sebastian
1971 "Transforming Free Time." Pp. 25–60 in Rosenberg and White.
Durkheim, Emile
1933 The Division of Labor in Society. (Translated by George Simpson).
New York: Free Press.
1966 Suicide. (Translated by John A. Spaulding and George Simpson).
New York: Free Press.
Fromm, Erich
1945 Escape from Freedom. New York: Rinehart.
Greenberg, Clement
1960 "Avant-Garde and Kitsch." Pp. 98–107 in Rosenberg and White.
Gusfield, Joseph R.
1962 "Mass Society and Extremist Politics." American Sociological Review
27 (February):19–30.
Henry, Jules
1963 Culture Against Man. New York: Random House.
Hoffer, Eric
1966 The True Believer. New York: Harper & Row (Perennial Library).
Israel, Joachim
1971 Alienation: From Marx to Modern Sociology. Boston: Allyn & Bacon.
Kornhauser, William
1959 The Politics of Mass Society. New York: Free Press.
Macdonald, Dwight
1953 "A Theory of Mass Culture." Diogenes 3 (Summer):1–17.
McGinniss, Joe
1969 The Selling of the President 1968. New York: Trident Press.
Merton, Robert K.
1963 Social Theory and Social Structure. Revised ed. Glencoe, Ill.: Free
Press.
1965 "Durkheim's Division of Labor in Society." Pp. 105–112 in Nisbet.
Mills, C. Wright
1951 White Collar. New York: Oxford University Press.
1956 The Power Elite. New York: Oxford University Press.
Mott, Frank Luther
1960 "Is There a Best Seller Formula?" Pp. 113–118 in Rosenberg and
White.
Nisbet, Robert A.
1953 The Quest for Community. New York: Oxford University Press.
1965 Emile Durkheim. Englewood Cliffs, N.J.: Prentice-Hall.
Parsons, Talcott
1951 The Social System. Glencoe, Ill.: Free Press.

Pinard, Maurice
1968 "Mass Society and Political Movements: A New Formulation." American Journal of Sociology 73 (May):682–690.
Redfield, Robert
1941 The Folk Culture of Yucatan. Chicago: University of Chicago Press.
Reich, Charles A.
1970 The Greening of America. New York: Bantam.
Riesman, David (with Nathan Glazer and Reuel Denney)
1955 The Lonely Crowd: A Study of the Changing American Character. Abridged ed. Garden City, N.Y.: Anchor Books.
Rosenberg, Bernard
1960 "Mass Culture in America." Pp. 3–12 in Rosenberg and White.
1971 "Mass Culture Revisited I." Pp. 3–12 in Rosenberg and White.
Rosenberg, Bernard, and David Manning White
1960 Mass Culture. New York: Free Press.
1971 Mass Culture Revisited. New York: Van Nostrand Reinhold.
Selznick, Philip
1960 The Organizational Weapon. Glencoe, Ill.: Free Press.
Simmons, J. L., and Barry Winograd
1968 "The Hang-Loose Ethic." Pp. 383–393 in J. Alan Winter, Jerome Rabow, and Mark Chesler (eds.), Vital Problems for American Society. New York: Random House.
Slater, Philip
1971 The Pursuit of Loneliness. Boston: Beacon.
Tönnies, Ferdinand
1963 Community and Society (Gemeinschaft und Gesellschaft). (Translated and edited by Charles P. Loomis). New York: Harper & Row.
White, David Manning
1971 "Mass Culture Revisited II." Pp. 13–21 in Rosenberg and White.
Whyte, William H., Jr.
1956 The Organization Man. Garden City, N.Y.: Anchor Books.

INTRODUCTION TO THE READINGS

The readings have been selected to illustrate two recurrent issues in the study of mass society: the professionalization of leisure and the conflict between mass culture and high culture.

The first selection is both humorous and tragic. Lionel S. Lewis and Dennis Brissett suggest that in mass society the line between work and play is blurred to the point where leisure becomes work and is measured by the same standards. No longer content to simply enjoy leisure, Americans are driven to master and excel in leisure activities. As a result, a vast market has emerged for "avocational counselors" and other experts who specialize in teaching the public how to have fun and enjoy leisure. This paper shows that the area of sex has not been insulated from these trends. Americans are so busy reading about sex and mastering coital techniques that there is little time to enjoy the activity. Sex has become work.

The second reading deals with the new culture that appears to be emerging from mass society. The new "populist culture," according to Kingsley Widmer, challenges both mass culture and "power-preservative" culture (high culture). High culture is elitist, seeking to preserve culture for the powerful segments of society; popular culture (mass culture) is exploitative and manipulative, marketing culture as a product to be painlessly consumed and digested by the masses. Populist culture provides a glimmer of hope for the common man; it is within the reach of all. The new culture, ironically, provides greater opportunity for leisure, in the classical sense, than the old. Man is ideally free to pursue his own interests without invoking a sharp distinction between work and play.

Sex as work: a study of avocational counseling

LIONEL S. LEWIS and
DENNIS BRISSETT

It is commonly accepted that America is a society of leisure. The society is said to have shifted from one of production to one of consumption.[1] The American of today spends little time working; he has a great deal of time to play.

With this surfeit of leisure, Americans have been called upon to engage in forms of consumption quite unknown to their inner-directed predecessors. There exist extensive opportunities for play, but little knowledge of how to conduct oneself in this play. As Riesman has remarked, "To bring the individual into unfrightening contact with the new range of opportunities in consumption often requires some guides and signposts."[2] Knowing how to play has become problematic; it is something the individual must learn. He must, in a word, be socialized into the art of play.

Faced with this necessary socialization, the consuming American seeks out persons to teach him how to play. Very often this involves engaging the

services of avocational counselors. The term avocational counseling ". . . describe[s] the activities undertaken by a number of relatively rapidly growing professions in the United States, including travel agents, hotel men, resort directors, sports teachers and coaches, teachers of the arts, including dancing teachers, and so on."[3] Each of the various counselors supplies the American public with advice on play and leisure. The advice of one such group of counselors is the subject matter of this paper.

Quite recently, Nelson Foote has observed that sex, since it is becoming increasingly dissociated from procreation, is becoming more and more a kind of play activity. He states that "the view that sex is fun can . . . hardly be called the invention of immoralists; it is every man's discovery."[4] The arena of consumption is extended to include the realm of man's sexual activity, and the avocational counselor finds himself a place advising people on the vicissitudes of sex as play.

Concomitant with this increasing amount of leisure time, and the attendant problem of learning how to play, it has been observed that the play of most Americans has become a laborious kind of play. "Fun, in its rather unique American form, is grim resolve. . . . We are as determined about the pursuit of fun as a desert-wandering traveler is about the search for water. . . ."[5] Consumption, to

[1] Leo Lowenthal, "The Triumph of Mass Idols," in Literature, Popular Culture, and Society, Englewood Cliffs, New Jersey: Prentice-Hall, 1961, pp. 109–140.

[2] David Riesman (with Nathan Glazer and Reuel Denney), The Lonely Crowd, Garden City, New York: Doubleday Anchor Books, 1953, p. 341.

[3] Riesman, loc. cit.

[4] Nelson Foote, "Sex as Play," in Eric Larrabee and Rolf Meyersohn, editors, Mass Leisure, Glencoe, Illinois: Free Press, 1958, p. 335.

[5] Jules Henry, Culture Against Man, New York: Random House, 1963, p. 43.

From Lionel S. Lewis and Dennis Brisset, "Sex as Work: A Study of Avocational Counseling," Social Problems, Vol. 15, no. 1, Summer 1967, pp. 9–18. Reprinted with permission of the Society for the Study of Social Problems and the authors.

most Americans, has become a job. Like work, play has become a duty to be performed. This interpretation is supported by the emergence of what Wolfenstein has labeled a "fun morality." Here "play tends to be measured by standards of achievement previously applicable only to work . . . at play, no less than at work, one asks: 'Am I doing as well as I should?' "[6] Consumption very definitely has become production.

It is the purpose of this paper to examine the products of the avocational counselors of marital sex and to inquire as to their depiction of man's sexual behavior. If it is true that play is becoming work in the mass society, it might be necessary to amend Foote's notion of the character of sexual play. In focusing on how marital sex is handled by these avocational counselors, we will show how sex, an area of behavior usually not thought of as involving work, has been treated as such. We will emphasize how general work themes are presented as an essential part of sexual relations, and how the public is advised to prepare for sex just as they are advised to prepare for a job.

MARRIAGE MANUALS

The avocational counselors of sex with the widest audience are those who write what are frequently referred to as marriage manuals. These manuals are designed to explain all aspects of the sexual side of marriage. Their distribution is wide: many are in paperback and are readily available in drug stores; many can be found in multiple copies in public and university libraries; and some are distributed by facili-

ties which offer services in sex, fertility, and contraception, such as Planned Parenthood clinics.

Fifteen manuals were selected from a listing of almost 50 for analysis in this study. They are listed in Appendix A. The first criterion for using a manual was wide circulation. This was determined by number of printings and number of copies sold. For example, one volume (15) in 1965 was in its forty-fifth printing and had sold more than one-half million copies in the United States; a second (13) was in its forty-eighth printing and had sold almost six hundred thousand; a third (3) was in its thirtieth printing[7] and has "been read by" two million eight hundred thousand[8]; and a fourth (5) advertises on its cover "over a million and a half copies in print." Other criteria were that the book be still read and available. The fifteen volumes ranged from 14 page pamphlets to full-sized, indexed, hardbound books.

Each manual was read by both authors, and principal themes were recorded. Notes were taken, compared, and classified. Only material about whose meaning both authors agreed was utilized in drawing conclusions about the themes in a book.

WORKING AT SEX

Marital sex, as depicted by the marriage manuals, is an activity permeated with qualities of work. One need not even read these books, but need only look at the titles or the chapter headings to draw this conclusion. Thus, we have books titled *The Sex Technique*

---

[6] Martha Wolfenstein, "The Emergence of Fun Morality," in Eric Larrabee and Rolf Meyersohn, *op. cit.*, p. 93.

[7] We were unable to obtain this most recent printing, and our copy was the twenty-ninth printing.

[8] These figures were published in *Newsweek*, October 18, 1965, p. 100.

in Marriage (10), *Modern Sex Techniques* (14), *Ideal Marriage: Its Physiology and Technique* (15). There are also chapters titled "How to Manage the Sex Act (3)," "Principles and Techniques of Intercourse (7)," "The Fourth Key to Soundly Satisfying Sex: A Controlled Sexual Crescendo (5)."

From the outset, as we begin to read the books, we are warned not to treat sex frivolously, indeed not to play at sex:

An ardent spur-of-the-moment tumble sounds very romantic. . . . However, ineptly arranged intercourse leaves the clothes you had no chance to shed in a shambles, your plans for the evening shot, your birth control program incomplete, and your future sex play under considerable better-be-careful-or-we'll-wind-up-in-bed-again restraint (5, pp. 34–35).

In other words, marital sex should not be an impromptu performance.

Moreover, sex should not be approached with a casual mien. Rather, we are counseled, sexual relations, at least good sexual relations, are a goal to be laboriously achieved. It is agreed that "satisfactory intercourse is the basis for happy marriage." However, it is added, "It does not occur automatically but must be striven for (12, p. 39)." In the plain talk of the avocational counselor, "Sexual relations are something to be worked at and developed (7, p. 6)."

This work and its development are portrayed as a taxing kind of endeavor; as behavior involving, indeed requiring, a good deal of effort. That sex involves effort is a pervasive theme in the 15 manuals. From the start one is advised to direct his effort to satisfying his or her mate so that mutual climax is achieved, sexual activity is continual, and one's partner is not ignored after climax. Thus, we are told:

Remember, *couple* effort for *couple* satisfaction! That's the key to well-paced, harmonious sex play (5, p. 62).

Certain positions of intercourse are also seen as particularly taxing, in fact so taxing that certain categories of people are advised not to use them. One author, in discussing a particularly laborious position, remarks that "This is no position for a couple of grandparents, no matter how healthy and vigorous they are for their age, for it takes both effort and determination (4, p. 201)." Quite obviously, certain kinds of marital sex are reserved only for those persons who are "in condition."

The female is particularly cautioned to work at sex, for being naturally sexual seems a trait ascribed only to the male. The affinity of sex to her other work activities is here made clear: "Sex is too important for any wife to give it less call upon her energy than cooking, laundry, and a dozen other activities (5, p. 36)." To the housewife's burden is added yet another chore.

Even the one manual that takes great pains to depict sex as sport, injects the work theme. It is pointed out that

You certainly can [strive and strain at having a climax]—just as you can . . . help yourself to focus on a complex musical symphony. . . . Just as you strive to enjoy a party, when you begin by having a dull time at it. Sex is often something to be worked and strained at— as an artist works and strains at his painting or sculpture (6, p. 122).

Sex, then, is considered a kind of work; moreover, a very essential form of labor. Regular sexual activity is said, for instance, to contribute to "physical and mental health (7, p. 27)," and to lead to *spiritual unity* (14, frontpiece)." In the majestic functionalist tradition, "A happy, healthy sex life is vital to wholesome family life, which in turn is fundamental to the welfare of the community and of society (1, XIII)." Marital sex, most assuredly, is the cornerstone of humanity, but not any kind of marital sex—only that which leads to orgasm. "It is the orgasm that is so essential to the health and happiness of the couple . . . (10, p. 80)."

Indeed it is the orgasm which may be said to be the *product* of marital sexual relations. It is the *raison d'être* for sexual contact, and this orgasm is no mean achievement. In fact,

Orgasm occasionally may be the movement of ecstasy when two people together soar along a Milky Way among stars all their own. This moment is the high mountaintop of love of which the poets sing, on which the two together become a full orchestra playing a fortissimo of a glorious symphony (4, pp. 182–183).

In masculine, and somewhat more antiseptic terms, "ejaculation is the aim, the summit and the end of the sexual act (15, 133)." Woe be to the couple who fail to produce this state as there are dire consequences for the unsuccessful, particularly for the woman.

When the wife does not secure an orgasm, she is left at a high peak of sexual tension. If this failure to release tension becomes a regular thing, she may develop an aversion to starting any sex play that might lead to such frustrations. . . . Repeated disappointments may lead to headaches, nervousness, sleeplessness, and other unhappy symptoms of maladjustment (1, p. 65).

So important is it to reach orgasm, to have a product, that all the other sexual activities of marriage are seen as merely prosaic ingredients or decorative packaging of the product.

In fact, orgasm as a product is so

essential that its occasion is not necessarily confined to the actual act of intercourse, at least for the women. Numerous counselors indicate that it may be necessary for the man to induce orgasm in the woman during afterplay. "A woman who has built up a head of passion which her husband was unable to requite deserves a further push to climax through intensive genital caress . . . (5, p. 111)." Particularly in the early years of marriage, before the husband has learned to pace his orgasm, he may have to rely on the knack of digital manipulation. In one author's imagery, "Sometimes it may be necessary for the husband to withdraw and continue the stimulation of his wife by a rhythmic fondling of clitoris and vulva until orgasm is attained (1, p. 66)."

The central importance of experiencing orgasm has led many of the authors to de-emphasize the traditional organs of intercourse. The male penis (member) is particularly belittled. It is considered "only one of the instruments creating sensation in the female, and its greatest value lies as a mental stimulant and organ of reproduction, not as a necessary medium of her sexual pleasure." The same author adds, ". . . the disillusioning fact remains that the forefinger is a most useful asset in man's contact with the opposite sex . . . (14, p. 71)." Furthermore, this useful phallic symbol should be directed primarily to the woman's seat of sensation, the clitoris. Only a man who is ignorant of his job directs his digital attention to the vulva, the female organ that permits conventional union.

One must often deny himself immediate pleasure when manufacturing the orgasm. One author, in referring to an efficient technique to attain orgasm, states that: "Unfortunately, some men do not care for this position.

This, however, should be of little importance to an adequate lover, since his emotions are the less important of the two (14, p. 122)." Likewise, the woman may have to force herself in order to reach orgasm, even though she may not desire the activity which precedes it. It is specified that "If you conscientiously work at being available, you may ultimately find the feminine role quite satisfying even in the absence of ardor or desire (5, p. 38)." The work ethic of the sexual side of marriage, then, is one resting quite elaborately on what has been referred to as the "cult of the orgasm."

Still, one cannot easily perform one's job; its intricacies must first be mastered. After all, ". . . there is considerably more in the sexual relationship than . . . at first thought (8, p. 136)." "Remember that complete development of couple skills and adaptations takes literally years (5, p. 206)." There is a great deal to be learned. One author talks of eight steps "in order to facilitate sexual arousal and lead, finally, to satisfactory orgasm" and of seven "techniques which she and her mate may employ to help her attain full climax (6, pp. 124–126)."

All of this requires a good deal of mastery, a mastery that is necessary if the sex relationship is not to undergo "job turnover." Firstly, in the face of incompetence, the marriage partner may, at times, turn to auto-eroticism. One author stipulates that "There cannot be a shadow of a doubt that faulty technique, or a total lack of it on the man's part, drives thousands of wives to masturbation as their sole means of gratification (3, p. 140)." Moreover, if sexual skills are not acquired, the husband or wife may seek out new partners for sexual activity. The woman is admonished that adequate sexual relations will keep a man from

"The Other Woman . . . (4, pp. 264–265)." The male also must be proficient in sexual encounters for "it is the male's habit of treating . . . [sexual relationships] as such [mechanically] which causes much dissatisfaction and may ultimately drive the wife to someone who takes it more seriously (14, p. 77)."

LEARNING SEX: PASSIVE AND ACTIVE

Marital sex is said to necessitate a good deal of preparation if it is to be efficiently performed. In one author's words: "This [complete satisfaction] cannot be achieved without study, practice, frank and open discussion . . . (12, p. 45)." This overall preparation seems to involve both a passive and an active phase. The passive phase seems most related to an acquisition of information previous to engaging in sexual, at least marital sexual, relations. The active phase best refers to the training, one might say on-the-job training, that the married couple receive in the sexual conduct of wedlock.

The matter of passive preparation receives a great deal of attention from the avocational counselors. Thirteen of the fifteen books call attention to the necessity of reading, studying and discussing the various facets of sexual relationships. After listing a number of these activities, one author advises that "If the two of them have through reading acquired a decent vocabulary and a general understanding of the fundamental facts listed above, they will in all likelihood be able to find their way to happiness (1, p. 20)." Another counselor cites the extreme importance of reciprocal communication by noting that ". . . the vital problem . . . must be solved through intelligent, practical, codified, and instructive discussion . . . (14, p. 7)." The general purpose of all this learning is, of course, to dispel ignorance, as ignorance is said to lead to "mistakes at work," and such cannot be tolerated. The learning of the other partner's physiology is particularly emphasized, most counselors devoting at least one chapter and a profusion of illustrations to relieve the ignorance of the marriage partners. One author, however, quite obviously feels that words and pictures are insufficient. Presenting a sketch of the woman's genitals, he asserts that "It should be studied; on the bridal night . . . the husband should compare the diagram with his wife's genital region . . . (14, p. 18)."

Together with learning physiology, the various manuals also stress the critical importance of learning the methodology of marital sex. Sexual compatibility seems not a matter of following one's natural proclivities, but rather "The technique of the sexual relation has to be learned in order to develop a satisfactory sex life (13, p. 172)." One must know one's job if one is to be successful at it. Not surprisingly, to like one's job also requires a learning experience, particularly for the woman. As one book scientifically asserts:

There is a striking consensus of opinion among serious specialists (both men and women) that the average woman of our time and clime must *learn* to develop specific sexual enjoyment, and only gradually attains to the orgasm in coitus. . . . they [women] have to *learn how* to feel both voluptuous pleasure and actual orgasm (15, p. 262).

In summary, then, passive learning involves the mastering of physiology and techniques. By the desexualized female of the marriage manuals, the fine art of emotional experience and expression is also acquired. And the naturally inept male must learn, for

If the husband understands in even a general way the sexual nature and equipment of his wife, he need not give the slightest offense to her through ignorant blundering (1, p. 20).

This learning process, according to most of the manuals, eventually becomes subject to the actual experience of matrimonial sex. The marriage bed here becomes a "training" and "proving" ground. Again, wives seem particularly disadvantaged: "Their husbands have to be their guides (3, p. 108)." However, generally the training experience is a mutual activity. As one author suggests in his discussion of the various positions for coitus,

In brief, the position to be used is not dictated by a code of behavior but should be selected as the one most acceptable to you and your mate. To find this you will examine your own tastes and physical conformations. By deliberate application of the trial and error method you will discover for yourselves which is most desirable for you both (11, p. 11).

In training, rigorous testing and practice is a must. In the words of one manual "experimentation will be required to learn the various responses within one's own body as well as those to be expected from one's beloved . . . (9, p. 7)," and also, "After a variable time of practice, husband and wife may both reach climax, and may do so at the same time (11, p. 10)."

Both the husband and wife must engage in a kind of "muscular control" training if the sex act is to be efficiently performed. The woman's plight during intercourse is picturesquely portrayed with the following advice. "You can generally contract these muscles by trying to squeeze with the vagina itself . . . perhaps by pretending that you are trying to pick up marbles with it (5, p. 97)." Fortunately, the man is able to practice muscular control at times other than during intercourse.

Indeed, the man, unlike the woman, is permitted to engage in activities not normally related to sexual behavior while he is training. It is advised that "You can snap the muscles [at the base of the penile shaft] a few times while you are driving your car or sitting in an office or any place you happen to think of it . . . (5, p. 96)." The practice field, at least for the male, is enlarged.

In general, then, a careful learning and a studied training program are necessary conditions for the proper performance of marital sex. As seems abundantly true of all sectors of work, " 'Nature' is not enough. . . . Man must pay for a higher and more complex nervous system by study, training, and conscious effort . . . (7, p. 34)."

THE JOB SCHEDULE

As in most work activities, the activity of marital sex is a highly scheduled kind of performance. There is first of all a specification of phases or stages in the actual conduct of the sex act. Although there is disagreement here, some authors indicating four or five distinct phases (15, p. 1), the consensus of the counselors seems to be that "Sexual intercourse, when satisfactorily performed, consists of three stages, only one of which is the sex act proper (11, p. 7)."

The sexual act therefore is a scheduled act and the participants are instructed to follow this schedule. "All three stages have to be fitted into this time. None of them must be missed and none prolonged to the exclusion of others (8, p. 155)." Practice and study is said to insure the proper passage from one phase to another (12, p. 42). Moreover, to guarantee that none of the phases will be excluded, it is necessary to engage in relations

only when the sexual partners have a sizable amount of time during which they will not be distracted: ". . . husbands and wives should rarely presume to begin love-play that may lead to coitus unless they can have an hour free from interruptions (1, p. 51)." Even then, however, the couple must be careful, for there is an optimal time to spend on each particular phase. For instance, "Foreplay should never last less than fifteen minutes even though a woman may be sufficiently aroused in five (14, p. 43)." Likewise, the epilogue to orgasm should be of sufficient duration to permit the proper recession of passion.

Given this schedule of activity, the marriage manuals take great pains to describe the various activities required at each particular phase. It is cautioned, for instance, that "all contact with the female genital region . . . should be kept at an absolute minimum (14, pp. 42–43)" during foreplay. The man is warned furthermore to "refrain from any excessive activity involving the penis (14, p. 77)" if he wishes to sustain foreplay. Regarding afterplay, the advice is the same; the partners must not permit themselves "any further genital stimulation (15, p. 25)."

The "job specification" is most explicit, however, when describing the actual act of intercourse. It is particularly during this stage that the sexual partners must strain to maintain control over their emotions. Innumerable lists of "necessary activities" are found in the various manuals. The adequate lovers should not permit themselves to deviate from these activities. Sometimes, in fact, the male is instructed to pause in midaction, in order to ascertain his relative progress:

After the penis has been inserted to its full length into the vagina, it is usually best for the husband to rest a bit before allowing himself to make the instinctive in-and-out movements which usually follow. He needs first to make sure that his wife is comfortable, that the penis is not pushing too hard against the rear wall of the vagina, and that she is as ready as he to proceed with these movements (1, p. 61).

TECHNIQUES

The "labor of love" espoused by the avocational counselors is one whose culmination is importantly based on the proper use of sexual technique. In fact, ". . . *miserable failure results from ignorance of technique* (3, p. 49)." Indeed "no sex relationship will have permanent value unless technique is mastered . . . (8, p. 177)." Thirteen of the fifteen books devote considerable space to familiarizing the reader with the techniques of sexual activity. These discussions for the most part involve enumerating the various positions of intercourse, but also include techniques to induce, to prolong, to elevate, and to minimize passion. Many times the depiction of particular coital positions takes on a bizarre, almost geometric, aura. In one such position, "The woman lies on her back, lifts her legs at right angles to her body from the hips, and rests them on the man's shoulders; thus she is, so to speak, doubly cleft by the man who lies upon her and inserts his phallus; she enfolds both his genital member and his neck and head. At the same time the woman's spine in the lumbar region is flexed at a sharp angle . . . (15, p. 218)." Often, however, the mastery of sexual technique seems to involve little more than being able to keep one's legs untangled, ". . . when the woman straightens her right leg the man, leaving his right leg between both of hers, puts his left one outside her right, and rolls over onto his left side facing her (1, 58)."

At times, in order to make love adequately, it is required of the participants that they supplement their technique with special equipment. Some of this equipment, such as lubricating jellies, pillows, and birth control paraphernalia, is simple and commonplace. Others are as simple but not as common, such as chairs, foot-high stools, and beds with footboards or footrails. Some, like aphrodisiacs, hot cushions, medicated (carbonic acid) baths, and sitz baths, border on the exotic. Still others actually seem to detract from the pleasure of intercourse. In this vein would be the rings of sponge rubber which are slipped over the penis to control depth of penetration and the various devices which make the male less sensitive, such as condoms and a local anesthetic applied to the glans.

This equipment that minimizes stimulation, while not particularly inviting, might be said to give greater pleasure than still other techniques that are suggested to add variety to the sex life. The latter, in fact, seem cruelly painful. For instance,

. . . both partners tend to use their teeth, and in so doing there is naught abnormal, morbid or perverse. Can the same be said of the real love-bite that breaks the skin and draws blood? Up to a certain degree —yes (15, p. 157).

Indeed, a certain amount of aggression should be commonplace.

. . . both of them can and do exult in a certain degree of male aggression and dominance. . . . Hence, the sharp gripping and pinching of the woman's arms and nates (15, p. 159).

At times, the authors seem to go so far as to indicate that the proper performance of the sex act almost requires the use of techniques that create discomfort. The element of irksomeness becomes an almost necessary ingredient of the conduct of marital sex.

CONCLUDING REMARKS

The kinds of impressions assembled here seem to support the notion that play, at least sexual play in marriage, has indeed been permeated with dimensions of a work ethic. The play of marital sex is presented by the counselors quite definitely as work.

This paradox, play as work, may be said to be an almost logical outcome of the peculiar condition of American society. First of all, it seems that in America, most individuals are faced with the problems of justifying and dignifying their play. In times past, leisure was something earned, a prize that was achieved through work. In the present era, it might be said that leisure is something ascribed or assumed. Indeed, as Riesman and Bloomberg have noted, "leisure, which was once a residual compensation for the tribulations of work, may become what workers recover from at work."[9]

The American must justify his play. It is our thesis that he has done this by transforming his play into work. This is not to say that he has disguised his play as work; it is instead to propose that his play has become work.[10] To consume is, in most cases, to produce. Through this transformation of play, the dignity of consumption is seemingly established; it is now work, and work is felt to carry with

it a certain inherent dignity. The individual now is morally free to consume, and moreover free to seek out persons to teach him how to consume, for learning how to play is simply learning how to do one's job in society.

This transformation of play into work has been attended by another phenomenon that is also quite unique to contemporary American society. Given the fact that work has always been valued in American society, a cult of efficiency has developed. As a consequence, the productive forces in America have become very efficient, and an abundance of consumer goods have been created. So that such goods will be consumed, Americans have been socialized into being extremely consumption oriented. As Jules Henry[11] has noted, the impulse controls of most Americans have been destroyed. The achievement of a state of general satisfaction has become a societal goal. To experience pleasure is almost a societal dictum.

Thus there seem to be two antagonistic forces operating in American society. On the one hand, there is an emphasis on work and, on the other hand, there is an emphasis on attaining maximum pleasure. These two themes were recurrent in the fifteen manuals which we read, and as one writer put it:

. . . it may well be that the whole level of sexual enjoyment for both partners can be stepped up and greatly enriched if the man is able to exercise a greater degree of deliberation and management (1, p. 33).

It was as if the avocational counselors were trying to solve a dilemma for their audience by reminding them to both "let themselves go" while cautioning them that they should "work at

[9] David Riesman and Warner Bloomberg, Jr., "Work and Leisure: Tension or Polarity," in Sigmund Nosow and William H. Form, editors, *Man, Work, and Society,* New York: Basic Books, Inc., 1962, p. 39.

[10] Many investigators have observed the intertwining of work and play. We are here only interested in one aspect of admixture, the labor of play.

[11] Henry, *op. cit.,* pp. 20–21.

this." If sex be play, it most assuredly is a peculiar kind of play.

APPENDIX A

1. Oliver M. Butterfield, Ph.D., *Sexual Harmony in Marriage*, New York: Emerson Books, 1964 (sixth printing).
2. Mary Steichen Calderone, M.D., M.S.P.H., and Phyllis and Robert P. Goldman, *Release from Sexual Tensions*, New York: Random House, 1960.
3. Eustace Chesser, M.D., *Love Without Fear*, New York: The New American Library, 1947 (twenty-ninth printing).
4. Maxine Davis, *Sexual Responsibility in Marriage*, New York: Dial Press, 1963.
5. John E. Eichenlaub, M.D., *The Marriage Art*, New York: Dell Publishing Co., 1961 (fourteenth printing).
6. Albert Ellis, Ph.D., *The Marriage Bed*, New York: Tower Publications, 1961.
7. Bernard R. Greenblat, B.S., M.D., *A Doctor's Marital Guide for Patients*, Chicago: Budlong Press, 1964.

8. Edward F. Griffith, *A Sex Guide to Happy Marriage*, New York: Emerson Books, 1956.
9. Robert E. Hall, M.D., *Sex and Marriage*, New York: Planned Parenthood-World Population, 1965.
10. Isabel Emslie Hutton, M.D., *The Sex Technique in Marriage*, New York: Emerson Books, 1961 (revised, enlarged, and reset edition following thirty-fifth printing in 1959).
11. Lena Levine, M.D., *The Doctor Talks with the Bride and Groom*, New York: Planned Parenthood Federation, 1950 (reprinted, February 1964).
12. S. A. Lewin, M.D., and John Gilmore, Ph.D., *Sex Without Fear*, New York: Medical Research Press, 1957 (fifteenth printing).
13. Hannah M. Stone, M.D., and Abraham Stone, M.D., *A Marriage Manual*, New York: Simon and Schuster, 1953.
14. Robert Street, *Modern Sex Techniques*, New York: Lancer Books, 1959.
15. Th. H. Van de Velde, M.D., *Ideal Marriage: Its Physiology and Technique*, New York: Random House, 1961.

The electric aesthetic and the short-circuit ethic: the populist generator in our mass culture machine*

KINGSLEY WIDMER

"Monuments, museums, permanencies, and ponderosities are all anathema," angrily commented D. H. Lawrence on the imposed order and passionless deadness of much of our traditional culture. Some such rejection of the preservative and power-protective emphasis seems to be essential in the quest for greater individual responsiveness and communal liberation. The sought for experiences are kinesthetic, an intense ritualization of bodily immediacy and relatedness, in arts open and celebratory. Responsiveness must be energetic and social rather than passive and distanced, as in the usual aesthetic appreciation. The festival rather than the monument, the exalted sensation rather than the museum object, the playfulness rather than the permanency, the quick impulses of being rather than the ponderous markers of knowing, connect the genuinely popular and protesting currents which should be recognized as part of our post-industrial mass culture.

In contrast, the power-preservative culture controls sensibility by the withdrawal of art into awesome and exclusive objects with prescribed values. These achieve fixity and scarcity, and thus authority, as masterpieces and other precious commodities and as specialist techniques and painfully learned and restricted styles. Trained mediators—we institutionalized critics and teachers—insist on a preparatory "connoisseurship" and ascetic spiritualization as the controlled way of access to aesthetic experience. We suspect the arts of the uncultivated young just as we doubt the learning of the uninstitutionalized autodidact. We can recognize "popular culture" as controlled solace and exploitation aimed at the inner barbarians but not as collective innovation and vitality. What we prefer to think of as "high culture" can be defended, with some partial justice, by claims to immutable and lonely profundity. But socially, the rejection of such cultural permanency and ponderosity is also a revolt against the elitist and repressive control of sensibility. Preservative cultural processing serves social domination. The hierarchies of high culture, of values as well as of persons, fuse with those of institutional control and general social power. Culture becomes forms of power, and corrupts.

* This is the author's revision of two articles, "The Electric Aesthetic and the Short-Circuit Ethic," *Arts in Society*, X (Summer, 1970), and "McLuhanism," *The Village Voice* (Dec. 30, 1969), and continuous with several earlier studies, such as "The Role of the Rebellious Culture," in C. H. Anderson, ed., *Sociological Essays* (Dorsey Press, 1970). Reprinted by permission of the publishers and the author.

Abridged from Kingsley Widmer, "The Electric Aesthetic and the Short-Circuit Ethic: The Populist Generator in our Mass Culture Machine," pp. 102–109 and 117–119 in Bernard Rosenberg and David Manning White (eds.), *Mass Culture Revisited*. New York: Van Nostrand Reinhold, 1971. Reprinted with permission of the author.

Popular and protesting culture resists controls and affirms other values less by preserving and protecting than by re-creating, by, literally, lively recreation. Given the amorphously pervasive controls and corruptions of contemporary culture, esoteric as well as popular, the dissident less assault them than attempt to outflank authority and power by furthering populist subcultures. Not surprisingly, this now gets identified—and patronizingly subsumed—as mere youthful waywardness which serves the mass culture industries. For the charged-up young seem to be threatening to blow out social control by short-circuiting the controls and corruptions of cultural processing.

The custodians of high culture, like a junta directorate denouncing guerrilla revolutionaries as "mere bandits," often refuse to acknowledge that what they war with constitutes art and meaningful culture and authentic human responses. Since they rightly see the new artistic responsiveness and variant sensibility as an implicitly powerful social movement, involving energetic and undomesticated masses, the sycophants of power—a majority of the learned—hasten to denigrate the "weird youth culture," the "drop-out aesthetic" exploited by the media, just "another student madness," "the drug-entertainment scene," which is "largely a generational pathology" now built into a "sub-establishment" or "counter-establishment." Some small truths lurk in most such charges but we would serve the rhetoric of manipulation and domination if we were only to discuss our popular protesting culture within the petty terms of such "social problems." Our sense of the more lively currents within mass culture will be weak and contemptuous if it centers on drugs or entertainment or adolescence. That would be like discussing the delightful Medieval Goliard poets only in terms of unemployment and alcoholism (they did not have clerical sinecures and treated wine as a *sumum bonum*), or reducing the mordantly perceptive outsider view of the picaresque literary tradition to an issue of vagrancy laws (poetic wanderers and hoboes and beatniks are of course dirty and disruptive migrants), or vulgarizing the Greco-Roman Cynic philosophers and the Radical Reformation preachers into the sociology of educational surplus and delinquency. Movements of populist culture require rather more awareness than that allowed in textbook discussions of "social disorganization." Sadly, some of our pot-vague and rock-happy young dissidents seem to have been taken in by their patronizing elders and so themselves misrationalize their own freshness of artistic experience and libertarian social motives as just accusatory symptoms. It is embarrassing to hear the young smugly spouting about "the generation gap." In fact, the free-wheeling mockeries and joyous affirmations of our dissident culture go quite beyond such suburban sociology. Though we should recognize the limitations and ambiguities of the populist side of the mass culture, we must start by emphasizing the genuineness of its artistic impetus and the importance of its cultural role.

Partly for historical reasons, I prefer "populist culture" to "counter culture." For one thing, the imperatives are not "new" in the sense of unprecedented or unidentifiable. Partly a recurrence of Western populist romanticism, partly an expansion of the minority styles of several generations (American bohemian-beat-hippyrebels), and partly a cyclic recrudescence of ancient antinomian-utopian religious and social revolt, its newness comes from its curious relations to technology and its mass spread by way of the electronic media. The populist music, for example, variously combines traditional forms of the rural folk, the impassioned artistry and anguish of the ghettos, and the modes of urban-industrial entertainment, along with some of the eclecticism and exhibitionism we should expect in a late and overdone civilization. Most responsive observers agree that contemporary rock-folk-blues music results in some of the most lively and intriguing *popular* music since industrial organization effectively smashed indigenous folk arts. The populist literary imagination takes lesser ways, not least because our culture-of-the-word remains more fully controlled by the hierarchs of indoctrinating education and exploitative publishing and programming. The word arts stay within limited rhetorical forms: lyrics, titles, slogans, subjective reportage (the "personal" or "participatory" journalism of the hundreds of "underground" newspapers), broadsides, improvisational theatre, but rarely novels, contemplative essays, elaborate poetry, or intellectual dialectics. The emphasis upon transitory, parodistic, cursing, and burlesque styles assumes a great skepticism about our word culture so generally falsified for institutional rationalization and indoctrination. In contrast to the modernist aesthetic movements of the recent past, our present dissident culture no longer treats the man-of-letters as a hero. Pretty obviously, literacy has lost much of its magic. (And its transcendental egotism, as a wry contrast may suggest. In despairing moods, a noted but rather solitary literary artist I know thumbs through the inch-thick library card-catalogue of works by and about himself, or pursues the dry immortality of index references to himself. He is puzzled to the threshold of rage by some former writing students who distribute their satiric verses as anonymous broadsides and edit and write a radical and community-oriented biweekly newspaper under varied instant nicknames—collective outcast "monicker" style revived and widespread in the current underculture.)

The hundreds of "underground newspapers," with a readership of at least several millions in 1970, don't, contrary to the electronic priests of mass culture, indicate a total refusal of the written word. But they do point up some rather different styles of spreading, and parodying, the Word in their mocking variations on journalism and programming and advertising and other institutional rhetoric. Heterodox styles of sermon and prayer came back in vogue, as any observer of protest rallies and other underculture rituals can testify. While most of the populist papers seem as tiresome as seventeenth century sectarian pamphlets, with their neo-Leninist gospels and quasi-Learyist rituals, they service in rather burlesque forms of the other media a mass audience. The real news from underground is that there exists another nation, other communities, than those presented in the mass gospels of mainstream America.

The visual arts of the populist culture largely consist of costume and decoration and mixed media and transitory icons (posters, banners, graffiti) which usually "pastiche," in a surreal heightening, historical and museum motifs. The psychedelic styles, fortunately fading, were mostly *retardataire*, whether as forty-point illegible type or as arts nouveau imitation patterns. But the aesthetics of visual involvement, fracturing, and intensification continue.

We have previously experienced most of these elements of musical, verbal, and visual art but not in such peculiarly mixed, massive and electrifying ways. Part of the distinctiveness of these arts from the under-culture, when they become popularized, resides in what might be summarized as their "electric increment." Traditional musical elements become one with their electronic mixture, amplification, distortion, and intensification. The otherwise historic iconology takes similar, and somewhat grotesque, visual proportions because of mergence with new techniques (day-glo paints, strobe lights, synthetic materials, etc.) and normatively gratuitous application (to automobiles, kites, human bodies). Idiomatic speech, especially that derived from minority and outcast defiance, gets heightened by unexpected enlargement (the headline obscenity), by bizarrely imaginative nomenclature (the rock group names), and by a poeticization in which quotidian technical terms transpose into ecstatic gestures (as "electrical vibrations" become spiritual "vibes"). These electric-increments characterize a post-technological popular and protesting culture which turns the media to its own imperatives, and thus carries out considerable humanization.

Much of what stands out here seems to be the *playful* use of technology. The technical gets turned into the fantastic, humorous, grotesque. Traditional aesthetic elements combine with electronics and synthetics. The significance should be seen less in either source, the technological and the traditional, than in the fusion itself. Rebellious imperatives don't just use technology for reproduction and distribution but make something different of it. By playing with the electronic and synthetic, and not only when paradoxically mocking "plastic culture," they tend to twistingly absorb and artfully invert the more usual mass media sensibility. Our most advanced technological modes become sheer sensation and game and mystery and defiance and communion.

Perhaps here may be found some watershed points in the perplexed relations of modern technology and culture. Our prevalent theories of culture versus technology may have obscured what has been happening. For example, our allegiance to past heroic artists led us, properly enough, to see humane and imaginative culture as struggling for autonomy from the "Satanic mills." William Blake was considerably right, of course, in demanding "mental warfare" against an exploitative and dehumanizing industrial order and the science ("Newton's single-vision") on which it rested. Later cultivated allegiance to conservative craftsmen and reactive aesthetes and *symboliste* explorers of artistic autonomy furthered resistance to technocratic sensibility. They justly rejected what we now widely recognize as the lunar pieties and self-worshipping monumentalities of production for its own destructive sake. But though the scientistic and technistic certainly lack fully human dimensions, art cannot itself provide an alternative production and social order and, in the long run, countering art cannot even provide sufficient culture. In the past two centuries, artistic styles as well as media never successfully resisted for long the pressures of technological transformation. In spite of repeated attempts at archaizing and almost mystical efforts to stay with the traditional means (instruments, easels, class performances, genteel and metrical language, and all the rest), art ended up imitating technology. Even the distinctive "modernist" movements in the arts could not long defend themselves from subservient entertainment and power-preservative academicization. The break with the traditional aesthetics did not achieve a new autonomy from class or mass culture. By the middle of the twentieth century, the modernist culture of the preceding three or four generations was not only exploited by the technological media but merged with the elitist cultural depositories of museum and theater and journal and academy. Avant-gardist careerism clearly came to serve the sensibility and social order of technological society. If modernism in the arts won its battles for succession with the traditional aesthetics, succeeding in its "adversary" intellectualism, it also became merely new-traditional and lost much of its campaign for humanization. Modernism merely systematized the schizophrenia between sensitive culture and technological order. Consequently, artful protest against dehumanization today no longer pursues artistic modernism.

Now, apparently, we move within "post-modernist" responses, including the sense that the old conflicts of art and technology end Pyrrhic. But technological sensibility even more desperately needs to be humanized, transformed into the tolerable and various and responsive and communal. Culture which cannot serve tangible and social ways of living will not do it. The arts, our young make clear, must be immediate and involving, sensual and communal, to be humanly effective. They require an enlivening of the technological order, not an archaic or modernist split from the reality we inhabit.

Why is the effort to humanize the technological not recognized? Uncomfortable "liberal" members of the preservative culture plaintively qualify their attempts at sympathy for the populist art experiences: if only the music weren't so loud, the costumes so outrageous, the hair and nudity so sexually peculiar, the drugged lives so impractical, the gestures and language

so gross, the gatherings so lemminglike, the parasitism on society so patent. . . . But the populist currents in the mass culture reveal an amoral strategy, a take-over rather than a fastidious withdrawal from our social realities, from our noise, affluence, polymorphous sexuality, massization, distorted language, rootlessness, and other absurdities—and our technology. The populist culture takes much of what is and makes it aesthetic experience—re-creates the dominating things-as-they-are into delightful things-in-themselves. By embracing rather than rejecting, it would transpose our social realities into realms of imagination and feeling and communion. The enlightened moralist objections, though reasonable and appealing in cast, rest on the schizophrenia between culture and technology, refined art and the mass media, and must therefore miss the connections the "new people" make.

To the degree that there is a new culture within the mass culture, it operates by what we must call an inverted "aestheticizing." In this, the official becomes pure game just as the technical becomes pure sensation. For the young especially, such misuse becomes an art. The mechanical and electrical apparatus loses its depersonalized utility and reductive control when hedonistically exploited. Our spurious commodities cease to alienate by being turned into toys. An awesome administrative center (our technological cathedral) becomes proper scene for noise, graffitti, begging, lovemaking, and other humanizing irreverance. The woozy public event becomes a sacred festival, the earnest political occasion a comic ritual, the pious ceremony a saturnalia—or vice versa, when inappropriate. (The famous front page pictures of the sixties, such as the bearded and denimed student smoking a stolen cigar and with his feet on a university president's desk, or the pacifist rally with pranksters dressed in guerilla-type clothes firing toy machine-guns, or the stoned, peace-medalioned and guitar-playing soldier leaning against the armoured recon car in Vietnam, or the entwined young bodies on the littered floor of a computer center—among others— illustrate the style.) To the horror of the technologically pious, the young treat machines less in terms of their function than of decoration and destruction. Science properly reverts to direct magic, or so loses its ascetic mystification and is so derided that a great technologue fearfully warns of the end of technological advance within a generation. The ideologies of patriotism and productive submission and traditional legitimacy which support the technological order get turned, literally, into grotesque and obscene comic mythologies. The decorum of "dressing up"—always an important cultural key—becomes defiantly flamboyant costuming. The "impractical" becomes normative. The pharmaceutical provides madness rather more than medicine. Our current popular but intense arts—that itself is an inversion —come within, by and through, the dominant counterfeit culture, manipulative technology, and dehumanized organization. By such reversals reality becomes art, the realm of necessity reveals itself the realm of freedom, and the mass technological culture becomes expressive, fantastic, comic, sensational, lively, communal, and subverted.

I am highlighting, of course, certain currents as the populist side of the mass culture and would readily grant that they are often only partial and ambiguous, and their future uncertain. Yet surely they have been present for some time, for those willing to hear and see and, I suppose, properly vi-

brate. Often cultivated responses can only lead to misapprehension. "Show me," says a long-time competent and politically conscious artist, "the key masterpieces of this populist culture, and I will predict its future." But there are no such uniquely defining works. If our populist arts produce any "masterpieces" they will be as incidental to it as those we now discover in the ceremonial artifacts of neolithic tribes. To claim otherwise usually falsifies the actual work of, say, Kesey or Dylan or Cobb or Hendrix. Or it would be to substitute a psychedelic bus for a Romanesque altar or the Grateful Dead for the London Philharmonic or *Avatar* for the New York *Times* or a California underground collective for the Pentagon—a confusion of realms and dominions.

Quite appropriate to a culture which does not seek the preservative and the masterpiece and the powerful order is the renewed emphasis on applied arts, the exceptional rise in pottery and weaving and decoration of so many kinds. This shows yet again the turn away from both the hierarchies of preservative culture and the utilities of technological organization. Accessible style, rather than rare artifact or pure function, provide the aim and end of the new craftsmen. Surely it is production for use but, as we suddenly see the contrast of much of the rest of our culture, the populist ways do not aspire to transcendental art, science, or power.

Nor will the populist culture likely produce new ideas, any more than new inventions or new masterpieces. Indeed, it implicitly questions why we should even want such things. In such culture, intellectual disinterest and aggrandizement and dialectics must be subordinated to the kinetic and communal. You can groove with, join in, the populist culture and its group art experiences, but thinking will not make it. Perhaps protectively, entree comes from a mixture of game temper —"hang loose" in an ecstatic "cool," "do your thing but don't get up-tight" —and from the electricity of touch, of communal relation. The historian can catalogue the "ideas," ranging from mystical nature doctrines to the hero-ization of the urban outcast and poor, but the derivations are less important than the tone, manner, and relation-ship, which will allow many incom-patible ideas. Intellectual criticism and dialectic, those hostile arts, do not pro-vide such connections and commu-nions.

We intellectuals must feel irritation when faced with much of the populist culture. One of its senior mentors, for example, now bitterly mocks the re-sults, the drastic severance and denial of authority, the ignorance and lack of high culture. Paul Goodman (in *New Reformation*) even smugly points out the aesthetic contradictions in-volved in playing "primitive folk mu-sic" on "electronically amplified in-struments." Left-Hegelian Herbert Marcuse wants to be programmatically sympathetic to such "liberating imag-ination"; but, also as a good European, he really feels that culture means Bach rather than rock, and the dia-lectics of liberation demand tough or-ganizational cadres, and technological mastery. Even a learned anarchist his-torian, George Woodcock, ended with a vociferous condemnation of the "counter-culture" for its parasitism on the technological society and its lack of "classical heroic individualism"—a strangely conservative way of negating the anarchist movement of his own time. Each of these libertarian intellec-tuals must miss essential imperatives of the populist culture in breaking with the preservative culture in the quest for community. Marcuse's Hegal,

Homer (cited by Woodcock), and Milton (cited by Goodman) cannot possibly provide the aesthetic elec-tricity. Also a sticking point each time is the paradoxical relation to technol-ogy, the renaturing it by play. This has some forerunners, as in dadaism, but generally contrasts with the all-too-grim attempts to fuse art and technol-ogy, as in objectivist abstraction and functionalist design, and electronic musical neoclassicism and positivistic documentary literature. In contrast, the populist culture properly subordi-nates the techno-order by not taking it seriously. . . .

Will the populist current in the mass culture also short out? It constantly threatens to, but the hunger for its art and communion, and the basic human inadequacy of the mainstream techno-logical mass culture, restore the ener-gies. The cultural vacuum demands it, as we finally learn in practice that mass schooling and higher learning cannot successfully and satisfyingly impose much preservative culture on every-one. Granted, in protective coloration as well as in desperation for control, the manipulative institutions would and do take it over. Populist artists become rich celebrity businessmen and, in spite of a sometimes remark-able insouciance, sink into show-biz fatuousness and the usual commercial fraudulence. Our exhaustive processing of culture, like our endless bureau-cratization of learning, certainly re-moves autonomy and difference from the populist culture and would pacify it into rococo irrelevence. Yet the populist culture has a curious elusive-ness in which sleazy entertainment events become ecstatic religious festi-vals and in which styles start out by already ambiguously parodying them-selves and those who would take them over. The weird disproportions in-digenous to such minority cultures disrupt the logic of counterfeiting and control. Thus a minor indulgence such as pot becomes a politics and metaphysics. In curious defensive reversals, we have ardent youths claiming moral revelations from fatuous exoticism, e.g., from the revival of astrology and other forms of the occult, while passing off as mere youthful games revolutionary insurrections. But which of our cultures in the most mad mirror-world can be left open?

Still, an adversary culture must finally go beyond play, inversion, parody, grotesquery, and ambiguity and become something more, a full sensibility and continuing way of life. Though hardly ever in full synchronization in modern civilization, culture finally belongs to society. In the usual cultural theory, change in power allows change in institutions which then allows a change in sensibility, from political to social to cultural revolution. However, our present cultural conflicts imply that the last be first, that a change in sensibility will change the order of the world. Such is the positive force, the awesome dialectic, suggested by so many manifestations of our populist culture. And we must admit the remarkable vitality and the widespread social effects. However, direct change in institutional and other political power seems absurdly slight. Essentially the same denaturing processes, and the same types, considerably control education and entertainment. Even the populist culture's delightful revival of American utopian imagination, made tangible in some hundreds of communes and in many thousands of collectives and other tribal ways of domesticity (crucial modifications of our great anxiety machine, the competitive suburban family), often seems ambiguous. Frequently, we can suspect that marijuana substitutes for martinis, middling rock for middle-

brow schmaltz, whole-earth-catalogue salesmanship for the thing of ancient hucksters, and the new messiness for the old morality. Instead of alternatives to technological organization and its passively reductive consciousness, we may find that collectives of young technologues week-end for cheap therapy and that the mass culture peddles new anesthetics.

Does the populist culture finally reveal itself as fully subordinate to the power culture? The evidence in the early seventies should leave one, I believe, rather uncertain. Surely the genuine and desirable impetus to new ways of life and more vital sensibility and communitarian order would need more rigor and fullness than they now show in order to counter the technological processing and the apathetic consciousness that demands. But at least temporarily, the populist culture has led to some significant de-powering of not only the mass culture but of some institutions, e.g., familial and educational. Still, that will hardly transform a large part of technological mass culture, much less re-create our other institutions. Those who sardonically compare the populist currents with old fashioned rebelliousness and its minority art, alienated criticism, and moral intransigence certainly have a case. Taken in itself, our countering culture often seems a soft, vulgarized, and declining version of the culture of revolt, i.e., jazz down to rock, abstractionism and expressionism down to psychedelic decoration, bohemian literature reduced to underground journalism, philosophical radicalism reduced to ecological sentimentality, ecstatic prophecy condensed to drug "highs," and heroic nihilism to adolescent hedonism. But a popular and protesting culture must serve different purposes and roles and is therefore not comparable. For as a humane civilization we must also have an intense, kinesthetic, communal, and youthful popular culture, not just a preservative high culture (however modernist) and a piously exploitative and mind-rinsing technological mass culture. If the current populist culture gets altogether short-circuited into thin arts of passivity, surrogate experience, and institutional submission, if it is fully processed into mainstream mass culture and its technocratic ideology, then there will have to be another populist culture. Our openness to real change, to the possibilities of lively sensibility and more humane consciousness, and to communal relations are being tested by a relatively new cultural and social populism. Are we so far gone that it can have no authentic and enduring possibilities? The alternatives seem to be a violent apocalypse or a combination of a mortuary culture and a technological mass culture which will serve a fully authoritarian and debasing order. Our populist culture at least generates against this currents of a richer and freer life.

PART TWO

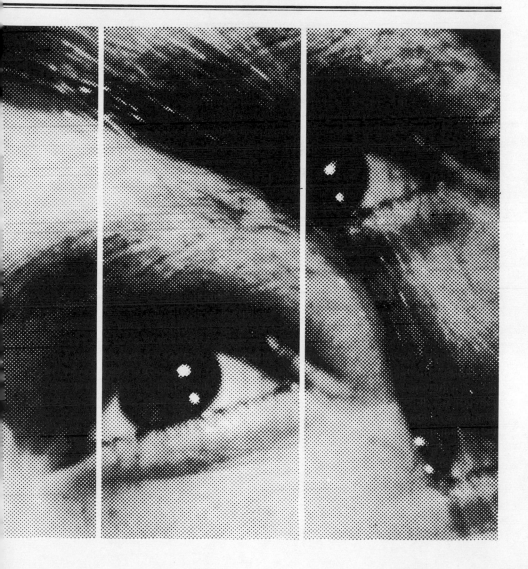

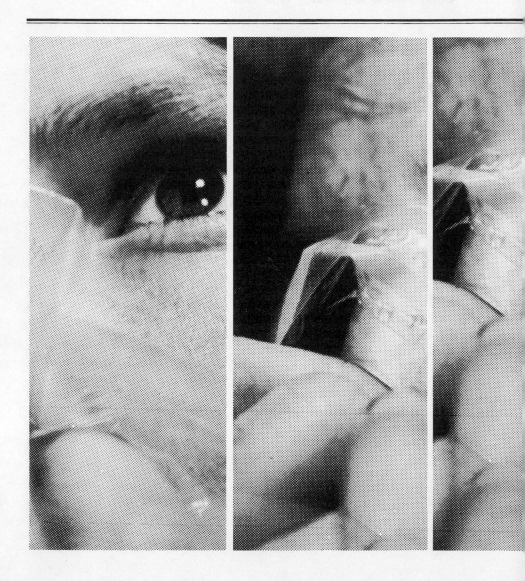

Deviant behavior approach

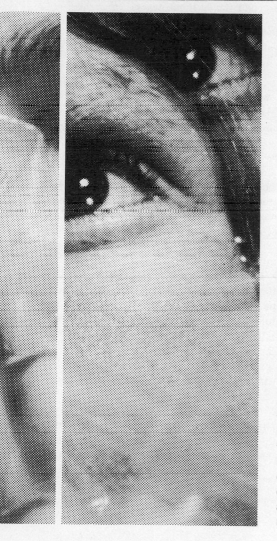

INTRODUCTION

The founders of sociology, it will be recalled, had a strong commitment to the amelioration of societal ills (Hinkle and Hinkle, 1961:4). American sociologists, in particular, were imbued with a pragmatist philosophy that led them to seek solutions to social problems. After World War I, however, sociology entered a new era: "Viewing the second period of American sociology as a whole, it appears to have been as preoccupied with making the discipline scientific as the earlier period was devoted to ameliorating social conditions and accelerating progress" (Hinkle and Hinkle, 1961:40). Many sociologists felt that social problems could not be resolved through the conventional social reform perspective; instead sociology had to first establish a sound empirical and theoretical basis. The discipline entered the era of scientific sociology, which was to continue and reach its peak during the late 1950s and early 1960s. Adherents to this position aligned themselves with natural science, believing that the scientific method could be applied to social phenomena in the same manner that it was applied to natural phenomena. In retrospect this was a sensitive, almost defensive era, with too much energy exerted in trying to demonstrate that sociology was a science and too little in developing theoretical models and testing research hypotheses. The value-free ethic discussed in the Introduction to Part One was an important corollary to scientific sociology. The sociologist was expected to be a "pure" scientist, impartial toward his data or subjects and devoid of value positions.[1] This position was expounded by George Lundberg (1947:50):

Social scientists, as scientists, had better confine themselves to three tasks: First and foremost, they should devote themselves to developing reliable knowledge of what alternatives of action exist under given conditions and the probable consequences of each. Secondly, social scientists should, as a legitimate part of their technology as well as for its practical uses, be able to gauge reliably what the masses of men want under given circumstances. Finally, they should, in the applied aspects of their science, develop the administrative or engineering techniques of satisfying most efficiently and economically these wants, regardless of what they may be at any given time, regardless of how they may change from time to time, and regardless of the scientists' own preferences.

The impartiality of the value-free position, however, was used to camouflage values that support the status quo.

The deviant behavior approach flourished during the era of scientific sociology. Social problems courses were offered, but they were mostly shunned by respectable sociologists. The field of deviant behavior provided the opportunity to study relevant subject matter while retaining a somewhat detached, value-free position. Deviant behavior could be defined operationally as behavior that fails to conform to specified standards. The deviant behavior approach was also consistent with the theory of cultural relativity, which had gained wide acceptance. To say that behavior is deviant does not imply that it is somehow inferior. One of the underlying tenets of the approach was that deviance is not a quality of individuals but of social norms; consequently, all of us are deviant relative to certain norms.

The study of deviant behavior is intricately related to the development of social psychology. American sociology, in contrast to European sociology, has from its inception had a strong social-psychological orientation (Hinkle and Hinkle, 1961:14–17; Simpson, 1954:36). It is therefore not surprising that American sociologists would show a strong interest in deviance. The study of deviant behavior is basically social-psychological in that it seeks to ascertain the conditions under which persons will conform to social norms. Although sociologists asserted that "all of us are deviant," they set out to study drug addicts, criminals, delinquents, and others who were regarded as deviant by larger societal norms (Liazos, 1972:104).

The deviant behavior approach is the most clearly defined and well developed of the three approaches. The approach, however, has been both social-psychological and microscopic, focusing on interpersonal, face-to-face relations, and neglecting large-scale conditions. Thus despite the

---

[1] This position was of course not accepted by all sociologists. C. Wright Mills (1959), for example, was an outspoken critic of scientific sociology and the value-free ethic. For more recent critiques of value-free sociology see, Gouldner (1962), Becker (1967), and Hoult (1968).

richness of the literature on deviant behavior it has become increasingly clear that a number of societal conditions are not reducible to deviant behavior. Societal problems such as overpopulation, poverty, and mass society and alienation cannot be adequately understood using the deviant behavior model. Little is gained in understanding, for example, by calling black rioters or student protesters "deviants."

The purpose of differentiating among the three approaches is not to suggest that one is somehow better or worse, but rather that they are distinctive, with different origins, assumptions, and foci. The social problems approach is better suited for looking at broad societal conditions, the deviant behavior approach for looking at the relationship between the individual and social norms. Just as the deviant behavior approach is inadequate for understanding societal problems, so the social problems approach cannot be used to explain deviant behavior.

ALTERNATIVE APPROACHES TO DEVIANCE

Although the sociological approach to deviant behavior is a relatively recent development, concern with human aberration is probably as old as man. Both Plato and Aristotle, for example, discussed deviant behavior and crime. Aristotle maintained that "poverty engenders rebellion and crime" (Quinney, 1970:44). Attempts to explain deviant behavior have ranged from moralistic and religious views to biological theories. Despite the diversity of these views, they tend to share an important characteristic in that the study of deviant behavior is generally the study of deviant or aberrant individuals.

Moralistic

From prehistoric times man has employed demonological interpretations of unknown or complex phenomena. Deviance was frequently seen as the work of demons or other evil spirits (Vold, 1958:5–6). Judeo-Christian teaching reinforced the belief that deviant or antisocial attitudes were the product of demons (Knudten, 1970:223). Belief in demonism was especially prevalent during the Middle Ages, and much of the rationale behind the Spanish Inquisition was based on demonological thought.

Demonological thought was modified during the eighteenth century by the classical school of criminology and, particularly, by its founder Cesare Beccaria. In traditional demonological explanations deviant acts were controlled by external forces; the classical school believed, on the other hand, that deviance was very much within the control of the individual. Man had free will and was capable of exercising moral responsibility. Since the actions of individuals were not predetermined, they were free to choose between good or evil. Man was also basically hedonistic, seeking to maximize pleasure and minimize pain. Deterrents to deviance must therefore be sufficient to discourage violation of the law, but not excessive or arbitrary. Punishment, according to the classical school, should fit the crime. Beccaria and others campaigned to bring about legal reform and to eliminate the arbitrary use of punishment by the state. Many of the beliefs of the classical school have been discarded, yet its impact on our criminal legal system is evident to this day.

Biological

During the nineteenth century a new school, variously known as the Italian or positivistic school of criminology, challenged the classical school. Cesare Lombroso is undoubtedly the best known exponent of this position, and he and Enrico Ferri and Raffaelle Garofalo are generally recognized as the founders of the Italian school. Lombroso and his contemporaries, seeking to develop a criminology modeled after the natural sciences, applied the positivistic method to the study of crime. This provided a sharp departure from the classical school. "While the classical school emphasized the idea of the choice of right and wrong, the positive school placed the emphasis on the determinism of conduct" (Quinney, 1970:58). The Italian positivists sought to take criminology out of the realm of mysticism and religion and to place it within the realm of science. The study of crime was viewed as deterministic in that whether a man was good or evil (criminal or non-criminal) was determined by natural forces over which he had little if any control.

Lombroso, an Italian military physician, came to believe after extensive study of cadavers and living persons that the criminal constituted a distinctive biological type. He advanced the theory of the born criminal, an atavistic throwback to primitive man. *Homo sapiens* had evolved from an earlier, inferior form called *Homo delinquens*. The criminal type was characterized by distinctive physical stigmata such as shifty eyes, long arms, large ears, and cranial or facial asymmetry (Vold, 1958:50–51). The criminal was assumed to be a reversion to an earlier, primitive type of man who could not adjust to modern European civilization. In later work Lombroso modified this view substantially by acknowledging other criminal types such as insane criminals and criminaloids. The latter category included criminals whose crimes resulted from environmental and situational influences (Lombroso, 1911:373–375).

The biological approach to deviance originated with the study of crime, but over the years it has been applied to other forms of deviance such as homosexuality, prostitution, delinquency, and drug addiction. Despite the lack of evidence to support Lombroso and subsequent biological theorists, the biological approach to deviance continues to have a strong appeal. A number of contemporary writers attribute deviant behavior to body build, extra chromosomes, and other biophysical factors. These works will be discussed more fully in Chapter 5, but for now it is important to point out that the various biological theories of deviance share a common conception of the deviant as inferior or somehow lacking in normal development. The deviant is abnormal not only for violating social norms but also in his physical make-up.

Although contemporary sociologists tend to reject the biological approach to deviant behavior, the positivistic school did much to advance the scientific study of deviant behavior by applying the scientific method to criminology. The major contribution of positivism, therefore, is in the method It advanced rather than in its substance.

Psychological

The psychological approach to deviance evolved from the biological approach. Early psychological studies followed the lead established by the biological approach of attempting to demonstrate the inferiority of the deviant. A number of studies, for example, set out to prove that the criminal was mentally defective. In the latter part of the nineteenth century and the first part of the twentieth century there were many attempts to show that deviance resulted from feeble-mindedness. It was argued that the person of low mental capacity was unable to cope with the demands of society. The most celebrated studies of this type were those that tried to establish a hereditary link to deviance among certain families. The Jukes (Dugdale, 1877; Estabrook, 1916), the Kallikaks (Goddard, 1912), and the Nams (Estabrook and Davenport, 1912) were among the families in which feeble-mindedness presumably produced a long series of social misfits. While these case histories were admittedly bizarre, they do not in and of themselves "prove" that crime or deviance are inherited characteristics. One could use the same case histories to "prove" that crime is socially transmitted.

Attempts to link mental deficiency to deviance were fostered by the development of tests to measure intelligence during the early part of the twentieth century. Many scholars concluded from studies of inmate populations that feeble-mindedness was a primary cause of crime. Goddard, one of the leading exponents of this view, asserted that "it is no longer to be denied that the greatest single cause of delinquency and crime is low grade mentality, much of it within the limits of feeble-mindedness" (Goddard, 1920:73). In general it is important to note that these studies committed a major error in assuming that the average mental age of the general population was sixteen. By comparison the prevalence of feeble-mindedness (assumed to be a mental age of twelve or less) in the prison population appeared excessive. Subsequent tests of army draftees during World War I revealed that the average mental age of the population as a whole was much lower (about thirteen) than previously assumed. Today, there is little doubt that differences in IQ between prisoners and the rest of the population are negligible (for an excellent discussion of this literature see Vold, 1958:75–89). If one assumes that those criminals who are caught and prosecuted are generally less capable than those who go undetected, it is interesting to speculate about the possibility that criminals might on the average be more intelligent than noncriminals! With the development of a more sophisticated methodology, however, the view that deviants are mentally inferior lost much of its support. The deviant, nevertheless, continued to be viewed as deficient in more subtle ways. As psychiatry gained in acceptance, the dominant view of the deviant shifted from mentally deficient to emotionally disturbed.

The person who undoubtedly has had the most significant impact on the development of psychiatry, especially as it pertains to the study of deviant behavior, is Sigmund Freud (1920, 1927, and 1930). In order to understand the psychiatric approach to deviant behavior it is necessary to provide at least a skeletal sketch of Freud and psychoanalytic theory. One of the most central concepts in psychoanalysis is the unconscious. Although the concept was not originated by Freud, it is the cornerstone of his theory. Accordingly, much of man's behavior results from deeply rooted unconscious motives that can be uncovered only through in-depth psychoanalysis. Another important element in psychoanalytic theory is the conflict between man's biological urges and the demands of society. Freud outlined three basic components of the personality: (1) the *id* corresponds to man's instinctive biological urges; (2) the *superego* corresponds to the internalized demands of society; and (3) the *ego* corresponds to the rational component of the personality. The id is the seat of the instincts, unlearned, unconscious and out of touch with reality, being motivated by the pleasure principle rather than reason or ideals. The two primary instincts in man are the *libido* (the force of sexual energy) and the instinct for survival. The ego is the rational, conscious and deliberating component of the personality, the thinking or reasoning quality in man. Unlike the id, which is motivated by pleasure, the ego is in touch with reality and motivated by it. The superego is the moral dimension of the personality, the internalization of societal standards of right and wrong. According to Freud, within man there wages a never-ending battle among the id, the ego, and the superego. One of the primary functions of the ego is to arbitrate between the conflicting demands of the body (id) and society (superego). Normal personality development requires the establishment of a delicate balance among the three components of the personality. Psychic and emotional disorders result when there is an imbalance among these forces.

In psychoanalytic theory deviant or aberrant behavior takes various forms. It may occur, for example, when repressed complexes are released, as in crime and other deviant forms, which serve as symbolic or substitute acts for repressed desires (Vold, 1958:119). While this form of deviance is a product of an "overly developed" superego, another form results from a "poorly developed" superego. Some persons, for one reason or another, fail to develop a conscience or to internalize the norms of society. The most extreme example of a poorly developed superego is the psychopathic personality (Schur, 1969:70–72).

One of the major difficulties with psychoanalytic theory is that its assumptions and propositions almost defy scientific verification.

A methodology (as in psychoanalysis) under which only the patient knows the "facts" of the case, and only the analyst understands the meaning of those "facts" as revealed to him by the patient, does not lend itself to external, third person, impersonal verification or to generalization beyond the limits of any particular case (Vold, 1958:125).

Psychoanalytic explanations involve the ex post facto imposition of unconscious motives to earlier actions. While psychoanalytic case studies are interesting and persuasive, their validity cannot be established.

Sociological

It is difficult to talk about a sociological approach to deviance, since in reality there are numerous sociological approaches. One can, however, outline some of the major assumptions shared by these various approaches. One characteristic, already noted, of the sociological approach to deviance is that it has been predominantly social-psychological in focus. The study of deviance is concerned with the interaction between the individual and society, seeking to determine the conditions under which individuals will conform to social norms. While earlier perspectives such as the biological and psychological saw deviance as the study of deviant individuals, for sociologists the essence of deviance is in social norms. Social norms are standards shared by group members. They involve expectations as to the appropriateness of behavior under given conditions. Norms do not generally specify certain acts, but rather set parameters for acceptable action. Such expectations are not static; they change rapidly over time. Since social norms are created by society, deviance must ultimately be created by society.

The study of deviance has come a long way from the early demonological explanations of deviant behavior as the work of spirits or demons. The view was largely discarded during the nineteenth century as the desirability of applying science to human affairs was recognized. Given the wide acceptance of evolutionary theory it was not surprising that many scientists turned to biological explanations of human deviation. It was reasoned that if man is a biological organism, his behavior (both normal and abnormal) must be a product of his biological make-up. Since human evolution represents a linear movement toward progress, persons who engage in aberrant action must be biological misfits. With the emergence of behavioral sciences, particularly psychology during the twentieth century, biological theories were increasingly discarded in favor of theories that saw mental and emotional disturbances as the source of deviance.

Despite their obvious differences both the biological and psychological views saw deviance as emanating from within the individual. Sociology was to make a critical leap by shifting the study of deviance from the individual to the society. One of the logical fallacies of the biological and psychological approach is that they failed to recognize the social nature of deviance. Biology, for example, can affect human behavior, but it cannot produce deviant behavior as such. In the last analysis it is society, not biology, that determines whether an act is deviant. The term "deviant" is a label attached to certain actions by society. Such labels are subject to variation across societies and over time. In short, the biological view of deviant behavior is absolute, the sociological relativistic.

Although sociologists are in general agreement over the basic components of a sociological perspective, there are some significant differences among them. Today we can identify two basic schools, or traditions, in the study of deviance. One tradition, anomie theory, is usually traced to Émile Durkheim, while the other, labeling theory (the "interactionist" perspective), is said to have originated with the work of Max Weber (Jacobs, 1972:1–3).

Durkheim sought to make sociology into an objective science (for a more extended discussion of Durkheim see the Introduction to this book). For Durkheim sociology was the study of social facts. Social facts are "ways of acting, thinking, and feeling, external to the individual, and endowed with a power of coercion . . ." (1964:3). Since social facts are external to the individual, they cannot be explained by individual facts. Sociology is the study of societal tendencies, or rates, not individual tendencies. Durkheim is credited with starting a tradition that attempts to explain objective rates of deviant behavior by looking at the relationship of these rates to the organization of society. The concept of anomie was central to Durkheim's work. As was mentioned earlier, it referred to a state of normlessness, or disorganization, in society. His sociological method was illustrated in a classic study of suicide (1966). Suicide was to be understood not as an expression of biological, psychological, or climatic factors, but rather as a social fact, determined by social forces (see the Introduction).

The concept of anomie has been revised and expanded by Robert K. Merton, who in an excellent essay, "Social Structure and Anomie" (1963: 131–160), developed a typology of deviant behavior based on a means-ends scheme. Merton, like Durkheim, rejected biological and psychological explanations of deviance, suggesting instead that the social structure exerts pressure on certain individuals to engage in deviant behavior. The two critical concepts in the typology are "cultural goals" and "institutionalized means." Cultural goals are the things worth striving for in society; institutionalized means are the legitimate avenues for achieving these goals. While there is usually some correspondence between cultural goals and means, "the cultural emphasis placed upon certain goals varies independently of the degree of emphasis upon institutionalized means" (1963: 133). One of Merton's basic points is that when either cultural goals or institutionalized means are emphasized without a corresponding emphasis on the other, deviant behavior ensues. Anomie, a situation in which cultural goals are emphasized without a corresponding emphasis on legitimate means, is especially problematic in American society. This imbalance between goals and means creates a state of normlessness, a dog-eat-dog world, where individuals pursue goals without social regulation. In sports the emphasis is on winning at any cost; in economic activity wealth is attained through the most expedient means. Merton noted that in the economic area our society puts pressure on certain persons, especially social minorities and the poor, to engage in nonconforming activity (e.g., crime). The society tells them to reach out for success goals, not to be quitters; yet the society blocks their access to legitimate means. The table that follows presents the typology.

Modes of adaptation	Culture goals	Institutionalized means
I. Conformity	+	+
II. Innovation	+	−
III. Ritualism	−	+
IV. Retreatism	−	−
V. Rebellion	±	±

[a] + signifies acceptance, − rejection, and ± rejection of prevailing values and substitution of new values.

The second tradition is usually linked to Weber. Although Weber payed relatively little attention to deviant behavior, the labeling perspective adopted his sociological method. With the concept *verstehen* (sympathetic understanding) Weber stressed that sociological understanding can only come about through the subjective interpretation of social acts (Gerth and Mills, 1958:55–61). While Durkheim believed that sociology studied objective, and impersonal, social facts, Weber stressed the subjective interpretation of social phenomena.

It is fashionable today to link Durkheim to anomie theory and Weber to the interactionist, or labeling, perspective. The link, however, is not so direct. Since Weber actually failed to study deviant behavior, the link to these traditions is found in the method of their work, not in the content. Durkheim, on the other hand, was very much concerned with deviance. Moreover, his conception of deviance, particularly his theory of crime (see Chapter 6) is consistent with contemporary labeling theory.

Anomie theory focuses on the relationship of social structure to deviant behavior. Traditionally, it has attempted to explain differential rates of deviant behavior (e.g., crime, suicide, delinquency) among segments of the society. The approach is more purely sociological (rather than social-psychological), focusing on rates of deviation and neglecting the subjective meaning attached to behavior in an interactional context. Although the approach looks at collective tendencies toward deviance, as opposed to individual deviation, the focus of the study of deviance is still on deviant actors who violate social norms. The labeling perspective, on the other hand, shifts the focus from the deviant actor to the process through which behavior is defined as deviant. Deviance is a label attached by an audience to behavior. In order to understand deviance one must go beyond rates and look at the interactional setting within which deviance is defined. Labeling theory is associated with the work of a number of contemporary sociologists including Lemert (1951 and 1967), Becker (1966), Kitsuse (1962), and Erikson (1962). Becker succinctly summarizes the labeling perspective:

. . . *social groups create deviance by making the rules whose infraction constitutes deviance*, and by applying those rules to particular people and labeling them as outsiders. From this point of view, deviance is *not* a quality of the act the person commits, but rather a consequence of the application by others of rules and sanctions to an "offender." The deviant is one to whom that label has successfully been applied; deviant behavior is behavior that people so label (1966:9).

The distinction between *primary* and *secondary* deviation is especially critical to labeling theory.[2] Primary deviation involves the violation of a social norm or law. A person may engage in nonconforming behavior and yet not be defined by himself or others as deviant. "The secondary deviant, as opposed to his actions, is a person whose life and identity are organized around the facts of deviance" (Lemert, 1967:41). Under secondary deviation a person adopts the deviant role ascribed by society and assumes a role consistent with this label. Thus while the deviant behavior approach and the labeling perspective, in particular, have done much to humanize and

---

[2] For further discussion of the labeling perspective see Douglas (1970), Schur (1971), Filstead (1972), and Rubington and Weinberg (1973).

destigmatize the deviant, the focus of sociological research on deviance is still on persons who are labeled as "odd," "weird," or "perverted" by dominant societal standards. Despite the assertion that deviance is a "normal" phenomenon, emphasis in American society is on dramatic and bizarre acts that violate middle-class morality.

By focusing on the dramatic forms, as we do now, we perpetuate most people's beliefs and impressions that such "deviance" is the basic cause of many of our troubles, that these people (criminals, drug addicts, political dissenters, and others) are the real "troublemakers;" and, necessarily, we neglect conditions of inequality, powerlessness, institutional violence, and so on; which lie at the bases of our tortured society (Liazos, 1972:119).

REFERENCES

Becker, Howard S.
1966 Outsiders. New York: Free Press.
1967 "Whose Side Are We On?" Social Problems 14 (Winter):239–247.
Douglas, Jack D.
1970 Deviance and Respectability. New York: Basic Books.
Dugdale, Richard L.
1877 The Jukes. New York: Putnam.
Durkheim, Emile
1964 The Rules of Sociological Method. (Translated by Sarah A. Solovay and John H. Mueller, ed. by George E. G. Catlin). New York: Free Press.
1966 Suicide (Translated by John A. Spaulding and George Simpson). New York: Free Press.
Erikson, Kai T.
1962 "Notes on the Sociology of Deviance." Social Problems 9 (Spring):307–314.
Estabrook, A. H.
1916 The Jukes in 1915. Washington, D.C.: Carnegie Institute.
Estabrook, A. H., and C. B. Davenport
1912 The Nam Family. Lancaster, Pa.: New Era Publishing Co.
Filstead, William J.
1972 An Introduction to Deviance. Chicago: Markham.
Freud, Sigmund
1920 A General Introduction to Psychoanalysis. New York: Boni and Liveright.
1927 The Ego and the Id. London: Hogarth.
1930 Civilization and Its Discontents. New York: Cape and Smith.
Gerth, Hans H., and C. Wright Mills
1964 From Max Weber: Essays in Sociology. New York: Oxford University Press.
Goddard, Henry Herbert
1912 The Kallikak Family. New York: Macmillan.
1920 Human Efficiency and Levels of Intelligence. Princeton, N.J.: Princeton University Press.
Gouldner, Alvin W.
1962 "Anti-Minotaur: The Myth of a Value-Free Sociology." Social Problems 9 (Winter):199–213.
Hinkle, Roscoe C., Jr., and Gisela J. Hinkle
1961 The Development of Modern Sociology. New York: Random House.
Hoult, Thomas Ford
1968 ". . . Who Shall Prepare Himself to the Battle?" The American Sociologist 3 (February):3–7.

Jacobs, Jerry
1972 Getting By: Illustrations of Marginal Living. Boston: Little, Brown.
Kitsuse, John I.
1962 "Societal Reaction to Deviant Behavior: Problems of Theory and Method." Social Problems 9 (Winter): 247–256.
Knudten, Richard P.
1970 Crime in a Complex Society: An Introduction to Criminology. Homewood, Ill.: Dorsey.
Lemert, Edwin M.
1951 Social Pathology. New York: McGraw-Hill.
1967 Human Deviance, Social Problems, and Social Control. Englewood Cliffs, N.J.: Prentice-Hall.
Liazos, Alexander
1972 "The Poverty of the Sociology of Deviance: Nuts, Sluts, and Preverts." Social Problems 20 (Summer):103–120.
Lombroso, Cesare
1911 Crime: Its Causes and Remedies. (Translated by Henry P. Horton). Boston: Little, Brown.
Lundberg, George A.
1947 Can Science Save Us? New York: Longmans, Green.
Merton, Robert K.
1963 Social Theory and Social Structure. Revised ed. Glencoe, Ill.: Free Press.
Mills, C. Wright
1959 The Sociological Imagination. New York: Oxford University Press.
Quinney, Richard
1970 The Problem of Crime. New York: Dodd, Mead.
Rubington, Earl, and Martin S. Weinberg
1973 Deviance, The Interactionist Perspective. Second ed. New York: Macmillan.
Schur, Edwin M.
1969 Our Criminal Society. Englewood Cliffs, N.J.: Prentice-Hall.
1971 Labeling Deviant Behavior. New York: Harper & Row.
Simpson, George
1954 Man in Society: Preface to Sociology and the Social Sciences. New York: Random House.
Vold, George B.
1958 Theoretical Criminology. New York: Oxford University Press.

Juvenile delinquency

5

HISTORY OF THE JUVENILE COURT

Although societies have been concerned with the problem of juvenile delinquency for centuries, it was not recognized as a legal category until the latter part of the nineteenth century. Societal interest in delinquency stems from at least two distinctive problems. First is the problem of intergenerational conflict and the desire by adults to control the young. Adolescence, at least in Western nations, is frequently an age of conflict and rebellion. A high level of delinquency is taken by adults as an indication that social norms are breaking down and, consequently, as a threat to sacred societal values. The second problem is the need of society to protect itself from persons, adult or juvenile, who are perceived as presenting a threat to the society. The society needs to devise ways of dealing with persons who violate the criminal law but who are considered too young to be subjected to the same treatment as adult offenders.

Before the juvenile court was established, minors either received the same treatment as adults or were not subject to the criminal law.[1] The treatment of young offenders was based on English common law, which stipulated that children under the age of seven were incapable of criminal intent. Those between seven and fourteen were also incapable of criminal intent unless it could be demonstrated that they understood the consequences of their actions. The common law, however, did not make special provisions for juvenile offenders. A young person judged capable of criminal intent was handled like an adult; those not capable of criminal intent were not subject to criminal prosecution.

The first juvenile court in the United States was established in April 1899 when the Illinois legislature passed the Juvenile Court Act. "The juvenile court emerged from the confluence of several streams of thought and practice, some of them centuries old, others relatively recent responses to changing social conditions" (President's Commission, 1967b:2). The earliest source of the idea of the juvenile court is the concept of *parens patriae*, which developed under feudalism in Great Britain. Under this system the chancery court exercised substantial authority over children in the name of *pater patriae*, the king. Although initially court jurisdiction was limited mostly to children whose property rights were jeopardized, in the United States it was also expanded to include protection from personal injury. Thus the juvenile court had some precedent in the English chancery court. There was, however, an important difference in that the chancery court was limited to neglected or dependent children and did not have jurisdiction over criminal violations.

A second source of the juvenile court is a nineteenth-century social movement in the United States that sought general reforms in the treatment of children. A number of individuals, including philanthropists, intellectual feminists, penologists, and social scientists, were able to dramatize the vulnerability of children. Of special concern was the excesses that occurred when children were placed in the same correctional institutions as adult criminals. The reformers were successful "first in establishing separate institutions for youth and substituting noninstitutional supervision wherever feasible, then in adopting physically separate court proceedings, and finally in altering the very philosophy underlying judicial handling of children" (President's Commission 1967b:3). Within a few years after 1899 a number of states followed the lead of Illinois and by 1925 there were juvenile courts in all but two states. The underlying view of the delinquent was that of a wayward child whose best interests and rights were to be secured by the court. The juvenile court was to have jurisdiction not only over cases involving neglect and dependency but also over delinquency.

From the outset the juvenile court was given great latitude in handling cases. The proceedings were to consist of hearings rather than a formal trial. While the chief objective of the criminal court is to punish criminals,

---

[1] Much of the discussion of the juvenile court in this section is based on the President's Commission on Law Enforcement and Administration of Justice (1967b).

the juvenile court was designed to help children in trouble and to rehabilitate them. A terminology consistent with these goals was introduced: there was a "petition on behalf of the child" rather than an indictment, "disposition of a case" rather than sentence, and "training" schools replaced prisons. However, the juvenile court has come under considerable criticism in recent years. The humanitarianism of the court was more apparent than real. Despite its liberal rhetoric, the juvenile court functions very much like the criminal court. Persons are accused, judged, deprived of their freedom, and punished through incarceration. One of the basic criticisms of the court is that adolescents are denied basic constitutional guarantees. In 1967 the Supreme Court ruled in the *Gault* case that juveniles are entitled to counsel, the right to confront and cross-examine witnesses against them, and the right to timely notice of the charges. This decision, however, has not really been implemented, and most juveniles are still subject to the arbitrary discretion of the courts.

The juvenile court was created to help the child, not to punish him or to label him "criminal." The delinquent is in fact labeled "delinquent" by the court and, subsequently, by the schools, employers, and other agencies. The broad discretion given the court means that about half of the cases are handled informally. The court, however, operates with a distinctive class bias. Middle-class adolescents are subjected to more lenient treatment and are placed on probation or released to the custody of their parents, since they are not perceived as hard-core delinquents. Lower-class adolescents are likely to be regarded as "delinquent," "incorrigible," or "leading a life of idleness and crime."

The informality of the juvenile court places an adolescent in an ambiguous position. He is subject to prosecution by the juvenile court not only for violations of the criminal law but also for a host of other acts, attitudes, and dispositions, which are not criminal when committed by adults. Ideally, a juvenile is judged delinquent when he commits an act that is a crime when it is committed by an adult. In practice, of course, the juvenile court has much broader jurisdiction. It handles cases of dependency and neglect as well as delinquency. A child may be adjudicated as delinquent for violations of the criminal law, of ordinances that apply only to children, or because he is "incorrigible or ungovernable." Cohen lists a number of more specific offenses for which a child could be labeled "delinquent":

1. Is habitually truant.
2. Is incorrigible.
3. Is growing up in idleness or crime.
4. Conducts himself immorally or indecently.
5. Habitually uses vile, obscene or vulgar language in a public place.
6. Habitually wanders about railroad yards or tracks.
7. Smokes cigarettes or uses tobacco in any form.
8. Makes indecent proposals.

9. Attempts to marry without consent in violation of the law.
10. Is given to sexual irregularities (Cohen, 1970:368).

The experience of the juvenile court illustrates how well-meaning social reform can produce unanticipated consequences. The goals of the juvenile court are laudable, indeed: to protect, help, and rehabilitate the wayward child. The court has failed, however, to attain these goals. It was granted broad powers in order to protect the interests of the juvenile, but it is now necessary to institute reforms that will curb its power and ensure due process for the accused.

CONCEPTIONS OF DELINQUENCY

Despite the wide usage of the term "juvenile delinquency," there is little agreement not only over the definition of "delinquent" but also over who constitutes a "juvenile." In most states eighteen is the upper limit of juvenile status, but in some the limit is sixteen and in others it is twenty-one. Thus whether or not one is subject to the jurisdiction of the juvenile court depends, at least partly, on the state in which an act is committed. The term "delinquency" is even more difficult to define. It varies across states and among jurisdictions and is, in the last analysis, an arbitrary decision imposed by the police and the courts.

Some investigators conceive of delinquency as *behavior*, whereas others regard it as a quality or attribute of *persons* (Voss, 1970:2). The first conception looks at unofficial delinquency in that a person is termed "delinquent" when he commits certain acts, whether or not such acts are detected. Under the second conception behavior is secondary to the delinquent label. The labeling of a person as "delinquent" is only partly dependent on his actions. The essence of delinquency, according to a sociological labeling perspective, lies not in delinquent behavior but in the application of a label by society to certain persons and the internalization of this label. An adolescent may commit acts for which he could be adjudicated as delinquent, but if he is not defined as delinquent (by himself or others), he is not "socially" delinquent. A third, related conception is that of delinquent subcultures (Voss, 1970:2). Proponents of this position argue that since delinquency is ultimately a group phenomenon, one gains a true understanding of delinquency not by looking at isolated individuals, but rather by studying delinquent groups or gangs.

There is yet another factor that complicates the definition of delinquency. At what point does an adolescent who is in violation of the law become delinquent? Is one delinquent when an act is committed, once it is known to the police, or when he is adjudicated by the court? If a delinquent is anyone who commits an act for which he *could* be adjudicated as delinquent by the court, almost all adolescents would be delinquent—the estimate given by the President's Commission (1967a:55) is 90 percent. Such a conception renders the term "delinquency" meaningless, since there is virtually no nondelinquent group against which to compare delinquents. It does, however, caution us not to treat adolescents as two dichotomous groups, one delinquent and the other nondelinquent.

Most sociological studies have examined only official delinquency, that is, adolescents defined as delinquent by either the police or the courts. Considerable diversity exists even among official delinquents. At one extreme are those placed in correctional institutions by the court; at the other are those whose cases are handled informally by the police. Between these extremes are adolescents placed on probation or referred to another agency by the court. There are some who maintain that a person is delinquent only if he is so defined by the juvenile court. While this position is technically correct, it poses a number of problems. First, it ignores behavior that goes undetected by authorities or is handled informally. Second, an official definition of delinquency underestimates the amount of delinquency in the middle class, since middle-class delinquent acts are less likely to be detected by the police and, when detected, likely to be handled informally (Short and Nye, 1957–58). Finally, it does not consider the effects of "treatment" on delinquency. Arrest, appearance in court, and institutionalization undoubtedly influence one's self-conception and attitude toward society (Voss, 1970:4). It is impossible to know, therefore, the extent to which factors such as broken homes and emotional disturbances, which are treated as causes of delinquency, are really *caused by* delinquency, or more accurately by institutionalization (Short and Nye, 1957–58).

A number of investigators have suggested the use of self-reports in order to overcome some of the difficulties inherent in official conceptions of delinquency (Short and Nye, 1957–58). Such studies question the use of non-institutionalized adolescents as a nondelinquent control group. Actually, most of these nondelinquents have engaged in acts for which they could be judged delinquent by the juvenile court (Voss, 1970:4). Short and Nye (1957–58) have devised a paper-and-pencil scale that can be administered anonymously to groups of students. This method has certain obvious advantages. First, and most important, it uncovers much hidden delinquency and indicates better than either police reports or court records the number of delinquent acts committed. Second, it does much to reduce the bias against the lower class prevalent in studies of official delinquents. Third, it reduces the effect of treatment or institutionalization on delinquency. Finally, it treats delinquency as a variable rather than a quality or trait of persons. Studies of official delinquency make the dubious assumption that there are two kinds of adolescents in the world—delinquent and nondelinquent.

Self-reports are not a panacea, however. Are such measures valid and reliable indicators of delinquency? Do these studies underrepresent the most delinquent-prone persons, who are more apt to be institutionalized, truant, or school dropouts? Finally, and most critically, can we really measure delinquency by simply counting the number of offenses committed? If the essence of delinquency lies in the fact that it is a deviant label, self-reports are missing the point. One is not socially delinquent if he is not so labeled. In view of the maze of conceptions and the numerous controversies, one might expect the field of delinquency to be in a state of chaos. In fact, the study of delinquency has benefited from these diverse conceptions. It is now clear that we can no longer continue to reify delinquency, searching for a single true or correct conception. Delinquency is a complex phenomenon, variable and taking different forms. We can study official delinquency if we are aware of its limitations. But if we wish to study undetected delinquency, self-reports are in order. The point is that these conceptions are supplementary and complementary—one cannot substitute one for another. Hopefully, differences and similarities between official and unofficial delinquency will be drawn out by future studies.

CORRELATES OF DELINQUENCY

One of the strongest correlates of delinquency is sex. Both official statistics and self-reports (Short and Nye, 1958) indicate that delinquency is far more common among boys than girls, although delinquency among girls is probably slightly underreported by official data. Boys are arrested about five times more frequently than girls and referred to the juvenile court four times more often (President's Commission, 1967a:56). Despite the higher rate of delinquency among boys, sex differences in delinquency appear lower in the United States than in most other countries. This finding is consistent with the hypothesis that the rate of crime and delinquency among females approaches that of males in countries where women have more equality with men (Sutherland and Cressey, 1970:127). When girls are referred to the juvenile court, it is likely to be (in order of frequency) for running away, ungovernable behavior, larceny, and sex offenses, whereas boys are referred mostly for larceny, burglary, and auto theft (President's Commission, 1967a:56).

Another factor that has been consistently related to delinquency is urban-rural place of residence. Delinquency is highest in large metropolitan areas and lowest in small rural areas (President's Commission, 1967a:56). Rural-urban differences in delinquency rates may not, however, reflect real differences in delinquent behavior. Cases are more likely to be disposed of informally in rural areas, and many juvenile offenses are not recorded officially. Official rates of delinquency tend to be high among members of deprived racial and ethnic minorities such as black Americans, Mexican Americans, Puerto Ricans, and American Indians. There is reason to believe, however, that an adolescent's socioeconomic status and the area of the city where he resides are more important determinants of delinquency than racial and ethnic background. Deprived racial and ethnic groups usually reside in inner-city ghettos where crime and delinquency are high;

but as their economic positions improve and they move out of the inner-city, the rate of delinquency in these groups decreases (Shaw et al., 1929; Shaw and McKay, 1969; Gordon, 1967).

A question remains unanswered: Do the higher rates of delinquency among economically deprived groups reflect actual differences in delinquent behavior or differences in the behavior of the police and the courts? The President's Commission on Law Enforcement and Administration of Justice concluded that: "It is likely that the official picture exaggerates the role played by social and economic conditions. . . . But there is still no reason to doubt that delinquency, and especially the most serious delinquency, is committed disproportionately by slum and lower-class youth" (1967a:57). Despite the boldness of this assertion, studies of self-reported delinquency do not support the hypothesis that socioeconomic status and delinquency are inversely related. Nye, Short, and Olson found that "there is no sig-nificant difference in delinquent behavior of boys and girls in different socioeconomic strata" (1958:388). A number of other studies have also questioned the presumed relationship between socioeconomic status and delinquency (Voss, 1966 and 1970:60). The only thing that can be said with certainty is that lower-class adolescents have higher rates of official delinquency. Whether this finding reflects real differences in behavior can only be answered by future studies that compare rates of official delinquency with self-reports and control significant variables (Empey, 1967). We can, however, hazard an educated guess as to the nature of this relationship. On the basis of available research social class differences in the overall volume of delinquency seem doubtful. Most likely there are differences in the type of delinquent activities engaged in by adolescents in different strata. Lower-class adolescents are more likely to be arrested and brought before the juvenile court not only because their families lack power and influence but because they engage in the type of delinquent activity that is viewed as more "serious" or "dangerous" by public officials (Voss, 1970:60). "Delinquency," according to the labeling perspective, is a label that is applied by representatives of the community power structure (the police and judges) to the behavior of juveniles. The police and judges for the most part have a preconceived notion of delinquency that they employ in handling delinquents. The disposition of a case is determined more often by whether the adolescent fits this preconception of a true delinquent than by the offense committed. Piliavin and Briar (1964) found that the police exercised a great deal of latitude in deciding which juveniles were true delinquents to be brought before the court and which were "good kids in trouble" (see the reading selection by Irving Piliavin and Scott Briar at the end of the chapter). Somewhat independently of the acts committed, boys who demonstrated a demeanor or appearance that was judged un-cooperative or tough were much more likely to be arrested, especially if they were black.

THEORIES OF DELINQUENCY

Few topics have aroused more interest than the study of juvenile delinquency. A host of theories have emerged ranging from those that treat delinquency as the result of a chromosome imbalance to those that treat it as learned social behavior. Space limitations permit only a general overview of these theories.

Psychobiological theories

A number of contemporary disciples of Lombroso have sought to validate a psychobiological theory of delinquency, termed "constitutional psychiatry." The best-known, and most controversial, exponent of constitutional psychiatry is William Sheldon (1949). According to Sheldon somatotypes (body types) are related to temperament and behavior. He proposed three basic body types: endomorphic, mesomorphic, and ectomorphic. The endomorphic body build is one in which the dominant body tissue is fat. Not only is this type fat, but he is also soft, round, small boned and has short tapering limbs (Vold, 1958:71). The endomorph is typically jolly, relaxed, easygoing, and extroverted. The mesomorph, on the other hand, has a predominance of muscle and bone. He has a large trunk and heavy chest, as well as large hands and wrists. The mesomorph is an active, aggressive, and energetic person. The last body type, the ectomorph, is lean, linear, and thin. The dominant body tissue is skin. Ectomorphs are characteristically fragile, delicate, nervous, and excitable. The type is introverted and concerned more with mental than with physical activity (for a summary of these characteristics see Vold, 1958:71).

Although Sheldon placed heavy emphasis on these three types, they are not to be considered as distinct entities, but rather as interrelated variables. Each dimension is given a value on a scale which ranges from 1 to 7. Every respondent receives three somatotype scores—the first for endomorphy, the second for mesomorphy, and the third for ectomorphy. A person high on endomorphy, for example, might score 7-3-1, whereas one high on mesomorphy might score 2-7-1. One who is average on each dimension would score about 4-4-4.

Sheldon has tried to link body type and temperament to delinquency, hypothesizing that mesomorphy is an important determinant of delinquency. The strong and aggressive mesomorph is more likely to engage in delinquent activities than either the jovial endomorph or the withdrawn ectomorph. After comparing 200 "more or less" delinquent boys and young men who had been treated by a Boston welfare agency with a group of nondelinquents, Sheldon claimed support for his basic hypothesis. His research, however, has been the object of much controversy and criticism (Washburn, 1951). "Critical analysts have concluded that Sheldon's own data did not justify such a conclusion, let alone his accompanying interpretations of inferiority and inherited tendency toward crime" (Schur,

1969:58). One major criticism is that since the same investigators rated both physique and temperament, a self-fulfilling prophecy may have been built into the study (Munn, 1956:164). There is also some question about the representativeness of his sample. The criterion for including some delinquents and excluding others is not clear. There is an additional problem in that his definition of delinquency is not made explicit. Delinquency is defined as "disappointingness" or "disappointing" behavior (Cortés and Gatti, 1972:15). Finally, does body type change over one's lifetime, and if it does, how does one determine a person's true body type?

Interest in Sheldon's work was revived by a more methodologically sophisticated study carried out by Sheldon and Eleanor Glueck (1950, 1956, and 1962). The Gluecks compared a group of institutionalized delinquents with a carefully selected control group of matched nondelinquent working-class boys. They found that 60.1 percent of the delinquents were predominantly mesomorphic, whereas only 30.7 percent of the nondelinquents were mesomorphic (Glueck and Glueck, 1956:9). Although the Gluecks study supported Sheldon's hypothesis, their findings cannot be accepted as conclusive. First, the use of delinquents committed to correctional institutions may introduce a bias (Cortés and Gatti, 1972:18). The rigors, strains, and competitiveness of institutionalization may produce mesomorphy. Second, the study is subject to many of the same criticisms as Sheldon's work in that the Gluecks relied on his method of somatotyping. Finally, the use of adolescents who have not reached puberty is questionable (their respondents ranged from nine to seventeen years), since their somatotype is subject to change (for a more detailed discussion of Sheldon and the Gluecks see Cortés and Gatti, 1972:13–20).

A more recent study of body type and delinquency has been carried out by Cortés and Gatti (1972). Using Parnell's method of somatotyping, which is reputedly more objective than Sheldon's, they compared 100 adolescents convicted and sentenced by the court, 100 seniors from a private high school in the Boston area, and 20 convicted felons (mean age 33.8). Delinquents were decidedly more mesomorphic than nondelinquents, and the convicted felons scored higher on mesomorphy than either adolescent group (Cortés and Gatti, 1972:25–30).

From the time of Lombroso social scientists have been reluctant to accept biological explanations of crime and delinquency. Today enough evidence has been accumulated to draw our attention to such studies. Let us assume, for the moment, that body build is related to delinquency. Must we then conclude that body build causes delinquency? Whereas the more extreme biological theorists such as Lombroso and Hooten felt that criminality is inherited and criminals are biologically inferior, most contemporary constitutional theorists take a more cautious view. They argue that body build, rather than being a determinant of delinquency, is instead a predisposing factor. The assertiveness, aggressiveness, and high energy level of the mesomorph is assumed to be consistent with the demands of the delinquent role. Such a view of the relationship between body type and delinquency is compatible with sociological theory. In fact, it provides an excellent illustration of the labeling perspective. Since society expects males with a muscular body build to be physically aggressive and assertive, their involvement in delinquent activities may result from their internalization of this expectation. Muscular individuals may be dominant and assertive, and endomorphs jolly and easygoing, not because these characteristics are biologically determined but because they are expected socially. This is a classic example of the self-fulfilling prophecy in society.

A number of questions have not been answered adequately by studies of somatotype and delinquency. First, to what extent does delinquency produce mesomorphy? Can we assume that body build leads to delinquency, or do delinquent activities and institutionalization produce mesomorphy? Second, the somatotype theory assumes that criminal activities require physical strength and aggressiveness. Many, if not most, criminal activities can be performed by persons who are not mesomorphic. The confidence game, check forging, embezzlement, and burglary, for example, require more skill and finesse than muscle. Most constitutional theorists appear to have a stereotyped, and erroneous, conception of the criminal. Finally, even if we grant that criminal activities satisfy aggressive and assertive needs, other noncriminal activities could satisfy the same needs. There is no explanation for why a mesomorphic boy becomes a delinquent instead of an athlete.

This discussion suggests a composite picture of the relationship between body type and delinquency. Muscular lower-class adolescents are expected to be assertive and aggressive. In trying to prove that they are tough they are likely to get into trouble, come to the attention of the police, and be institutionalized. Involvement in delinquent activities further intensifies their mesomorphic tendencies. The competitive world of correctional institutions is particularly conducive to the development of mesomorphy. A critical test of the hypothesis that body build leads to criminality would entail a study of noninstitutionalized delinquents or criminals. There is evidence that indicates that while the more physically aggressive and unskilled criminals are imprisoned, those who rely on skill and intelligence typically go undetected (Roebuck and Johnson, 1962 and 1964).

Sociological theories

In response to the biological and psychological theories that dominated the study of delinquency during the latter part of the nineteenth century and the first part of the twentieth century, sociologists proposed a variety of theories to explain delinquent activities. Although these theories rejected the view of delinquency as an individual pathology and saw it instead as a social phenomenon, there is great diversity among them.

A pioneer in the study of delinquency, Edwin H. Sutherland, proposed a theory that would explain not only delinquency but all criminal behavior. The theory of differential association was set forth in the 1939 edition of

Principles of Criminology and revised in subsequent editions. According to Sutherland, crime is normal behavior that can be understood through the same principles that are used to explain noncriminal behavior. Criminal behavior is learned in face-to-face association with significant others. "The process by which one becomes delinquent—the acquiring of attitudes favorable to delinquency and the learning of the appropriate behavior patterns— is no more normal or abnormal than the process by which one becomes a law-abiding citizen. The difference lies in the content, not the process of learning" (Voss, 1970:151). Sutherland rejected the concept of social disorganization and suggested instead the concept of differential social organization. Within a heterogeneous society some groups are organized around norms and values that support legal codes, while others are organized around definitions that are favorable to violation of the law. He summarized the theory of differential association in nine basic propositions (Sutherland and Cressey, 1970:75–76):

1. Criminal behavior is learned.
2. Criminal behavior is learned in interaction with other persons in a process of communication.
3. The principal part of the learning of criminal behavior occurs within intimate personal groups.
4. When criminal behavior is learned, the learning includes (a) techniques of committing the crime, . . . (b) the specific direction of motives, drives, rationalizations, and attitudes.
5. The specific direction of motives and drives is learned from definitions of the legal codes as favorable or unfavorable.
6. A person becomes delinquent because of an excess of definitions favorable to violation of law over definitions unfavorable to violation of law.
7. Differential associations may vary in frequency, duration, priority, and intensity.
8. The process of learning criminal behavior by association with criminal and anticriminal patterns involves all of the mechanisms that are involved in any other learning.
9. While criminal behavior is an expression of general needs and values, it is not explained by those general needs and values, since noncriminal behavior is an expression of the same needs and values.

Differential association was accepted for many years as a model sociological theory of crime. Today, however, it is clear that the theory suffers from a number of weaknesses. Differential association cannot account for the isolated crimes that occur with no apparent association with definitions favorable to violation of the law. Moreover, it does not explain why some persons exposed to criminal definitions commit crimes while others do not. Policemen, for example, frequently have the same kinds of childhood associations as criminals. How can we account for a family in which one brother becomes a policeman and the other a criminal? Perhaps the most important criticism is that differential association is so broad that it is not a theory at all but a set of self-validating assumptions and definitions. What Sutherland considered the major strength of the theory—that it could account for both criminal and noncriminal acts—may be its major weakness. Critics argue that the theory simply restates some basic sociological assumptions about human behavior without really explaining criminality. A final, related criticism, is that although a few studies of delinquency have operationalized differential association (Reiss and Rhodes, 1964; Short, 1957, 1958, and 1960; Voss, 1964 and 1969), sociologists have found it difficult to apply Sutherland's basic propositions to concrete studies of crime (for further discussion of differential association see Chapter 6). With the benefit of hindsight it is easy to find fault with Sutherland's work. Nonetheless, differential association remains a classic statement of the sociological perspective on crime. Its value lies not so much in its ability to explain specific criminal acts but in shifting the focus of criminology from attributes of the individual to sociocultural forces.

Some researchers have applied the theory of differential association to the study of self-conceptions among delinquent youth. Reckless, Dinitz, and their associates attacked a question that was unanswered by differential association: How do certain adolescents who reside in areas with high rates of delinquency refrain from delinquent activities? Their research suggested that an adolescent's self-conception may serve as an insulator against delinquency. Those who have socially appropriate self-conceptions, view themselves as good boys and resist delinquency. The authors attempt to use differential self-conceptions, or containment theory, to explain both the low rates of delinquency among middle-class adolescents and the presence of nondelinquent youth in high-delinquency areas. More recently, Voss (1969) has tried to show that containment theory provides a useful extension of differential association. He found that the joint effects of differential association and containment account more fully for delinquency than does the separate effect of either variable (1969:391).

Despite the apparent usefulness of containment theory, it is subject to several criticisms. One of the most important is a definite middle-class bias. Studies of self-conception have for the most part neglected the role played by agents of social control in defining delinquency. Boys who have "socially appropriate" self-conceptions are probably less likely to be defined as delinquent somewhat independently of whether or not they violate the law. Another criticism is that self-conception may be an effect rather than a cause of delinquency. Those boys who are defined as delinquent by the community may come to define themselves as "bad."

Following in the tradition established by differential association, which postulates that crime is learned within the context of social groups, a number of sociologists have proposed subcultural theories of delinquency. One of the most prominent of these is Albert Cohen's theory of the delinquent subculture. His theory of the emergence of the delinquent subculture was first proposed in the book *Delinquent Boys* (1955). According to Cohen, the crucial condition for the emergence of a subculture "is the existence, *in effective interaction with one another, of a number of actors with similar problems of adjustment"* (1955:59). Lower-class adolescents face such problems of adjustment. In many situations, particularly the school, they are asked to compete according to middle-class standards and are judged by middle-class persons. These standards are not, however, peculiar to the middle class. "They express the dominant American value system; they pervade the mass media; and they are also applied, although in a less throughgoing way, by 'respectable' working-class people" (Cohen, 1966:65). Verbal fluency, academic intelligence, achievement, deferred gratification, good manners, and neatness, for example, are valued. Lower-class adolescents who do not meet these standards are doomed to failure, since their early socialization does not prepare them adequately for this competition. Cohen describes the adjustment made by lower-class adolescents to their failure and humiliation:

One way they can deal with this problem is to repudiate and withdraw from the game . . . to set up new games with their own rules or criteria of status— rules by which they *can* perform satisfactorily. . . . They not only reject the dominant value system, but do so with a vengeance. They "stand it on its head"; they exalt its opposition . . . (1966:65–66).

Thus much delinquent behavior is malicious and spiteful and appears to have no point of utility. The theory helps to explain why delinquency is more prevalent in the lower class and why much of it is nonutilitarian.

A basic difficulty of Cohen's work is that the theory of the emergence of the delinquent subculture is impossible to test, since it requires historical data concerning the psychological characteristics of an unknown past population (Kitsuse and Dietrick, 1959). While the theory of emergence cannot be tested, the theory of maintenance can (Kitsuse and Dietrick, 1959). Does the delinquent subculture maintain itself by resolving, for participants, those problems that were the bases for its emergence? From the theory one would expect that those lower-class adolescents who are least equipped to compete with middle-class standards are most likely to join the delinquent subculture. When one focuses on the problem of maintenance, the theory of delinquent subcultures becomes a useful tool for testing some basic propositions of differential association. One might hypothesize, for instance, that "the individual learns the values of the delinquent subculture through his participation in gangs which embody that subculture" (Kitsuse and Dietrick, 1959:214).

While Cohen sees the delinquent subculture as a reaction to middle-class norms, for Walter Miller (1958) it originates within lower-class culture. Miller maintains that we can understand delinquency without turning to concepts such as delinquent subculture, social strain, or social disorganization. The values embodied by lower-class gangs are deviant from the standpoint of middle-class norms, but they conform to lower-class culture. More specifically, Miller sets forth a set of six focal concerns (issues that command a great deal of interest and emotional commitment) characteristic of lower-class culture: "trouble," "toughness," "smartness," "excitement," "fate," and "autonomy." The activities of lower-class street gangs center on the satisfaction of these focal concerns. The gang satisfies two additional focal concerns, the need for "belonging" and for "status." Since the nuclear family is allegedly weak in the lower class and youth lack significant contact with adult males, the peer group plays an important part in socializing adolescents into the male role.

Miller's theory assumes that lower-class culture is inherently deviant or criminal (Valentine, 1968:43–45). As such, it is somewhat reminiscent of the culture of poverty perspective and subject therefore to the same criticisms (see Chapter 2). There is also no compelling evidence that these focal concerns are limited to the lower class. The focal concerns are so broad and ill-defined that one could argue that middle-class persons are also concerned about trouble, toughness (i.e., proving masculinity), smartness, excitement, fate, and autonomy.

Despite the apparent differences between Cohen and Miller, they are similar in that delinquent activities for both result from the violation of middle-class or larger societal norms. Merton's anomie theory (discussed more fully in the Introduction to Part Two) sees delinquency as resulting from adherence to larger societal values. The lower-class delinquent (or criminal) would fall under the innovative pattern in that he accepts the value of economic success but selects deviant means to reach this goal. This framework has been expanded and applied to delinquency by several sociologists, most notably Richard Cloward and Lloyd Ohlin (1960). They, like Merton, believe that success-goals are not class bound, but rather cut across the entire society. Lower-class adolescents, however, are pressured toward delinquency by a marked discrepancy between their aspirations and their opportunities. For some lower-class boys legitimate opportunities for success are open (e.g., professional athletics or entertainment), but avenues to success are limited for most. When the discrepancy between unfulfilled aspirations and opportunities becomes intense, they are likely to turn to illegitimate alternatives (Cloward and Ohlin, 1960:86). The delinquent response, however, is determined not only by the availability of legitimate means but also by the availability of illegitimate opportunities (Cloward and Ohlin, 1960:148). Even illegitimate opportunities are not equally available to all. In well-integrated and cohesive slum neighborhoods youngsters are likely to turn to a criminal pattern. Stable lower-class neighborhoods have a well-developed criminal subculture. This provides adult role models and an alternative opportunity structure for youngsters who adopt the criminal subculture. The conflict pattern is likely to emerge in more poorly integrated areas of the city. Slum areas with high rates of social and geographical mobility, characterized by transiency and instability, limit "access to stable criminal opportunity systems . . ." (Cloward and Ohlin, 1960:172). Under such conditions violence becomes an alternative means settings. Some drugs are approved and others are not. We seem to oppose drugs that are taken for pleasure and recreation and that alter our mental and emotional state; we seem to approve drugs that are taken as "medicine."

A "normal" drug user is one of the millions of persons who use drugs on a regular basis in a socially approved setting. The drugs are legitimate or approved, and such drug use is considered neither illegal nor deviant. The drugs used in this context include coffee, tea, alcohol, sleeping pills, and various other stimulants and depressants. When these drugs are taken under medical care or in a socially sanctioned setting, the drug user is not defined as deviant. Normal drug use is usually not considered part of the drug problem. Most Americans, for example, do not even regard alcohol and tobacco as drugs (National Commission on Marihuana and Drug Abuse, 1973:10).

Mainliners

Mainliners are persons who are physically dependent on heroin or another opium derivative. Sociologists have identified a subculture of mainline addicts. Members of this subculture are typically young males who reside in the urban slums of large cities. About 46 percent of the addicts known to the Bureau of Narcotics (1967:23) are between the ages of twenty-one and thirty. The subculture seems to flourish in urban areas having high crime rates (DEA, 1973b:21–23).

Although some members of the subculture are white, the mainline subculture is epitomized by the society of black, drug-using "cats." Finestone (1964) has presented an excellent description of young, black addicts, based on a study in Chicago. The young addict identifies with an elite "society of cats."[5] The cat is cool in demeanor and dress. He is smart and tries to outwit or con others, avoiding the use of force and violence. The cat has disdain for work and for the "square," who lives by routine and works hard at a regular job. Every cat maintains his "kick" through a lucrative "hustle." Heroin has great appeal to the cat and is regarded as the ultimate kick. Since heroin is frowned upon by conventional society, "regular heroin use provides a sense of maximal social differentiation from the 'square' " (Finestone, 1964:285). This description of the society of cats is supported by a study of black narcotic law offenders. Roebuck (1962) found that, compared to other offender types, narcotics offenders were younger, more intelligent, verbally fluent, soft-spoken, and non-aggressive. They disliked the use of violence, and few of their arrests were for nonnarcotic violations. Most of them took pride in their ability to outfox and outsmart other persons.

---

[5] Cloward and Ohlin's (1960) "retreatist" subculture discussed in Chapter 5 is based on Finestone's description of the society of cats.

Mind-Expanding drug users

In recent years a distinctive mind-expanding subculture has emerged. Although there is substantial variation within the subculture, it possesses certain features that distinguish it from other drug-using groups and from straight society. First, drugs are used for pleasure or recreation. Drug use is defined as a pleasurable experience, not as a way of maintaining a habit or as medical treatment. "The drug is used occasionally for the pleasure the user finds in it, a relatively casual kind of behavior in comparison with that connected with the use of addicting drugs" (Becker, 1966:43). A second, related characteristic is that neither tolerance nor drug dependence develops. Although critics of marijuana, including the Federal Bureau of Narcotics, have long argued that its use leads to the use of other drugs, there is no evidence of a causal relationship between smoking marijuana and the use of more dangerous drugs (National Commission on Marihuana and Drug Abuse, Appendix, 1972:422). While many heroin-dependent persons have tried marijuana, only a small proportion of those who smoke marijuana go on to use heroin. Members of the subculture generally frown on the use of heroin and other drugs that produce dependence. "The narcotics addict is viewed with scorn and pity specifically because of his loss of cool" (Goode, 1969:60). He fails to exercise choice. In a sense, both the addict and the straight person are unduly restricted. Third, the use of drugs is typically a shared social experience. "Grass" is seldom smoked alone (Goode, 1969:55), and group "tripping" is a common phenomenon. The passing of a joint is a symbolic expression of good will, friendship, and in-group solidarity. Smoking typically occurs among friends or casual acquaintances with whom one shares basic values. "Brotherhood is an element in the marijuana ritual, as is the notion of sharing something treasured and esteemed" (Goode, 1969:55). Finally, the mind-expanding subculture was, at least in its inception, a counter-culture whose values challenged traditional beliefs and values. Smoking and tripping were activities carried out by fringe or deviant groups such as artists, musicians, and "hip" or street people. Today the use of mind-expanding drugs has spread to many groups whose values are not particularly radical or deviant— teeny boppers, members of college fraternities and sororities, middle-class suburbanites, and captains of industry.

Although drug use has become more prevalent and is not necessarily indicative of membership in the counter-culture, there is reason to believe that drug experience is generally still associated with adherence to the hang-loose ethic (see Chapter 4). Suchman (1968) found that drug-using college students were more likely than other students to be antagonistic toward the educational system, attend "happenings" and political protests, and see themselves as cynical, apathetic, rebellious, and "hippie."

From this discussion it is clear that there is considerable diversity among persons who use mind-expanding drugs. It would be a mistake to equate a person who has tried marijuana once with one whose whole life revolves around drugs. This is like equating the occasional drinker with the alcoholic (Keniston, 1968–69:99). Of the 24 million persons who have ever tried marijuana only about a third are currently using the drug. The majority of persons who have used mind-expanding drugs are occasional users or "tasters." Keniston (1968–69:100) maintains that "if we eliminate the tasters from the ranks of student drug users, we are left with a contingent of probably less than five percent of the college population." While this figure may be somewhat low, there is no doubt that only a minority of the population are regular users of mind-expanding drugs. Among these regular users three distinctive subtypes can be distinguished: (1) recreational users, (2) "heads," and (3) "freaks."

Most regular users of mind-expanding drugs are recreational users (Carey, 1968:122). They use drugs on a regular and repetitive basis, but their lives do not revolve exclusively, or even predominantly, around drugs. "They see themselves as liberals or radicals politically, and most of them have participated in political action of one kind or another during the past year" (Carey, 1968:122). Members of this group are generally "secret deviants," moving freely between the world of drugs and straight society. Their use of drugs is limited mostly to grass; its use is planned and considered a special event that can take place at parties, concerts, or movies. "Marihuana particularly is felt to be a drug that not only produces a different state of mind but one which improves upon one's chances to enjoy certain kinds of activities" (Carey, 1968:123). Recreational users do not flaunt their drug use, fearing detection by straights (family and friends) and prosecution by the police. A person is considered "cool" if he can relate to both straight persons and drug users (Carey, 1968:133). This ambivalent or marginal position is characteristic of the recreational user, who tends to be critical of established society and yet participates in that society without totally repudiating it.

Some members of the drug subculture refer to themselves and are recognized by others as "heads." The head experiments with a variety of drugs. His most distinctive characteristic, however, is not the variety of drugs used or the quantity consumed but the meaning attached to use (Carey, 1968:145). The term "head" implies a concern with mental activity. The head uses drugs not as an end in themselves or as a pure source of pleasure but as a means of gaining greater self-awareness and attaining a new level of consciousness (Davis, 1968:160). The head has a more casual orientation to drug use, especially marijuana. Grass is smoked with little or no preparation, at different times and in many settings, except where there is a high probability of a bust (Carey, 1968:146). LSD is taken more seriously and with more preparation. ". . . many heads see LSD as an avenue for very profound, sometimes religious, experiences that should not be played with as one plays with marihuana" (Carey, 1968: 147). The ideology of the head seems to be based on existential philosophy, particularly that of Jean Paul Sartre:

Identity is constructed in situations where choices are made. Choices are directly related to "being." Heads speak of "having being" which points to the experience of being wherein one's choices lead to understanding of the true meaning of existence, to the truth of life (Carey, 1968:158).

Whereas heads are searching to reach a new level of spirituality and consciousness,[6] "freaks," on the other hand, strive to attain pleasure. ". . . the term 'freak' refers usually to someone in search of drug kicks as such, especially if his craving carries him to the point of drug abuse where his health, sanity and relations with intimates are jeopardized" (Davis, 1968:160). The entire world of the drug freak centers on the hedonistic pursuit of drugs (Goode, 1972:135). To "freak out" implies that one becomes ill, violent, and paranoid (Davis, 1968:160). While LSD is the drug typically associated with heads, methedrine ("speed") is the drug of freaks. Methedrine produces body stimulation and aggression rather than mind expansion. Heads experiment with many drugs, but they generally condemn the use of speed (Carey, 1968:146–147). The saying **"speed kills"** reflects the attitude of many heads toward speed (Davis, 1968:162). The freak seeks body stimulation; the head seeks personality development and mind expansion.

This discussion of types of drug users suggests that the social context within which drugs are used is most important in determining the meaning of the experience, both for participants and outsiders. The consequences of drug use are dependent on the meaning attached to the situation by the user and by others. There is a tremendous difference between a man who becomes addicted to morphine in the course of medical treatment and a "cool cat" who gets high on heroin, even though the two drugs are very similar pharmacologically. Societal response to drug use is also conditioned by the context of use. A person who takes amphetamines under medical care is "sick"; one who takes them for "kicks" is deviant or immoral. Negative response to LSD came only after it was perceived that the drug was being used to "turn people on" rather than for medical treatment as originally proposed.

DRUGS AND THE LAW

In American society today we are faced with the paradoxical situation in which some drugs are used extensively by members of the society and others are condemned. Our reaction cannot be attributed solely to the properties of the drugs, for the same drugs are approved in one setting and disapproved in another. Societal reaction to drug use is most intense when it is viewed as a threat to the traditional values embodied in the Protestant Ethic. Our Puritan heritage extols the virtues of hard work,

---

[6] For discussions of drugs and spiritualism and higher consciousness see Weil (1973) and Watts (1971).

thrift, and achievement. The use of drugs for pleasure or recreation challenges these traditional values (National Commission on Marihuana and Drug Abuse, 1972:96–102). We approve of drugs when used to treat an "illness" but not when used to attain hedonistic pleasure or to expand our minds. Some drugs, however, are consistent with the dominant American value system. Alcohol is widely used and approved, despite the fact that it is clearly more harmful to society than any illegal drug and, perhaps, than all drugs combined (Gay and Way, 1972:53). Although heroin is considered to be the most harmful drug by many Americans, its effects are quite mild compared to those of alcohol. Alcohol withdrawal, for example, can be fatal, but heroin withdrawal is much easier and never fatal (Weil, 1973:42). The long-term effects of alcohol on the body are also much more harmful (Weil, 1973:43; Gay and Way, 1972:53). In addition to the physical harm caused by alcohol, it is responsible for thousands of injuries and fatalities on the highway, and more persons, one out of three, are arrested for drunkenness than for any other single offense (President's Commission, 1967a:20). There is a strong association between alcohol and the commission of violent crimes (National Commission on Marihuana and Drug Abuse, 1973:157). ". . . alcohol 'fits' better into complex society because of its tension reduction properties and facilitation of interpersonal relationships. Drugs, on the other hand, tend to turn the person inward—back on the self. In a competitive, impersonal, urban society, turning in on the self (retreatism) and privatizing one's life are incomprehensible to many" (Dinitz et al., 1969:277).

Our attitude toward drugs has been extremely punitive. We have tried to control the problem by passing more laws and by stronger enforcement. The war on drugs, however, has not reduced the drug problem but instead has created a series of other problems. Much of the so-called drug problem can be traced to our official government policy toward drugs. Many of the stereotypes and misconceptions about drugs originated with the Bureau of Narcotics, which has perpetuated a drug-fiend mythology since 1930 (Lindesmith, 1965:243–246). The traditional attitude of the Bureau of Narcotics has been that addicts are dangerous criminals, who should be treated like other criminals. The view that addicts are sick and need medical treatment has been opposed by law-enforcement groups and other segments of society. It appears, as Durkheim suggested in his discussion of crime (see Chapter 6), that we are more interested in punishing the addict for flaunting societal norms than in curing his addiction or alleviating the drug problem. Alexander Trocchi, an ex-addict and writer, has noted how the drug addict becomes an easy scapegoat:

It's a nice tangible cause for juvenile delinquency. And it lets a lot of people out because they're alcoholics. There's an available pool of wasted-looking bastards to stand trial as the corrupters of their children. It provides the police with something to do, and as junkies and potheads are relatively easy to apprehend because they have to take so many chances to get hold of their drugs, a heroic police can make spectacular arrests, lawyers can do a brisk business, judges can make speeches, the big peddler can make a fortune, the tabloids can sell millions of copies. John Citizen can sit back feeling exonerated and watch evil get its deserts . . . (quoted in Lindesmith, 1965:268).

Everyone except the addict, profits from our punitive laws. The police and other law-enforcement agencies can request more funds in order to attack the drug problem. Politicians can wage a war on drugs at the same time that organized crime reaps many profits from the illicit drug market. According to Gus Tyler, Puritanism in our society produces:

a whole range of illegal commodities and services, for which there is a widespread demand. Into the gap between what people want and what people can legally get leaps the underworld as purveyor and pimp. . . . Puritanism gives the underworld a monopoly on a market with an almost insatiable demand. . . . (Tyler, 1962:333).

Addicts are placed in a position in which they cannot obtain drugs under medical supervision as part of a treatment program and must turn to criminal activities in order to pay for expensive illicit drugs. There has been considerable opposition to proposals that seek to reform our system. One proposal is that we adopt a program similar to the British system under which addicts would be registered and receive drugs at a nominal cost as part of a program of withdrawal (Lindesmith, 1965:270–302). Under such a program addiction would no longer be concentrated among the disadvantaged in society but instead would cut across various groups (Schur, 1964). In short, the addict subculture, now composed of the poor, the young, blacks, and men, would disappear. ". . . most observers agree that the current British system is functioning reasonably well. The relatively small population of addicts has apparently not increased over the past two years" (BNDD, 1972:33; Goode, 1972:216). Even if a medical program failed to reduce the number of addicts, it would eliminate other problems associated with addiction. Addicts would no longer have to commit property crimes in order to support an expensive habit. Many would be able to pursue regular jobs and to lead a more normal family life (Schur, 1964:73–74). Since there would be less motivation for the addict to sell drugs and turn someone else on (Schur, 1964:75–77), the police and the Bureau of Narcotics could concentrate on the more limited illegal drug trade.

Mind-expanding drugs and marijuana present a different problem. Not only are these the drugs of the more affluent, but they can be obtained with relative ease and at a modest cost. In the case of marijuana, tolerance does not develop, and the user does not have to increase his use of the drug in order to get the same high. In fact, there appears to be a "reverse tolerance"; that is, the experienced smoker can get high on a smaller dosage or even on a placebo (NIMH, 1972:16). Mind-expanding drugs do not generally produce dependence, and one can abstain without incurring physical discomfort. These factors make the mind-expanding drug traffic less lucrative than the heroin traffic.

Recently there has been considerable controversy over the legalization of marijuana. Many persons, but particularly the young and educated, argue that marijuana is a relatively innocuous drug that is much less harmful than other legalized drugs. Others, especially law-enforcement agencies, view it as an evil weed that is harmful to one's physical and mental health, leads to crime, increases permissiveness, and decays the moral fiber of the community. Marijuana and mind-expanding drugs can be termed "moral" drugs in that opposition to them seems to be grounded in the belief that they alter a person's level of consciousness. Opposition to marijuana is based on a moral position and emotional judgments rather than scientific evidence. Many persons, including some prominent politicians, have taken the position that they will oppose legalization of marijuana regardless of the findings of commission reports and other studies. On one level this fear seems irrational but on another it is not, since the drug is viewed as a threat to the dominant value system and to traditional morality. Marijuana smoking has been linked to an unconventional life style that challenges cherished American beliefs. Marijuana smokers are viewed as long-haired hippy radicals who seek to corrupt the youth of America and to undermine the American way of life. Alarm over the increased use of "pot" is due more to a fear of this life style or counter-culture than to concern over negative physiological effects of smoking. It is precisely because the drug subculture retreats or escapes from the dominant society that it is regarded as being most threatening to that society.

Concern with the drug problem has led some observers to the erroneous conclusion that widespread drug use is a condition peculiar to contemporary American society. Not only have drugs been a common feature of most cultures, but use has frequently been approved and regulated by society. Many Amazonian Indian societies use hallucinogenic drugs such as DMT without the attendant problems found in our society (Weil, 1973: 100). Drugs are not taken to rebel against elders, to drop out of society, or to injure oneself, but for mind expansion and to attain altered states of consciousness (Weil, 1973:100–101). Since these drugs are similar to the mind-expanding drugs in our own culture, their use in a socially approved setting destroys the "chemicalistic fallacy," which holds that the negative effects of drugs are attributable to their pharmacological properties (Goode, 1972:198). Andrew Weil (1973:10–11), for example, believes that our present way of thinking about drugs is the greatest obstacle to resolving the drug problem. While our society condemns attempts to alter consciousness as dangerous and unnatural, Weil postulates that the "drive to experience periodic episodes of nonordinary consciousness" is universal (1973:13). Drugs have been used by all human societies to alter consciousness (Weil, 1973:17). Even our society approves the use of certain drugs, to be used by certain persons, in certain settings. Drugs are potentially a means of attaining states of mind expansion and higher consciousness, although they are not the only, nor necessarily the most desirable, manner of attaining these states. Thus drugs are not inherently harmful or undesirable. Whether drugs are a detriment or benefit to humanity is ultimately dependent on societal definition and response.

REFERENCES

Anslinger, Harry J., and Will Oursler
1961 The Murderers. New York: Farrar, Straus & Giroux.
Associated Press
1972 "Repeal of Jail Terms for Smoking Pot Urged." Grand Forks Herald, Grand Forks, N.D. (March 22):1.
Becker, Howard S.
1966 Outsiders. New York: Free Press.
Blum, Richard H.
1967a "Mind-Altering Drugs and Dangerous Behavior: Dangerous Drugs." Pp. 21–39 in The President's Commission on Law Enforcement and Administration of Justice (1967b) Appendix A-1.
1967b "Mind-Altering Drugs and Dangerous Behavior: Narcotics." Pp. 40–63 in The President's Commission on Law Enforcement and Administration of Justice (1967b) Appendix A-2.
Bureau of Narcotics
1967 Traffic in Opium and Other Dangerous Drugs. U.S. Treasury Department. Washington, D.C.: GPO.
Bureau of Narcotics and Dangerous Drugs (BNDD)
1969 LSD-25: A Factual Account. U.S. Department of Justice. Washington, D.C.: GPO.
1971 Drug Usage and Arrest Charges. U.S. Department of Justice, Drug Control Division. Washington, D.C.: GPO.
1972 Alternative Approaches to Opiate Addiction Control: Costs, Benefits and Potential. U.S. Department of Justice, Drug Control Division. Washington, D.C.: GPO.
Carey, James T.
1968 The College Drug Scene. Englewood Cliffs, N.J.: Prentice-Hall.
Clausen, John A.
1971 "Drug Use." Pp. 185–226 in Robert K. Merton and Robert Nisbet (eds.), Contemporary Social Problems. Third ed. New York: Harcourt.
Cohen, Maimon M., Michelle J. Marinello, and Nathan Back
1967 Chromosomal Damage in Human Leukocytes Induced by Lysergic Acid Diethylamide." Science 155 (March 17):1417–1419.
Cloward, Richard A., and Lloyd E. Ohlin
1960 Delinquency and Opportunity: A Theory of Delinquent Gangs. New York: Free Press.
Davis, Fred (with Laura Munoz)
1968 "Heads and Freaks: Patterns and Meanings of Drug Use Among Hippies." Journal of Health and Social Behavior 9 (June):156–164.

Dihotsky, Norman I., William D. Loughman, Robert E. Mogar, and Wendell R. Lipscomb
1971 "LSD and Genetic Damage." Science 172 (April 30):431–440.

Dinitz, Simon, Russell R. Dynes, and Alfred C. Clarke
1969 Deviance. New York: Oxford University Press.

Drug Enforcement Administration (DEA)
1973a "Drug Abuse." Fact Sheets. U.S. Department of Justice. Washington, D.C.: GPO, pp. 15–16.
1973b "Drug Abuse Warning Network" (Dawn I Analysis). U.S. Department of Justice, Special Programs Division. Washington, D.C.: GPO.

Finestone, Harold
1964 "Cats, Kicks, and Color." Pp. 281–297 in Howard S. Becker (ed.), The Other Side. New York: Free Press.

Gallup, George
1972 "Use of LSD, Other Hallucinogens Continues to Grow." Grand Forks Herald, Grand Forks, N.D., (February 10):10.

Gay, Anne C., and George R. Gay
1972 "Evolution of a Drug Culture in a Decade of Mendacity." Pp. 13–31 in Smith and Gay.

Gay, George R., and E. Leong Way
1972 "Pharmacology of the Opiate Narcotics." Pp. 45–58 in Smith and Gay.

Geller, Allen, and Maxwell Boas
1971 The Drug Beat. New York: McGraw-Hill.

Ginsberg, Allen
1966 "The Great Marijuana Hoax." The Atlantic Monthly (November): 104, 107–112.

Goode, Erich
1969 "Multiple Drug Use Among Marijuana Smokers." Social Problems 17 (Summer):48–64.
1972 Drugs in American Society. New York: Knopf.

Keniston, Kenneth
1968–69 "Heads and Seekers: Drugs on Campus, Counter-Cultures and American Society." The American Scholar 38 (Winter):97–112.

Kramer, John C.
1972 "A Brief History of Heroin Addiction in America." Pp. 32–44 in Smith and Gay.

Lindesmith, Alfred R.
1965 The Addict and the Law. New York: Vintage Books.

McGrath, John H., and Frank R. Scarpitti
1970 Youth and Drugs: Perspectives on a Social Problem. Glenview, Ill.: Scott, Foresman.

National Commission on Marihuana and Drug Abuse
1972 Marihuana: A Signal of Misunderstanding. First Report. Washington, D.C.: GPO.
1973 Drug Use in America: Problem in Perspective. Second Report. Washington, D.C.: GPO.

National Institute of Mental Health (NIMH)
1971 Marihuana and Health. A Report to the Congress from the Secretary of Health, Education, and Welfare. Washington, D.C.: GPO.

1972 Marihuana and Health. Second Annual Report to Congress from the Secretary of Health, Education, and Welfare. Washington, D.C.: GPO.

O'Donnell, John A.
1966 "Narcotic Addiction and Crime." Social Problems 13 (Spring): 374–385.

President's Commission on Law Enforcement and Administration of Justice
1967a The Challenge of Crime in a Free Society. Washington, D.C.: GPO.
1967b Task Force Report: Narcotics and Drug Abuse. Washington, D.C.: GPO.

Roebuck, Julian B.
1962 "The Negro Drug Addict as an Offender Type." Journal of Criminal Law, Criminology, and Police Science 53 (March):36–43.

Schur, Edwin M.
1964 "Drug Addiction Under British Policy." Pp. 67–83 in Howard S. Becker (ed.), The Other Side. New York: Free Press.

Smith, David E., and George R. Gay
1972 "It's So Good Don't Even Try It Once": Heroin in Perspective. Englewood Cliffs, N.J.: Prentice-Hall.

Smith, David E., and Donald R. Wesson
1973 Uppers and Downers. Englewood Cliffs, N.J.: Prentice-Hall.

Suchman, Edward A.
1968 "The 'Hang-Loose' Ethic and the Spirit of Drug Use." Journal of Health and Social Behavior 9 (June):146–155.

Tyler, Gus
1962 "The Roots of Organized Crime." Crime and Delinquency 8 (October): 325–338.

Watts, W. David, Jr.
1971 The Psychedelic Experience. Beverly Hills, Calif.: Sage Publications.

Weil, Andrew
1973 The Natural Mind. Boston: Houghton Mifflin.

Weil, Andrew T., Norman E. Zinberg, and Judith M. Nelsen
1968 "Clinical and Psychological Effects of Marihuana in Man." Science 162 (December 13):1234–1242.

Winick, Charles
1961 "Physician Narcotic Addicts." Social Problems 9 (Fall):174–186.

INTRODUCTION TO THE READINGS

The first reading exemplifies what has been for many years the position of the Bureau of Narcotics on marijuana. Harry Anslinger, as head of the Bureau from 1930 to 1962, did much to perpetuate many myths about marijuana and its effects. During the early thirties he used his position to protect the public from this "evil weed":

As the marijuana situation grew worse, I knew action had to be taken to get proper control legislation passed. By 1937, under my direction, the Bureau launched two important steps: First, a legislative plan to seek from Congress a new law that would place marijuana and its distribution directly under federal control. Second, on radio and at major forums, . . . I told the story of this evil weed of the fields and river beds and roadsides. I wrote articles for magazines; our agents gave hundreds of lectures to parents, educators, social and civil leaders. In network broadcasts I reported on the growing list of crimes, including murder and rape (Anslinger and Oursler, 1961:38).

The uncorroborated testimony of Anslinger and other law-enforcement officials led in 1937 to passage of the Marijuana Tax Act. In this selection Anslinger gives the "facts" on marijuana, showing how it increases aggression and causes many heinous crimes. Marijuana, according to Anslinger, is ultimately an "assassin of youth."

The second selection is science fiction. In "What to Do Until the Analyst Comes" Frederik Pohl presents a humorous but fascinating analysis of societal reactions to mind-altering substances. Although control mechanisms are not discussed directly in this fictional account, one cannot help but wonder about societal reaction to Cheery-Gum. Would societal response parallel the current response to marijuana and LSD? Would attempts be made to prove that the substance is harmful or that it leads to crime? Is it likely that legislation would be passed to make Cheery-Gum illegal?

Marijuana, assassin of youth

HARRY J. ANSLINGER

The sprawled body of a young girl lay crushed on the sidewalk the other day after a plunge from the fifth story of a Chicago apartment house. Everyone called it suicide, but actually it was murder. The killer was a narcotic known to America as marijuana, and to history as hashish. It is a narcotic used in the form of cigarettes, comparatively new to the United States and as dangerous as a coiled rattlesnake.

How many murders, suicides, robberies, criminal assaults, holdups, burglaries, and deeds of maniacal insanity it causes each year, especially among the young, can be only conjectured. The sweeping march of its addiction has been so insidious that, in numerous communities, it thrives almost unmolested, largely because of official ignorance of its effects.

Here indeed is the unknown quantity among narcotics. No one can predict its effect. No one knows, when he places a marijuana cigarette to his lips, whether he will become a philosopher, a joyous reveler in a musical heaven, a mad insensate, a calm philosopher, or a murderer.

That youth has been selected by the peddlers of this poison as an especially fertile field makes it a problem of serious concern to every man and woman in America.

There was the young girl, for instance, who leaped to her death. Her story is typical. Some time before, this girl, like others of her age who attend our high schools, had heard the whispering of a secret which has gone the rounds of American youth. It promised a new thrill, the smoking of a type of cigarette which contained a "real kick." According to the whispers, this cigarete could accomplish wonderful reactions and with no harmful aftereffects. So the adventurous girl and a group of her friends gathered in an apartment, thrilled with the idea of doing "something different" in which there was "no harm." Then a friend produced a few cigarettes of the loosely rolled "homemade" type. They were passed from one to another of the young people, each taking a few puffs.

The results were weird. Some of the party went into paroxysms of laughter; every remark, no matter how silly, seemed excruciatingly funny. Others of mediocre musical ability became almost expert; the piano dinned constantly. Still others found themselves discussing weighty problems of youth with remarkable clarity. As one youngster expressed it, he "could see through stone walls." The girl danced without fatigue, and the night of unexplainable exhilaration seemed to stretch out as though it were a year long. Time, conscience, or consequences became too trivial for consideration.

Other parties followed, in which inhibitions vanished, conventional barriers departed, all at the command of this strange cigarette with its ropy, resinous odor. Finally there came a gathering at a time when the girl was behind in her studies and greatly worried. With every puff of the smoke the feeling of despondency lessened.

From Harry J. Anslinger (with Courtney Ryley Cooper), "Marijuana, Assassin of Youth," American Magazine, Vol. 124, July 1937, pp. 18–19, 150–152. Reprinted with permission of the author.

Everything was going to be all right—at last. The girl was "floating" now, a term given to marijuana intoxication. Suddenly, in the midst of laughter and dancing, she thought of her school problems. Instantly they were solved. Without hesitancy she walked to a window and leaped to her death. Thus can marijuana "solve" one's difficulties.

The cigarettes may have been sold by a hot tamale vendor or by a street peddler, or in a dance hall or over a lunch counter, or even from sources much nearer to the customer. The police of a Midwestern city recently accused a school janitor of having conspired with four other men, not only to peddle cigarettes to children, but even to furnish apartments where smoking parties might be held.

A Chicago mother, watching her daughter die as an indirect result of marijuana addiction, told officers that at least fifty of the girl's young friends were slaves to the narcotic. This means fifty unpredictables. They may cease its use; that is not so difficult as with some narcotics. They may continue addiction until they deteriorate mentally and become insane. Or they may turn to violent forms of crime, to suicide or to murder. Marijuana gives few warnings of what it intends to do to the human brain.

The menace of marijuana addiction is comparatively new to America. In 1931, the marijuana file of the United States Narcotic Bureau was less than two inches thick, while today the reports crowd many large cabinets. Marijuana is a weed of the Indian hemp family, known in Asia as *Cannabis Indica* and in America as *Cannabis Sativa*. Almost everyone who has spent much time in rural communities has seen it, for it is cultivated in practically every state. Growing plants by the thousands were destroyed by law-enforcement officers last year in Texas, New York, New Jersey, Mississippi, Michigan, Maryland, Louisiana, Illinois, and the attack on the weed is only beginning.

It was an unprovoked crime some years ago which brought the first realization that the age-old drug had gained a foothold in America. An entire family was murdered by a youthful addict in Florida. When officers arrived at the home they found the youth staggering about in a human slaughterhouse. With an ax he had killed his father, his mother, two brothers, and a sister. He seemed to be in a daze.

"I've had a terrible dream," he said. "People tried to hack off my arms!"

"Who were they?" an officer asked.

"I don't know. Maybe one was my uncle. They slashed me with knives and I saw blood dripping from an ax."

He had no recollection of having committed the multiple crime. The officers knew him ordinarily as a sane, rather quiet young man; now he was pitifully crazed. They sought the reason. The boy said he had been in the habit of smoking something which youthful friends called "muggles," a childish name for marijuana.

Since that tragedy there has been a race between the spread of marijuana and its suppression. Unhappily, so far, marijuana has won by many lengths. The years 1935 and 1936 saw its most rapid growth in traffic. But at least we now know what we are facing. We know its history, its effects, and its potential victims. Perhaps with the spread of this knowledge the public may be aroused sufficiently to conquer the menace. Every parent owes it to his children to tell them of the terrible effects of marijuana to offset the enticing "private information" which these youths may have received. There must be constant enforcement and equally constant education against this enemy, which has a record of murder and terror running through the centuries.

The weed was known to the ancient Greeks and it is mentioned in Homer's *Odyssey*. Homer wrote that it made men forget their homes and turned them into swine. Ancient Egyptians used it. In the year 1090, there was founded in Persia the religious and military order of the Assassins, whose history is one of cruelty, barbarity, and murder, and for good reason. The members were confirmed users of hashish, or marijuana, and it is from the Arabic "*hashshashin*" that we have the English word "assassin." Even the term "running amok" relates to the drug, for the expression has been used to describe natives of the Malay Peninsula who, under the influence of hashish, engage in violent and bloody deeds.

Marijuana was introduced into the United States from Mexico, and swept across America with incredible speed.

It began with the whispering of vendors in the Southwest that marijuana would perform miracles for those who smoked it, giving them a feeling of physical strength and mental power, stimulation of the imagination, the ability to be "the life of the party." The peddlers preached also of the weed's capabilities as a "love potion." Youth, always adventurous, began to look into these claims and found some of them true, not knowing that this was only half the story. They were not told that addicts may often develop a delirious rage during which they are temporarily and violently insane; that this insanity may take the form of a desire for self-destruction or a persecution complex to be satisfied only by the commission of some heinous crime.

It would be well for law-enforcement officers everywhere to search for marijuana behind cases of criminal and sex assault. During the last year a young male addict was hanged in Baltimore for criminal assault on a ten-year-old girl. His defense was that he was temporarily insane from smoking marijuana. In Alamosa, Colo., a degenerate brutally attacked a young girl while under the influence of the drug. In Chicago, two marijuana-smoking boys murdered a policeman.

In at least two dozen other comparatively recent cases of murder or degenerate sex attacks, many of them committed by youths, marijuana proved to be a contributing cause. Perhaps you remember the young desperado in Michigan who, a few months ago, caused a reign of terror by his career of burglaries and holdups, finally to be sent to prison for life after kidnapping a Michigan state policeman, killing him, then handcuffing him to the post of a rural mailbox. This young bandit was a marijuana fiend.

A sixteen-year-old boy was arrested in California for burglary. Under the influence of marijuana he had stolen a revolver and was on the way to stage a holdup when apprehended. Then there was the nineteen-year-old addict in Columbus, Ohio, who, when police responded to a disturbance complaint, opened fire upon an officer, wounding him three times, and was himself killed by the returning fire of the police. In Ohio a gang of seven young men, all less than twenty years old, had been caught after a series of 38 holdups. An officer asked them where they got their incentive.

"We only work when we're high on 'tea,'" one explained.

"On what?"

"On tea. Oh, there are lots of names for it. Some people call it 'mu' or 'muggles' or 'Mary Weaver' or 'moocah' or 'weed' or 'reefers'—there's a million names for it."

"All of which mean marijuana?"

"Sure. Us kids got on to it in high school three or four years ago; there must have been twenty-five or thirty of us who started smoking it. The stuff was cheaper then; you could buy a whole tobacco tin of it for fifty cents. Now these peddlers will charge you all they can get, depending on how shaky you are. Usually though, it's two cigarettes for a quarter."

This boy's casual story of procurement of the drug was typical of conditions in many cities in America. He told of buying the cigarettes in dance halls, from the owners of small hamburger joints, from peddlers who appeared near high schools at dismissal time. Then there were the "booth joints" or Bar-B-Q stands, where one might obtain a cigarette and a sandwich for a quarter, and there were the shabby apartments of women who provided not only the cigarettes but rooms in which girls and boys might smoke them.

"But after you get the habit," the boy added, "you don't bother much about finding a place to smoke. I've seen as many as three or four high-school kids jam into a telephone booth and take a few drags."

The officer questioned him about the gang's crimes: "Remember that filling-station attendant you robbed—how you threatened to beat his brains out?"

The youth thought hard. "I've got a sort of hazy recollection," he answered. "I'm not trying to say I wasn't there, you understand. The trouble is, with all my gang, we can't remember exactly what we've done or said. When you get to 'floating,' it's hard to keep track of things."

From the other youthful members of the gang the officer could get little information. They confessed the robberies as one would vaguely remember bad dreams.

"If I had killed somebody on one of those jobs, I'd never have known it," explained one youth. "Sometimes it was over before I realized that I'd even been out of my room."

Therein lies much of the cruelty of marijuana, especially in its attack upon youth. The young, immature brain is a thing of impulses, upon which the "unknown quantity" of the drug acts as an almost overpowering stimulant. There are numerous cases on record like that of an Atlanta boy who robbed his father's safe of thousands of dollars in jewelry and cash. Of high-school age, this boy apparently had been headed for an honest, successful career. Gradually, however, his father noticed a change in him. Spells of shakiness and nervousness would be succeeded by periods when the boy would assume a grandiose manner and engage in excessive, senseless laughter, extravagant conversation, and wildly impulsive actions. When these actions finally resulted in robbery the father went at his son's problem in earnest—and found the cause of it a marijuana peddler who catered to school children. The peddler was arrested.

It is this useless destruction of youth which is so heartbreaking to all of us who labor in the field of narcotic suppression. No one can predict what may happen after the smoking of the weed. I am reminded of a Los Angeles case in which a boy of seventeen killed a policeman. They had been great friends. Patrolling his beat, the officer often stopped to talk to the young fellow, to advise him. But one day the boy surged toward the patrolman with a gun in his hand; there was a blaze of yellowish flame, and the officer fell dead.

"Why did you kill him?" the youth was asked.

"I don't know," he sobbed. "He was good to me. I was high on reefers. Suddenly I decided to shoot him."

In a small Ohio town, a few months ago, a fifteen-year-old boy was found wandering the streets, mentally deranged by marijuana. Officers learned that he had obtained the dope at a garage.

"Are any other school kids getting cigarettes there?" he was asked.

"Sure. I know fifteen or twenty, maybe more. I'm only counting my friends."

The garage was raided. Three men were arrested and 18 pounds of marijuana seized.

"We'd been figuring on quitting the racket," one of the dopesters told the arresting officer. "These kids had us scared. After we'd gotten 'em on the weed, it looked like easy money for a while. Then they kept wanting more and more of it, and if we didn't have it for 'em, they'd get tough. Along toward the last, we were scared that one of 'em would get high and kill us all. There wasn't any fun in it."

Not long ago a fifteen-year-old girl ran away from her home in Muskegon, Mich., to be arrested later in company with five young men in a Detroit marijuana den. A man and his wife ran the place. How many children had smoked there will never be known. There were 60 cigarettes on hand, enough fodder for 60 murders.

A newspaper in St. Louis reported after an investigation this year that it had discovered marijuana "dens," all frequented by children of high-school age. The same sort of story came from Missouri, Ohio, Louisiana, Colorado—in fact, from coast to coast.

In Birmingham, Ala., a hot-tamale salesman had pushed his cart about town for five years, and for a large part of that time he had been peddling marijuana cigarettes to students of a downtown high school. His stock of the weed, he said, came from Texas and consisted, when he was captured, of enough marijuana to manufacture hundreds of cigarettes.

In New Orleans, of 437 persons of varying ages arrested for a wide range of crimes, 125 were addicts. Of 37 murderers, 17 used marijuana, and of 193 convicted thieves, 34 were "on the weed."

One of the first places in which marijuana found a ready welcome was in a closely congested section of New York. Among those who first introduced it there were musicians, who had brought the habit northward with the surge of "hot" music demanding players of exceptional ability, especially in improvisation. Along the Mexican border and in seaport cities it had been known for some time that the musician who desired to get the "hottest" effects from his playing often turned to marijuana for aid.

One reason was that marijuana has a strangely exhilarating effect upon the musical sensibilities (Indian hemp has long been used as a component of "singing seed" for canary birds). Another reason was that strange quality of marijuana which makes a rubber band out of time, stretching it to unbelievable lengths. The musician who uses "reefers" finds that the musical beat seemingly comes to him quite slowly, thus allowing him to interpolate any number of improvised notes with comparative ease. While under the influence of marijuana, he does not realize that he is tapping the keys with a furious speed impossible for one in a normal state of mind; marijuana has stretched out the time of the music until a dozen notes may be crowded into the space normally occupied by one. Or, to quote a young musician arrested by Kansas City officers as a "muggles smoker":

"Of course I use it—I've got to. I can't play any more without it, and I know a hundred other musicians who are in the same fix. You see, when I'm 'floating,' I *own* my saxophone. I mean I can do anything with it. The notes seem to dance out of it—no effort at all. I don't have to worry about reading the music—I'm music-crazy. Where do I get the stuff? In almost any low-class dance hall or night spot in the United States."

Soon a song was written about the drug. Perhaps you remember:

Have you seen
That funny reefer man?
He says he swam to China;
Any time he takes a notion,
He can walk across the ocean.

It sounded funny. Dancing girls and boys pondered about "reefers" and learned through the whispers of other boys and girls that these cigarettes could make one accomplish the impossible. Sadly enough, they can—in the imagination. The boy who plans a holdup, the youth who seizes a gun and prepares for a murder, the girl who decides suddenly to elope with a boy she did not even know a few hours ago, does so with the confident belief that this is a thoroughly logical action without the slightest possibility of disastrous consequences. Command a person "high" on "mu" or "muggles" or "Mary Jane" to crawl on the floor and bark like a dog, and he will do it without a thought of the idiocy of the action. Everything, no matter how insane, becomes plausible. The underworld calls marijuana "that stuff that makes you able to jump off the tops of skyscrapers."

Reports from various sections of the country indicate that the control and sale of marijuana has not yet passed into the hands of the big gangster syndicates. The supply is so vast and grows in so many places that gangsters perhaps have found it difficult to dominate the source. A big, hardy weed, with serrated, swordlike leaves topped by bunchy small blooms supported upon a thick, stringy stalk, marijuana has been discovered in almost every state. New York police uprooted hundreds of plants growing in a vacant lot in Brooklyn. In New York State alone last year 200 tons of the growing weed were destroyed. Acres of it have been found in various communities. Patches have been revealed in back yards, behind signboards, in gardens. In many places in the West it grows wild. Wandering dopesters gather the tops from along the right of way of railroads.

An evidence of how large the traffic may be came to light last year near La Fitte, La. Neighbors of an Italian family had become amazed by wild stories told by the children of the family. They, it seemed, had suddenly become millionaires. They talked of owning inconceivable amounts of money, of automobiles they did not possess, of living in a palatial home. At last their absurd lies were reported to the police, who discovered that their parents were allowing them to smoke something that came from the tops of tall plants which their father grew on his farm. There was a raid, in which more than 500,000 marijuana plants were destroyed. This discovery led next day to another raid on a farm at Bourg, La. Here a crop of some 2000 plants was found to be growing between rows of vegetables. The eight persons arrested confessed that their main source of income from this crop was in sales to boys and girls of high-school age.

With possibilities for such tremendous crops, grown secretly, gangdom has been hampered in its efforts to corner the profits of what has now become an enormous business. It is to be hoped that the menace of marijuana can be wiped out before it falls into the vicious protectorate of powerful members of the underworld.

But to crush this traffic we must first squarely face the facts. Unfortunately, while every state except one has laws to cope with the traffic, the powerful right arm which could support these states has been all but impotent. I refer to the United States government. There has been no national law against the growing, sale, or possession of marijuana.

As this is written a bill to give the federal government control over marijuana has been introduced in Congress by Representative Robert L. Doughton of North Carolina, Chairman of the House Ways and Means Committee. It has the backing of Secretary of the Treasury Morgenthau, who has under his supervision the various agencies of the United States Treasury Department, including the Bureau of Narcotics, through which Uncle Sam fights the dope evil. It is a revenue bill, modeled after other narcotic laws which make use of the taxing power to bring about regulation and control.

The passage of such a law, however, should not be the signal for the public to lean back, fold its hands, and decide that all danger is over. America now faces a condition in which a new, although ancient, narcotic has come to live next door to us, a narcotic that does not have to be smuggled into the country. This means a job of unceasing watchfulness by every police department and by every public-spirited civic organization. It calls for campaigns of education in every school, so that children will not be deceived by the wiles of peddlers, but will know of the insanity, the disgrace, the horror which marijuana can bring to its victim. And, above all, every citizen should keep constantly before him the real picture of the "reefer man"—not some funny fellow who, should he take the notion, could walk across the ocean, but—

In Los Angeles, Calif., a youth was walking along a downtown street after inhaling a marijuana cigarette. For many addicts, merely a portion of a "reefer" is enough to induce intoxication. Suddenly, for no reason, he decided that someone had threatened to kill him and that his life at that very moment was in danger. Wildly he looked about him. The only person in sight was an aged bootblack. Drug-crazed nerve centers conjured the innocent old shoe-shiner into a destroying monster. Mad with fright, the addict hurried. to his room and got a gun. He killed the old man, and then, later, babbled his grief over what had been wanton, uncontrolled murder.

"I thought someone was after me," he said. "That's the only reason I did it. I had never seen the old fellow before. Something just told me to kill him!"

That's marijuana.

What to do until the analyst comes

FREDERIK POHL

I just sent my secretary out for a container of coffee and she brought me back a lemon Coke.

I can't even really blame her. Who in all the world do I have to blame, except myself? Hazel was a good secretary to me for fifteen years, fine at typing, terrific at brushing off people I didn't want to see, and the queen of them all at pumping office gossip out of the ladies' lounge. She's a little fuzzy-brained most of the time now, sure. But after all!

I can say this for myself, I didn't exactly know what I was getting into. No doubt you remember the ——— Well, let me start that sentence over again, because naturally there is a certain doubt. Perhaps, let's say, *perhaps* you remember the two doctors and their headline report about cigarettes and lung cancer. It hit us pretty hard at VandenBlumer & Silk, because we've been eating off the Mason-Dixon Tobacco account for twenty years. Just figure what our fifteen percent amounted to on better than ten million dollars net billing a year, and you'll see that for yourself. What happened first was all to the good, because naturally the first thing that the client did was scream and reach for his checkbook and pour another couple million dollars into special promotions to counteract the bad press, but that couldn't last. And we knew it. V.B. & S. is noted in the trade as an advertising agency that takes the long view; we saw at once that if the client was in danger, no temporary spurt of advertising was going to pull him out of it, and it was time for us to climb up on top of the old mountain and take a good long look at the countryside ahead.

The Chief called a special Plans meeting that morning and laid it on the line for us. "There goes the old fire bell, boys," he said, "and it's up to us to put the fire out. I'm listening, so start talking."

Baggott cleared his throat and said glumly, "It may only be the paper, Chief. Maybe if they make them without paper . . ." He's the a.e. for Mason-Dixon, so you couldn't really blame him for taking the client's view.

The Chief twinkled: "If they make them without paper they aren't cigarettes any more, are they? Let's not wander off into side issues, boys. I'm still listening."

None of us wanted to wander off into side issues, so we all looked patronizingly at Baggott for a minute. Finally Ellen Silk held up her hand. "I don't want you to think," she said, "that just because Daddy left me a little stock I'm going to push my way into things, Mr. VandenBlumer, but— well, did you have in mind finding some, uh, angle to play on that would take the public's mind off the report?"

You have to admire the Chief. "Is that your recommendation, my dear?" he inquired fondly, bouncing the ball right back to her.

She said weakly, "*I* don't know. I'm confused."

"Naturally, my dear," he beamed. "So are we all. Let's see if Charley here can straighten us out a little. Eh, Charley?"

He was looking at me. I said at once, "I'm glad you asked me for an opinion, Chief. I've been doing a little thinking, and here's what I've come up with." I ticked off the points on my fingers. "One, tobacco makes you cough. Two, liquor gives you a hangover. Three, reefers and the other stuff —well, let's just say they're against the law." I slapped the three fingers against the palm of my other hand. "So what's left for us, Chief? That's my question. Can we come up with something new, something different, something that, one, is not injurious to the health, two, does not give you a hangover, three, is not habit-forming and therefore against the law?"

Mr. VandenBlumer said approvingly, "That's good thinking, Charley. When you hear that fire bell, you really jump, boy."

Baggott's hand was up. He said, "Let me get this straight, Chief. Is it Charley's idea that we recommend to Mason-Dixon that they go out of the tobacco business and start making something else?"

The old man looked at him blandly for a moment. "Why should it be Mason-Dixon?" he asked softly, and left it at that while we all thought of the very good reasons why it *shouldn't* be Mason-Dixon. After all, loyalty to a client is one thing, but you've got an obligation to your own people too.

The old man let it sink in, then he turned back to me. "Well, Charley?" he asked. "We've heard you pinpoint what we need. Got any specific suggestions?"

They were all looking at me to see if I had anything concrete to offer.

Unfortunately, I had.

I just asked Hazel to get me the folder on Leslie Clary Cloud, and she came in with a copy of my memo putting him on the payroll two years back. "That's all there was in the file," she said dreamily, her jaw muscles moving

rhythmically. There wasn't any use arguing with her, so I handed her the container of lemon Coke and told her to ditch it and bring me back some *coffee*, C-O-F-F-E-E, coffee. I tried going through the files myself when she was gone, but *that* was a waste of time.

So I'll have to tell you about Leslie Clary Cloud from memory. He came in to the office without an appointment and why Hazel ever let him in to see me I'll never know. But she did. He told me right away, "I've been fired, Mr. McGory. Canned. After eleven years with the Wyoming Bureau of Standards as a senior chemist."

"That's too bad, Dr. Cloud," I said, shuffling the papers on my desk. "I'm afraid, though, that our organization doesn't ———"

"No, no," he said hastily. "I don't know anything about advertising. Organic chemistry's my field. I have a, well, a suggestion for a process that might interest you. You have the Mason-Dixon Tobacco account, don't you? Well, in my work for my doctorate I ———" He drifted off into a fog of long-chain molecules and short-chain molecules and pentose sugars and common garden herbs. It took me a little while, but I listened patiently and I began to see what he was driving at. There was, he was saying, a substance in a common plant which, by cauliflamming the whingdrop and di-tricolating the residual glom, or words something like that, you could convert into another substance which appeared to have many features in common with what is sometimes called hop, snow or joy-dust. In other words, dope.

I stared at him aghast. "Dr. Cloud," I demanded, "do you know what you're suggesting? If we added this stuff to our client's cigarettes we'd be flagrantly violating the law. That's the most unheard-of thing I ever heard of! Besides, we've already looked into this matter, and the cost estimates are ————"

"No, no!" he said again. "You don't understand, Mr. McGory. This isn't any of the drugs currently available, it's something new and different."

"Different?"

"Non-habit-forming, for instance."

"Non-habit-forming?"

"Totally. Chemically it is entirely unrelated to any narcotic in the pharmacopeia. Legally—well, I'm no lawyer, but I swear, Mr. McGory, this isn't covered by any regulation. No reason it should be. It doesn't hurt the user, it doesn't form a habit, it's cheap to manufacture, it ————"

"Hold it," I said, getting to my feet. "Don't go away—I want to catch the boss before he goes to lunch."

So I caught the boss, and he twinkled thoughtfully at me. No, he didn't want me to discuss it with Mason-Dixon just yet, and yes, it did seem to have some possibilities, and certainly, put this man on the payroll and see if he turns up with something.

So we did; and he did.

Auditing raised the roof when the vouchers began to come through, but I bucked them up to the Chief and he calmed them down. It took a lot of money, though, and it took nearly six months. But then Leslie Clary Cloud called up one morning and said, "Come on down, Mr. McGory. We're in."

The place we'd fixed up for him was on the lower East Side and it reeked of rotten vegetables. I made a mental note to double-check all our added-chlorophyll copy and climbed up the two flights of stairs to Cloud's private room. He was sitting at a lab bench, beaming at a row of test tubes in front of him.

"This is it?" I asked, glancing at the test tubes.

"This is it." He smiled dreamily at me and yawned. "Excuse me," he blinked amiably. "I've been sampling the little old product."

I looked him over very carefully. He had been sampling something or other, that was clear enough. But no whisky breath; no dilated pupils; no shakes; no nothing. He was relaxed and cheerful, and that was all you could say.

"Try a little old bit," he invited, gesturing at the test tubes.

Well, there are times when you have to pay your dues in the club. V.B. & S. had been mighty good to me, and if I had to swallow something unfamiliar to justify the confidence the Chief had in me, why I just had to go ahead and do it. Still, I hesitated for a moment.

"Aw," said Leslie Clary Cloud, "don't be scared. Look, I just had a shot but I'll take another one." He fumbled one of the test tubes out of the rack and, humming to himself, slopped a little of the colorless stuff into a beaker of some other colorless stuff—water, I suppose. He drank it down and smacked his lips. "Tastes awful," he observed cheerfully, "but we'll fix that. Whee!"

I looked him over again, and he looked back at me, giggling. "Too strong," he said happily. "Got it too strong. We'll fix that too." He rattled beakers and test tubes aimlessly while I took a deep breath and nerved myself up to it.

"All right," I said, and took the fresh beaker out of his hand. I swallowed it down almost in one gulp. It tasted terrible, just as he said, tasted like the lower floors had smelled, but that was all I noticed right away. Nothing happened for a moment except that Cloud looked at me thoughtfully and frowned.

"Say," he said, "I guess I should have diluted that."

I guess he should have. *Wham.*

But a couple of hours later I was all right again.

Cloud was plenty apologetic. "Still," he said consolingly, standing over me as I lay on the lab bench, "it proves one thing. You had a dose about the equivalent of ten thousand normal shots, and you have to admit it hasn't hurt you."

"I do?" I asked, and looked at the doctor. *He* swung his stethoscope by the earpieces and shrugged.

"Nothing organically wrong with you, Mr. McGory—not that I can find, anyway. Euphoria, yes. Temporary high pulse, yes. Delirium there for a little while, yes—though it was pretty mild. But I don't think you even have a headache now."

"I don't," I admitted. I swung my feet down and sat up, apprehensively. But no hammers started in my head. I had to confess it: I felt wonderful.

Well, between us we tinkered it into what Cloud decided would be a "normal" dosage—just enough to make you feel good—and he saturated some sort of powder and rolled it into pellets and clamped them in a press and came out with what looked as much like aspirins as anything else. "They'd probably work that way too," he said. "A psychogenic headache would melt away in five minutes with one of those."

"We'll bear that in mind," I said.

What with one thing and another, I couldn't get to the old man that day before he left, and the next day was the weekend and you *don't* disturb the Chief's weekends, and it was Monday evening before I could get him alone for long enough to give him the whole pitch. He was delighted.

"Dear, dear," he twinkled. "So much

out of so little. Why, they hardly look like anything at all."

"Try one, Chief," I suggested.

"Perhaps I will. You checked the legal angle?"

"On the quiet. It's absolutely clean."

He nodded and poked at the little pills with his finger. I scratched the back of my neck, trying to be politely inconspicuous, but the Chief doesn't miss much. He looked at me inquiringly.

"Hives," I explained, embarrassed. "I, uh, got an overdose the first time, like I said. I don't know much about these things, but what they told me at the clinic was I set up an allergy."

"Allergy?" Mr. VandenBlumer looked at me thoughtfully. "We don't want to spread allergies with this stuff, do we?"

"Oh, no danger of that, Chief. It's Cloud's fault, in a way; he handed me an undiluted dose of the stuff, and I drank it down. The clinic was very positive about that: Even twenty or thirty times the normal dose won't do you any harm."

"Um." He rolled one of the pills in his finger and thumb and sniffed it thoughtfully. "How long are you going to have your hives?"

"They'll go away. I just have to keep away from the stuff. I wouldn't have them now, but—well, I liked it so much I tried another shot yesterday." I coughed, and added, "It works out pretty well, though. You see the advantages, of course, Chief. I have to give it up, and I can swear that there's no craving, no shakes, no kick-off symptoms, no nothing. I, well, I wish I could enjoy it like anyone else, sure. But I'm here to testify that Cloud told the simple truth: It isn't habit-forming."

"Um," he said again; and that was the end of the discussion.

Oh, the Chief is a cagey man. He

gave me my orders: Keep my mouth shut about it. I have an idea that he was waiting to see what happened to my hives, and whether any craving would develop, and what the test series on animals and Cloud's Bowery-derelict volunteers would show. But even more, I think he was waiting until the time was exactly, climactically right.

Like at the Plans meeting, the day after the doctors' report and the panic at Mason-Dixon.

And that's how Cheery-Gum was born.

Hazel just came in with the cardboard container from the drug store, and I could tell by looking at it—no steam coming out from under the lid, beads of moisture clinging to the sides—that it wasn't the coffee I ordered. "Hey!" I yelled after her as she was dreamily waltzing through the door. "Come back here!"

"Sure 'nough, Massa," she said cheerfully, and two-stepped back. "S'matter?"

I took a grip on my temper. "Open that up," I ordered. "Take a look at what's in it."

She smiled at me and plopped the lid off the container. Half the contents spilled across my desk. "Oh, dear," said Hazel, "excuse me while I get a cloth."

"Never mind the cloth," I said, mopping at the mess with my handkerchief. "What's in there?"

She gazed wonderingly into the container for a moment then she said, "Oh, honestly, boss! I see what you mean. Those idiots in the drug store, they're gummed up higher than a kite, morning, noon and night. I always say, if you can't handle it, you shouldn't touch it during working hours. I'm sorry about this, boss. No lemon! How can they call it a lemon Coke when they forget the ———"

"Hazel," I said, "what I wanted was coffee. Coffee."

She looked at me. "You mean I got it wrong? Oh, I'm sorry, Mr. McGory. I'll go right down and get it now." She smiled repentantly and hummed her way toward the door. With her hand on the knob, she stopped and turned to look at me. "All the same, boss," she said, "that's a funny combination. Coffee and Coke. But I'll see what I can do."

And she was gone, to bring me heaven knows what incredible concoction. But what are you going to do?

No, that's no answer. I know it's what you would do. But it makes me break out in hives.

The first week we were delighted, the second week we were triumphant, the third week we were millionaires.

The sixth week I skulked along the sidewalks all the way across town and down, to see Leslie Clary Cloud. Even so I almost got it when a truckdriver dreamily piled into the glass front of a saloon a yard or two behind me.

When I saw Cloud sitting at his workbench, feet propped up, hands clasped behind his head, eyes half-closed, I could almost have kissed him. For his jaws were not moving. Alone in New York, except for me, he wasn't chewing Cheery-Gum.

"Thank heaven!" I said sincerely.

He blinked and smiled at me. "Mr. McGory," he said in a pleasant drawl. "Nice of you."

His manner disturbed me, and I looked more closely. "You're not—you're not gummed up, are you?"

He said gently, "Do I looked gummed up? I never chew the stuff."

"Good!" I unfolded the newspaper I had carried all the way from Madison Avenue and showed him the inside pages—the ones that were not a mere smear of ink. "See here, Cloud. Planes crashing into Radio City. Buses driving off the George Washington Bridge. Ships going aground at the Battery. We did it, Cloud, you and I!"

"Oh, I wouldn't get upset about it, old man," he said comfortably. "All local, isn't it?"

"Isn't that bad enough? And it isn't local—it can't be. It's just that there isn't any communication outside the city any more—outside of any city, I guess. The shipments of Cheery-Gum, that's all that ever gets delivered anywhere. Because that's all anybody cares about any more, and we did it, you and I!"

He said sympathetically, "That's too bad, McGory."

"Curse you!" I shrieked at him. "You said it wasn't a drug! You said it wasn't habit-forming! You said ———"

"Now, now," he said with gentle firmness. "Why not chew a stick yourself?"

"Because I can't! It gives me hives!"

"Oh, that's right." He looked self-reproachful. "Well," he said dreamily at last, "I guess that's about the size of it, McGory." He was staring at the ceiling again.

"*What* is?"

"What is what?"

"What's about the ——— Oh, the devil with it. Cloud, you got us into this, you have to get us out of it. There must be some way of curing this habit."

"But there isn't any habit to cure, McGory," he pointed out.

"But there is!"

"Tem-per," he said waggishly, and took a corked test tube out of his workbench. He drank it down, every drop, and tossed the tube in a wastebasket. "You see?" he demanded severely. "*I* don't chew Cheery-Gum."

So I appealed to a Higher Authority.

In the eighteenth century I would have gone to the Church, in the nineteenth, to the State. I went to an office fronting on Central Park where the name on the bronze plaque was *Theodor Yust, Analyst.*

It wasn't easy. I almost walked out on him when I saw that his jaws were chewing as rhythmically as his secretary's. But Cloud's concoction is not, as he kept saying, a drug, and though it makes you relax and makes you happy and, if you take enough of it, makes you drunk, it doesn't make you unfit to talk to. So I took a grip on my temper, the only bad temper left, and told him what I wanted.

He laughed at me—in the friendliest way. "Put a stop to Cheery-Gum? Mr. McGory!"

"But the plane crashes ———"

"No more suicides, Mr. McGory!"

"The train wreck ———"

"Not a murder or a mugging in the whole city in a month."

I said hopelessly, "But it's *wrong!*"

"Ah," he said in the tone of a discoverer, "now we come down to it. Why is it wrong, Mr. McGory?"

That was the second time I almost walked out. But I said "Let's get one thing straight: I don't want you digging into my problems. That's not why I'm here. Cheery-Gum *is* wrong, and I am *not* biased against it. You can take a detached view of collisions and sudden death if you want to, but what about slow death? All over the city, all over the country, people are lousing up their jobs. Nobody cares. Nobody does anything but go through the motions. They're happy. What happens when they get hungry because the farmers are feeling too good to put in their crops?"

He sighed patiently. He took the wad of gum out of his mouth, rolled it neatly into a Kleenex and dropped it in the wastebasket. He took a fresh stick out of a drawer and unwrapped it, but stopped when he saw me looking at him. He chuckled. "Rather I didn't, Mr. McGory? Well, why not oblige you? It's not habit-forming, after all." He dropped the gum back into the drawer and said: "Answering your questions, they won't starve. The farmers are farming, the workers are working, the policemen are policing, and I'm analyzing. And you're worrying. Why? Work's getting done."

"But my secretary ———"

"Forget about your secretary, Mr. McGory. Sure, she's a little fuzzy-brained, a little absent-minded. Who isn't? But she comes to work, because why shouldn't she?"

"Sure she does, but ———"

"But she's happy. Let her be happy, Mr. McGory!"

I looked scandalized at him. "You, a doctor! How can you say that? Suppose *you* were fuzzy-brained and so on when a patient desperately needed ———"

He stopped me. "In the past three weeks," he said gently, "you're the first to come in that door."

I changed tack: "All right, you're an analyst. What about a G.P. or a surgeon?"

He shrugged. "Perhaps," he conceded, "perhaps in one case out of a thousand—somebody ·hurt in an accident, say—he'd get to the hospital too late, or the surgeon would make some little mistake. Perhaps. Not even one in a thousand—one in a million, maybe. But Cheery-Gum isn't a drug. A quarter-grain of sodium amytol, and your surgeon's as good as new." Absent-mindedly he reached into the drawer for the stick of gum.

"And you say," I said accusingly, "that it's not habit-forming!"

He stopped with his hand halfway to his mouth. "Well," he said wryly, "it *is* a habit. Don't confuse semantics, Mr. McGory. It is not a narcotic addiction. If my supply were cut off this minute, I would feel bad—as bad as if I couldn't play bridge any more for some reason, and no worse." He put the stick of gum away again and rummaged through the bottom drawers of his desk until he found a dusty pack of cigarettes. "Used to smoke three packs a day," he wheezed, choking on the first drag.

He wiped his streaming eyes. "You know, Mr. McGory," he said sharply, "you're a bit of a prig. You don't want people to be happy."

"I ———"

He stopped me before I could work up a full explosion. "Wait! Don't think that you're the only person who thinks about what's good for the world. When I first heard of Cheery-Gum, I worried." He stubbed the cigarette out distastefully, still talking. "Euphoria is well and good, I said, but what about emergencies? And I looked around, and there weren't any. Things were getting done, maybe slowly and erratically, but they were getting done. And then I said, on a high moral plane, that's well and good, but what about the ultimate destiny of man? Should the world be populated by cheerful near-morons? And that worried me, until I began looking at my patients." He smiled reflectively. "I had 'em all, Mr. McGory. You name it, I had it coming in to see me twice a week. The worst wrecks of psyches you ever heard of, twisted and warped and destroying themselves; and they stopped. They stopped eating themselves up with worry and fear and tension, and then they weren't my patients any more. And what's more they weren't morons. Give them a stimulus, they respond. Interest them, they react. I played bridge the other night with a woman who was catatonic last month; we had to put the first stick of gum in her mouth. She beat the hell out of me, Mr. McGory. I had a mathematician coming here who—well, never mind. It was bad. He's happy as a clam, and the last time I saw him he had finished a paper he began ten years ago, and couldn't touch. Stimulate them—they respond. When things are dull—Cheery-Gum. What could be better?"

I looked at him dully, and said, "So you can't help me."

"I didn't say that. Do you want me to help you?"

"Certainly!"

"Then answer my question: Why don't you chew a stick yourself?"

"Because I can't!" It all tumbled out, the Plans meeting and Leslie Clary Cloud and the beaker that hadn't been diluted and the hives. "A terrific allergy," I emphasized. "Even antihistamines don't help. They said at the clinic that the antibodies formed after a massive initial ————"

He said comfortably, "Soma over psyche, eh? Well, what would you expect? But believe me, Mr. McGory, allergies are psychogenic. Now, if you'll just ————"

Well, if you can't lick 'em, join 'em, that's what the old man used to say.

But I can't join them. Theodor Yust offered me an invitation, but I guess I was pretty rude to him. And when, at last, I went back, ready to crawl and apologize, there was a scrawled piece of cardboard over the bronze nameplate; it said: *Gone fishing.*

I tried to lay it on the line with the Chief. I opened the door of the Plans room, and there he was with Baggott and Wayber, from Mason-Dixon. They were sitting there whittling out model ships, and so intent on what they were doing that they hardly noticed me. After a while the Chief said idly, "Bankrupt yet?" And moments passed, and Wayber finally replied, in an absent-minded tone:

"Guess so. Have to file some papers or something." And they went on with their whittling.

So I spoke sharply to them, and the minute they looked up and saw me, it was like the Rockettes: The hands into the pockets, the paper being unwrapped, the gum into the mouth. And naturally I couldn't make any sense with them after that. So what are you going to do?

No! I can't!

Hazel hardly comes in to see me any more, even. I bawled her out for it—what would happen, I demanded, if I suddenly had to answer a letter. But she only smiled dreamily at me. "There hasn't been a letter in a month," she pointed out amiably. "Don't worry, though. If anything comes up, I'll be with you in a flash. This stuff isn't a habit with me, I can stop it any time, you just say the word and ol' Hazel'll be there. . . ."

And she's right because, when you get right down to it, there's the trouble. It isn't a habit.

So how can you break it?

You can stop Cheery-Gum any time. You can stop it this second, or five minutes from now, or tomorrow.

So why worry about it?

It's completely voluntary, entirely under your control; it won't hurt you, it won't make you sick.

I wish Theodor Yust would come back. Or maybe I'll just cut my throat.

Sexual deviance

8

SOCIAL NORMS AND SEXUAL DEVIANCE

Few topics have fascinated man more than his own sexual behavior. Even early cave paintings depict human sexuality (Bell and Gordon, 1972:2). This interest is understandable, since sex is one of the most powerful biological drives. The sex drive is, of course, not peculiar to man. The behavior of many animals is determined by biological sexual drives or instincts. Man differs from other animals precisely in that much of his sexuality is not innate but rather is shaped by sociocultural forces (Edwards, 1972:7). While man's sexual drive or impulse is biologically rooted, sexual expression is controlled by society.

Although we tend to normalize those forms of sexual expression which are prescribed in our own society and to view divergent forms as aberrations or pathologies, cross-cultural comparisons reveal great diversity in sexual practices. Incest, for example, is considered an aberration in American society, but it was prescribed by the Dahomey of West Africa, the Incas, and royal families in ancient Egypt, Sumeria, and Hawaii (Murdock, 1965:266; Edwards, 1972:1). Some societies have also been relatively tolerant and accepting of homosexuality. Almost any practice that is taboo in one socio-cultural context is approved in another. No sexual act is inherently deviant or normal. Its meaning is derived from the cultural context within which it occurs.

Cultural variability in sexual behavior does not mean that sexual behavior is controlled in some societies and uncontrolled in others. Our sex norms may appear capricious and arbitrary, but they are no more so than the sex norms of other societies. A society that condones premarital intercourse regulates adolescent sexual behavior as much as one that condemns this practice. An adolescent who is virginal in such a society will suffer much shame and ridicule. The point is simply that all societies attempt in some way to control sexual behavior. As long as there is society and norms are established to regulate sexual conduct, there will also be sexual deviance. This is an interesting societal paradox—regulation of sexual behavior creates cross-cultural variation in sexual expression. The sexual behavior of other animals, controlled by biological forces, is much less variable than the sexual behavior of man.

TYPES OF SEXUAL DEVIANCE

The United States and other Western societies appear to be more sexually repressive than most other societies (Bell and Gordon, 1972:2). They have traditionally attempted to restrict sexual behavior to the marital bed (Bell and Gordon, 1972:2). Those individuals who do not adhere to this pattern are viewed as deviating from official morality. Western cultures are especially conspicuous in their effort to control premarital sex, since most societies have either permitted or encouraged premarital coitus (Murdock, 1965:265). Most societies do not, however, allow complete sexual freedom. Premarital permissiveness is generally "accompanied by other norms which seek to insure the eventual marriage of those involved (not necessarily marriage to each other)" (Edwards, 1972:7). Similarly, some form of extramarital relation is approved in about 39 percent of societies around the world (Ford and Beach, 1951:113). Men, in particular, are able to engage in adulterous relations in many societies (Edwards, 1972:8).

Norms that attempt to limit sex to marriage are difficult to enforce in a large, complex, and impersonal society. When informal controls fail to regulate sexual activity, formal controls come into effect. In the United States numerous laws have been passed in an attempt to control sexually deviant acts. Under such laws all forms of sexual behavior other than coitus between husband and wife are defined as unnatural or aberrant sex acts. We have already noted in the discussion of crime (Chapter 6) that there is always some incongruity between law, norms, and behavior. By interrelating these levels of analysis one can derive three basic types of sexual deviance: "normal," "pathological," and "group."[1]

"Normal deviance" involves cases in which there is a low correspondence among norms, law, and behavior. Premarital sex, masturbation, and heterosexual mouth-genital contact are "normal" from at least three perspectives: (1) the behavior is engaged in by a large proportion of the population, (2) it is at least tacitly approved, and (3) the acts can be carried out privately and do not openly challenge public morality. Acts that fall under this category then are considered deviant by society but not as much as other sexually deviant acts. The society is ambivalent toward them because they serve a socially useful purpose. Masturbation, for example, may be viewed as a lesser evil than illicit heterosexual coitus. It also provides a sexual release when members of the opposite sex are not available. Mouth-genital contact in marriage serves to reduce sexual inhibitions. Premarital coitus is frequently the outcome of the increasing intimacy that is expected in courtship. Although these acts are legally proscribed, violators are seldom prosecuted.

In the second type, "pathological deviance," there is a high correspondence among the law, norms, and behavior. This type is called pathological because few persons engage in such activities, and society views the acts with general disapproval. Rape, child molesting, and incest would fall under this category. Pathological deviance is condemned not only by the legal system but also by the normative structure. Despite the obvious differences between normal and pathological deviance, they share a common characteristic—the deviant acts are not articulated with a group structure. In the third type, "group deviance," there is less correspondence among law, norms, and behavior than in pathological deviance but more than in normal deviance. The two prominent examples of group, or collective, deviance are homosexuality and prostitution. While some homosexuals have minimal contact with other homosexuals ("closet queens") and a prostitute may be isolated from other prostitutes, both activities characteristically occur within a deviant community. Because of the collective nature of homosexuality and prostitution sociologists have shown more interest in these activities than in other forms of sexual deviance.

Normal deviance

The private nature of most acts of normal sexual deviance makes knowledge of such behavior extremely limited. Masturbation is widely proscribed in the United States by organized religion and other segments of society, but it is not a criminal offense. Such condemnation has not been effective in controlling masturbation, which is an important sexual outlet. Nonetheless, those who masturbate are aware of the social stigma that is attached to the activity, and many experience guilt and shame.

[1] These types are discussed more fully by Gagnon and Simon (1967:1–12).

Although most males and nearly two out of every three females masturbate at some point in their lives (Kinsey, 1953:173; Gagnon and Simon, 1967:4), there are important sex differences in levels of masturbation. Men masturbate more than women, starting earlier and masturbating more regularly (Simon and Gagnon, 1969:13). There is also evidence that suggests that masturbation in women involves direct physical stimulation with fewer masturbatory fantasies[2] (Kinsey, 1953:164–165). Males, on the other hand, fantasize extensively, and their fantasies often provide the initial stimulus to masturbate (Kinsey, 1953:165). ". . . about half of the females who masturbate do so only *after* having experienced orgasm in some situation involving others" (Bartell, 1971:55). This pattern is consistent with the general tendency of women to experience orgasm later and less frequently than men.

The acceptance of masturbation also varies according to one's educational level and social class standing. There seems to be greater acceptance of masturbation in the middle and upper classes and among the college educated (Albert Reiss, 1967:56). Kinsey noted that "although most lower level boys masturbate during their early adolescence, many of them never have more than a few experiences or, at the most, regular masturbation for a short period of months or years, after which they rarely again depend on such self-induced outlets" (1948:375). Masturbation is typically viewed by the lower class as an abnormality or perversion, and the person who relies on it is ridiculed. For many middle-class men, however, masturbation serves as a regular sexual outlet not only during adolescence but also after marriage. About 30 percent of college-educated males continue to masturbate regularly after marriage (Simon and Gagnon, 1969: 17). The rejection of masturbation by the lower class seems to be part of a broader pattern of rejection of all techniques of sexual arousal other than coitus. Kinsey found that rates of premarital intercourse were higher among men of low educational levels than those at high educational levels (1948:377–379). The college-educated male was more likely to engage in petting and to develop proficiency in a number of noncoital techniques of sexual arousal. This pattern continues after marriage as upper-level couples employ a wide variety of sexual techniques including mouth-genital contact, anal intercourse, and manual manipulation (Wheeler, 1967:88). In marital relations, for example, oral stimulation of the female (cunnilingus) occurred in about 60 percent of couples who were college educated, 20 percent of those who attended high school, and only 11 percent of those who did not go beyond grade school (Kinsey, 1948:576–577). Thus while the lower class is more likely to experience coitus before marriage, it frequently views other techniques of sexual arousal as unnatural perversions.

---

[2] This does not mean that women do not have sexual fantasies. One study found that it was common for married women to have erotic fantasies, during intercourse with their husbands (Hariton, 1973).

Despite the apparent class differences in premarital coital experiences, attitudinal studies do not support the view that lower-class persons are more permissive toward premarital intercourse. Two surveys conducted by the Roper organization between 1939 and 1943 suggest that lower-class persons are *less* accepting of premarital coitus (Wheeler, 1967:89–90). Ira Reiss (1965), using data from a national adult sample and two state student samples, found no significant social class differences on a premarital sexual permissiveness scale. These findings suggest a complex relation among social class, attitudes toward premarital coitus, and behavior. Lower-class persons may have attitudes less accepting of coitus before marriage, but "at the same time, the objective life situation of lower socio-economic groups may predispose them to greater pressure for engaging in the activity" (Wheeler, 1967:91). Pressure to engage in coitus may be especially strong on the female, who frequently uses sex as a means of attracting males when other resources are limited. But if the lower-status girl has intercourse with a number of males, she stands to lose her reputation as a "nice girl" and to reduce her marriageable status (Albert Reiss, 1967:50). Nice girls can exchange sex for a steady affectionate relationship with a boy.

It was noted earlier that the United States, unlike most other societies, attempts to control premarital coitus. Adults have characteristically tried to enforce the norm of premarital chastity, especially among females, through a variety of institutional structures including religious groups, the schools, and legal statutes. Today there is much concern that these controls are becoming increasingly less effective in regulating sexual conduct. While many seem to accept more liberal attitudes toward sex, the evidence supporting increasing permissiveness is not conclusive. There is little doubt that we have undergone considerable liberalization of sexual attitudes and beliefs. We speak more openly about sex and are more tolerant of premarital coitus, but it is not clear if changes in behavior have kept pace with changes in attitudes. Kinsey found that there was a significant difference in premarital coital experience between females born before 1900 and those born after 1900. "Among the females in the sample who were born before 1900, less than half as many had had pre-marital coitus as among the females born in any subsequent decade" (Kinsey, 1953:298). The findings of a number of other studies suggest that rates of premarital intercourse did not change appreciably between about 1920 and 1960 (Reiss, 1960:77; Bell, 1966:57; Gagnon and Simon, 1970:100). On the basis of these studies it appeared that the rates of premarital coitus reported by Kinsey (about 80 percent for men[3] and 50 percent for women) had

[3] This figure is an estimate since the rate of premarital intercourse varies according to educational attainment, and Kinsey (1953:330) does not give a total rate of incidence for males. He reports the rate of incidence to be 98 percent for men with an eighth-grade education or less, 85 percent for those with nine to twelve years of schooling, and 68 percent for those who attended college.

stabilized. More recent studies have found increases in premarital coitus in the past decade or so. While the rate of coital experience has remained relatively stable for men, the rate for women has risen consistently (Leslie, 1973:384–389; Packard, 1968:160–162; Bell and Chaskes, 1970; Christensen and Gregg, 1970).

If one can talk of a "sexual revolution," the revolution seems to have centered on the sexual attitudes and behavior of women. A large proportion of males have always experienced premarital coitus. Men continue to have intercourse prior to marriage, but increasingly it is with companions rather than with prostitutes or lower-status women. Kinsey noted that males born in more recent generations were less likely to use prostitutes as a sexual outlet (1953:300). Despite the increased permissiveness of women, their premarital sexual experiences are still more limited than those of men. Men usually have orgasm earlier and outside the context of an emotional relationship. For women, on the other hand, sexual relations are generally the outgrowth of romantic involvement and intimate courtship (Ira Reiss, 1967:47; Ehrmann, 1959:169; Bell, 1966:105–106). This pattern, however, is changing. As women are liberated from their traditional role, "the commitment of engagement has become a less important condition for many coeds engaging in premarital coitus as well as whether or not they will have guilt feelings about that experience" (Bell and Chaskes, 1970: 84).

A number of other factors have been related to premarital sexual permissiveness. There is reason to believe that blacks are more sexually permissive than whites (Ira Reiss, 1967:38–55). Religious involvement tends to decrease premarital permissiveness. Ira Reiss found that white students, especially females, who attend church regularly are less permissive than other students (1967:42–45). Kinsey and others report "that those with no religious affiliation have higher rates of premarital coitus than do those with religious affiliations" (Bell, 1966:126). These findings are not surprising of course, since in American society religion is probably the dominant institution for controlling illicit sexual activities. Another factor that relates to premarital permissiveness is the emotional involvement of the parties. Ira Reiss found that white students who believed in "romantic love" were less permissive than those who did not, while the opposite was true of black students (1967:45). Each of these associations was stronger for women than for men. Similarly, among white students frequency of falling in love is related to permissiveness, but the relationship varies according to the sex of the respondent (Ira Reiss, 1967:47–48). For women, permissiveness increases with number of times in love; for men, those who have been in love only once are less permissive than those who have never been in love or those who have been in love twice or more.

Pathological deviance

Although almost any form of sexual deviance could be interpreted as a violation of a legal statute, some are more vigorously enforced than others.

Pathological deviance involves acts that are condemned by most members of society. When violations are detected, they are likely to be prosecuted and to receive strong, negative sanctions.

Incest is perhaps the only sexual activity that is universally disapproved. Variations from this pattern have occurred only in a few societies in which some persons have been exempted from the generalized incest taboo (e.g., nobility and the upper class).[4] The taboo forbids intercourse and marriage among members of the nuclear family—father and daughter, mother and son, or brother and sister (Murdock, 1965:12). In some societies the prohibition is extended to blood relatives outside the nuclear family. Incest is so strongly proscribed in American society that detection is virtually impossible. It occurs in private and is kept secret by the family. An additional difficulty in detecting incest is that the relationship is typically entered voluntarily, or at least semivoluntarily, by the parties involved (Gebhard et al., 1965:267). One study of incestuous relations between father and daughter found that the mother at least tacitly approved of the relationship (Kaufman, Peck, and Tagiuri, 1954). The daughters tended to assume the social and sexual role of the mother.

The incest taboo is enforced in most societies not by the threat of external controls but by the internalization of values and norms that make incest inconceivable to most persons. Despite these prohibitions the taboo is violated occasionally. Perhaps the most complete study of incest offenders has been carried out by S. Kirson Weinberg. According to Weinberg, incest is a very low-volume offense in English-speaking nations, with about one incest offender per million inhabitants (1955:249).[5] Some of the major findings from his study of 203 cases of incest in Illinois are listed below:

1. An overwhelming majority of the cases (159) involved father and daughter relations.
2. In father-daughter incest the daughter was usually the informant.
3. Not all offenders were convicted (only 49.4 percent of the fathers and 25.6 percent of the brothers).
4. Relative to their numbers in the population, blacks and foreign-born whites were overrepresented in incest cases.
5. The average age of the fathers was 43.5 years, of the daughters 15.3 years, of the brothers 24 years, and of the sisters 19.3 years.
6. About 55 percent of the participants were in the lowest socioeconomic level (43 percent of the fathers were unemployed).

[4] There are some who differ with this view. Lester (1972:269), for example, claims that incest was generally approved for all members of society in old Iran, Ancient Egypt, and among the Mormons.

[5] The incidence of unreported incest is probably considerably higher. Gebhard, et al., found that 3.9 percent of a control group, never convicted of anything beyond traffic violations, had been involved in incestuous relations (1965:572). It should be noted, however, that coitus with a first cousin and a sister-in-law were included and that the bulk of the cases were accounted for by first-cousin incest.

7. The fathers averaged about five years of formal education.
8. The eldest daughter was most likely to be victimized.
9. About half of the fathers had arrest records (mostly for petty theft, vagrancy, and disorderly conduct).
10. Many of the fathers were "disturbed," but few were psychotic.

These findings should be interpreted with caution, since they are based on cases that come to the attention of the police. A sample such as this underrepresents middle and upper socioeconomic groups and willing participants. Societal disapproval of incest is understandable, since uncontrolled sexual relations can be very disruptive to the nuclear family. Incest tends to confuse familial roles and to disrupt family relations:

Incest disrupts the function of the family as an agency of personality development. It confuses the child who has to submit or who even cooperates with the parent's sexual advances. It minimizes attitudes of deference to the parent. . . . It confuses the informal social roles in the family, intensifies rivalry between family members of the same sex . . . and markedly reduces family cooperation and family harmony (Weinberg, 1955:258).

Few offenses are more strongly condemned than incest, except perhaps rape and sexual assault. Wheeler has observed that the "strongest legal sanctions are directed to control of the *degree of consent* in the relationship, with many states allowing the death penalty for forcible rape" (1967: 79). Concern with the control of sex offenders has led to the passage of sexual psychopath laws that stipulate indefinite sentences for dangerous offenders. These laws are based on a number of stereotypes and misconceptions about sex offenders, including "the notion that all sex offenders were potentially dangerous, that they were very likely to repeat their offenses, that they can be accurately diagnosed and efficiently treated by psychiatrists" (Wheeler, 1967:96). Available evidence indicates that most sex offenders are not severely disturbed emotionally, that they are less apt to repeat their crimes than nonsexual offenders, and that few are dangerous to society (Tappan, 1960:417; Wheeler, 1967:96–98). Moreover, psychiatrists have had difficulty isolating the sex psychopath as a clinical entity (Tappan, 1960:412).

Aggressive sex offenses usually involve transgressions against an adult female (i.e., one who has reached puberty). Passive offenses, on the other hand, include noncoital sex play with children, exhibitionism, and voyeurism (Wheeler, 1967:98). Sexual psychopath laws were passed primarily to protect society from aggressive offenses such as rape and sexual assault, which represent a greater danger to society. Yet passive offenders are more likely to be emotionally disturbed and to have previous arrests for sexual offenses (Wheeler, 1967:98–99). The aggressive offender usually a lower-status offender shares many characteristics in common with other lower-status offenders. A study in California, for example, found that over half of the sex offenses committed by delinquents were gang motivated (Wheeler,

1967:99). Amir similarly found that 43 percent of the rapes involved multiple offenders (1967:55). Moreover, group rapes were most common among offenders in the fourteen- to nineteen-year-old category. There is therefore reason to believe that the behavior of aggressive sex offenders does not result from pathological sex motives, but rather is part of a broader subcultural system that emphasizes the use of force to attain desired ends. "It is the use of force, rather than any specifically deviant sexual motivation, that distinguishes these offenders from those who fall within the law" (Wheeler, 1967:101).

An extensive survey of sexual aggressors against adult females by the Indiana Institute for Sex Research supports the view that sexual aggressors do not differ significantly from other offenders (Gebhard et al., 1965:205). Persons convicted of heterosexual aggression against adult females (adult aggressors) were compared to several other groups: a group of nonsexual offenders (prison group), a group whose members had never been convicted of anything more serious than a traffic violation (control group), a group of heterosexual aggressors against children and minors, and a group convicted of sex offenses other than heterosexual aggression (voyeurs, exhibitionists, and homosexuals). Few factors distinguished adult sexual aggressors from these other groups except that adult aggressors were somewhat more likely to: (1) come from broken homes, (2) have a high frequency of masturbation before marriage, (3) experience mouth-genital contact both before and after marriage, (4) have higher rates of premarital coitus, (5) marry more than once, and (6) have a short courtship prior to marriage (Gebhard et al., 1965:180–197). The findings do not support the view of the adult sexual aggressor as a sex-starved psychopath. Most had an active sex life, and their rate of marital coitus was higher than other groups. They also devoted more time to precoital contact and did not rank their marriages as being especially happy or unhappy. Only 5 percent of the adult aggressors had been institutionalized for mental or emotional reasons. Most were in trouble with the law early, but there was little pattern in the crimes they committed, except for a tendency to commit offenses against persons.

Group deviance

Perhaps the best example of group deviance is homosexuality. Some homosexuals consider themselves to be "normal" members of society who deviate from the larger society only in their sexual preference (Newton, 1972:23). They are likely to carry out their sexual activities in private and avoid contact with the gay world.[6] Many homosexuals, however, identify with and participate in the gay world. Those whose lives and identity revolve around their homosexuality are what Lemert calls "secondary deviants"

[6] For an interesting study of "secret" and "overt" homosexuals see Leznoff and Westley (1956).

(Newton, 1972:23). One can find an active homosexual community, consisting of bars, clubs, steam baths, coffee houses, clothing stores, and restaurants, in every large city in the United States. The homosexual community is not a community in the traditional sense of the word, lacking a territorial base and basic social institutions. Nonetheless, certain residential areas do have a high concentration of homosexuals (Hooker, 1967).

The bar is probably the most important "institution" in the homosexual community (Achilles, 1967; Helmer, 1963). Although individual bars tend to have a relatively short life expectancy, the bar system is very stable (Achilles, 1967). Bars are closed periodically by the authorities, but since it is a lucrative business new bars spring up quickly to take their places. News of a new bar spreads rapidly throughout the homosexual world. The opening of a bar is sometimes marked with a celebration or party of some kind. Information of the opening is usually spread by word of mouth, but sometimes printed announcements are sent to persons on a mailing list (Achilles, 1967). Although bars generally represent a fairly broad cross-section of the homosexual community, some bars appeal to particular subgroups. The bartender usually helps to identify a bar. A bar that caters to effeminate "queens" will probably have a "limp-wristed" bartender, while a "leather bar" will have an overly masculine bartender (Achilles, 1967: 240). The bartender plays an important symbolic function. Many build up a following that they take with them as they move from one bar to another (Helmer, 1963).

The gay bar serves a number of important functions. It provides homosexuals with the opportunity to interact with others who are "secret" deviants and, as the saying goes, to "let their hair down" (Hooker, 1967: 181). For those who are new to the gay world, attendance at a gay bar may mark their debut or "coming out" as for the first time they publicly identify themselves as homosexual. Identification with the homosexual role is facilitated by knowledge that there are others in the same situation and that many are attractive and masculine looking (Hooker, 1967:178–179). The bar is a social institution then in the sense that it provides many services. "A particular bar, for example, may serve as a loan office, restaurant, message reception center, telephone exchange, and so forth" (Achilles, 1967:230). It is a place where one meets and talks with friends, exchanges gossip concerning the police and other matters, and perhaps, most importantly, carries out sexual transactions. Hooker has metaphorically referred to the gay bar as a "sexual market." It is "a place where agreements are made for the potential exchange of sexual services, for sex without obligation or commitment—the 'one night stand' " (Hooker, 1967: 175). Sexual transactions are frequently carried out through the exchange of glances. Persons may leave together without uttering a word or perhaps after only a brief verbal exchange. The details of the transaction such as the location and the sexual acts to be performed are worked out later (Hooker, 1967:176).

"Cruising" for sex partners may take place in a variety of locales including the bar, public toilet, bath, or the street corner. But wherever it takes place, it involves an impersonal sexual exchange without emotional or social commitment. Many homosexuals seek more stable and permanent unions, but characteristically homosexual relations are short-lived and promiscuous. While some attribute this promiscuity to a psychological abnormality, sociologists have identified a number of structural conditions that make homosexual relations unstable. Since homosexuality is proscribed by the larger society, homosexuals seek anonymity in their sexual relations (Hooker, 1967:177). Many adult homosexuals, for example, establish impersonal sexual liaisons with delinquent boys because both the boy and the adult male fellator wish to maintain secrecy (Reiss, 1961). Martin Hoffman (1970) suggests that much of the promiscuity in homosexual relations is due to the fact that the relationship involves two men. Women typically make a more emotional commitment to sexual relations (Hooker, 1967:177). "Without the stabilizing female the dyad tends to break up. When two females interact, as in lesbian relationships, the dyad tends to be more stable" (Hoffman, 1970:140).

The homosexual community has traditionally been a male community. There are lesbian bars, but they are few in number and much more conspicuous than male bars (Helmer, 1963). The lesbian bar, instead of being a sexual market, seems to be a place where one takes friends (Hoffman, 1970:140). The women who do participate in the open gay world are likely to be the more masculine, "butch" types who flaunt their homosexuality (Helmer, 1963). The low visibility of lesbians has led many to make the questionable assumption that lesbianism is a rare or uncommon phenomenon. The dominant sex norms of our society are actually more conducive to the establishment and maintenance of private homosexual relations among women than among men. We tolerate and sometimes even encourage physical contact among females (e.g., holding hands, hugging, and kissing). As one lesbian observed:

Once mother accepted the fact that I didn't want to live at home and that I wasn't going to get married, it worked out very well. I talk to them about once a week and go out every few weeks. My girl friend comes along and she gets along very well with the family. Mother, particularly, is pleased that I have such a well-educated and refined roommate. I am sure that she doesn't know. I don't think mother or father can conceive of something like homosexuality (Simon and Gagnon, 1967:268).

Whether a person is homosexual or heterosexual may be less significant than his gender in determining the pattern of inducement into sexual relations. Males, whether homosexual or heterosexual, are usually introduced to sex at an early age (Kinsey, 1953:330–332). The first sexual exploration by males is frequently of a homosexual nature. For men sex usually precedes love or emotional involvement, whereas for women sex follows emotional involvement. "Lesbians are exposed to the same subtle influences and experiences as heterosexual females, many of which occur before actual sexual experience" (Hedblom, 1972:35). It is therefore not surprising to find that lesbians have their first homosexual experiences in late adolescence or early adulthood and that, for most, sex follows an intimate emotional tie (Simon and Gagnon, 1967:251). The typical pattern seems to be for lesbians to move from friendship, to love or emotional involvement, and finally to sexual relations. Some female homosexuals have "had overt relationships for ten or fifteen years before they attempted any sort of genital stimulation" (Kinsey, 1953:659). Stable relations are the preferred pattern, and most lesbians are involved in a marriage arrangement (Hedblom 1972:48). Since lesbian behavior is private, women are probably slower to admit their homosexuality. The "coming-out" ritual that seems to help men to make the transition to the homosexual role is largely unavailable to women. Male homosexuality then is much more open and public than female homosexuality.

Because of her low detectability, furthermore, the lesbian has less often been the subject of research. Our knowledge of lesbianism is therefore limited, stereotyped, and distorted. "The most common image of the lesbian is probably that of a pseudomale, a female who, in her biological inability to be a male, is a caricature of maleness" (Simon and Gagnon, 1967:264). The lesbian, in short, is considered a "dyke," or an incomplete male. While a few females assume a masculine identity, entrance and maintenance of a homosexual career is characteristically feminine (Simon and Gagnon, 1967:251). A second, related assumption that is unsupported is that lesbians are unattractive women who turn to homosexuality as a result of unsuccessful heterosexual relations (Simon and Gagnon, 1967:258–259). About half of the respondents in one study had experienced sexual relations with a man, and almost half of those with such experience achieved orgasm (Hedblom, 1972:55). Lesbians also frequently engage in heterosexual dating in order to maintain a respectable appearance. These data suggest that the lesbian selects a homosexual career not because she is a heterosexual reject but because she prefers sex with another woman. Nonetheless, lesbians are "woman without men," and their occupational and achievement patterns are necessarily masculine (Hedblom, 1972:56; Simon and Gagnon, 1967:266).

A second dominant form of group deviance is prostitution. Some prostitution is carried out privately, but most occurs within a deviant subculture. Prostitution seems to be universal, found in some form in every known society past or present. There is, however, considerable disagreement over its definition. Some have defined it as the exchange of sex for financial considerations. According to such a definition, the contemporary housewife may in some respects be seen as a prostitute. Others have argued that the prostitute not only exchanges sex for financial considerations but that she does so impersonally and with many partners (Bell and Gordon,

1972:228). Prostitution will be defined here as the impersonal and indiscriminate exchange of sex for nonsexual considerations.

Society is ambivalent toward prostitution, simultaneously condemning and supporting it. Although prostitution is officially proscribed, it provides a sexual outlet for many persons who for one reason or another are not able to enter socially approved relations (Davis, 1971:341). It is somewhat ironic that prostitution tends to flourish in those societies that employ a "double standard" for men and women—that is, in societies in which men are expected to be sexually experienced and respectable women are expected to be virginal at marriage. As the status of women increases and they are granted more sexual freedom, the demand for prostitution appears to decrease (Davis, 1971:350). This view was supported by Kinsey, who found that males born in more recent generations were less likely to have sexual outlets with prostitutes and more likely to have intercourse with women who are not prostitutes (Kinsey, 1953:300). Other writers also maintain that contacts with prostitutes are declining (Packard, 1968:163; Winick and Kinsie, 1971:185–186). Although the frequency of sexual contact with prostitutes appears to be decreasing, there will probably always be some demand for prostitution. The prostitute provides an impersonal service without social obligations or entanglements in exchange for monetary compensation. The demand for prostitutes will continue as long as there are persons who are so socially repulsive that they cannot enter legitimate sexual relations, who are temporarily deprived of normal sexual outlets (e.g., conventioneers, military personnel), or who turn to the prostitute for sexual techniques that are considered immoral by society (Davis, 1971:346). Wayland Young has noted that males are able to release many of their repressed sexual desires with prostitutes (1964:177–178). The demand for these services should decrease, however, as more respectable women engage in previously taboo sexual activities (e.g., mouth-genital contact and anal intercourse).

There are variations in the wages of prostitutes, but generally they are well compensated. As Kingsley Davis has noted, given the wages of prostitutes "the interesting question is not why so many women become prostitutes, but why so few of them do" (1971:347). The prostitute is well compensated because she is expected to exchange financial rewards for social esteem. She is generally isolated and alienated from the larger society. Jackman, O'Toole, and Geis (1963) found that the prostitutes whom they interviewed were isolated from the society and alienated from their parents. The girls were especially alienated from their fathers. Despite their alienation, prostitutes are aware of larger societal values, and these values have some impact on them (Jackman et al., 1963). Their response is to develop rationalizations that help to justify their actions and neutralize societal norms (for a discussion of neutralization see Chapter 5). "The violation of sexual values is justified in two ways: (a) Everyone is rotten. Hence, prostitutes are no worse than other people, and they are less hypocritical. (b) Society doesn't really scorn prostitutes" (Jackman et al., 1963:153). The belief that the society is hypocritical is supported by the prostitute's daily contact with members of respectable society. There is variation among prostitutes in the extent to which they reject larger societal values. Jackman and his associates (1963) have isolated two value cultures of prostitution. In one, the criminal world contraculture, the prostitute identifies both with the world of prostitution and the world of crime. She is more contemptuous of members of "respectable" society and takes pride in her ability to move in "big business" circles and to associate with big spenders. Prostitutes of the second type, dual-worlds prostitutes, identify with their families and reject the world of prostitution. In a sense they are in the world of prostitution but not of it. They identify with and espouse middle-class values, claiming to be "good mothers" and subscribing to religious values. Dual-worlds prostitutes do not associate with many other prostitutes or criminals. They are able to participate in the world of prostitution and identify with middle-class morality by dichotimizing the two worlds and dissociating themselves psychologically from their activities.

Because the prostitute engages in deviant sexual activities, we tend to view prostitution as an unskilled occupation that is entered with little or no training. Bryan (1965) has shown that call girls typically undergo a period of apprenticeship that is directed by another prostitute or by a pimp. The training period may last as long as eight months, but usually it is completed in two or three months. The setting for the training is usually the apartment of the older prostitute. The novice is introduced not only to the "dos and don'ts" of the trade but also to a general value system. According to this value system, the customer is exploitative, but he is to be exploited before he exploits. Interaction with the John (customer) is kept to a minimum. The girl learns how to make a telephone "pitch," talk to customers, collect the fee, and use personal hygiene. There is, however, little instruction in sexual techniques. One of the most significant values that is learned during the apprenticeship is a sense of honesty and fairness toward other prostitutes and pimps. Although the learning of the "dos and don'ts" and of values is important, the most important function of the training period seems to be the development of an adequate clientele. Once the trainee builds up a list of customers, the apprenticeship period ends abruptly.

Prostitution is a group or collective phenomenon in part because transactions with customers, contacts with the police, and relations with members of straight society are best carried out within a deviant subculture. ". . . this is a network of social relationships that both facilitates and, in some measure, determines the sexual and the social activity of the prostitute" (Gagnon and Simon, 1967:10). The subculture of prostitution provides a collective solution to the problems of adjustment faced by individual prostitutes.

EXTRAMARITAL RELATIONS

The last category of sexual behavior to be discussed, extramarital relations, is not easily classified as either "normal," "pathological," or "group" deviance; it contains elements of all three categories. Adulterous relations in the United States appear more common, or at least more visible, than in the past. Under certain circumstances, such as when a couple is separated for a prolonged period of time or one spouse is incapacitated, we are relatively tolerant of infidelity. Yet one can hardly call adultery normal deviance or equate it with masturbation. Considerable stigma is still attached to extramarital relations, which are criminal offenses (although few persons are prosecuted) and the only grounds for divorce found in every state. Nonetheless, we are much more accepting of adultery than of acts of pathological deviance such as rape or incest. Finally, extramarital relations may be private individual acts or a group or collective phenomenon. Most "affairs" are carried out privately and secretly by the parties involved, but "swinging" is a subcultural activity that resembles other forms of group deviance such as prostitution and homosexuality.

Although some societies permit sexual relations outside of marriage, cross-culturally extramarital relations are more restricted than premarital relations. A majority of known societies have had prohibitions against sex outside of marriage.[7] There are at least two reasons for the stronger sanctions against extramarital relations: (1) The married person is considered to have a legitimate sexual outlet, and (2) adultery is seen as a threat to the institution of marriage, which is valued by society (Bell and Gordon, 1972:96). Adulterers are usually secret deviants, making it extremely difficult to gather accurate information on the incidence of adultery in American society. Kinsey (1953:437) found that about 50 percent of the males and 26 percent of the females had been involved in extramarital relations by the age of forty (1953:437). More recently the Kinsey Institute for Sex Research (Baguedor, 1973:123) has estimated that perhaps as many as 50 percent of the married population have engaged in adulterous relations (about 60 percent of the men and 40 percent of the women).[8] If a majority of married persons have engaged in adulterous relations, can we then speak of a taboo against extramarital relations? Some would say that we are hypocritical and continue to pay lip service to a standard that has become obsolete. The problem is of course more complicated than this statement would suggest. Although a majority of the population

---

[7] The specific figure varies according to the study. Ford and Beach give a figure of about 60 percent (1951:113), while Murdock says it is closer to 80 percent (1965: 265).

[8] Paul Gebhard (1973) of the Institute for Sex Research emphasized in a personal communication that this is an "educated guess" that has been neither substantiated nor refuted by concrete data.

probably does violate the taboo against extramarital relations, the taboo is effective in limiting most sexual behavior to marriage. Extramarital relations are frequently sporadic and of short duration. Many are literally "one-night stands" in which the participants may not even know each other's names. Extramarital relations probably account for no more than 10 percent of the total sexual outlet of married persons. Kinsey (1953: 437) found that for persons twenty-one to twenty-five extramarital coitus accounted for 3 percent of the total outlet for females and 7 percent for males; for those thirty-six to forty it was 10 percent for females and 8 percent for males; and for those forty-six to fifty it was 13 percent for females and 9 percent for males.

Extramarital relations is a broad category that encompasses a variety of behavioral patterns ranging from a single act of petting with someone other than the spouse to an enduring sexual and emotional relationship outside of marriage. One of the most important distinctions to be made is between "affairs," which are carried out privately and individually, and "swinging," which is a joint or collective endeavor. Swinging is a form of group deviance in that spouses jointly and deliberately exchange mates with one or more couples, and the activity is buttressed and supported by subcultural norms and values. Most extramarital relations would probably be classified as affairs. Although the persons involved usually try to keep the affair secret from the spouses, this is not always the case. Sometimes a spouse suspects, and in other cases he or she knows and approves of the relationship. One woman, for example, sanctioned an affair between her husband and a neighbor for over ten years:

About ten years ago I noticed that my husband and the woman next door discovered a compelling interest in trimming the roses and the hedge between our houses. They had practically trimmed all the leaves off. She's a fine person and I guessed they would like to know each other better. I knew they both liked bowling and I suggested they go bowling together. . . . Since then, on two nights a week my husband and this woman go bowling together. . . . They usually come home about two. We don't say much about it, although everything is perfectly clear to all four of us directly concerned. . . . I would say that I am in love with my husband and the woman next door is in love with hers. Also, of course, she and my husband are in love with each other. . . . I don't think this has had any effect on our sex life as far as I can see (Cuber and Harroff, 1965:159–160).

A number of factors contribute to spouse approval of adultery. Sometimes the marriage is admittedly bad and is kept together only for appearances or because of children. Approval also frees the other spouse to become involved in affairs or other activities (Cuber and Harroff, 1965:106–131). Cuber (1969:191–192) has isolated three basic types of adulterous relationships. Type I refers to relations that compensate for what is regarded as a bad marriage by the adulterous partner. In Type II, extramarital relations are the outcome of a discontinuous marriage in which spouses are physically separated for an extended period of time. These separations can range from prolonged absences due to military duty to extensive travel for business. Type II extramarital encounters are most likely to be "forgiven," since one's spouse is, at least temporarily, unavailable. They are also likely to be short-lived affairs that lack emotional involvement. In Type III the couple has a satisfying marriage, but husband and wife do not limit themselves to monogamous relations. They work out an arrangement in which both parties feel free to pursue other social and sexual relations, although their primary commitment is to one another (O'Neill and O'Neill, 1972:254–257). Type III affairs most closely resemble swinging. The basic difference is that in swinging not only is there mutual consent but the activity is engaged in jointly. Swinging is in a very real sense an extension of the marital relationship; it is planned, entered into, and carried out jointly. The activity usually takes place in one's home or in the home of friends. Although our knowledge of swinging is somewhat limited, a fairly consistent pattern of the typical swinger has emerged. Swingers are usually white, middle-class suburbanites, with moderate to high incomes[9] (Bartell, 1971:24–45). They are in their late twenties or early thirties, and most have two or three children (Bartell, 1971:24–45). In fact, except for their sexual practices, swingers are extremely conventional. Denfeld and Gordon have concluded that "the swinging suburban party differs, then, from the conventional cocktail party only in that it revolves around the sexual exchange of mates" (1970:97).

Swinging is in many ways compatible with monogamy. It is a joint activity, and one partner is not regarded as "cheating" on another. Moreover, since one swings with many different couples, most of them strangers, jealousy and competitive emotional relations do not usually develop. Jealousy is also minimized by swinging only with other married couples (O'Neill and O'Neill, 1970:105). Swinging does not necessarily have an adverse effect on the marital relation—it may liven and sometimes even strengthen what was previously an unsatisfying marriage. It is interesting to note that although women frequently enter swinging reluctantly, usually at the urging of their husbands, they "are better able to make the necessary adjustments to sexual freedom after the initial phases of involvement than are men . . ." (Smith and Smith, 1970:136). Swinging is basically a group activity. Swingers are part of a subculture having a distinctive value system, the "swinging philosophy," and fairly explicit rules that govern their relations (O'Neill and O'Neill, 1970:106). Magazines and clubs play an important role in the subculture. The magazines perpetuate

[9] Although swinging is primarily a middle-class activity, extramarital relations, at least among males, are probably more prevalent in the lower class (Edwards, 1973: 212). Extramarital involvement also appears to be greater among persons who are not religiously devout, reside in urban areas, have extensive premarital experience, have been married for a longer period of time, are not satisfied with their marriage, and have a high sense of alienation (Edwards, 1973).

the swinging philosophy by carrying articles on swinging, advertisements for various sex-related products, and, most important, classified ads that are used to meet other swingers (Bartell, 1971:60–78). In addition to using the magazine ads, swingers make arrangements to meet other swingers by visiting swingers' bars, joining swinging clubs, and through interpersonal contacts (Bartell, 1971:79).

There are at least two very different types of swingers. The most publicized, and the one that has been discussed so far, is the recreational swinger. Recreational swingers swing for fun or pleasure, but they are not interested in making basic changes in the social order (Symonds, 1968: 5–6; Walshok, 1971; Stephenson, 1973). The behavior of the recreational swinger is conforming in most spheres.[10] For the utopian swinger, on the other hand, swinging is part of a new life style that challenges conventional values in nonsexual areas. The utopian swinger advocates communal living and retreating from the society and its values (Symonds, 1968). One would also expect the utopian swinger to be more interested in developing meaningful emotional relations and less interested in sex per se. The utopian swinger is likely to reject the nuclear family and advocate its replacement by some form of group marriage or by "free love."

THE SEXUAL REVOLUTION: REALITY OR MYTH

It is said that we are currently in the midst of a sexual revolution. Americans are flooded by a continuous barrage of sexual stimuli. Sex, once taboo, is now discussed openly and freely. With the relaxation of censorship one can see nudity and a wide assortment of sex acts depicted on the screen and the stage. Nudity has also become commonplace in magazines. The "Playboy Philosophy," which has long exploited female nudity, has now been extended to include the "Playgirl Philosophy," which seeks to market male nudity. If we can speak of a sexual revolution, which hardly seems warranted, it is more a revolution in the realm of attitudes rather than behavior. We speak more openly about sex and probably are less likely to prohibit books, magazines, films, and plays that previously would have been called obscene, indecent, or pornographic. The liberalization of sexual attitudes has produced an interesting phenomenon that might be termed, for lack of a better name, the "everybody's-doin'-it" syndrome. This is a situation in which sexual attitudes are ahead of, or more liberal than, sexual behavior. Private morality becomes more conservative than

---

[10] There is undoubtedly internal variation among swingers. The respondents studied by the Smiths (1970), for example, were less structured and conforming than those studied by the Bartells (1971). Walshok (1971) and Stephenson (1973) have proposed interesting theories to explain the emergence of swinger among conventional middle-class persons.

public morality. Under such circumstances one would expect that feelings of relative sexual deprivation would increase as individuals assume that their sexual experiences are more limited than the experiences of others. The psychological costs should be greater for persons who are not getting "a piece of the action" in the sexual revolution than they would be in a society in which public morality is less liberal. Such feelings of relative deprivation are similar to the feelings experienced by the poor in an affluent society.

The so-called sexual revolution has undoubtedly had its greatest impact on the sexual attitudes and behavior of women. We have witnessed the gradual erosion of the double standard and its replacement with a more equalitarian standard. Increasingly, the same standard is being applied to the behavior of men and women. It is women who have benefited most from the liberalization of sexual attitudes and behavior, since men have always been allowed considerable latitude to deviate from official morality.

There is much concern in American society with increasing sexual permissiveness, or what is commonly regarded as the decline in the moral fiber of society. Many, particularly among the older generation, depict the United States as a sexually loose and sinful society. When our sexual standards are compared to the standards of other societies, however, the United States appears restrictive rather than permissive. If we are undergoing a sexual revolution, it is only relative to our past repression, not relative to most other societies. Perhaps it is only because ours is a puritanical society with a history of sexual repression that recent changes are viewed as revolutionary. Many societies, some which we might call backward or underdeveloped, have long taken a casual attitude toward nudity and sex outside marriage.

REFERENCES

Achilles, Nancy
　　1967 "The Development of the Homosexual Bar as an Institution." Pp. 228–244 in Gagnon and Simon.
Amir, Menachem
　　1967 "Forcible Rape." Federal Probation 31 (March):51–58.
Baguedor, Eve
　　1973 "Is Anyone Faithful Anymore?" McCall's C (February):73, 123–126.
Bartell, Gilbert D.
　　1971 Group Sex. New York: Peter H. Wyden.
Bell, Robert R.
　　1966 Premarital Sex in a Changing Society. Englewood Cliffs, N.J.: Prentice-Hall.
Bell, Robert R., and Jay B. Chaskes
　　1970 "Premarital Sexual Experience Among Coeds, 1958 and 1968." Journal of Marriage and the Family 32 (February):81–84.

Bell, Robert R., and Michael Gordon
1972 The Social Dimension of Human Sexuality. Boston, Mass.: Little, Brown.

Bryan, James H.
1965 "Apprenticeships in Prostitution." Social Problems 12 (Winter):287–297.

Christensen, Harold T., and Christina F. Gregg
1970 "Changing Sex Norms in America and Scandinavia." Journal of Marriage and the Family 32 (November):616–627.

Commission on Obscenity and Pornography
1970 The Report of the Commission on Obscenity and Pornography. New York: Bantam.

Cuber, John F.
1969 "Adultery: Reality Versus Stereotype." Pp. 190–196 in Gerhard Neubeck (ed.), Extramarital Relations. Englewood Cliffs, N.J.: Prentice-Hall.

Cuber, John F., and Peggy B. Harroff
1965 The Significant Americans. New York: Appleton.

Davis, Kingsley
1971 "Sexual Behavior." Pp. 313–360 in Robert K. Merton and Robert Nisbet (eds.), Contemporary Social Problems. Third ed. New York: Harcourt.

Denfeld, Duane, and Michael Gordon
1970 "The Sociology of Mate Swapping: Or the Family That Swings Together Clings Together." Journal of Sex Research 6 (May):85–100.

Edwards, John N.
1972 Sex and Society. Chicago: Markham.
1973 "Extramarital Involvement: Fact and Theory." The Journal of Sex Research 9 (August):210–224.

Ehrmann, Winston
1959 Premarital Dating Behavior. New York: Holt, Rinehart & Winston.

Ford, Clellan S., and Frank A. Beach
1951 Patterns of Sexual Behavior. New York: Harper & Row.

Gagnon, John H., and William Simon
1967 Sexual Deviance. New York: Harper & Row.
1970 "Prospects for Change in American Sexual Patterns." Medical Aspects of Human Sexuality 4 (January):100–117.

Gebhard, Paul H.
1973 Personal Communication. (January 24).

Gebhard, Paul H., John H. Gagnon, Wardell B. Pomeroy, and Cornelia V. Christenson
1965 Sex Offenders. New York: Harper & Row.

Hariton, E. Barbara
1973 "The Sexual Fantasies of Women." Psychology Today 6 (March): 39–44.

Hedblom, Jack H.
1972 "The Female Homosexual: Social and Attitudinal Dimensions." Pp. 31–64 in Joseph A. McCaffrey (ed.), The Homosexual Dialectic. Englewood Cliffs, N.J.: Prentice-Hall.

Helmer, William J.
1963 "New York's 'Middle-Class' Homosexuals." Harper's Magazine 226 (March):85–92.
Hoffman, Martin
1970 "Homosexuality and Social Evil." Pp. 137–141 in James V. McConnell (ed.), Readings in Social Psychology Today. Del Mar, Calif.: CRM Books.
Holloway, Mark
1966 Heavens on Earth. Second ed. New York: Dover.
Hooker, Evelyn
1967 "The Homosexual Community." Pp. 168–184 in Gagnon and Simon.
Jackman, Norman R., Richard O'Toole, and Gilbert Geis
1963 "The Self-Image of the Prostitute." Sociological Quarterly 4 (Spring): 150–161.
Kaufman, Irving, Alice L. Peck, and Consuelo K. Tagiuri
1954 "The Family Constellation and Overt Incestuous Relations Between Father and Daughter." American Journal of Orthopsychiatry 24 (April):266–277.
Kinsey, Alfred C., Wardell B. Pomeroy, and Clyde E. Martin
1948 Sexual Behavior in the Human Male. Philadelphia: Saunders.
Kinsey, Alfred C., Wardell B. Pomeroy, Clyde E. Martin, and Paul H. Gebhard
1953 Sexual Behavior in the Human Female. Philadelphia: Saunders.
Leslie, Gerald R.
1973 The Family in Social Context. Second ed. New York: Oxford University Press.
Lester, David
1972 "Incest." The Journal of Sex Research 8 (November):268–285.
Leznoff, Maurice, and William A. Westley
1956 "The Homosexual Community." Social Problems 3 (April):257–263.
Murdock, George P.
1965 Social Structure. New York: Free Press.
Newton, Esther
1972 Mother Camp: Female Impersonators in America. Englewood Cliffs, N.J.: Prentice-Hall.
O'Neill, George C., and Nena O'Neill
1970 "Patterns of Group Sexual Activity." The Journal of Sex Research 6 (May):101–112.
O'Neill, Nena, and George O'Neill
1972 Open Marriage: A New Life Style for Couples. New York: M. Evans.
Packard, Vance
1968 The Sexual Wilderness: The Contemporary Upheaval in Male-Female Relationships. New York: McKay.
Reiss, Albert J., Jr.
1961 "The Social Integration of Queers and Peers." Social Problems 9 (Fall): 102–120.
1967 "Sex Offenses: The Marginal Status of the Adolescent." Pp. 44–77 in Gagnon and Simon.
Reiss, Ira L.
1960 Premarital Sexual Standards in America. New York: Free Press.

1965 "Class and Premarital Sexual Permissiveness." American Sociological Review 30 (October):747–756.

1967 The Social Context of Premarital Sexual Permissiveness. New York: Holt, Rinehart & Winston.

Simon, William, and John H. Gagnon

1967 "The Lesbians: A Preliminary Overview." Pp. 247–282 in Gagnon and Simon.

1969 "Psychosexual Development." Transaction 6 (March):9–17.

Smith, James R., and Lynn G. Smith

1970 "Co-Marital Sex and the Sexual Freedom Movement." The Journal of Sex Research 6 (May):131–142.

Stephenson, Richard M.

1973 "Involvement in Deviance: An Example and Some Theoretical Implications." Social Problems 21 (Fall):173–190.

Symonds, Carolyn

1968 Pilot Study of the Peripheral Behavior of Sexual Mate Swappers. Unpublished Master's Thesis, University of California, Riverside.

Tappan, Paul W.

1960 Crime, Justice and Correction. New York: McGraw-Hill.

Walshok, Mary Lindenstein

1971 "The Emergence of Middle-Class Deviant Subcultures: The Case of Swingers." Social Problems 18 (Spring):488–495.

Weinberg, S. Kirson

1955 Incest Behavior. New York: Citadel.

Wheeler, Stanton

1967 "Sex Offenses: A Sociological Critique." Pp. 78–102 in Gagnon and Simon.

Winick, Charles, and Paul M. Kinsie

1971 The Lively Commerce. Chicago: Quadrangle.

Young, Wayland

1964 Eros Denied. New York: Grove.

INTRODUCTION TO THE READINGS

The first selection in this chapter is concerned with pornography, a form of sexual deviance that has been almost totally neglected by sociologists. While pornography is generally repudiated by society, it is apparently found universally. Polsky attempts to explain the universality of pornography by suggesting that it plays a function analogous to that of prostitution. Both provide an outlet for the expression of what is considered deviant or anti-social sex, prostitution a direct physical outlet and pornography an indirect vicarious outlet. Pornography then is normal deviance. The behavior is officially condemned, but it is engaged in by a large proportion of the population and reinforces rather than challenges traditional societal values that support monogamous marriage. From this perspective pornography serves a safety-valve function by providing a safe institutionalized outlet for aberrant desires. Thus the consumers of pornography are not depraved sex criminals but normal and respectable middle-class citizens, and, moreover, pornography is no longer the exclusive domain of the male (Commission on Obscenity and Pornography, 1970:144–168). Many couples, for example, find that pornography enhances marital sex.

The second selection is taken from the *History of American Socialisms,* a classic work on nineteenth-century utopian societies. The author, John Humphrey Noyes, was the founder and charismatic leader of the Oneida Community. Noyes and his followers were "utopian" swingers in the true sense of the word, and the ideology espoused by members of Oneida contrasts sharply with that of contemporary recreational swingers. Recreational swinging is not particularly threatening to the nuclear family; the recreational swingers, as was mentioned previously, swings for fun or pleasure without commitment to a deviant or radical value system. Noyes adhered to the doctrine of perfectionism, believing that since the Second Coming of Christ had taken place in 70 A.D., man should work to perfect himself on this earth, to create "Heaven on Earth" (Holloway, 1966:179–185). The community introduced a pattern of complex marriage according to which any two consenting adults could engage in sexual relations. The ultimate goal was to abolish monogamous marriage.

On the sociology of pornography*

NED POLSKY

Samuel Johnson once informed James Boswell that he could recite a complete chapter of a book called *The Natural History of Iceland*. The chapter was entitled "Concerning Snakes," and consisted in its entirety of the following: "There are no snakes to be met with throughout the whole island." I can be similarly brief concerning studies on the sociology of pornography: there are no such studies to be met with throughout the whole of sociology.

What we do have, first of all, is an abundance of offhand "sociologizing" about pornography, on the part of contemporary journalists, cultural historians, psychiatrists, literary critics, lawyers, and judges—especially if they are of liberal inclination and don't like censorship. This material isn't worth much. In fact its chief interest for sociologists, as I shall elaborate below, is that the sociological interpretations most often found in it are demonstrably wrong.

Secondly, we have some published data on consumers of pornography and their social backgrounds. The best material of this sort, as on most matters sexual, comes (as you might expect) from the Institute for Sex Research.[1]

Thirdly, we have a particular sociological theory—I would call it a theory of the upper-middle range—that was not developed to explain the place of pornography in society but nevertheless serves, I think, to explain that place very well.

There are many special aspects of the sociology of pornography, and in what follows I shall not even mention most of them, much less pursue them. Instead, I shall try to spell out how that theory of the upper-middle range gives a sociological overview of pornography within which more specialized investigations might proceed.

I

In his study of prostitution Kingsley Davis demonstrated, with cogent reasoning and much evidence that I cannot rehearse here, the following main argument: (a) the goals of sexual behavior in man are not inherently social;

[1] Cf. Alfred Kinsey, Wardell Pomeroy, and Clyde Martin, *Sexual Behavior in the Human Male* (Philadelphia: W. B. Saunders, 1948), pp. 363, 510; and Kinsey, Pomeroy, Martin, and Paul Gebhard, *Sexual Behavior in the Human Female* (Philadelphia: W. B. Saunders, 1953), pp. 652–72. N. B. that most Kinsey findings on male use of pornography are presented in the volume on females, along with comparative data on females.

* Most of this chapter was presented at the annual meeting of the American Sociological Association, Miami Beach, August, 1966. I offered a sketchy first version of some of it at a public symposium, "Pornography and Literature," in which I participated with Alfred Chester, Benjamin De Mott, Ephraim London, and Hubert Selby, at the YMHA Poetry Center, New York City, March, 1966.

but (b) societies need to hook sexuality onto social ends, particularly the ends of bearing and raising children, by restricting the morally legitimate expression of sex to the institution of the family; and (c) this conflict between sexual inclinations and social requirements is ameliorated by prostitution, which helps to maintain the family as an institution by acting as a safety-valve for the expression of antisocial coitus—i.e., impersonal, transitory, nonfamilial coitus—that cannot be fully suppressed.[2] Davis thus sees the family and prostitution as complementary institutions, each requisite to the other.

I suggest that Davis's theory applies, *mutatis mutandis*, to pornography. Prostitution and pornography occur in every society large enough to have a reasonably complex division of labor; and although pornography develops in only a rudimentary way in preliterate societies (by means of erotic folktales and simple pictorial or sculptural devices), whenever a society has a fair degree of literacy and mass-communication technology then pornography becomes a major functional alternative to prostitution.

In saying that prostitution and pornography are, at least in modern societies, functional alternatives, I mean that they are different roads to the same desired social end. Both provide for the discharge of what society labels antisocial sex, i.e., impersonal, nonmarital sex: prostitution provides this via real intercourse with a real sex object, and pornography provides it via masturbatory, imagined intercourse with a fantasy object.

[2] Cf. Kingsley Davis, "Prostitution," in Robert Merton and Robert Nisbet (Eds.), *Contemporary Social Problems* (New York: Harcourt, Brace & World, 1961), pp. 262–88.

Although societies use both alternatives, the degree to which one is used in preference to the other seems to vary considerably from one society to the next, in ways and for reasons that remain to be investigated. There is also variation within a given society, of at least two kinds: First, there is variation in what is considered appropriate in different social situations; for example, a group of adolescent boys might collectively visit a prostitute but masturbate to pornography only singly and in private, with group contemplation of pornography serving merely to convey sex information or as the occasion for ribald humor. A second kind of variation has to do with what is considered appropriate in different subcultures. The main such variation in our own society, revealed by the Kinsey data, is that masturbating to pornographic books or pictures is largely a phenomenon of the better-educated classes; at the lower levels of our society, this is generally put down (as is long-term masturbation *per se*), and, conversely, prostitutes are visited much more often.

Prostitution, as Davis noted, presents a great paradox of social life: on the one hand it is so nearly a cultural universal[3] that it seems to fill a need

[3] [*Addendum, 1968:* Mario Bick has pointed out to me that prostitution and pornography are not fully cross-cultural phenomena, and that Davis and I have been misled simply because these occur in various Eastern societies (such as China, Japan, India) as well as Western ones. Mr. Bick notes that (a) all the examples we can cite are from long-time monetary economies, and (b) in nonmonetary, polygynous societies such as those of Africa, prostitution appears to be unknown before European contact and/or urbanization, and erotic depictions do not have the pornographic function they have in monetary economies.]

endemic to complex societies, but on the other hand the prostitute is, except in very special circumstances, generally and highly stigmatized. Davis's theory resolves the paradox, and does so in a way that applies equally to pornography: both prostitutes and pornographers are stigmatized because they provide for the socially illegitimate expression of sex, yet their very existence helps to make tolerable the institutionalizing of legitimate sex in the family.

An additional relation between the functioning and the stigmatizing of prostitutes and pornographers, a relation at once more general and more intimate than that given by Davis, may be inferred from the neo-Durkheimian theory of deviance recently proposed by Kai Erikson. He observes:

The only material found in a system for marking [moral] boundaries is the behavior of its participants; and the kinds of behavior which best perform this function are often deviant. . . . In this sense, transactions between deviant persons and agencies of social control are boundary-maintaining mechanisms. . . . Each time the group censures some act of deviation it sharpens the authority of the violated norm. . . . [Instances of publicity about deviants, as in the old public parading of them or in the modern newspaper] constitute our main source of information about the normative contours of society.[4]

In Erikson's view, then, one function of prostitutes and pornographers would lie precisely *in* the fact that they are stigmatized.

II

The use of pornography is by no means limited to its role as an adjunct to masturbation. For example, as al-ready indicated, pornography may sometimes serve rather as a sex instruction manual. (Conversely, a sex instruction manual may serve as pornography.) And sometimes pornography, far from stimulating masturbation, may be used to stimulate real intercourse, as in, say, the case of whorehouse murals from Pompeii to the present. Granted all that, and other uses as well, people given to using pornography do so for the most part as a means of facilitating masturbation. This is the primary use of pornography. It is summed up in the classic definition of pornographic books as "the books that one reads with one hand."

The consumption of pornography is a sort of halfway house between sexual intercourse and erotic response to purely private mental fantasies. Masturbation to pornography is more "social" than masturbation simply to inner pictures, i.e., pornography offers the masturbator erotic imagery that is external to himself, a quasi-real "other" to whom he can more "realistically" respond. That is why even lower-class males frequently use pornography for masturbatory release—and here the Kinsey findings need qualification—when they are deprived of their usual sexual outlets: people in prisons are overwhelmingly from the lower class, and the masturbatory use of pornography is widespread in prisons and a continual headache for any prison administrator who wants to make it one.[5] Sociologists, however, in their fascination with the way pris-

---

[4] Kai Erikson, "Notes on the Sociology of Deviance," *Social Problems*, Vol. 9 (Spring, 1962), pp. 307–14.

[5] Cf. Charles Smith, "Prison Pornography," *Journal of Social Therapy*, Vol. 1 (1955), pp. 126–29, and Stanley B. Zuckerman, "Sex Literature in Prison," *ibid.*, pp. 129–31. I cite these articles merely to document the widespread prison use of pornography.

oners turn toward homosexuality, seem to have neglected the prisoners' turn toward pornography.

As my reference to jailhouse pornography implies, a great deal of pornography exists unpublished, in the form of manuscript writing or drawing. Even outside the prison context, an enormous number—perhaps even the majority—of pornographic works are in manuscript.[6] The important thing to realize about such manuscripts is that mostly they are produced neither for publication nor for circulation as manuscripts, but for self-enjoyment. Here we have a major difference between prostitution and pornography: hardly any man can, as it were, be his own prostitute (although many try, by attempting auto-fellation),[7] but every man can be his own pornographer. Even a good deal of published pornography was written initially to aid the masturbation of the writer. For example, Jean Genet indicates that this was why he wrote *Our Lady of the Flowers*.[8] And it is apparently to this motivation that we owe the pornography produced by the most noted pornographer of them all, the Marquis de Sade. Here is a letter from Sade to his

wife, written from prison in 1783—a date, note well, that is several years after Sade had begun writing nonpornographic works but before he had written any pornography:

I'll bet you thought you had a brilliant idea in imposing a revolting abstinence on me with regard to the sins of the flesh. Well, you were all mistaken. You brought my brain to the boiling point. You caused me to conjure up fanciful creatures which I shall have to bring into being.

Over the years that followed, most of them spent in jail, Sade devoted himself to setting down those fanciful creatures on paper. As Albert Camus put it, Sade "created a fiction in order to give himself the illusion of being."[9]

Of course Genet and Sade wrote most of their pornography while in prison. But especially when it comes to sexuality, society imprisons everyone in a number of ways; that is the starting point of Kingsley Davis's argument and mine—and also and originally and profoundly, though Davis is silent on the matter, of Sigmund Freud's. Let us now consider one of those ways—and here my point of departure is Freud rather than Davis—that seems especially germane to our subject.

III

Prostitution and pornography, as we have seen, allow the expression of antisocial sex—impersonal, transitory, non-familial sex. But both institutions also provide for antisocial sex in another, deeper sense—one that is merely mentioned in passing by Kingsley Davis but is nevertheless a key function of prostitution as well as pornog-

---

[6] This seems to be the implication of a statement about quantities made in the Kinsey volume on females, *op. cit.*, p. 672. See also Wladimir Eliasberg, "Remarks on the Psychopathology of Pornography," *Journal of Criminal Psychopathology*, Vol. 3 (1942), pp. 715–20, although on other points, as note 20 below may indicate, Eliasberg is unreliable.

[7] Kinsey *et al.* report in their volume on males, *op. cit.*, p. 510, that "a considerable portion" of males attempt autofellation, at least in early adolescence, but that it is anatomically impossible for all except two or three males in a thousand.

[8] Cf. Jean Genet, *Our Lady of the Flowers* (New York: Bantam Books, 1964), e.g., pp. 59–61.

[9] I take the Sade and Camus quotations from Georges May, "Fiction Reader, Novel Writer," *Yale French Studies*, No. 35, "Sade" (December, 1965), p. 7.

raphy: these institutions permit "poly-morphous perverse" and other sexual behaviors so highly stigmatized as to be labelled deviant even within the institution of marriage and morally inhibited from expression therein.

In other words, sex is socialized by being placed in a double constraint—the marital relationship on the one hand and a specified selection of possible sex acts on the other. It is important to see that the function of prostitution and pornography in alleviating the latter constraint is clearly distinct from their providing merely for coitus *per se* (real or imaginary) in an impersonal and transitory relationship.

No real house of prostitution has perhaps approached the logically ultimate one depicted in Genet's play *The Balcony*, where each client buys a custom-made social scene that conforms in all particulars to any wishful sexual fantasy he chooses to select. But many such houses, as well as freelance prostitutes, have specialized in catering to customers who wanted to indulge in sadism, masochism, orgies, intercourse with children, anal or oral intercourse, voyeurism, intercourse with the aid of mechanical contraptions, fetishism, and so on. Among one city's documented examples that come to mind are: London's Victorian houses of child prostitutes, including (a sub-specialty of the house) the providing of prepubescent virgins[10]; the advertisement by London prostitutes, in their *Ladies Directory* of 1959–1960, offering themselves in rubber or leather clothing; and the many more advertisements, in the same periodical, by prostitutes offering "corrective treatment" and signing themselves with such sobriquets as "Ex-governess, strict

disciplinarian" and "Miss Whyplash."[11] In a study of 732 American clients of prostitutes (574 clients were married, 158 single), the motivation for patronage that the clients indicated most frequently (78 percent of the clients) was that they "got something different" from a prostitute, and 10 percent of these further volunteered the information that the difference was in the type of sexual act performed.[12] Other studies have shown that even the prostitute having no desire to specialize must learn, and quite early in her career, that she will encounter a goodly share of customers presenting "kinky" or "freaky" sexual requests.[13] There is an enormous amount of this sort of material on prostitution (far more than I have mentioned), but, although most of it was available when Davis wrote, he ignores all of it.[14]

---

[10] Cf. W. T. Stead's series of articles, "Maiden Tribute of Modern Babylon," in issues of the *Pall Mall Gazette* for 1885.

[11] Published monthly in Soho, the *Ladies Directory* was transparently disguised as a directory of "models" in an attempt to circumvent the new ban on open soliciting. At least nine issues appeared. The prosecution of its publisher is described in, e.g., the London *Evening Standard* of July 26, 1960.

[12] Cf. Charles Winick, "Clients' Perceptions of Prostitutes and of Themselves," *International Journal of Social Psychiatry*, Vol. 8 (1961–62), pp. 289–97.

[13] Cf. John Murtagh and Sara Harris, *Cast the First Stone* (New York: McGraw-Hill, 1957), pp. 180–86; James Bryan, "Apprenticeships in Prostitution," *Social Problems*, Vol. 12, No. 3 (Winter, 1965), pp. 287–97.

[14] There are many other defects in Davis's account of prostitution. Most are matters of detail—e.g., Davis thinks the attempt to control pimps arises only with industrialized societies, though Pompeo Molmenti could have told him that in twelfth-century Venice "pimps were imprisoned, branded, tortured, and banished"—but one is crucial: Davis insists

For our purpose, the point is this: as prostitution goes with respect to perversity, so goes pornography—only more so. Possibly the "more so" derives from the fact that "freaky" sexual

---

that *promiscuity* is the fundamental defining element of prostitution, with commercial and emotionally indifferent aspects of the role being distinctly secondary. But against this emphasis we can put the following considerations: (1) The typical prostitute undertakes intercourse for money or valuables. (2) Even the untypical prostitute, such as one whose prostitution is a religious duty, works for some remuneration, albeit largely for what the economist calls "psychic income." (3) Davis ignores the fact that nymphomaniacs, free souls, and others who literally "give it away" may be stigmatized by the society but are not generally classified as prostitutes either by law enforcers or by laymen (for example, cf. W. F. Whyte, "A Slum Sex Code," *American Journal of Sociology*, Vol. XLIX [July, 1943], pp. 24–31). (4) Davis also ignores the fact that, conversely, some women not promiscuous in the slightest degree, such as concubines, are usually regarded as special types of prostitutes, although they carry lesser stigma. (5) Davis finds support for his "promiscuity" thesis in the fact that the prostitute's stigma is lessened whenever promiscuity is lessened (as in the case of *geisha*, who were selective about customers); but with equal logic one can note that the prostitute's stigma is lessened whenever she is not "strictly commercial," even if she is highly promiscuous (as in the case of temple prostitutes). A definition of prostitution that would best fit all these points—while excluding the woman who "marries for money" as well as the girl who consents to intercourse only after a fancy dinner and is, as Kinsey remarks, "engaged in a more commercialized relationship than she would like to admit"—is the following: Prostitution is the granting of nonmarital sex *as a vocation*.

interests, being much more highly stigmatized than simple nonmarital coitus, lie closer to total repression or suppression and thus are more often banished strictly to fantasized interaction; possibly other factors account for the difference. In any event, it seems clear that although much pornography depicts sexual relations whose only deviance consists of their nonmarital status, an extraordinary amount of this material offers fantasy involvement in sex acts that society proscribes as "unnatural." The history of pornography provides endless examples, and in this regard it makes no difference whether one thinks of the "hard core" tradition from, say, the *Priapea* of ancient Rome to such current paperbacks as *Perverted Lust Slave*, or of the "art" tradition from, say, Petronius to *Histoire d'O*.

IV

From a sociological standpoint our society's current distinction between "genuine" or "hard core" pornography and highly erotic art is specious in a more fundamental respect.

In recent years the U.S. federal courts have tended to second and extend the view—a view advanced by defense lawyers, literary critics, *et al.*—that certain extremely erotic books and films are not really pornographic because they show over-all serious artistic intent and/or contain other redeeming social virtues, that is, because they seem not to be simply "dirt for dirt's sake." The courts in various ways have reaffirmed and amplified the doctrine, first set forth clearly in Judge John Woolsey's 1933 decision on Joyce's *Ulysses* and the 1934 confirming opinion of Augustus Hand, that highly realistic descriptions of sex cannot be judged pornographic in isolation, but must be viewed within the context of the work as a whole.[15] And except for a handful of diehard clergymen, our social critics, literary scholars, journalists, and the like—our "sociologizers" about pornography—have fallen in line.[16] But the sociologist, at any rate this sociologist, must disagree with such "contextual" arguments and maintain that a work like, say, Henry Miller's *Tropic of Cancer* is pornographic, whatever else it may be in addition.

Granted that in one type of sociological analysis—what is loosely called the "labelling" approach—pornography is neither more nor less than what the society's decisive power groups say it is at any given time, and if our society now chooses officially to label *Tropic of Cancer* nonpornographic, that's that.[17] Such a conceptual framework does lead to many useful discoveries, along the lines indicated by W. I. Thomas's famous dictum that if people define a situation as real, it is real in its consequences. But this mode of analysis has its limitations, as can be seen when we turn to another and equally legitimate mode, functional analysis, and define pornography in terms of what it actually does to or for society—what are its particular uses and effects on people, intended or otherwise.[18]

Pornography obviously has many functions; and some of these are not even sexual, e.g., the providing of paid work for pornography producers and sellers, as well as for their professional opponents. But as we have seen, por-

[15] Judge Woolsey's decision is most readily available in the front matter of the Modern Library edition of *Ulysses*. For Augustus Hand's superb affirming decision, which languishes unreprinted, see 72 F. (2d) 705.

[16] Among many recent examples of this kind of reasoning, the best known is probably Eberhard and Phyllis Kronhausen, *Pornography and the Law* (New York: Ballantine Books, 1959).

[17] The "labelling" viewpoint, associated with publications in recent years by Edwin Lemert, Howard Becker, John Kitsuse, *et al.*, is actually a reinvention of a viewpoint formulated and applied in sociology at least as far back as Wilhelm Lange-Eichbaum's *The Problem of Genius* (1931), and in the sociology of deviance at least as far back as Frank Tannenbaum's *Crime and the Community* (1938; see Tannenbaum on "the dramatization of evil"). As a "literary" insight into the workings of society its history goes back much further, e.g., the Spanish inquisitor Salazar Frias wrote in 1611 that "there were neither witches nor bewitched until they were written and talked about." The topic is worthy of a Shandean postscript, but I forbear.

[18] As other parts of this essay should indicate, I am hardly arguing for functionalist theory *against* labelling theory, and rather believe that the two theories apply at different levels of analysis and that both have great explanatory power. But unfortunately some "labellers," in their initial zeal for the reinvented theory, fail to see its limitations. They have overly reified W. I. Thomas's dictum, and are in danger of falling into the same trap W. Lloyd Warner fell into when he concluded that social class is "really" what people say it is.

Thomas's insight is true, but only half the truth. The other half is that social life, though profoundly affected by the participants' linguistic interpretation of it, is not identical with or completely determined by such interpretation. In other words, a real situation has some real consequences even if people *don't* define it as real. That fact is often lost sight of by those who take a "labelling" stance (see, for example, my remarks on Korn and McCorkle in Chapter 3). It is never lost sight of by functionalists; in fact, their recognition of it underlies two of the most useful analytic concepts of modern sociology, the concept of latent function and the concept of functional alternatives.

nography's main function at the societal level (as distinguished from the individual-psychological level) is to help preserve society's double institutionalizing of legitimate sex—within marriage and within a specified few of the possible sex acts—by providing sexual depictions that literally drain off the other, socially illegitimate sexual desires of the beholder. Any sexual depiction (written, recorded, pictorial) that facilitates such masturbatory involvement is thus pornographic. And when pornography is defined in this way, it becomes clear that the courts and the literary critics are wrong, viz., their assumption that pornography and art are mutually exclusive is patently false. For in contemplating naturalistic erotic art, people can and do easily respond to the erotic qualities as such, in utter disregard of the "artistic context." The stock of every pornography store confirms this. Thus the user of written pornography, for example, gets his pornography from "hard core" literature or from erotic "art" literature; so far as he is concerned, the only significant difference is that in the latter he usually gets less for his money.[19]

Let me suggest at this point that my readers think back to their early adolescence and recall the so-called "dirty books" that were used for adolescent masturbation. (Rather, I ask males among my readers to do this. As the Kinsey data reveal, only a small minority of females are sexually excited by pornography, much less masturbate to it, for reasons largely unknown.[20]) I think most will be able to recall not only "hard core" pornography, such as the little booklets containing pornographic versions of American comic strips, but also that there were so-called "dirty books" which were really for the most part "clean" and were read for their occasional "dirty pages," such as the books of Erskine Caldwell. At least, that was

---

attributes they can, i.e., become hypereffeminate homosexuals, they do not give up the male's interest in pornography (though of course the object changes and so their pornography consists of erotic depictions of males). And, conversely, when women take on as many male role attributes as they can, i.e., become tough "butch" lesbians, they do not typically lose the female's disinterest in pornography.

There are indeed many pornographic "lesbian" novels, but they are fakes. They are written by men and bought by men. (Both points have been made to me by Times Square pornography peddlers, and I have confirmed the latter from observation in their stores.) The genuine lesbian novel, whether the inartistic kind such as Radclyffe Hall's *Well of Loneliness* or the artistic kind such as Djuna Barnes's *Nightwood*, does not contain naturalistic description of sex but emphasizes the emotional-psychological aspect of sexual relationships. In this respect it is similar to the romantic literature that heterosexual women enjoy (on the latter, see the Kinsey volume on females, *op. cit.*, p. 670).

Apart from disinterest by females (heterosexual or homosexual) in pornography consumption, and the fact that "lesbian" pornography is actually produced by males for males, it has also been established beyond doubt that heterosexual pornography production by females is very rare. (Cf. Kinsey volume on females, *op. cit.*, p. 672.) Yet Wladimir Eliasberg, *op. cit.*, claims a striking feature of pornographic literature is that one cannot tell whether a man or woman is either the producer or consumer.

---

[19] Hanan Selvin has reminded me that the strong erotic appeal, as such, of much erotic art, is also noted in Sir Kenneth Clark's *The Nude*.

[20] Note that theories of the female "role" won't do to explain this, for even when men take on all the female role

true not only for my own early adolescence but for that of most every other middle-class boy I knew at the time.

I know of no evidence to indicate that people erotically interested in naturalistic descriptions of sex—whatever their age—are seriously impeded by, or even give much thought to, the overall non-erotic context in which such descriptions might be embedded; and this applies to highly artistic works as well as any other. Can one seriously maintain, for example, that most of the Americans in Paris who smuggled back copies of *Lady Chatterley's Lover* and *Tropic of Cancer* did so out of interest in the "artistic" or "other social redeeming" qualities of these books rather than out of "prurient interest"? Or when it comes to the people—adolescent or adult—who masturbate to such books, can one seriously claim that they used these works for masturbatory purposes only so long as our society labelled them pornographic and stopped such masturbating when the label changed? Clearly we must modify W. I. Thomas's dictum, which is the "labelling" dictum writ small, to read that if people define a situation as real (erotic book X is non-pornographic), it is real in some of its consequences (erotic book X can be sold over the counter) but not in others (people don't stop masturbating to it).

And clearly society has always permitted the dissemination of some kinds of material that are functionally pornographic. In our own society one of the major ways it currently does so, as previously indicated, is to non-label such material as pornographic if it is packaged between significant amounts of non-erotic material—as in, say, the pages of *Playboy*.

The social processes involved in deciding which pornography shall be permitted, and even some (though by no means all) of the selective criteria used, are roughly analogous to the way that—as Sutherland showed us—our society permits certain types of criminals, notably businessmen who commit crimes in their corporate capacities, to escape penological consequences and even public stigma.[21] The recent case of the magazine *Eros* notwithstanding, the classier the pornography the more likely it is to be permitted.[22] What is big news about the publisher of *Eros* is precisely what is big news about those price-fixing G.E. officials: such people are rarely the kind who get rapped.

V

At the same time that society permits the dissemination of pornography, it officially denounces it. There is good reason for it to do both at once: from the desire to maintain a restrictive societal definition of "legitimate" sex, it naturally follows that pornography should be stigmatized and harassed yet tolerated as a safety-valve, in the same way that, as Davis demonstrates, society stigmatizes and otherwise harasses prostitution but never really abolishes it.

[21] Cf. Edwin Sutherland, *White Collar Crime* (New York: Holt, Rinehart & Winston, 1949), especially pp. 42 ff. Of course there are also special selective factors operating at more mundane levels of pornography production. For example, in the recent case of a Michigan hard-core pornographer who was not only fined $19,000 but sentenced to ten years in prison, I assume that the severity of the sentence was not unrelated to the title of his masterpiece: *The Sex Life of a Cop.* (Cf. New York *Daily News*, April 7, 1966, p. 13, col. 1).

[22] On the case of *Eros* and the prison sentence given to its publisher, see, for example, *The New York Times*, March 27, 1966, p. 8E, cols. 1–2.

And just as Davis indicates for prostitution, the stigma attached to pornography is lessened when pornography is tied to some other socially valued end, such as art or science. One important result is this: when the "situation" being defined by society is a naturalistic depiction of sex, the most real consequence of a definition that labels it something other than pornographic is to increase its pornographic use in the society by reducing the inhibitions on acquiring it. This is obvious from the libraries of countless souls who avidly buy highly erotic work that society labels "art" or "literature" or "science" or "scholarship," but who take care not to buy "real" pornography.

And if the non-labelling of an erotic depiction as pornographic actually increases its pornographic use in the society, de-labelling increases such usefulness still more. As any publisher can tell you (I speak as a former publisher), it is much better for sales to have an erotic book that was once labelled pornographic and then got delabelled than to have one that never got labelled at all. Thus such works as *Lady Chatterley* or *Tropic of Cancer* are, functionally, among our society's most pornographic books of all.

All of this could, as Albert Cohen has suggested to me, simply indicate that many if not most Americans label *Playboy* or erotic art or sexual scholarship as "pornography" even if the courts and others don't. But such an interpretation depends on a dubious double hypothesis—that the courts have largely deluded themselves in claiming to follow community opinion and have also failed to mold opinion. It might still be truer than mine, and only empirical data we don't yet have can settle the question. However, I think it more reasonable to suppose this: If the behavior of people often

contradicts their attitudes (and social research is forever stumbling against that one), then it can be just as discrepant with their labelling or definition of the situation, and, moreover, such discrepancy is widespread in areas of life involving socially encouraged hypocrisy and unawareness, as in the case of sex behavior.

And even clearer, and more fundamental, discrepancy between social reality and the social definition or labelling of the situation has to do with highly erotic depictions that make no claim to art or science and are not enwrapped in non-erotic contexts, depictions that society calls "real" or "hard core" pornography or "dirt for dirt's sake." Such a label means that the material is, in the words of Mr. Justice Brennan, "utterly without redeeming social importance." That definition of the situation is obviously upheld by the great majority of our society; it is entertained equally by the courts, by assorted professional experts (such as literary critics and psychiatrists), and by the lay public. It is, nevertheless, mistaken. To the extent that society, in restricting morally legitimate sex to certain specified acts within marriage, cannot count fully on the mechanisms of repression and suppression, to that extent it must provide stigmatized safety-valve institutions such as prostitution and pornography.[23] As Thomas

[23] The historical and comparative sociology of the part that "safety-valve" institutions play in social control has yet to be written. We do not even have an adequate general theory of these functions—merely scattered remarks about *panem et circenses*—although Freud has provided many psychological underpinnings for such a theory. Here I note only that in our society major historical changes in safety-valve mechanisms have involved other than sexual institutions; for example, there has been a decrease in displace-

Aquinas put it—he was explaining prostitution—"A cesspool is necessary to a palace if the whole palace is not to smell."[24]

VI

As I mentioned at the beginning of this chapter, there are many special aspects of the sociology of pornography. One involves a hypothesis I am currently testing and for which I have already found a bit of confirmation, namely, that organized crime is more and more associating itself with the production and distribution of hard core pornography, particularly but not exclusively the most profitable part of it, pornographic movies. This would represent a coming together of organized crime's traditional interest in providing illegal goods and services, with a change in American consumption patterns that is having fateful consequences for the technology of pornography: the great increase, over the past fifteen years, in private ownership of 8 mm. movie projectors.

Until roughly 1950, the pornographic movie business consisted largely in renting films for showing at stag dinners, fraternity parties, and the like, but since then it has been increasingly, and is now overwhelmingly, a matter of outright sale of prints to individual customers.[25] Consequently, over the past decade and a half, the pornographic movie business has had one of the highest growth rates of any business in the United States (legal or illegal); and organized crime is now well aware of that fact if the general public is not. It is true that the pornographic movie industry, like the pornography industry generally, is still mostly in the hands of individual entrepreneurs; but if present trends continue, investment in this industry by organized crime may one day reach the takeoff point, that is, the stage where muscle is applied to make independents fall in line or get out.

There are other special hypotheses about the sociology of pornography that need investigating, dozens of them. What I have tried to do here is offer a general framework within which such investigations might be made.[26]

---

ment of secular goals onto an afterlife (a decline in "pie in the sky" or "opium of the people" functions of religion), and an increase in spectatorship for competitive sports as a means of draining off potential public violence.

[24] This view of prostitution—which, shorn of its moralism, is the essence of Davis's sociological view—can be found in many writers beside St. Thomas, e.g., in Horace's *Satires* and Mary Wollstonecraft's *A Vindication of the Rights of Woman*. Of these functionalist explanations prior to Davis, the ablest are in Bernard Mandeville's "An Inquiry into the Origin of Moral Virtue" (his preface to the 1714 edition of *Fable of the Bees*) and his *A Modest Defence of Publick Stews* (1724).

[25] I am informed by pornography distributors in Soho, London, that a similar shift has taken place in England.

[26] *Addendum:* A detailed scholarly study of mid-Victorian sexuality and pornography, based on the Kinsey collection, was published after this book went to press: Steven Marcus, *The Other Victorians* (New York: Basic Books, 1966). At various places in his book Mr. Marcus discusses the relation of pornography to Victorian society, and his concluding chapter is, in design and in the words of the publisher, "an essay propounding a general theory of pornography as a sociological [i.e., social] phenomenon." In this late note I cannot demonstrate, but only asseverate, that *The Other Victorians* is a prime instance of rubbishy "sociologizing" about pornography, "sociologizing"

of the sort produced by that growing band of American literary critics who believe they are experts on society simply because they live in it.

One brief example: Mr. Marcus seems ignorant of statistical reasoning and, worse, of its possible relevance to his argument. Hence one cannot learn from his book that the Victorian era's tremendous upsurge in the growth rate of pornography publishing, which he finds so strange, was equalled and usually surpassed by increases in growth rates for every other kind of publishing. (Indeed, he even seems innocent of the distinction between growth and growth rate.) Nor can one learn that all this had some relation to England's having perfected, in the first decade of the nineteenth century, the Fourdrinier machine for cheap papermaking, nor the fact that, over the following decades, while England's population grew nearly fourfold its *literate* population grew thirty-two-fold.

Heaven on earth: From The Oneida Community

JOHN HUMPHREY NOYES

. . .

Showing that Marriage is not an institution of the Kingdom of Heaven, and must give place to Communism.

. . . In the Kingdom of Heaven, the institution of marriage, which assigns the exclusive possession of one woman to one man, does not exist. Matt. 22: 23–30.

In the Kingdom of Heaven the intimate union of life and interest, which in the world is limited to pairs, extends through the whole body of believers; i.e. complex marriage takes the place of simple. John 17: 21. Christ prayed that all believers might be one, even as he and the Father are one. His unity with the Father is defined in the words, "All mine are thine, and all thine are mine." Ver. 10. This perfect community of interests, then, will be the condition of all, when his prayer is answered. The universal unity of the members of Christ, is described in the same terms that are used to describe marriage unity. Compare 1 Cor. 12: 12–27, with Gen. 2: 24. See also 1 Cor. 6: 15–17, and Eph. 5: 30–32.

The effects of the effusion of the Holy Spirit on the day of Pentecost, present a practical commentary on Christ's prayer for the unity of believers, and a sample of the tendency of heavenly influences, which fully confirm the foregoing proposition. "All that believed were together and had all things common; and sold their possessions and goods, and parted them to all, as every man had need." "The multitude of them that believed were of one heart and of one soul; neither said any of them that aught of the things which he possessed was his own; but they had all things common." Acts 2: 44, 45, and 4: 32. Here is unity like that of the Father and the Son: "All mine thine, and all thine mine."

Admitting that the Community principle of the day of Pentecost, in its actual operation at that time, extended only to material goods, yet we affirm that there is no intrinsic difference between property in persons and property in things; and that the same spirit which abolished exclusiveness in regard to money, would abolish, if circumstances allowed full scope to it, exclusiveness in regard to women and children. Paul expressly places property in women and property in goods in the same category, and speaks of them together, as ready to be abolished by the advent of the Kingdom of Heaven. "The time," says he, "is short; it remaineth that they that have wives be as though they had none; and they that buy as though they possessed not; for the fashion of this world passeth away." 1 Cor. 7: 29–31.

The abolishment of appropriation is involved in the very nature of a true relation to Christ in the gospel. This we prove thus: The possessive feeling which expresses itself by the possessive pronoun *mine*, is the same in essence when it relates to persons, as when it relates to money or any other property. Amativeness and acquisitiveness are only different channels of one stream. They converge as we trace them to

From John Humphrey Noyes, "The Oneida Community," in *History of American Socialisms* (New York: Dover, 1966), pp. 624–629, 638–640.

their source. Grammar will help us to ascertain their common center; for the possessive pronoun *mine*, is derived from the personal pronoun *I*; and so the possessive feeling, whether amative or acquisitive, flows from the personal feeling, that is, it is a branch of egotism. Now egotism is abolished by the gospel relation to Christ. The grand mystery of the gospel is vital union with Christ; the merging of self in his life; the extinguishment of the pronoun *I* at the spiritual center. Thus Paul says, "I live, yet not I, but Christ liveth in me." The grand distinction between the Christian and the unbeliever, between heaven and the world, is, that in one reigns the We-spirit, and in the other the I-spirit. From *I* comes *mine*, and from the I-spirit comes exclusive appropriation of money, women, etc. From *we* comes *ours*, and from the We-spirit comes universal community of interests.

The abolishment of exclusiveness is involved in the love-relation required between all believers by the express injunction of Christ and the apostles, and by the whole tenor of the New Testament. "The new commandment is, that we love one another," and that, not by pairs, as in the world, but *en masse*. We are required to love one another fervently. The fashion of the world forbids a man and woman who are otherwise appropriated, to love one another fervently. But if they obey Christ they must do this; and whoever would allow them to do this, and yet would forbid them (on any other ground than that of present expediency), to express their unity, would "strain at a gnat and swallow a camel"; for unity of hearts is as much more important than any external expression of it, as a camel is larger than a gnat.

The abolishment of social restrictions is involved in the anti-legality of the gospel. It is incompatible with the state of perfected freedom toward which Paul's gospel of "grace without law" leads, that man should be allowed and required to love in all directions, and yet be forbidden to express love except in one direction. In fact Paul says, with direct reference to sexual intercourse—"All things are lawful for me, but all things are not expedient; all things are lawful for me, but I will not be brought under the power of any"; (1 Cor. 6: 12) thus placing the restrictions which were necessary in the transition period on the basis, not of law, but of expediency and the demands of spiritual freedom, and leaving it fairly to be inferred that in the final state, when hostile surroundings and powers of bondage cease, all restrictions also will cease.

The abolishment of the marriage system is involved in Paul's doctrine of the end of ordinances. Marriage is one of the "ordinances of the worldly sanctuary." This is proved by the fact that it has no place in the resurrection. Paul expressly limits it to life in the flesh. Rom. 7: 2, 3. The assumption, therefore, that believers are dead to the world by the death of Christ (which authorized the abolishment of Jewish ordinances), legitimately makes an end of marriage. Col. 2: 20.

The law of marriage is the same in kind with the Jewish law concerning meats and drinks and holy days, of which Paul said that they were "contrary to us, and were taken out of the way, being nailed to the cross." Col. 2: 14. The plea in favor of the worldly social system, that it is not arbitrary, but founded in nature, will not bear investigation. All experience testifies (the theory of the novels of the contrary notwithstanding), that sexual love is not naturally restricted to pairs. Second marriages are contrary to the one-love theory, and yet are often the happiest marriages. Men and women find universally (however the fact may be concealed), that their susceptibility to love is not burnt out by one honeymoon, or satisfied by one lover. On the contrary, the secret history of the human heart will bear out the assertion that it is capable of loving any number of times and any number of persons, and that the more it loves the more it can love. This is the law of nature, thrust out of sight and condemned by common consent, and yet secretly known to all.

The law of marriage "worketh wrath." 1. It provokes to secret adultery, actual or of the heart. 2. It ties together unmatched natures. 3. It sunders matched natures. 4. It gives to sexual appetite only a scanty and monotonous allowance, and so produces the natural vices of poverty, contraction of taste and stinginess or jealousy. 5. It makes no provision for the sexual appetite at the very time when that appetite is the strongest. By the custom of the world, marriage, in the average of cases, takes place at about the age of twenty-four; whereas puberty commences at the age of fourteen. For ten years, therefore, and that in the very flush of life, the sexual appetite is starved. This law of society bears hardest on females, because they have less opportunity of choosing their time of marriage than men. This discrepancy between the marriage system and nature, is one of the principal sources of the peculiar diseases of women, of prostitution, masturbation, and licentiousness in general.

. . .

FREE LOVE

"This terrible combination of two very good ideas—freedom and love—was first used by the writers of the Oneida Community about twenty-one years ago, and probably originated with them. It was however soon taken up by a very different class of speculators scattered about the country, and has come to be the name of a form of socialism with which we have but little affinity. Still it is sometimes applied to our Communities; and as we are certainly responsible for starting it into circulation, it seems to be our duty to tell what meaning we attach to it, and in what sense we are willing to accept it as a designation of our social system.

"The obvious and essential difference between marriage and licentious connections may be stated thus:

"Marriage is permanent union. Licentiousness deals in temporary flirtations.

"In marriage, Communism of property goes with Communism of persons. In licentiousness, love is paid for as hired labor.

"Marriage makes a man responsible for the consequences of his acts of love to a woman. In licentiousness, a man imposes on a woman the heavy burdens of maternity, ruining perhaps her reputation and her health, and then goes his way without responsibility.

"Marriage provides for the maintenance and education of children. Licentiousness ignores children as nuisances, and leaves them to chance.

"Now in respect to every one of these points of difference between marriage and licentiousness, *we stand with marriage*. Free Love with us does *not* mean freedom to love to-day and leave to-morrow; nor freedom to take a woman's person and keep our property to ourselves; nor freedom to freight a woman with our offspring and send her down stream without care or help; nor freedom to beget children and leave them to the street and the poorhouse. Our Communities are *families*, as distinctly bounded and separated from promiscuous society as ordinary households. The tie that binds us together is as permanent and sacred, to say the least, as that of marriage, for it is our religion. We receive no members (except by deception or mistake), who do not give heart and hand to the family interest for life and forever. Community of property extends just as far as freedom of love. Every man's care and every dollar of the common property is pledged for the maintenance and protection of the women, and the education of the children of the Community. Bastardy, in any disastrous sense of the word, is simply impossible in such a social state. Whoever will take the trouble to follow our track from the beginning, will find no forsaken women or children by the way. In this respect we claim to be in advance of marriage and common civilization.

"We are not sure how far the class of socialists called 'Free Lovers' would claim for themselves any thing like the above defense from the charge of reckless and cruel freedom; but our impression is that their position, scattered as they are, without organization or definite separation from surrounding society, makes it impossible for them to follow and care for the consequences of their freedom, and thus exposes them to the just charge of licentiousness. At all events their platform is entirely different from ours, and they must answer for themselves. *We* are not 'Free Lovers' in any sense that makes love less binding or responsible than it is in marriage."*

* We observe that the account of the Oneida Community given in the Supplement to Chambers' Encyclopædia, begins thus: "*Perfectionists* or *Bible Communists*; popularly known as Free Lovers or preachers of Free Love." The whole article, covering several pages, is very careless in its geographical and other details, and not altogether reliable in its statements of the doctrines and morals of the Communists. As materials that get into Encyclopædias may be presumed to be crystallizing for final history, it is to be hoped that the Messrs. Chambers will at least get this article corrected by some intelligent American, for future editions.

PART THREE

Social disorganization approach

INTRODUCTION

It was noted in the Introduction to Part Two that the deviant behavior approach is social-psychological in orientation. The last approach to be discussed, social disorganization, is most consistent with a purely sociological perspective. Although the social disorganization approach did not come into its own until the middle of the twentieth century, its intellectual roots are found in the work of pioneering nineteenth-century sociologists. One cannot discuss the development of the social disorganization approach without also discussing the development of the school of sociological thought known as functionalism or structural-functionalism. The concept of social disorganization follows directly from structural-functional analysis (for a discussion of functionalism as it pertains to stratification see Chapter 3).

If there is any one individual whose work represents the first systematic formulation of structural-functionalism it is Emile Durkheim. In his analysis of numerous phenomena (e.g., the division of labor, crime, suicide, and religion), Durkheim sought to establish the contribution made by "social facts" to the maintenance or change of the social system (Coser and Rosenberg, 1965:616).[1] Functionalism was applied and developed by early twentieth-century social anthropologists, especially the British anthropologists A. R. Radcliffe-Brown (1952:178–187) and Bronislaw Malinowski (1926 and 1945:41–51). The work of Radcliffe-Brown in particular reveals the influence of Durkheim. Further advances in structural-functional thought have been made by a number of contemporary sociologists including Robert Merton (1963), Talcott Parsons (1951), Kingsley Davis (1959), and Marion Levy (1952).

The origins of structural-functionalism can be traced to the "organismic" school of sociology, which was prevalent during the nineteenth century, although most contemporary functionalists disavow any connection with the earlier school, which has long since fallen into disrepute (see Martindale, 1960:448; Turner, 1974:15–18). The organismic view was based on an analogy between social systems and biological systems (Radcliffe-Brown, 1952:178). Concepts such as structure, function, and organ, which previously had been applied to biological organisms, were now applied to societies. It was believed that the various parts or organs of society were organized into a stable structure and that the system was maintained through the performance of critical functions. Organicism was closely linked to evolutionary thought, especially the idea that "progress" was inevitable. The Frenchman Auguste Comte, sometimes called the father of sociology, believed that sociology stood at the apex of the hierarchy of sciences. Social progress would take place only after the systematic formulation of social laws (Hinkle and Hinkle, 1961:4–5). Since biology stood just below sociology in the evolutionary hierarchy of sciences, much of sociology (especially its method) was modeled after biology. "Just as society is viewed as an organism, so social structure and change are studied like anatomy and physiology" (Hinkle and Hinkle, 1961:5). Sociology was to be divided into two broad areas—social statics and social dynamics. Statics is concerned with the structure of society or the conditions that make for social order, dynamics with change or progress from one evolutionary stage to another (Timasheff, 1963:22). The primary unit of analysis for Comte was society. The basic organs of society are its social institutions. Societies, however, differ from biological organisms in important respects. While biological organisms are basically immutable, societies are subject to considerable change and improvement through the application of the scientific method (Timasheff, 1963:23).

Despite Comte's affinity for the organismic analogy, it remained for him largely an analogy. The pioneering British sociologist Herbert Spencer (1851, 1887, and 1920), on the other hand, was so immersed in organicism that, in his work, the distinction between biological organisms and human societies is frequently blurred (Turner, 1974:17). Although Spencer acknowledged some differences between biological and social systems, he believed that the same principles or laws applied to both.

---

[1] Durkheim's contribution to sociology is covered in various chapters. The division of labor is discussed in Chapter 4, anomie in the Introduction to the book and in Chapter 4 and the Introduction to Part Two, suicide in the Introductions to the book and to Part Two, and crime and punishment in Chapter 6.

So completely is society organized on the same system as an individual being that we may perceive something more than analogy between them; the same definition of life applies to both. Only when one sees that the transformation passed through during the growth, maturity, and decay of a society, conforms to the same principles as do the transformations passed through by aggregates of all orders, inorganic and organic, is there reached the concept of sociology as a science (Timasheff, 1963:35–36).

Spencer isolated three types of phenomena—inorganic (physical), organic (biological), and superorganic (social), each representing matter in motion and subject to the laws of evolution (1887:3–7). He, like Comte, believed that social evolution would bring about moral progress, or survival of those patterns that are most beneficial to society. Spencer therefore opposed governmental interference with the "natural development" of society (see Chapter 2 for his views on poverty).

Spencer observed that as societies become larger, they become more complex and internally differentiated (1887:459–465). The evolutionary movement from homogeneous to heterogeneous societies is accompanied by increasing complexity and interdependence in societal structures and functions. Just as the parts of simpler organisms are more similar to one another, so members of simpler societies are easily interchangeable (except of course for certain obvious differences between the sexes). When a worm is bisected, it forms two worms, each capable of survival independently of the other. But in more complex organisms and societies, division or elimination of a critical part is usually fatal (Spencer, 1887: 476–477).

The major assumptions of contemporary structural-functionalism, therefore, are found in organicism. First, there is the belief in the primacy of the whole over its parts. The basic unit of analysis is society, not individuals or biological organisms, and society is an organic whole that is greater than the sum of its parts. Second, there is the emphasis on the structure, or organization, of society. Third, there is the concern with the contribution made by the parts of society to the maintenance of the whole. Structure thus refers to the relation between parts, while function is the contribution made by the parts to the maintenance of the system (Radcliffe-Brown, 1952:180–181). Finally, there is the emphasis on institutions as the basic subunits of society.

THE MEANING OF FUNCTION

Since there is much confusion over the term "function," it is necessary to discuss its various meanings.[2] Function may be used in a mathematical sense as when one says that x is a function of y (i.e., the value of x is determined by y). A second usage is function as useful activity. This meaning is so broad and ambiguous that it adds little to our understanding of society. It confuses need with function. Durkheim noted that "to show how a fact is useful is not to explain how it originated or why it is what it is. The uses which it serves presuppose the specific properties charac-

[2] The four uses of function discussed here are taken from Martindale (1960:443–446).

terizing it but do not create them" (1964:90). Furthermore, "a fact can exist without being at all useful . . ." (Durkheim, 1964:91). The third usage is that of appropriate activity. The problem with this conception is that since the appropriateness of action is socially determined, an act may be functional without being appropriate or appropriate without being functional. The final meaning of function is "system-determined and system-maintaining activity." This usage is most consistent with structural-functional analysis. "The critical property of this position is the view that social life is fundamentally incorporated in systems. In these systems, any item is to be judged in terms of its determination by the system and its place in maintaining the system" (Martindale, 1960:445).

A major difficulty with functional analysis is that often one term is used to represent different concepts and in other cases a single concept is represented by different terms (Merton, 1963:20). Some of the varying meanings of the term "function" have already been discussed. We will now examine terms that have been used interchangeably with function. Much confusion has been generated by the indiscriminate use of terms such as "goal," "purpose," "motive," "aim," and "function." Merton believes that the distinction between goals or purposes and functions is critical. "Social function refers to *observable objective consequences*, and not to *subjective dispositions* (aims, motives, purposes)" (Merton, 1963:24). Functions, according to Merton, are viewed from the perspective of the observer and not necessarily that of participants. Participants may or may not be aware of the objective consequences of sociocultural phenomena. Moreover, the reasons or explanations that people give for their actions are not always the same as the societal consequences of their actions. We cannot assume "that the *motives* for entering into marriage ('love,' 'personal reasons') are identical with the *functions* served by families (socialization of the child)" (Merton, 1963:24). In attempting to take into account the relation between intended motives and objective effects, Merton has introduced the concepts of manifest and latent function. Manifest functions are "those objective consequences for a specified unit (person, subgroup, social or cultural system) which contribute to its adjustment or adaptation and were so intended"; latent functions are "unintended and unrecognized consequences of the same order" (Merton, 1963:63). In manifest functions there is a close correspondence between intended motives and objective consequences, while in latent functions the two vary, independently of one another. Hopi rain ceremonies, for example, do not meet the manifest function of producing rain, but they do have important latent consequences for the group. Such ceremonies help to reinforce societal norms and to increase cohesion. The concept of latent function helps to make sense of much behavior that may appear at first to be irrational or contradictory to avowed purposes.

POSTULATES OF FUNCTIONAL ANALYSIS

Although functional analysis has made some important contributions to sociological theory, it has been the object of much criticism and controversy. One criticism has been that the functional unity of a system is frequently treated as a given rather than as a hypothesis to be tested. Durkheim, for example, observed:

. . . If the usefulness of a fact is not the cause of its existence, it is generally necessary that it be useful in order that it may maintain itself. For the fact that it is not useful suffices to make it harmful, since in that case it costs effort without bringing in any returns. If, then, the majority of social phenomena had this parasitic character, the budget of the organism would have a deficit and social life would be impossible. Consequently, to have a satisfactory understanding of the latter, it is necessary to show how the phenomena comprising it combine in such a way as to put society in harmony with itself and with the environment external to it (1964:97).

Radcliffe-Brown was influenced by Durkheim, but he modified Durkheim's conception of function. While Durkheim defined the function of an institution as the correspondence between it and the needs of the total system, Radcliffe-Brown substituted the term "necessary conditions of existence" for the term "needs" (1952:178). Function is the contribution made by one element to the maintenance of the total system. "Such a view implies that a social system . . . has a certain kind of unity, which we may speak of as a functional unity. We may define it as a condition in which all parts of the social system work together with a sufficient degree of harmony or internal consistency . . ." (Radcliffe-Brown, 1952:181). He was quick to note, however, that the functional unity of a system is a hypothesis that may or may not be supported by the facts (Radcliffe-Brown, 1952:181).

A second assumption of functional analysis that has been challenged by critics is what Merton terms the "postulate of universal functionalism" (1963:30). According to this postulate, "all standardized social or cultural forms have positive functions" (Merton, 1963:30). Malinowski (1926:133), for example, asserts: "The functional view of culture insists therefore upon the principle that in every type of civilisation, every custom, material object, idea and belief fulfills some vital function . . ." (1926:133). Kluckhohn similarly maintains that "no cultural forms survive unless they constitute responses which are adjustive or adaptive, in some sense . . ." (1944:79). The postulate of universal functionalism is based on the questionable teleological assumption that cultural elements must be functional or else they would not persist. This view makes the functionality of a cultural item a question of definition rather than one of empirical test. Items that persist are, by definition, functional. One would be hard pressed, however, to explain the functionality of certain items such as neckties or ornamental buttons on sportscoats. The assertion that items that persist are universally functional not only questions our sensibility but also goes beyond social science knowledge. As Merton has observed, "although any item of culture or social structure *may* have functions, it is premature to hold unequivocally that every such item *must* be functional" (1963:31).

A related postulate of functionalism is that of "indispensability" (Merton, 1963:32). Many functional analysts have suggested, either explicitly or implicitly, that certain cultural forms or functions are indispensable to the maintenance of a social system. Malinowski believed that every cultural item played an "indispensable part within a working whole" (1926:133). Less extreme exponents of this view propose that *some* but not *all* cultural items are indispensable. Whether they are referring to the indispensability of cultural items (structures) or of the functions performed by such items is frequently unclear (Merton, 1963:32). Davis and Moore (1945: 246), for example, assert that religion is necessary because it "plays a unique and indispensable part in society" (see Chapter 3 for a detailed discussion of their functional theory of stratification). Is it religion per se or the functions performed by religion that are essential to the maintenance of society? Even if one accepts the assumption that certain functions are indispensable, there is little or no support for the view that such functions *must* be fulfilled by a given structure. ". . . *just as the same item may have multiple functions, so may the same function be diversely fulfilled by alternative items*" (Merton, 1963:33–34). A number of social scientists who are dissatisfied with the postulate of indispensability have suggested the concept of functional alternative or equivalent. According to this view, essential societal functions may be fulfilled by various structures.

From this brief review of the common postulates of structural-functionalism it is clear why this theory or perspective has been severely criticized. Functionalism, however, becomes a useful perspective when the functional unity of a system and the functionality of particular cultural items are treated as hypotheses, and it is recognized that the same function may be fulfilled by alternative structures.

THE CONCEPT OF SOCIAL DISORGANIZATION

One of the most frequent criticisms of structural-functionalism is that it is a conservative ideology designed to maintain the status quo. An extreme functionalist perspective can be used to justify any and all existing practices on the grounds that they are somehow "functional." Such a view cautions against tampering with the natural system that has evolved in society. Those religious, familial, and political structures that have evolved are the best, or at least, the most functional. Sociology is accordingly reduced to a discipline that simply describes the structure and function of existing social forms.

Critics argue that a functional perspective cannot adequately account for social change or deviant behavior, since the social system is seen as constantly seeking a state of equilibrium or homeostasis (Appelbaum, 1970:67). Questions such as when or how social change takes place in the system tend to be ignored, relegated to secondary importance, or answered in a manner that destroys the question. Change is seen as a natural, evolutionary process that occurs by trial and error and through natural selection (i.e., the survival of those elements that are most functional to the maintenance of the system). Deviant behavior is an anomaly or pathology in the system. ". . . equilibrium theory . . . can neither explain the occurrence of radical changes in society nor account for the phenomena which accompany them. . . . Nothing new and unique, no important transformations ever happen in the normal world of equilibrium theory" (Guessous, 1967:34).

The assertion that functional theorists have not been concerned with social change or deviant behavior can be shown to be patently false. Durkheim is one of the earliest and most influential sociological functionalists. His concept of anomie recognizes that the degree of organization or functional unity of a social system is a hypothesis to be tested. Systems vary in the extent to which they are organized from those that are extremely cohesive to those that are in a state of anomie. Merton has further developed and applied the concept of anomie and introduced a related term— "dysfunction." A cultural item may be functional, dysfunctional, or nonfunctional (Merton, 1963:51). Dysfunctions are "those observed consequences which lessen the adaptation or adjustment of the system" (Merton, 1963:51). Dysfunction implies that there is strain, stress, or tension in the system.[3] Thus dysfunction refers to the contribution (or lack of it) of a cultural element or structure to the maintenance of the system, anomie refers to the general state of organization of the system.

While many assert that functional analysis (and the concept of social disorganization or anomie) is a conservative ideology, others accuse functionalism of being a radical ideology. Richard LaPiere in his classic work on collective behavior noted:

The functional approach to collective behavior will, undoubtedly, affront all those who believe that specific sociopsychological structures have inherent values. Thus, to those who believe that a church service is good because it is a church service, the statement that some church services are formal motions which are devoid of religious significance, that others are functionally comparable to theatrical performances, and that still others are a form of revelry and are therefore comparable to a drunken spree will be an affront to common sense, an attack upon the integrity of decent people, or, at the least, the ravings of a poor fool (1952:82).

The fact that functional analysis has been accused of adhering to polar ideological positions is not surprising, for this has been the history of many theoretical systems. Karl Marx's dialectical materialism has similarly been the object of conflicting and contradictory interpretations (Merton, 1963: 39–41). That functional analysis is "seen by some as inherently conservative and by others as inherently radical suggests that it may be *inherently* neither one nor the other . . . functional analysis may involve no *intrinsic* ideological commitment although . . . it can be infused with any one of a wide range of ideological values" (Merton, 1963:39).

Social institutions are structures of roles and norms centered around the fulfillment of essential societal functions. The three institutions included in this part—family, education, and religion—are among the most basic to human societies. While a functional perspective is employed, the focus is on stress, strain, and change within institutions and in society at large.

[3] Levy uses dysfunction in a manner "roughly equivalent" to Merton's usage but he suggests substituting the term eufunction for function. ". . . *eufunction* is defined as a condition, or state of affairs, that . . . increases or maintains adaptation or adjustment of the unit . . ." (Levy, 1952:77). Each type of function has a corresponding structure: "(1) eustructures are structures such that operation in terms of them result in eufunctions, and (2) dysstructures are structures such that operation in terms of them results in dysfunctions" (Levy, 1952:82).

REFERENCES

Appelbaum, Richard P.
1970 Theories of Social Change. Chicago: Markham.
Coser, Lewis A., and Bernard Rosenberg
1965 Sociological Theory: A Book of Readings. Second ed. New York: Macmillan.
Davis, Kingsley
1959 "The Myth of Functional Analysis as a Special Method in Sociology and Anthropology." American Sociological Review 24 (December):757–772.
Davis, Kingsley, and Wilbert E. Moore
1945 "Some Principles of Stratification." American Sociological Review 10 (April):242–249.
Durkheim, Emile
1964 The Rules of Sociological Method. (Translated by Sarah A. Solovay and John H. Mueller, ed. by George E. G. Catlin.) New York: Free Press.
Guessous, Mohammed
1967 "A General Critique of Equilibrium Theory." Pp. 23–35 in Wilbert E. Moore and Robert M. Cook (eds.), Readings on Social Change. Englewood Cliffs, N.J.: Prentice-Hall.
Hinkle, Roscoe C., and Gisela J. Hinkle
1961 The Development of Modern Sociology. New York: Random House.
Kallen, Horace M.
1931 "Functionalism." Pp. 523–525 in Encyclopaedia of the Social Sciences 6. New York: Macmillan.
Kluckhohn, Clyde
1944 Navaho Witchcraft. Boston: Beacon.
LaPiere, Richard T.
1938 Collective Behavior. New York: McGraw-Hill.
Levy, Marion J., Jr.
1952 The Structure of Society. Princeton, N.J.: Princeton University Press.
Malinowski, Bronislaw
1926 "Anthropology." Pp. 132–139 in Encyclopaedia Britannica First Supplementary Volume. London and New York.
1945 The Dynamics of Culture Change. New Haven, Conn.: Yale University Press.
Martindale, Don
1960 The Nature and Types of Sociological Theory. Boston: Houghton Mifflin.
Merton, Robert K.
1963 Social Theory and Social Structure. Revised ed. New York: Free Press.
Parsons, Talcott
1951 The Social System. New York: Free Press.
Radcliffe-Brown, A. R.
1952 Structure and Function in Primitive Society. New York: Free Press.
Spencer, Herbert
1851 Social Statics. London: John Chapman (reprinted by Augustus M. Kelley Publishers, 1969).
1887 The Principles of Sociology. Third ed. Vol. I. New York: Appleton.
1920 First Principles. Sixth ed. New York: Appleton.
Timasheff, Nicholas S.
1963 Sociological Theory: Its Nature and Growth. Revised ed. New York: Random House.
Turner, Jonathan H.
1974 The Structure of Sociological Theory. Homewood, Ill.: Dorsey.

Family disorganization

9

THE FUNCTIONS OF THE FAMILY

The family is the oldest and most basic of all social institutions, found universally in all societies and at all times (Murdock, 1965:2).[1] The nuclear unit, consisting of husband, wife, and children,[2] fulfills a number of essential societal functions. Among these are procreation, the care and socialization of children, defining the legitimacy of children, establishing rules of descent, and the production and consumption of goods and services (Malinowski, 1945:50). The family also provides emotional gratification for its members and a regular sexual outlet for

[1] There have been some experimental attempts to abolish the family as we know it. The Oneida Community, discussed in Chapter 8, replaced the nuclear family with complex marriage. Other attempts include the Soviet experiment to eliminate the family following the Bolshevik revolution, and the Israeli kibbutz (see Leslie, 1973:123–151; Gordon, 1972:59–142).

[2] Some "families," of course, are childless, and others have only one parent, but these are the exception rather than the rule. What is important is that society moves toward the "ideal" of two parents and their children (Leslie, 1973:13).

adults. All societies permit, and usually actively encourage, sexual inter-course between husband and wife (Murdock, 1965:4). The expectation of coitus between husband and wife seems to be universal. Persons some-times enter sexual unions outside of marriage and a man and woman may establish a division of labor without sexual exchange but marriage is unique in that it combines these functions (Murdock, 1965:8). One cannot over-state the importance of the functions fulfilled by the family. The sexual, economic, reproductive, and socialization functions are essential for the maintenance of society. Society would not persist beyond a single genera-tion without the first and the third functions. The second is essential for the maintenance of life, and the fourth for the transmission of culture (Murdock, 1965:10).

Despite the apparent universality of the family, there is considerable variation in the structure and function of the family in various cultures. In our own society the nuclear family is largely isolated from other kin relations. It usually occupies a separate residence and is structurally inde-pendent. But in most societies the nuclear family has existed within a larger system of reciprocal kin relations. Of the 192 societies studied by Murdock (1965:2), 47 had the nuclear family only, 53 had polygamous families, and 92 had some form of the extended family.

The best example of the extended kinship system is probably the tradi-tional Chinese family.[3] The Chinese family was patriarchal, family cen-tered, and male dominated. The male head of the household was the ultimate authority, exercising almost total control over his wife, children, and all descendants of his children and their spouses. More specifically, the extended family system contained the following essential features:

1. Emphasis on the father-son relationship
2. Family pride
3. Encouragement of the large family
4. The cult of ancestor worship
5. Common ownership of property by the family (Lee, 1953:272–273).

Although this was the ideal pattern, it was only the more wealthy members of the gentry-scholar class who were able to maintain it (Lee, 1953:272). Peasants identified with and imitated the pattern but seldom were able to maintain large households. Ideally, six generations of a family were to live under one roof, and the division of property was to occur only after nine generations; but in practice seldom did more than three or four generations live together, and property was frequently divided after the death of the patriarch. There is evidence that indicates that the average household was

---

[3] For further discussion of the traditional Chinese family see Levy (1968), Leslie (1973:80–122), Ho (1965), Lee (1953), and Queen and Habenstein (1967:88–115). The modern family in China has undergone substantial changes. For a discussion of the family, women, and child care in Red China, see Sidel (1973).

not much larger than the average household in the contemporary United States. Ping-ti Ho (1965:18) maintains that a respectable census in 2 A.D. showed that the average household size was 4.87 and that this figure has remained relatively stable.

The authority of the family was maintained by both tradition and law. Much of the power of the family was tied to its control over economic resources. The family controlled not only the distribution of property and wealth but also the means of obtaining a livelihood (Lee, 1953:274). Crafts and other occupational skills were passed on from father to son. Although the father was depicted as the ultimate and absolute authority in the Chinese family, the mother probably had a considerable amount of influence. Legal clauses that affirmed the authority of the father usually made mention of the mother. "The authority was therefore not the father's alone but that jointly held by the parents, which by definition included more senior direct patrilineal ascendants. For the basic legal and ethical principle regulating the traditional Chinese family was based not so much on sexes as on senior-junior relationships" (Ho, 1965:23).

THE AMERICAN FAMILY IN TRANSITION

The contemporary American family provides an interesting contrast with the Chinese family. The Chinese family was a relatively self-sufficient, multifunctional, and stable institution; the American family is dependent, unifunctional, and unstable. The extended family seems to flourish in stable agricultural societies in which wealth and social position are determined largely by one's relation to the land. Persons are dependent on the extended unit, which determines their social and economic position. The nuclear family system, on the other hand, usually predominates in urban-industrial societies and in hunting and gathering societies (Nimkoff and Middleton, 1960:216–217).

The American family still fulfills the two most basic and universal functions—sexual gratification of adults and reproduction. Most adults marry at some point in their life, and the societal ideal holds that families will have children. Although, as noted in Chapter 8, there is considerable variation from the norm that limits sex to marriage, married persons limit most of their sexual outlets to marital relations. Equally significant, but more obvious, is the expectation that married persons engage in coitus. Reproduction continues to be the most basic function of the American family. The birth rate has stabilized in recent years, but there is little danger of the nuclear family not replacing itself in future generations.

The economic function of the family has been largely supplanted by other institutions. The contemporary American family is not a unit of economic production. This is not to suggest that it has no economic function. There is still a division of labor—one parent, usually but not necessarily the male, is the primary breadwinner, and the other parent cares for the children and maintains the household. The family is also a unit of consumption and the primary mechanism for distributing goods and services.

The family continues to play a significant, although admittedly declining, role in the care and training of children. It is generally acknowledged that the first five years of life are probably the most critical. The bases for personality structure, values, intellectual development, and views of the world are laid in these formative years. Later experiences are also significant, but they build on those tendencies that are implanted early. There is no doubt that the family is still the most important single influence on the intellectual and moral development of the child. A child's first and most meaningful relationship is with his mother, who nurses, protects, and cares for him. The family, but especially the mother, is the primary agent for the transmission of culture. Despite the importance of the family, however, the socialization function is being increasingly assumed by other institutions and agencies. Two competing agencies of socialization are the school and the peer group. With the liberation of women and their greater involvement in the labor force much of the early socialization of children is being assumed by day-care centers, nursery schools, and baby sitters. The schools, which previously did not play a major role until children reached the age of five or six, are now assuming much of the care and training of preschool children (see Chapter 10 for a more detailed discussion of this trend). The impact of the school is felt earlier and is prolonged over a longer span of time.

As a result of these trends, not only are children and adolescents subject to greater influence by teachers and other adults, but they are also subject to greater influence by their peers. One consequence of the prolonged interaction among children from infancy to early adulthood has been the emergence of a distinctive youth culture. The peer group develops its own norms, standards, and values, which sometimes support or reinforce adult values but, at other times, contradict or challenge these values. The peer group is an alternative agent of socialization and, potentially, a competing source of allegiance for the family.

SOURCES OF FAMILY DISORGANIZATION

Those who argue that the family in the United States is disorganized frequently cite increases in premarital intercourse, illegitimacy, adultery, and divorce as evidence of the demise of the family. Each of these sources of family disorganization will be considered in turn, and an attempt will be made to assess the merits of the arguments in each case.

Premarital intercourse

Available evidence regarding increases in the incidence of premarital intercourse indicate that while there has been a liberalization of attitudes toward sex before marriage, rates of premarital coital experience have remained remarkably stable.[4] Men have traditionally had premarital experience, and they continue to have this experience but increasingly their partners are companions or fiancées rather than prostitutes. Furthermore, there is no evidence that increasing levels of premarital coitus are necessarily threatening to or disruptive of the nuclear family. Such a view is based on the erroneous assumption that sexual gratification is the only, or even the most important, motivation for marriage. Many cultures allow considerable premarital sexual freedom, but persons are still encouraged to marry eventually and to establish families (Murdock, 1965:5–6).

Illegitimacy

Another source of family dissolution, it is alleged, is the increasing number of children born out of wedlock. Bronislaw Malinowski has observed that The Principle of Legitimacy, according to which each child must have a sociological father to serve as guardian and protector, is universal (1930: 137–138). While the rule is violated, it is significant that all societies consider it important and desirable that a child be legitimate. Societal concern with legitimacy is understandable, since rules of legitimacy place the child within a kinship network and ensure that responsibility for the care and socialization of children is assigned to a family. A child without a sociological father occupies an ambiguous position. Who is responsible for his care and training? What is his position in society? One should not be surprised then, of the greater disapproval of illegitimacy than of sex outside of marriage (Goode, 1964:20). Even those societies that allow considerable sexual freedom expect children to be born within marriage.

Despite the apparent universality of The Principle of Legitimacy, there is variation among and within societies in regard to tolerance of births out of wedlock. Generally, "the society will be less concerned with illegitimacy when it occurs in the lower social ranks, since their position is less significant for the larger social structure" (Goode, 1964:21). In the United States and most other societies rates of illegitimacy are highest among persons of lower social status. Much attention has been focused lately in the United States on the illegitimacy rates of the poor, particularly young lower-class black women. Opponents of public assistance for unwed mothers argue that welfare payments encourage and support illicit sexual relations. The evidence suggests, however, that over the past fifty or sixty years black illegitimacy rates have been reduced substantially (Goode, 1971:477). While the white rate of illegitimate births per 1000 unmarried women aged fifteen to forty-four has been increasing consistently since 1940, the rate for nonwhites has been declining consistently since 1960 when it reached an all-time high. The black illegitimacy rate is still considerably higher

[4] This topic was discussed extensively in the preceding chapter. The reader seeking a more detailed discussion is referred to Chapter 8.

than the white rate, but the gap between them is ˙apparently declining (U.S. Bureau of the Census, 1973:54).

Illegitimacy rates for the society as a whole have been increasing steadily in recent years (U.S. Department of Health, Education, and Welfare, 1974a:3). In 1968, 9.7 percent of all live births were illegitimate compared to 5.3 in 1960 and 3.5 in 1940 (U.S. Bureau of the Census, 1973:54). The rate per 1000 unmarried women ages fifteen to forty-four was 26.4 in 1970 (U.S. Department of Health, Education, and Welfare, 1974a:11), 21.8 in 1960, and 7.1 in 1940 (U.S. Bureau of the Census, 1973:54). Such increases may be misleading, however, reflecting greater acceptance of informal unions rather than a real increase in illegitimacy per se. Some unwed couples live together in a stable relationship, assuming all of the duties and responsibilities of marriage and parenthood. Many will marry formally at some point in the future, and others will establish common-law marriages.

Adultery

While reliable data on the incidence of adultery are not readily available, there are numerous indications that the proportion of married persons who engage in adulterous relations is increasing.[5] As with premarital relations, the most significant changes seem to involve the sexual behavior of women. Despite the apparent increase in extramarital sex, though, most of the sexual outlets of married persons are confined to marriage. Extramarital relations tend to be sporadic and short-lived. Moreover, while infidelity is a common ground for divorce, there is no evidence to support the popular view that it is a cause of either "unhappy marriages" or divorce. If anything, adultery may be the result rather than the cause of unsatisfactory marital relations. There are, for instance, no data that suggest that recreational swingers have a higher than normal rate of divorce or that participation in swinging has an adverse effect on the marital relation. Bartell believes that the rate of divorce among the swingers he studied is no higher than the national average (1971:26). A number of investigators suggest that swinging is compatible with the nuclear family and may in fact improve a monotonous or unsatisfying relationship (Bartell, 1971:279–282; Denfeld and Gordon, 1970:98; O'Neill and O'Neill, 1970:109–110). According to Denfeld and Gordon: ". . . for the couple committed to the martial relationship and for whom it still performs important functions for which no other relationship exists, mate swapping may relieve sexual monotony without undermining the marriage. ... swinging may support rather than disrupt monogamous marriage as it exists in this society" (1970:92–93, 98).

The evidence on the effects of "affairs" on marriage is less clear, but

[5] For a more complete discussion of extramarital relations see Chapter 8.

it is sufficient to challenge the conventional notion that the effect is always deleterious. A study of divorced women in Detroit found that only 16 percent listed another woman (a triangle) as one of the primary causes of their divorce (Goode, 1965:123). Cuber (1969:193) supports the view that affairs are not necessarily destructive of marriage. "Both for cases in which the spouse knew about the affair and where the affair was secret, we can document with a long list instances in which the spousal relationship remains at least as good qualitatively as within the average pair without adultery" (Cuber, 1969:193).

For many persons extramarital unions compensate for an unsatisfying marriage that is kept together for the sake of children, out of religious convictions, or as a result of community pressure. Under such circumstances the affair may help the person to make a better adjustment to the marriage. "Enduring affairs, especially, may be more psychologically fulfilling than marriages, thereby enhancing the adulterous partner's toleration for his marriage and fulfillment of the societal expectation that marriages should be permanent" (Edwards, 1972:219).

Divorce

No source of family disorganization has drawn more attention than divorce. Those who contend that the American family is on the demise cite increasing rates of divorce to support this claim. There can be little doubt that the rate of divorce in the United States has been increasing consistently. However, before concluding that the American family is a dying institution, it is necessary to examine carefully the data upon which such claims are based, compare rates of divorce in the United States with rates in other nations, and discuss the effects of divorce on the American family.

A number of analysts who are impressed by soaring divorce rates predict that one-third to one-half of all marriages in the United States will end in divorce (Otto, 1970:1). Such claims have been accepted as self-evident without substantive data to support them:

No reference is made, however, to the identity of the "analyst," nor to where the analyst got his information. One suspects that there is a circle of "analysts" who quote each other on divorce statistics, and whose quotes are in turn disseminated to millions . . . but that no one (including the experts) bothers to check the validity of anyone else's sources (Scanzoni, 1972:5).

The data on divorce present a more complicated picture than such analysts would lead us to believe. Both crude divorce rates (number of divorces per 1000 persons) and refined divorce rates (number of divorces per 1000 married women) show a consistent gradual increase from about 1920 to the present, with a peak attained after World War II (Scanzoni, 1972:7). The probability of divorce, however, is hardly alarming. The crude divorce rate is about 4.4 for each 1000 persons (U.S. Department of Health, Education, and Welfare, 1974b:2) in the population, and the refined rate about 17 divorces per 1000 married women 15 years old and over (U.S. Bureau of the Census, 1973:xiv).

A number of factors influence the divorce rate. With rising incomes more persons than in the past are able to dissolve an unhappy marriage through divorce rather than separation or desertion (sometimes referred to as "the poor man's divorce"). Decreases in the death rate for both men and women mean that marriages tend to be of longer duration than in the past. "Dissatisfactions in marriage that today might lead to divorce had perhaps less chance then to build up and bring about divorce, since death might intervene beforehand" (Scanzoni, 1972:12). In any given year about twice as many marriages are dissolved by death as by divorce. As a result of the declining death rate there has been a steady decrease since 1860 in the yearly rate of marital dissolution due to death and divorce combined (Scanzoni, 1972:13). Consequently, *"it seems safe to conclude that more Americans are spending more years in the marital situation than ever before in our history"* (Scanzoni, 1972:13).

What is the basis then for the claim that one out of two marriages will end in the divorce courts? Such claims are usually based on the naïve and misleading assumption that the ratio of current marriages to current divorces is a valid indicator of the probability of divorce for a given couple. The marriage-divorce ratio is computed by comparing the number of marriages per year with the number of divorces (Scanzoni, 1972:10). Thus if there are 500 divorces for every 1000 marriages, it is concluded that one out of two marriages will end in divorce! This is a vastly inflated measure, since a large majority of persons who divorce in a given year were married in previous years. Those who are alarmed by divorce in the United States also tend to overlook the fact that rates of divorce in the United States are increasing less rapidly than rates in most other nations. Our divorce rate is one of the highest among modern industrialized nations, and it continues to rise consistently, but the ratio of increase is among the lowest (Plateris, 1967:7). Other countries, in other words, are catching up, and the divorce rate in Russia has actually surpassed ours (Scanzoni, 1972:15).

Is a high divorce rate indicative of a disorganized or unstable family system? Many smaller and more stable societies have had high rates of divorce. George Murdock discovered that about 60 percent of the preliterate societies he studied had divorce rates that were higher than our own (1950:197). A number of literate nations have, according to William Goode (1971:482), also had divorce rates that were higher than the rate in the United States today (e.g., Israel between 1935 and 1944, Egypt between 1935 and 1954, and Japan between 1887 and 1919). High divorce rates in Arab nations have led some observers to conclude that divorce in such nations is the "poor man's polygyny" (Goode, 1971:484).

Some sociologists have advanced the view that a high divorce rate is functional in a large complex society. They point out, doomsday critics notwithstanding, that divorce is the result rather than the cause of an unhappy marriage. In fact, in the last analysis, marriage is itself the ultimate cause of divorce. If we expect all marriages to be satisfying and gratifying, we should also expect some to fail and to be dissolved. One could, as some countries have tried, outlaw divorce, but this would not solve the problem of unsuccessful marriages, since nothing would have been done to improve unsatisfactory relations. One way to reduce divorce is to improve the quality of the relationship; another is to lower the expectations that persons have in marriage (Goode, 1971:479). Our culture romanticizes marriage, and many enter it with the expectation that they will "live happily ever after" with all of their problems resolved. When expectations for happiness and personal fulfillment are high, disappointment will also be high. In the Chinese family system, on the other hand, in which more emphasis was placed on the larger kinship network than on the marital relation, happiness was not an important consideration in marriage. One could turn to other relatives for emotional gratification and support. If a man was not satisfied sexually in marriage, he was free to establish relationships with other women, and members of the gentry class could even bring a concubine into the home (Levy, 1968:98).

Another factor that seems to have affected the divorce rate is the attitude toward divorce itself. Societal tolerance of divorce seems to be increasing. Divorce is less likely to be seen as a social evil, and there is greater overall acceptance of divorce and the divorced. While divorce is not the ideal pattern, many consider it a more desirable alternative than tolerating an unhappy marriage (Goode, 1971:487). Women, in particular, are less likely today than in the past to uncritically accept an unsatisfying relationship. There is greater acceptance of the principle that marital relations that are not sexually or emotionally satisfying to either party should be dissolved.

THE ISOLATED NUCLEAR FAMILY

Anthropological descriptions usually assert that compared to the family in other cultures the American family is relatively isolated from extended kin relations. Husband and wife and their dependent children are expected to establish a separate household and to be economically independent of other relatives. Such cross-cultural comparisons have led some sociologists to conclude that the American family is isolated and independent of extended family ties (Parsons, 1943; Williams, 1958).[6] In a classic article, Talcott Parsons characterized the American family as an " 'open, multilineal, conjugal system' " (1943:24). This view has been challenged by a number of investigators who contend that the American family is not isolated from extended relatives. Sussman (1962) suggests that the "isola-

[6] For more detailed discussion and review of the isolated nuclear family hypothesis see Sussman (1962), Adams (1968:1–16), and Gibson (1972).

tion" of the nuclear family is more fiction than fact. In a study of a large metropolitan area, he uncovered extensive networks of mutual assistance and social activity among interlocking nuclear families. Greer (1956) found in two urban samples that visiting with kin was the single most important social relationship. A number of other studies support the view that the nuclear unit rather than being isolated is typically enmeshed in extended family relations (Axelrod, 1956; Litwak, 1960a, 1960b; Adams, 1968:30).

The isolated nuclear family hypothesis is based, at least in part, on the assumption that high levels of geographical and social mobility are disruptive of extended family relations. According to Eugene Litwak (1960a, 1960b), this assumption is unwarranted in that mobility strengthens rather than weakens extended family cohesion. He maintains that relatives promote mobility by providing help patterns and social support, and mobility in turn intensifies extended family bonds as relatives identify with the achievements of their upwardly mobile kin. Adams' (1968:170–171) findings are more complicated in that upwardly mobile persons were isolated relative to their social class of origin (stable blue collar) but not relative to their class of destination (stable white collar). Other researchers, on the other hand, argue that social mobility does disrupt extended family ties. Schneider and Homans contend that socially mobile persons maintain shallow ties with relatives (1955:1204). Their contention is supported by research findings that show that social mobility both intergenerational (Stuckert, 1963; Mirande, 1969 and 1973) and intragenerational (Bruce, 1970) is associated with a lower level of visiting with kin.[7]

The controversy over the isolated family hypothesis is due in part to confusion in levels of analysis. The hypothesis as originally derived by Parsons (1943) was based on a comparative cross-cultural anthropological perspective that proposed that the American family is isolated relative to families in less urbanized and industrialized societies. It asserted that the family is structurally and functionally isolated, not necessarily physically isolated. Societal norms, in other words, maintain that the nuclear unit should be economically and residentially independent of the extended family. There is nothing in this proposition that precludes the establishment of informal help or visiting patterns with kin, since one can establish such relations without undermining the structural autonomy and independence of the nuclear unit. In a sense then both proponents and critics of

[7] Intergenerational mobility refers to movement, up or down, between generations, and intragenerational to movement within a generation; for example, if a man is an M.D. and his father was a plumber, he is intergenerationally upwardly mobile. Similarly, a man who is a plumber in the early part of his work history and eventually becomes an M.D. is intragenerationally upwardly mobile. It should also be noted that Stuckert (1963) combined upward and downward mobility into a single category and that Mirande (1969 and 1973) found that only upward mobility is associated with isolation from kin.

the hypothesis may be correct in their basic assertions. The differences between the positions may be more apparent than real.

THE SEARCH FOR ALTERNATIVES

The search for alternatives to the nuclear family in contemporary American society is not a new or recent phenomenon. Throughout the history of this country there have been numerous utopian experiments that sought to bring about basic changes both in the family and the society at large. They ranged from attempts to replace the nuclear family with group marriage to experiments with celibacy. The communal movement in the United States has been concentrated in two major periods. The first occurred during the nineteenth century as hundreds of utopian communities, many with a religious basis, were established in the newly founded nation. We are currently in the midst of the second wave. Literally thousands of communes have emerged throughout the United States.[8]

Space limitations permit only a brief discussion of some of the better-known and most successful utopian experiments. Two of the communities to be discussed, the Shakers and the Oneida Community, were based in the United States; the other, the kibbutz, is found in Israel. These communities have been selected because of their attempts to make radical and interesting changes in the organization of the family. All together, they illustrate the great diversity that is to be found in communal experiments.

The kibbutz—children of the dream

There have been a number of experiments in communal or collective child-rearing, and whereas some have failed, others have been remarkably successful. One of the best known and most publicized of these experiments is the Israeli kibbutz.[9] The first kibbutzim were established in the 1880s by Russian Jews in what was then Palestine (Leslie, 1973:140). The founders of the kibbutz were European intellectuals who placed a high value on physical labor and established agricultural collectives that idealized the toiling of the soil. Today there are over 85,000 persons living in more than 200 kibbutzim throughout Israel (Leslie, 1973:140). Although there are differences among kibbutzim, they are generally characterized by collective ownership of property, a pooling of income, communal living arrangements, and collective child-rearing (Spiro, 1968:69).

Of particular interest is the kibbutz's attempt to revolutionize the family. The founders of the kibbutz rejected middle-class European morality, especially the subordination of women and the double sexual standard

[8] The student interested in utopian communities is referred to several excellent works on the subject. See, for example, Noyes (1966), Holloway (1966), Nordhoff (1966), Kanter (1972), Roberts (1971), Fairfield (1972), and Muncy (1973).

[9] This discussion of the kibbutz is based on Spiro (1968), Talmon (1965), Leslie (1973:140–146), and Queen and Habenstein (1967:116–137).

(Talmon, 1965:264–265). Since the family was viewed as a source of many societal evils, the kibbutz attempted systematically to eliminate it. As Talmon observed, *"there is a certain fundamental incompatibility between commitment to a radical revolutionary ideology and intensive collective identification on the one hand and family solidarity on the other"* (1965:260–261). The family was a competing source of allegiance to the radical ideology that was required for the kibbutz to survive under adverse conditions.

Men and women in the kibbutz are treated as equals, or near equals. There is some division of labor with men assuming tasks that require greater strength and women being concentrated in less physically demanding roles. Women are, however, relieved of the traditional domestic role that ties them to child-rearing. They work side by side with men in the fields and engage in many activities that were previously exclusively the domain of men. Differences between the sexes in dress and appearance are also minimized. The sexes are not segregated—men and women work and play together and sometimes share the same sleeping quarters. Nudity is commonplace but devoid of sexual or erotic significance. Marriage is permitted but de-emphasized. When a couple wants to marry, they simply request a separate room. A marriage ceremony usually takes place only after or just prior to the birth of the first child. Kinship lineage is also de-emphasized. Children belong to and are cared for by the community, and a woman is allowed to retain her maiden name.

At birth or shortly thereafter infants are taken from the mother and placed in communal nurseries. Women see their babies during feeding and visits, but the care and socialization of the children is assumed by a nurse (metapelet). The metapelet has four basic functions: (1) caretaker, (2) nurturer (giving love and affection), (3) transmitting kibbutz values, and (4) training children in basic discipline—feeding, toilet training, and independence training (Spiro, 1958:34). After the first year children move into the Toddler's House, where they stay until they enter kindergarten around the age of four or five (Spiro, 1958:9). Peers play an important role in socialization as the group of children who enter kindergarten, called the kevutza, will stay together until they reach high school. "This kevutza is in many ways the child's most important social group, not only because of its long duration, but also because of the frequency and intensity of interaction within it" (Spiro, 1958:10). Although children of the kibbutz are reared communally, they are not lacking in intimate or emotional contact. Not only do nurses frequently express their affection toward the children, but since the parental role is devoid of power and authority, the parent-child relation is warm and emotionally gratifying. "If anything, the attachment of the young children to their parents is greater than it is in our own society" (Spiro, 1968:74). Parents play the most influential role in the child's emotional development (Spiro, 1958:48).

The kibbutz is an important experiment because it questions some of our most fundamental assumptions about marriage and the family. Murdock, it will be recalled, asserts that marriage and the nuclear family are universal:

. . . marriage exists only when the economic and the sexual are united into one relationship, and this combination occurs only in marriage. Marriage, thus defined, is found in every known human society. In all of them, moreover, it involves residential cohabitation, and in all of them it forms the basis of the nuclear family (1965:8).

The kibbutz then is an exception to this universal rule, since only one of the two defining characteristics of marriage is present. A couple in the kibbutz enters into a socially sanctioned sexual union, but the relationship does not involve economic cooperation (Spiro, 1968:70). ". . . a division of labor based on sex is characteristic of the *kibbutz* society as a whole. This division of labor, however, does not characterize the relationship that exists between couples" (Spiro, 1968:70). Both the male and the female work in the kibbutz, but the fruits of such labor are shared by the entire community, not just one's spouse or children.

The family is also not present in the kibbutz, according to Murdock's definition. He defines the family as "a social group characterized by common residence, economic cooperation, and reproduction. It includes adults of both sexes, at least two of whom maintain a socially approved sexual relationship, and one or more children, own or adopted, of the sexually cohabiting adults" (Murdock, 1965:1). There is no single unit in the kibbutz that fulfills these four basic functions of the family: sexual, economic, reproductive, and educational. A couple enters a socially sanctioned sexual relationship with the aim of reproducing, but children and parents do not occupy a common residence. Moreover, parents do not engage in economic cooperation and most of the socialization function is assumed by the community as a whole (Spiro, 1968:72).[10]

It is paradoxical that while the kibbutz on the one hand challenges the universality of the family, it on the other hand supports Murdock's propositions concerning the universality of the functions performed by the family (Spiro, 1968:76). Murdock seems to have fallen into the functional trap of confusing the indispensability of functions with the indispensability of structures (see the Introduction to Part Three). The functions that are traditionally performed by the family are universal and essential for the maintenance of society, but they may, as in the kibbutz, be performed by

[10] Spiro acknowledges in an addendum to his earlier paper that whether or not "marriage" and the "family" are present in the kibbutz is largely a question of definition (1968:76–79). One could revise Murdock's definition, which may be too narrow, so that a couple in the kibbutz could be considered as a "marriage" and parents and their children as a "family." The point is that parents and children "constitute a unique group within the *kibbutz*, regardless of the term with which we may choose to designate it" (Spiro, 1968:78).

alternative structures. These functions are assumed by the entire community in the kibbutz, which in a sense acts as an extended family (Spiro, 1968:76). Members of the community are viewed as kin, and there is a tendency for them to seek mates outside of the group, although endogamy is not formally prohibited (Spiro, 1968:76).

The kibbutz continues to be a radical social experiment, but new patterns are emerging. As economic conditions have improved and the community has become more stable, there is apparently less emphasis on work, and individual families are permitted to accumulate personal possessions (Leslie, 1973:145). The strong antifamilistic sentiment also seems to be waning as children born in the kibbutz (sabras) reach adulthood. With the children of the founders establishing families, a full-scale three-generational structure has developed. Kin ties have become more important, and relatively cohesive kin networks are emerging (Talmon, 1965:280–281). Contacts with relatives are maintained, and children assume responsibility for sick or aging parents (Talmon, 1961). In short, in the more stable phase the family seems to have regained some of the functions that were lost during the revolutionary phase of the kibbutzim.

The Shakers—the family without sex

The Shakers are one of the oldest and most successful of American utopian communities. They differed from most utopias, however, in their attempt to enforce celibacy among their members. In this sense the Shaker community was a total attempt to abolish the nuclear family, seeking to eliminate not only its economic function as in the kibbutz but also its most basic sexual and procreative functions.

Ann Lee, later called Mother Ann by her followers, was the inspirational leader and founder of the United Society of Believers in Christ's Second Appearing—usually known as the Shakers. Ann Lee was born in Manchester, England, of humble parents, in 1736 (Nordhoff, 1966:118).[11] In 1758 she and her parents joined a group of religious revivalists headed by Jane and James Wardley. Members of this group were persecuted, some put in prison, as a result of their violent and frenzied physical movements. "At their religious meetings they shook and trembled, whirled like dervishes, danced, sang, and cried out in strange tongues derived from the spirit world" (Holloway, 1966:56). They came to be known as Shaking Quakers or, simply, Shakers. It was while Ann was in prison, during the summer of 1770, that " 'by a special manifestation of divine light the present testimony of salvation and eternal life was fully revealed to her . . .' " (Nordhoff, 1966:119). During this vision Jesus Christ ap-

---

[11] Much of this discussion of the Shakers is taken from Nordhoff (1966:117–256), a journalist who visited all of the communities in existence in 1874, and Holloway (1966:53–79).

peared and revealed to her a " 'full and clear view of the mystery of iniquity, of the root and foundation of human depravity, *and of the very act of transgression committed by the first man and woman in the garden of Eden*' " (Holloway, 1966:57). The way to salvation was clear. She viewed "the lustful gratifications of the flesh as the source and foundation of human corruption . . ." (Nordhoff, 1966:120).

Although Ann Lee married and gave birth to four children (who died in infancy), it is said that she expressed opposition to marriage from an early age (Nordhoff, 1966:125). "On reaching marriageable age, she began to express a particular hatred of the impure and indecent act of sexual union 'for mere gratification' " (Holloway, 1966:55). Mother Ann and her followers came to America in 1774 as a result of a vision that told her that the Church of Christ's Second Appearing would be established there. They settled at Niskeyuna (later called Watervliet), seven miles from Albany. Although her husband accompanied her on the journey, Ann had started practicing celibacy, and he eloped with another woman shortly after their arrival. They gathered many converts from the surrounding area, especially from religious revivals. Mother Ann died in 1784, at the age of forty-eight, three years before the formal organization of the first Shaker community in New Lebanon, New York. She had, however, laid the basic groundwork for a successful community, and by 1830 there were about 5000 members in 18 societies throughout the United States. New Lebanon, the first Shaker society and the last to fall, lasted until 1947 (Roberts, 1971:22).

Shaker theology was unique in proposing that God was bisexual. This bisexuality was:

. . . manifested in the creation of male and female "in our image," and dupli-
cated throughout nature in the vegetable as well as in the animal kingdom. All the angels and spirits were imbued with a male and a female element. There was, for instance, a Christ spirit, first clothed in the flesh of the man Jesus, son of a carpenter; and, secondly, entering the body of the girl, Ann Lee, daughter of a blacksmith (Holloway, 1966:64).

The Shakers regarded themselves as the "Church of the Last Dispensation," believing that Christ's Second Coming and the beginning of his kingdom on earth was dated by the establishment of their church. They were influenced by the Primitive or Pentecostal Church and claimed to "have returned to this original and perfect doctrine and practice" (Nordhoff, 1966:133). Five basic principles were adopted from the Pentecost Church: (1) common property, (2) celibacy, (3) nonresistance, (4) a separate and distinct government, and (5) power over physical disease. All but the last principle had been attained, and much progress was made in controlling disease.

Among the many justifications for the celibate life was the belief that

Shakers " 'are upstairs, above the rudimental state of men, which is the generative' " (Holloway, 1966:65). They frequently quoted Christ's statement that " 'there be eunuchs which have made themselves eunuchs for the Kingdom of heaven's sake' " (Holloway, 1966:66). Marriage and property were not treated as crimes or disorders, but rather as symbols of a lower order of society. Ironically, the Shakers were organized into "families" consisting of adult brothers and sisters and children. Members of a family lived in a large house with a wide hall separating the men's and women's dormitories. The kitchen, pantry, storerooms, and the common dining hall were located on the first floor of the building. Other buildings were devoted to the various activities and industries of the community. Each society usually consisted of four families; headed by two elders, male and female, who served as its spiritual leaders. "It also has deacons and deaconesses, who provide for the support and convenience of the family, and regulate the various branches of industry in which the members are employed. . . . Under the deacons are 'care-takers,' who are the foremen and forewomen in the different pursuits" (Nordhoff, 1966: 139).

The close proximity of the sexes was consistent with their belief in overcoming temptation and sin. Elaborate precautions were taken to avoid gratification of the flesh. "Brothers and sisters were not allowed to pass on the stairs or to shake hands with one another; they were not allowed to give each other presents; nor were they allowed to visit individuals of the opposite sex without being accompanied by companions of their own sex" (Holloway, 1966:67). Men and women worked, ate, and worshiped separately. When they came into contact, distance and reserve were maintained. Shaker life was ascetic, denying worldly pleasures and indulgence of the flesh. The society was well known for its wild and spirited dancing rituals, which contrasted sharply with their quiet, sedate, and monastic life. The rituals were characterized by trembling, shaking, twitching, stamping and rolling on the floor, and speaking and singing in strange tongues.

The nuclear family, as we know it, did not exist in Shaker society. There was a sharp division of labor along sex lines, but men and women did not cohabitate and, of course, sexual intercourse was forbidden. The closest thing to marriage was the practice of assigning each brother a sister who took care of and mended his clothing, did his laundry, told him when he needed new clothes, made sure that he was orderly, and generally overviewed his habits and needs (Nordhoff, 1966:140).

Shaker society was divided into two classes—the Noviate and the Church Order (Nordhoff, 1966:135). Children, usually orphans recruited from the outside, were housed along with new adult members in a Novitiate family. The care and training of children and new members was the responsibility of the entire family. It is interesting to note that the community had trouble retaining children once they grew up and apparently preferred recruiting adult members.

When men or women come to us at the age of twenty-one or twenty-two, then they make the best Shakers. The Society then gets the man's or woman's best energies, and experience shows us that they have then had enough of the world to satisfy their curiosity and make them restful (Nordhoff, 1966:158).

New members were usually taken in on a trial basis for one year. Before entering they were required to settle their debts and relinquish all property. If they were married, they could not enter without the consent of their spouse. Those who brought children into the society were separated from them and allowed to see them in private only once a year and then only with an elder present. Thus the bond between parents and children was severed.

The Shakers were one of the most successful utopian experiments in American history, enduring for over 150 years. They were revolutionary not only in their beliefs concerning sex and the family but also in their insistence on the equality of the sexes and their racial and religious tolerance (they admitted both Jews and blacks). They opposed war, slavery, and social iniquities. While it is difficult to isolate the factors that led to their demise, at least three seem to stand out. Economic factors, especially the impact of industrialism, seem to have played an important part in the decline of the Shakers (Roberts, 1971:22). Second, was the policy of enforced celibacy, which precluded their natural growth. Members were recruited from the outside, and children in particular were difficult to retain. Roughly 80 percent of the children left the community after learning a trade (Holloway, 1966:219). Their numbers declined so that by 1900 there were less than 1000 members and by 1940 their numbers had dwindled to less than 100 (Holloway, 1966:219–220). Finally, there was the split between liberal forces who wanted greater involvement with the outside world and conservatives who desired to remain separate and aloof (Roberts, 1971:22–23). Since wealth was accumulated and vested in out-farms, it became necessary to employ hired labor. The community was subjected to outside influence and to new and more liberal ideas. ". . . small luxuries began to appear; and extreme religious fervour became rare" (Holloway, 1966:219). Worldly books, music, and dancing were also introduced. In a sense, then, the prosperity of the community played an important part in its downfall as it became more difficult for the Shakers to retain the revivalist zeal and commitment to a life of austerity and sacrifice.

Oneida—sex without the family

The Oneida Community, it will be recalled, was founded by John Humphrey Noyes. Although a description of the religious basis of Oneida was included in Chapter 8, this utopian venture is of sufficient significance to warrant additional discussion.

"Complex marriage, a term coined by John Humphrey Noyes, was the most revolutionary of all social experiments associated with the communitarian movements of the nineteenth century in America" (Muncy, 1973: 160). Noyes and his followers began to experiment with communal living at Putney, Vermont, in 1846. Their radical views on sex and marriage, however, elicited a great deal of hostility, and they were forced to leave Putney (Nordhoff, 1966:260). Prior to his departure, Noyes had been indicted for adultery (Holloway, 1966:184). A new community was established at Oneida, in New York State in 1848. Eventually, branches of Oneida were set up at Wallingford, Connecticut, and Brooklyn, New York. Despite much opposition to the community and its basic principles, Oneida became one of the most prosperous communities in American history. The community gained fame for its excellent workmanship in producing steel traps, rustic furniture, silverware, and other items.

The basic religious tenet of Oneida was the belief in perfectionism, which held that heaven could be established on this earth since the Second Coming of Christ had already occurred. Noyes admired and was influenced by the Shaker experiment. Like the Shakers, the Noyesian Perfectionists believed that they were living in a state of regeneration after the Second Advent of Christ. If they were not yet in heaven, they were close enough to base their daily lives upon "heavenly conventions" (Holloway, 1966: 182). "One such convention for which Biblical authority existed was the absence of marriage in Heaven—where 'they neither marry nor are given in marriage' " (Holloway, 1966:182). While the Shakers had used this text to justify celibacy, Noyes and his followers used it to justify group marriage. Thus the same Biblical scripture supported very different ends. The Shakers and Oneida were similar, however, in rejecting exclusive, monogamous relations.

The Oneida community adopted a basic principle of the primitive Christian church—" 'the believers possessed one heart and one soul and had all things in common' " (Kanter, 1972:9). In practice, this meant that the community was founded on the principles of economic communism, communal child-rearing, and a government of mutual criticism. Noyes sought to institute a system of complete communism. Just as personal property was prohibited, so marriage and romantic love were believed to be selfish and possessive (Kanter, 1972:66). Under complex marriage all men in the community should love all women and all women should love all men. While this was the abstract principle, in practice no person was forced to have sexual relations with another. If a man desired sexual relations with a woman, he was to approach a Central Committee (or at least the chairman of the committee), who then would act as a go-between and convey his wishes (Kephart, 1972:67). The woman was free to accept or decline the invitation. If she accepted, the man would go to her room at bedtime and visit for an hour or so before returning to his room. Sex for recreation was sharply separated from sex for procreation (Muncy, 1973:181). Amative sex was considered superior, and conception was avoided in recreational sex through an ingenious method of birth control termed "male continence," or coitus without ejaculation. Men unable to master this technique were rebuked and avoided by women (Muncy, 1973:183). Young males were introduced to sex and learned self-control through intercourse with older women who had gone through menopause. As a general principle, young persons were introduced to sexual intercourse by older, experienced members of the opposite sex (Nordhoff, 1966:276).

Having been influenced by Darwin and other evolutionary theorists, Noyes introduced in 1869 a system of selective breeding—"stirpiculture." Fifty-three women and 38 men were selected for this eugenics program, and 58 children were born during the ten years that stirpiculture was in operation (Kephart, 1972:71). It is not clear what criteria were used in choosing persons for breeding, except that they were selected by committees on which Noyes served. Noyes was apparently not opposed to self-selection, since he is reputed to have fathered 12 of these children (Kephart, 1972:71). The program of selective breeding, however, was far from perfect in controlling reproduction. Some children were born in the community before the program was instituted, and some of the children born after the program were not the children of stirps (Kephart, 1972:72).

The nuclear unit was dissolved at Oneida. Exclusive and possessive relations were discouraged among both men and women and between parents and children. ". . . they strongly discourage, as an evidence of sinful selfishness, what they call 'exclusive and idolatrous attachment' of two persons for each other, and aim to break up by 'criticism' and other means every thing of this kind in the community . . ." (Nordhoff, 1966: 276). Children were separated from their mothers after they were weaned and then placed in a community nursery (Nordhoff, 1966:281). One nursery was designed for younger children, a second for those above three or four years (Nordhoff, 1966:281). Around the age of three, children remained in the Children's House away from their mothers even at night (Holloway, 1966:193). Although children had contact with their parents and could visit them in their rooms, the ultimate authority for child-rearing was in the hands of the heads of the children's department, not parents (Kanter, 1972:13–14). The heads of these departments were frequently called papa and mother (Kanter, 1972:14).

In addition to making child care a collective responsibility, much was done to equalize relations between the sexes and to remove women from their subordinate position (Muncy, 1973:160). There was some division of labor based on special skills, but most activities were rotated or shared (Kephart, 1972:62). Men and women worked side by side in various activities. "The community worked as a group whenever the nature of the job permitted, organizing the effort into 'bees'" (Kanter, 1972:11). Women served equally with men on the various committees that supervised and coordinated community projects (Nordhoff, 1966:280).

All indications are that morale was extremely high at Oneida. As noted earlier, certain tasks, such as "cleaning up" after a Sunday visit by outsiders, were accomplished collectively by members of the community organized into "bees." The integration of the group is illustrated by the comments of a person who was raised in the community:

I was a child in the old Community, and I can tell you that they were a happy group. They used to meet nightly in the Big Hall to socialize, discuss problems, etc. The outside world had their get-togethers on Saturday night. We had ours every night, and it was something to look forward to. Of course, I was only a child at the time—they disbanded before I was 10—and children like to glorify their childhood. Still, when anybody asks me about the old days, my dominant memory is one of contentment and happiness (Kephart, 1972:66).

The solidarity of the community was undoubtedly enhanced by the architectural design of Oneida. The entire community, including the children, was housed under one roof in a spacious building known as Mansion House. "Although each adult had a small room of his own, the building was designed to encourage a feeling of togetherness, hence the inclusion of a communal dining hall, recreation rooms, library, concert hall, outdoor picnic area, etc." (Kephart, 1972:60–61). Noyes' famous "home talks" were usually given in the Big Hall, and it was here that concerts, dramas, and other cultural events were held. In-group solidarity was also enhanced by antagonisms with the "outside" and by the sacrifice of personal property and abstinence from the selfish pleasures derived from coffee, alcohol, and tobacco (Kephart, 1972:63).

One of the most effective mechanisms for developing communality was their system of "mutual criticism." The system anticipated contemporary "sensitivity groups" and "encounter sessions." A member who showed signs of personal aggrandizement or selfishness came before a committee of peers who tried to objectively isolate his faults (Nordhoff, 1966:287–301). The system was not limited to social deviants but was open to any persons who desired self-improvement or feedback from the community (Kephart, 1972:62). Self-criticism was at the cornerstone of community life. As Nordhoff, a visitor to the community, noted, "It is in fact their main instrument of government; and it is useful as a means of eliminating uncongenial elements, and also to train those who remain into harmony with the general system and order" (1966:289).

The reasons for the fall of Oneida are many and complex. Certainly the absence of a charismatic leader to replace Noyes was a factor. In 1876 the aging Father Noyes attempted to appoint his agnostic son, Dr. Theodore Noyes, as his successor. The younger Noyes was opposed not only for his lack of religious convictions but for his aloofness (Holloway, 1966:195). The community became extremely disorganized after Noyes' resignation in 1877 (Kephart, 1972:74). Conflict with the surrounding world also played a part in the downfall of Oneida. Throughout its history Oneida was harassed and threatened by the outside (Muncy, 1973:192). There was much antagonism toward the community in 1879 when Noyes left for

Canada, apparently fearing prosecution for statutory sex offenses (Kephart, 1972:74). Although he never returned, Noyes never lost interest or communication with the community. In 1879 he recommended, among other things, that the community yield to public pressure and abandon the practice of complex marriage and that a system be established wherein marriage is permitted but celibacy preferred (Holloway, 1966:196). His recommendations were accepted, and several marriages were performed shortly after this. Monogamy presented a clear threat to communism (Muncy, 1973:194). Noyes had recommended that communism *not* be abandoned, but on January 1, 1881, the Oneida Community was transformed into a joint-stock company that is still in existence. Heaven was no longer to be found on this earth.

PROSPECTS FOR THE FUTURE

Predictions about the future are extremely hazardous not only because of deficiencies in our current knowledge but, more important, because the direction of the future is dependent to a considerable extent on the choices made by man. Since the future of the family is not immutable, our focus will be on isolating alternatives rather than "predicting" the future. Before discussing alternatives, however, it is necessary to evaluate the current status of the nuclear family. The American family, as we noted earlier, is believed by many to be a dying institution. The isolated and structurally independent family of the present is frequently compared to an idealized and nostalgic view of the family of the past:

It is a pretty picture of life down on grandma's farm. There are lots of happy children, and many kinfolk live together in a large rambling house. Everyone works hard. Most of the food to be eaten during the winter is grown, preserved, and stored on the farm. The family members repair their own equipment, and in general the household is economically self-sufficient. The family has many functions; it is the source of economic stability and religious, educational, and vocational training (Goode, 1963:6).

Closer analysis reveals that the "classical" family was not only rare, however, but largely mythical. Few farms were economically self-sufficient, and large aggregates of extended kin were rare (Goode, 1963:7). Most persons lived in relatively small dwellings, not on large farms. Although divorce was less common, there is no evidence that marriages were any "happier" than they are today (Goode, 1963:7).

Thus the basic structure and functions of the American family have not changed substantially since colonial times. Even though critics of the contemporary family cite increasing rates of premarital intercourse, illegitimacy, adultery, and divorce as evidence of family dissolution, perhaps these increases are indicative of increasing rather than decreasing functionality of the family. One would expect, for instance, that the level of premarital sexual involvement would be relatively high in a society that makes "love," mutual attraction, and sexual and personal compatibility important criteria for marriage. There is greater tolerance of unmarried persons living together but the motivation to marry is apparently not declining.

Divorce and adultery are important safety valves in a society that idealizes marriage and places a premium on individual satisfaction in the relationship. A high divorce rate reflects less tolerance for unsatisfying relations, not necessarily an increase in such relations. It would appear, in fact, that individual "happiness" is enhanced in a society having a high divorce rate. At least, fewer persons are required to tolerate unhappy marriages.

Many persons dissatisfied with the nuclear family are seeking alternative forms of family life. Those who accept the nuclear family but seek a variety of sexual partners have turned to swinging; others, however, seek more basic changes in structure of the family. In the thousands of communes that have emerged throughout the United States persons are searching not only for alternative family forms but also for alternative systems of social organization. Communes, however, vary widely:

There are small urban groups that share living quarters and raise their families together but hold outside jobs, and . . . rural farming communes that combine work and living. Some are formal organizations with their own business enterprises. . . . Others are loose aggregates without chosen names (Kanter, 1970:53).

With respect to sexual experimentation they run the gamut from weekend retreats for middle-class swingers to serious attempts to institute group marriage.

Despite the publicity surrounding sexual permissiveness in communes, where sex is reputedly free for the asking, there is reason to believe that sex norms in most communes do not deviate radically from larger societal norms. One study of 18 communes reported that only 3 granted what the researchers termed "much" sexual license, 8 had "some," and 7 permitted "little" (Krippner and Fersh, 1970). Another study found that while the idea of persons as sexual property is rejected, "stability and fidelity among couples is encouraged as a general pattern . . ." (Berger et al., 1971: 514). Thus while some communities encourage complete sexual freedom, the norm seems to be for relatively stable and permanent unions to form. Those communes that do attempt to institute group marriage or "free love" must overcome numerous difficulties.[12] First, is the problem of resocializing persons to accept sexual sharing and reject deeply engrained values of sexual possessiveness. Second, the community must withstand threats from the outside community, which is typically hostile toward sexual experi-

[12] One of the few systematic studies of group marriage has been carried out by Larry and Joan Constantine (1970 and 1972).

mentation (Houriet, 1969). Third, and perhaps most important, mechanisms need to be established for reducing jealousies and working out conflicts that inevitably arise. Rather than diminishing conflict and tension, according to Larry and Joan Constantine, group marriage " 'seems to bring out, highlight, possibly even aggravate, problem areas in individuals and prior two-person marriages' " (quoted in Roberts, 1971:124).

A second, less radical, alternative is the "joint family," consisting of several couples living together and sharing family functions but remaining monogamous. The joint family retains monogamous marriage but reduces the isolation of the nuclear unit. Unrelated persons function as an extended family, providing emotional support and sharing property, goods, and child-rearing. While there is considerable variation in the pattern developed by such communities, they all face certain basic common problems. In addition to instituting a division of labor, methods for producing and distributing goods and services must be established. Most communities seem to favor collective ownership of property (except for small personal items) and equal distribution of goods. They also must devise a system for the care and socialization of children.

Although contemporary communes are fascinating social experiments that provide alternatives for persons who are dissatisfied with the larger society, they are unlikely to supplant the nuclear family in the foreseeable future. One reason for this is that most Americans still prefer the conventional nuclear family. A second is that few intentional communities provide viable alternative social systems. Group marriage and other attempts to alter the nuclear family are, however, not inevitably doomed to failure. A number of earlier communities like the Shakers and the Oneida Community were able to radically alter the nuclear family. Such experiments, however, were supported by a distinctive ideology that bound members together and by structural mechanisms that minimized internal conflict and tension. Successful communities also instituted practices that demanded sacrifice and commitment from their members. Most contemporary communes, on the other hand, seek to maximize individual freedom and to avoid aversive external controls. Without developing mechanisms that elicit greater member commitment, the future of many of today's communes is in doubt (Kanter, 1970:78).

REFERENCES

Adams, Bert N.
1968 Kinship in an Urban Setting. Chicago: Markham.
Axelrod, Morris
1956 "Urban Structure and Social Participation." American Sociological Review 21 (February):13–18.
Bartell, Gilbert D.
1971 Group Sex. New York: Peter H. Wyden.

Berger, Bennett, et al.
1971 "Child-Rearing Practices of the Communal Family." Pp. 509–523 in Arlene S. Skolnick and Jerome S. Skolnick (eds.), Family in Transition. Boston, Mass.: Little, Brown.

Bruce, J. M.
1970 "Intragenerational Occupational Mobility and Visiting with Kin and Friend." Social Forces 49 (September):117–127.

Constantine, Larry L., and Joan M. Constantine
1970 "Where Is Marriage Going?" The Futurist 4 (April):44–46.
1972 "The Group Marriage." Pp. 204–222 in Gordon.

Cuber, John F.
1969 "Adultery: Reality Versus Stereotype." Pp. 190–196 in Gerhard Neubeck (ed.), Extramarital Relations. Englewood Cliffs, N.J.: Prentice-Hall.

Denfeld, Duane, and Michael Gordon
1970 "The Sociology of Mate Swapping: Or the Family That Swings Together Clings Together." The Journal of Sex Research 6 (May):85–100.

Edwards, John N.
1972 Sex and Society. Chicago: Markham.

Fairfield, Richard
1972 Communes USA. Baltimore, Md. Penguin.

Gibson, Geoffrey
1972 "Kin Family Network: Overheralded Structure in Past Conceptualizations of Family Functioning." Journal of Marriage and the Family 34 (February):13–23.

Goode, William J.
1963 World Revolution and Family Patterns. New York: Free Press.
1964 The Family. Englewood Cliffs, N.J.: Prentice-Hall.
1965 Women in Divorce. New York: Free Press.
1971 "Family Disorganization." Pp. 467–544 in Robert K. Merton and Robert Nisbet (eds.), Contemporary Social Problems. Third ed. New York: Harcourt.

Gordon, Michael
1972 The Nuclear Family in Crisis: The Search for an Alternative. New York: Harper & Row.

Greer, Scott
1956 "Urbanism Reconsidered: A Comparative Study of Local Areas in a Metropolis." American Sociological Review 21 (February):19–25.

Ho, Ping-ti
1965 "An Historian's View of the Chinese Family System." Pp. 15–30 in Seymour M. Farber, Piero Mustacchi, and Roger H. L. Wilson (eds.), The Family's Search for Survival. New York: McGraw-Hill.

Holloway, Mark
1966 Heavens on Earth. Second ed. New York: Dover.

Houriet, Robert
1969 "Life and Death of a Commune Called Oz." New York Times Magazine (February 16):30–31, 89, 92, 94, 100, 102–103.

Kanter, Rosabeth Moss
1970 "Communes." Psychology Today 4 (July):53–57, 78.
1972 Commitment and Community. Cambridge, Mass.: Harvard University Press.
Kephart, William M.
1972 "Experimental Family Organization: An Historico-Cultural Report on the Oneida Community." Pp. 59–77 in Gordon.
Krippner, Stanley, and Don Fersh
1970 "Mystic Communes." The Modern Utopian 4 (Spring): 2–10.
Lee, Shu-Ching
1953 "China's Traditional Family, Its Characteristics and Distintegration." American Sociological Review 18 (June):272–280.
Leslie, Gerald R.
1973 The Family in Social Context. Second ed. New York: Oxford University Press.
Levy, Marion J., Jr.
1968 The Family Revolution in Modern China. New York: Atheneum.
Litwak, Eugene
1960a "Occupational Mobility and Extended Family Cohesion." American Sociological Review 25 (February):9–21.
1960b "Geographical Mobility and Extended Family Cohesion." American Sociological Review 25 (June):385–394.
Malinowski, Bronislaw
1930 "Parenthood—the Basis of Social Structure." Pp. 113–168 in V. F. Calverton and Samuel D. Schmalhausen (eds.), The New Generation. New York: Citadel.
1945 The Dynamics of Culture Change. New Haven, Conn.: Yale University Press.
Mirande, Alfred M.
1969 "The Isolated Nuclear Family Hypothesis: A Reanalysis." Pp. 153–163 in John N. Edwards (ed.), The Family and Change. New York: Knopf.
1973 "Social Mobility and Participation: The Dissociative and Socialization Hypotheses." The Sociological Quarterly 14 (Winter):19–31.
Muncy, Raymond Lee
1973 Sex and Marriage in Utopian Communities: 19th Century America. Bloomington, Ind.: Indiana University Press.
Murdock, George P.
1950 "Family Stability in Non-European Cultures." Annals of the American Academy of Political and Social Science 272 (November):195–201.
1965 Social Structure. New York: Free Press.
Nimkoff, Meyer F., and Russell Middleton
1960 "Types of Family and Types of Economy." American Journal of Sociology 66 (November):215–225.
Nordhoff, Charles
1966 The Communistic Societies of the United States. New York: Dover.
Noyes, John Humphrey
1966 History of American Socialisms. New York: Dover.

O'Neill, George C., and Nena O'Neill
1970 "Patterns in Group Sexual Activity." The Journal of Sex Research 6 (May):101–112.
Otto, Herbert A.
1970 The Family in Search of a Future. New York: Appleton.
Parsons, Talcott
1943 "The Kinship System of the Contemporary United States." American Anthropologist 45 (January-March):22–38.
Plateris, Alexander A.
1967 Divorce Statistics Analysis, United States—1963. Public Health Service, Series 21, No. 13 (October). Washington, D.C.: GPO.
Queen, Stuart A., and Robert W. Habenstein
1967 The Family in Various Cultures. Third ed. New York: Lippincott.
Roberts, Ron E.
1971 The New Communes. Englewood Cliffs, N.J.: Prentice-Hall.
Scanzoni, John
1972 Sexual Bargaining: Power Politics in the American Marriage. Englewood Cliffs, N.J.: Prentice-Hall.
Schneider, David M., and George C. Homans
1955 "Kinship Terminology and the American Kinship System." American Anthropologist 57 (December):1194–1208.
Sidel, Ruth
1973 Women and Child Care in China. Baltimore, Md.: Penguin.
Spiro, Melford E.
1958 Children of the Kibbutz. Cambridge, Mass.: Harvard University Press.
1968 "Is the Family Universal?—The Israeli Case." Pp. 68–79 in Norman W. Bell and Ezra F. Vogel (eds.), The Family. Revised ed. New York: Free Press.
Stuckert, Robert P.
1963 "Occupational Mobility and Family Relationships." Social Forces 41 (March):301–307.
Sussman, Marvin B.
1962 "The Isolated Nuclear Family: Fact or Fiction." Pp. 49–57 in Robert F. Winch, Robert McGinnis, and Herbert R. Barringer (eds.), Selected Studies in Marriage and the Family. Revised ed. New York: Holt, Rinehart & Winston.
Talmon, Yonina
1961 "Aging in Israel, A Planned Society." American Journal of Sociology 67 (November):284–295.
1965 "The Family in a Revolutionary Movement—The Case of the Kibbutz in Israel." Pp. 259–286 in Meyer F. Nimkoff (ed.), Comparative Family Systems. Boston: Houghton Mifflin.
U.S. Bureau of the Census
1973 Statistical Abstract of the United States. Ninety-Fourth ed. Washington, D.C.
U.S. Department of Health, Education, and Welfare
1974a "Summary Report Final Natality Statistics, 1970." Monthly Vital Statistics Report 22 (March 20):1–14.

1974b "Births, Marriages, Divorces, and Deaths for January 1974." Monthly Vital Statistics Report 23 (March 27):1–8.

Williams, Robin M., Jr.
1958 "Kinship and the Family in the United States." Pp. 39–86 in American Society. Second ed. New York: Knopf.

INTRODUCTION TO THE READINGS

The readings in this chapter present the nuclear family from different perspectives. The first is taken from the novel *Couples* by John Updike. Piet and Angela are a "successful" upper middle-class couple whose relationship, once vibrant and satisfying, has now deteriorated. This account captures the strain felt by the nuclear unit in contemporary society and the frustration and anguish of many couples whose marriages have become empty.

In the second article the Herndons and the Sheas devise an alternative to monogamous relations, which they term "corporate marriage." While *Proposition 31* is fictional, it depicts the problems faced by persons who seek alternatives to the nuclear family. The problems encountered include the legitimacy of children, distribution of personal property and possessions, explaining group marriage to the children, sleeping arrangements, minimizing jealousy, and social and legal complications.

Welcome to tarbox: From Couples

JOHN UPDIKE

Now, thinking of this house from whose purchase he had escaped and from whose sale he had realized a partner's share of profit, Piet conservatively rejoiced in the house he had held. He felt its lightly supporting symmetry all around him. He pictured his two round-faced daughters asleep in its shelter. He gloated upon the sight of his wife's body, her fine ripeness.

Having unclasped her party pearls, Angela pulled her dress, the black décolleté knit, over her head. Its soft wool caught in her hairpins. As she struggled, lamplight struck zigzag fire from her slip and static electricity made its nylon adhere to her flank. The slip lifted, exposing stocking-tops and garters. Without her head she was all full form, sweet, solid.

Pricked by love, he accused her: "You're not happy with me."

She disentangled the bunched cloth and obliquely faced him. The lamplight, from a bureau lamp with a pleated linen shade, cut shadows into the line of her jaw. She was aging. A year ago, she would have denied the accusation. "How can I be," she asked, "when you flirt with every woman in sight?"

"In sight? Do I?"

"Of course you do. You know you do. Big or little, old or young, you eat them up. Even the yellow ones, Bernadette Ong. Even poor little soused Bea Guerin, who has enough troubles."

"You seemed happy enough, conferring all night with Freddy Thorne.

"Piet, we can't keep going to parties back to back. I come home feeling dirty. I hate it, this way we live."

"You'd rather we went belly to belly? Tell me"—he had stripped to his waist, and she shied from that shieldlike breadth of taut bare skin with its cruciform blazon of amber hair—"what do you and Freddy find to talk about for hours on end? You huddle in the corner like children playing jacks." He took a step forward, his eyes narrowed and pink, party-chafed. She resisted the urge to step backwards, knowing that this threatening mood of his was supposed to end in sex, was a plea.

Instead she reached under her slip to unfasten her garters. The gesture, so vulnerable, disarmed him; Piet halted before the fireplace, his bare feet chilled by the hearth's smooth bricks.

"He's a jerk," she said carelessly, of Freddy Thorne. Her voice was lowered by the pressure of her chin against her chest; the downward reaching of her arms gathered her breasts to a dark crease. "But he talks about things that interest women. Food. Psychology. Children's teeth."

"What does he say psychological?"

"He was talking tonight about what we all see in each other."

"Who?"

"You know. Us. The couples."

"What Freddy Thorne sees in me is a free drink. What he sees in you is a gorgeous fat ass."

She deflected the compliment. "He thinks we're a circle. A magic circle of heads to keep the night out. He told me he gets frightened if he doesn't see us over a weekend. He thinks we've made a church of each other."

"That's because he doesn't go to a real church."

"Well Piet, you're the only one who does. Not counting the Catholics." The Catholics they knew socially were the Gallaghers and Bernadette Ong. The Constantines had lapsed.

"It's the source," Piet said, "of my amazing virility. A stiffening sense of sin." And in his chalkstripe suit pants he abruptly dove forward, planted his weight on his splayed raw-knuckled hands, and stood upside down. His tensed toes reached for the tip of his conical shadow on the ceiling; the veins in his throat and forearms bulged. Angela looked away. She had seen this too often before. He neatly flipped back to his feet; his wife's silence embarrassed him. "Christ be praised," he said, and clapped, applauding himself.

"Shh. You'll wake the children."

"Why the hell shouldn't I, they're always waking me, the little bloodsuckers." He went down on his knees and toddled to the edge of the bed. "Dadda, Dadda, wake up-up, Dadda. The Sunnay paper's here, guess what? Jackie Kenneny's having a *ba*by!"

"You're so cruel," Angela said, continuing her careful undressing, parting vague obstacles with her hands. She opened her closet door so that from her husband's angle her body was hidden. Her voice floated free: "Another thing Freddy thinks, he thinks the children are suffering because of it."

"Because of what?"

"Our social life."

"Well I have to have a social life if you won't give me a sex life."

"If you think *that* approach is the way to a lady's heart, you have a lot to learn." He hated her tone; it reminded him of the years before him, when she had instructed children.

He asked her, "Why shouldn't children suffer? They're supposed to suffer. How else can they learn to be good?" For he felt that if only in the matter of suffering he knew more than she, and that without him she would raise their daughters as she had been raised, to live in a world that didn't exist.

She was determined to answer him seriously, until her patience dulled his pricking mood. "That's positive suffering," she said. "What we give them is neglect so subtle they don't even notice it. We aren't abusive, we're just evasive. For instance, Frankie Appleby is a bright child, but he's just going to waste, he's just Jonathan little-Smith's punching bag because their parents are always together."

"Hell. Half the reason we all live in this silly hick town is for the sake of the children."

"But we're the ones who have the fun. The children just get yanked along. They didn't enjoy all those skiing trips last winter, standing in the T-bar line shivering and miserable. The girls wanted all winter to go some Sunday to a museum, a nice warm museum with stuffed birds in it, but we wouldn't take them because we would have had to go as a family and our friends might do something exciting or ghastly without us. Irene Saltz finally took them, bless her, or they'd never have gone. I like Irene; she's the only one of us who has somehow kept her freedom. Her freedom from crap."

"How much did you drink tonight?"

"It's just that Freddy didn't let me talk enough."

"He's a jerk," Piet said and, suffocated by an obscure sense of exclusion, seeking to obtain at least the negotiable asset of a firm rejection, he hopped across the hearth-bricks worn like a passageway in Delft and sharply kicked shut Angela's closet door, nearly striking her. She was naked.

He too was naked. Piet's hands, feet, head, and genitals were those of a larger man, as if his maker, seeing that the cooling body had been left too small, had injected a final surge of plasma which at these extremities had ponderously clotted. Physically he held himself, his tool-toughened palms curved and his acrobat's back a bit bent, as if conscious of a potent burden.

Angela had flinched and now froze, one arm protecting her breasts. A luminous polleny pallor, the shadow of last summer's bathing suit, set off her surprisingly luxuriant pudenda. The slack forward cant of her belly remembered her pregnancies. Her thick-thighed legs were varicose. But her tipped arms seemed, simple and symmetrical, a maiden's; her white feet were high-arched and neither little toe touched the floor. Her throat, wrists, and triangular bush appeared the pivots for some undeniable effort of flight, but like Eve on a portal she crouched in shame, stone. She held rigid. Her blue irises cupped light cat-like, shallowly. Her skin breathed hate. He did not dare touch her, though her fairness gathered so close dried his tongue. Their bodies hung upon them as clothes too gaudy. Piet felt the fireplace draft on his ankles and became sensitive to the night beyond her hunched shoulders, an extensiveness pressed tight against the bubbled old panes and the frail mullions, a blackness charged with the ache of first growth and the suspended skeletons of Virgo and Leo and Gemini.

She said, "Bully."

He said, "You're lovely."

"That's too bad. I'm going to put on my nightie."

Sighing, immersed in a clamor of light and paint, the Hanemas dressed and crept to bed, exhausted.

. . .

Corporate marriage: From Proposition 31

ROBERT H. RIMMER

Most marriages that have lasted fifteen years might be compared to a novel that two people have been reading together. Midway through, perhaps still dimly hoping for a few unexpected climaxes and surprises, they adjust themselves to the slower pace of the second half. A few readers may get bored and try to discover a new story, but most plod quietly along, finding it easier and more comfortable to read through to the predictable ending.

Returning to San Pedro, to the same houses, we soon discovered that it wasn't easy to close the old book and concentrate on the new one. The new book didn't follow the formulas most people live by; it had no standard of social behavior to guide us. The accepted routines of monogamous living had vanished. Our combined intimacy, if it were to continue, forced us to reevaluate every detail of our lives. Even the impersonal aspects of our environment acquired a new coloring and sheen as we slowly substituted the group consciousness of the eight of us for our separate individualities. In some subtle way the exchange of our bodies depersonalized our possessions. Within a few weeks Tanya's dishes had moved into my house; the Herndons' phonograph records and books moved into hers. Carelessly discarded clothing ended up in one washing under an agreement that at least once a week we would tackle the whole mess together.

Tanya decided to continue working until April, and she convinced Tom Bayberry that after the baby was born she could still do fashion layouts at home. And the formal, priggish Nancy Herndon of less than a month ago, lonely and at our wit's end, came alive. I was caught up in a world of family living—bubbling, confused, messy, argumentative, but excitingly demanding and roaringly vital.

Tanya had stumbled on a book called, *Thank You, Doctor Lamaze*, a delightful, factual account of childbirth. I read it with her, identifying with both the author and Tanya. I became the pregnant mother, as well as the mother-in-law, anxious that her daughter should have a healthy child. Based on Pavlov's theories, and widely used in Russia and France, the book extolled natural childbirth without pain for the female who could master the technique. Tanya became so enthusiastic that she decided to have our baby (we told her she couldn't call it hers anymore) at home, suggesting, since we were all involved, that there was no good reason why we all couldn't watch and assist her.

"Even the children, why not?" she demanded hotly. "It'll be very valuable education for them." I don't know who was more shocked at the idea, myself, Horace, or David.

"Even in primitive tribes accouchement is a spectacle for women only," Horace protested. But he had to admit that the traditional practice excluded the father from a rather crucial marital experience.

"If you're referring to me as the particular father," David said, "then revise your statement to coincide with your principles. This is a family affair.

We should all be involved."

In most of our talk we skirted the whole business of whether the children should watch, since we hadn't been able to agree on a proper explanation, for them, of our involved marital relations. Tanya, meanwhile, engaged in a frustrating telephone search for a doctor willing to deliver a child at home, using the Lamaze techniques. She insisted she was a tough Swede, and that even if things didn't go according to plan, this time, at the birth of her third and last baby, she was damned if she was going to be asleep or even half-asleep. She said she was going to find out for herself if the final push is the thrill they say it is. But at first she had no luck in finding a doctor sympathetic to her idea.

We spent most of our first evenings back in California discussing our sleeping arrangements. It was obvious that unless we explained to the children, we had no choice but to attempt involved and clandestine bedtime meetings while maintaining the surface appearances of monogamous parents. Unless we came to grips with the problem, the habits of the old nuclear family arrangements of our two separate houses would overwhelm our daydream of a corporate family.

David summarized it for us a few days after we returned home. "Eating and fornicating under separate roofs," he said, and grinned at my displeasure at his choice of words, "splits us apart at the two vital centers of contact."

"Eating together is simple," I said sarcastically. "We could very easily eat together." I blushed as Horace smiled at the double meaning, and lamely added, "Food!"

Strangely, we all seemed to be embarrassed to face the sexual problem head on. "We can't sneak between bedrooms every night," Horace said.

"Even if we could," Tanya added,

"I'm not sleeping with David one night and Horace the next. It's too confusing; there's no continuity."

"Not to mention that it's demoralizing," David chuckled. "Some nights I just need to sleep. So where do we go from here, Horace? After the relative simplicity of New Hampshire, isn't it time we faced the facts?"

"Stating it without innuendo," I said coldly, "David hasn't slept with Tanya since we left the Chesley lodge." As I looked at Horace I tried to search his mind. "Probably the truth is that you've made your truce with conformity and would prefer to continue monogamously with Tanya."

Horace wasn't perturbed. "On the contrary, Nancy, the only reason I proposed the idea in the first place was to insure a future with *two* wives. Seriously, I miss our nightly arguments about the impossibility of the four of us working it out. Tanya is a more complacent bed-fellow."

"They weren't arguments; call them discussions," I said. "If that's all you miss, I'm sure I can accommodate you."

Tanya insisted we come out of the clouds. "Like tonight, for instance. If we agreed, how do we accomplish it? Mitch and Sam's bedrooms are right next to ours. You have the same problem in your house. They're going to be very surprised and confused kids if they wake up in the night and discover a strange mommy or daddy in the bedroom."

"We'll have to tell them," Horace said calmly.

"Tell them what?" I demanded. "That it's all right, because their daddies and mommies love each other? If I were Susan or the boys, I'd feel uneasy, sort of as if the rug were pulled out from under me. They may not be old enough to understand everything, but they're well aware that their friends' mothers and fathers don't exchange bed-mates, that a family has two parents, not four."

"I think we can gradually recondition them." Horace shrugged. "But before we get in too deep, we better be damned sure that we're in basic agreement. It would be disastrous to end up squabbling among ourselves."

"If you're asking that Nancy and I never become jealous of each other," Tanya said, "it's contrary to all female behavior. In a few months Nancy is going to be a more desirable sex partner than I will, with my bloated belly."

I scowled. "But after the baby is born, that's something else again."

"What do you mean?"

"You and David will have a stronger tie than Horace and I have."

Horace laughed. "Do you want me to get you pregnant? We could even things out."

"God, no! Five children to explain us to are enough," I sighed. "What we really need is something overriding, something equal to the commitment of monogamous marriage. When two people get married they soon discover that marriage is not all hearts and flowers, but the social and legal arrangements hold together the cracks in the walls."

While the others seemed more pragmatic than I, and appeared content to develop our future off the cuff, I was plagued with the fear that the whole business of calmly sleeping with each other's spouses was immoral. Our sleeping arrangements had now become haphazard; there was no predetermined pattern. Horace and David sneaked into each other's bedrooms late at night, but retreated to their own rooms by early morning.

In some way I was unable to define, I cared deeply for both David and Horace. Tanya and I discussed it together often. "I think they feel the same way," she told me. "When you think about the four of us, it's more amazing in reverse. I'll wager that if we could take a poll of females, we'd find that the typical female is much less jealous and possessive than her spouse. Females are basically amoral. Yet, as males, David and Horace think you and I are too subjective. We probe too much." Tanya looked at me with mild embarrassment. "At first, when David was in my arms, I couldn't stop thinking about you. I'd ask myself, did David respond in the same way to you as he was responding to me? I'd close my eyes and see him with you, and I wondered if there was a real distinction in his mind. Was there in mine? Or were we both just mechanical robots on whom someone had pushed the fuck button? Still, I was certain that with Horace I was a quite different female. Not quantitatively." Tanya grinned at my laughter. "Oh dear, I don't know if there are any words to pin any of us down. I think I discovered that my duality wasn't entirely real, or if it existed at all, was only partial. I was happy with both of them." Tanya shrugged. "Equally important, Sea, is to *dare* to explore my feelings with you."

I couldn't stop myself; I hugged her quickly. "That's the magic, really," I said. "We're friends. The wild passion, the blending with Horace wouldn't be possible for me with a stranger, or in a situation that didn't encompass the four of us. I'm female, and I've been naked with Horace in a way that I had never dared to be with David. Now, slowly, after years of marriage, I'm learning how to be an individual with David, too. I'm no longer just a wife; I'm Nancy, and I'm in love with us all. When I was shopping today, I couldn't help an inward smile. I was the only female among all those harried women who had two men in love with her. I felt like dancing and singing my joy, like shouting, 'Dull, stodgy world, wake up and love!' "

I suppose that explained my fears, too. We were not immoral in a sexual sense. I could no longer think of us as adulterers, as breaking the Seventh Commandment. As Horace pointed out, there was a better commandment in Leviticus: "Thou shalt love thy neighbor as thyself." To adulterate meant make corrupt, impure; to debase. We were adding to, purifying, cleansing, creating a new vital entity that enlarged us all.

When we returned to Graniteville for New Year's Eve with my family we took rooms as proper families at a nearby motel. Later, when we discussed the celebration and the New Year's Eve need for people to rediscover their emotional dependence on each other, we concluded that our dual relationship in New Hampshire was more basically honest than the sexual sparrings of suburbia. Even Mother had to admit it was a good thing Tanya and I were not relocating in Graniteville. Two new females, in the contained atmosphere of the Neighborhood Club, could fatally disturb an environment already shaken by numerous deviations from idealistic monogamy. By contrast, our immorality was simply against a morality that made it impossible for us to declare ourselves.

While we couldn't agree how to involve the children in the deeper aspects of our relationship, we decided that as a start toward reconditioning them we could blend our family meals by eating breakfast and dinner together. Neither the kitchen nor dining room in our twin houses was adequate to accommodate eight at a sitting, so we bought a large round table with center-leaf extensions, and turned the Herndon living room into a dining room. The kids were ecstatic. Slowly

we evolved a dining ritual which encompassed them in all our conversations. Whether it was discussing school, homework, David's business problems, Horace's teaching, Tanya's breathing exercises as she prepared for the baby, television, or what any of us had been reading, we purposely encouraged the children to participate and voice their opinions. After dinner, at Susan's suggestion, the table became a joint homework table. On weekday evenings while we read or answered questions or, later, played games with them before the children's bedtime, the television remained silent and happily neglected.

Since Tanya arrived home an hour or two before David and Horace, she and I decided to do our food shopping jointly. To eliminate argument over money, David and Horace contributed one hundred dollars each to our joint food fund and replenished it equally when it was gone.

Perhaps it was the food fund; perhaps it was David's continued reading of Ralph Borsodi; or perhaps it was our growing relatedness as a family of eight. Possibly it was our decision to bring the television out near the Sheas' swimming pool on Saturday night and watch the movies with the kids, while all of us, comfortably naked, swam, talked, and good-naturedly exchanged acrid comments about the drama we were only half watching. But who knows really what all the various origins and inspirations were for David's bombshell idea?

In the late evening, as he smiled and kissed and hugged each one of the kids good night, I intercepted a far-off, amused expression on his face. Tanya ruffled his hair. He ran his fingers lightly across the new curve of her belly as she passed by his chair and snapped off the television. I sat beside Horace, dangling my feet in the pool. For a moment we didn't say anything, but simply enjoyed the welcome silence of the television. The nervous throb of an automobile engine on the street in front of our houses seemed too near. Slowly it faded away; then it became pleasantly distant; soon there was a moment of absolute quiet.

"David seems lost in his thoughts." I smiled at him. "I think he should take us along with him into outer space."

He twinkled at me. "The truth is that I'm happy, and I'm surprised at the simplicity of happiness. It's the four of us, together here, indolent, content with the fact of each other's existence." He laughed and waved toward the top of the hill. "I don't know who the neighbors two streets above us are, but they've been watching us down here, either in awe or shock, for the past two hours."

"My God!" Tanya scowled at him. "You should have told us. I didn't realize they could look into this yard. One of these days we're going to be raided."

I agreed with her, though the men seemed unconcerned about our casual family nudity. Tanya and I had carefully cautioned the children not to make it a subject of discussion among their friends in the neighborhood or at school.

"We know," Susan had told us haughtily. "We're not stupid!"

"Do you think we are?" Tanya had asked.

Jimmy shook his head. "I think it's fun," he said. Mitch agreed. "The Materi kids never saw old lady Materi in her birthday suit." He laughed. "I think Sea and Tan are kind of interesting to look at."

I still had my doubts, but Horace insisted it was healthy for the children to grow up with a calm acceptance of us all as quite human beings who sometimes found it convenient to be naked.

"Forget the neighbors for a minute," David picked up the thread of his thoughts. "Since we've arrived at a point where we can discuss and solve most of our problems, except how to explain our sleeping arrangements to the kids, I'd like to propose an idea that's been flitting around in my mind for the past few weeks. It might be the step, if we dared to take it, that Nancy feels is so necessary. It would be a larger commitment to the belief that what we're doing is sound. I propose that we sell these two houses, pool all our resources, and incorporate as a joint family. If we did, we could build a home that made more sense for all of us. In the process we'd have to explain to the kids exactly what we hope to achieve."

Horace, stretched out on an air cushion, stared into the star-pricked sky. "How do you propose to do it?" he asked. He leaned on his elbow to examine my face and breasts, which were right-angled to his belly. "Nancy looks startled."

David shrugged. "Not with the idea. It's just that she can't believe the rugged Republican individualist she married could accept communal property sharing. It's an interesting fact that most middle class families, at least among themselves, have a greater reluctance to discuss their financial strength or lack of it than they do their sexual relations."

"Or lack of sex," Tanya grinned. "It's one problem we've overcome."

Horace trickled his fingers across my shoulders. "I'm not so rich that I care."

"I've known you three years," David said. "I could only guess at your earnings."

"Seventeen-five from Cal Institute." Horace laughed. "I'm in the ranks of the poorly paid pedagogues. Tanya has been earning seventy-five hundred. My father left an estate of seventy thousand, mostly in blue-chip stocks, which earn about thirty-five hundred in dividends. All told, discounting Tanya's salary for the long haul, about twenty-two to twenty-three thousand."

We spent the rest of the evening in an excited money discussion. David was earning twenty-four thousand from Herndon Showcase. If the company had a good year he could take a few thousand more, but more likely he should plow the money back into inventory and new machinery.

"My God," Tanya marveled. "Together we're filthy rich. We have a total income of nearly fifty thousand dollars."

As we explored in detail our total assets, we discovered that our combined savings totaled twenty-six thousand dollars, the equity in our houses came to thirty thousand dollars, and the paid-up value of our insurance policies was about eighteen thousand.

David estimated the Herndon Showcase Corporation was worth about two hundred fifty thousand dollars, and Horace pointed out that the Herndon assets were greater than his inheritance. David didn't think that was important. "We can't measure this merger by money values. We're four people in reasonably good health. The question is, do we have the nerve to love and cherish each other until death do us part?" David explained in detail Sub-Chapter S of the Internal Revenue Code, under which he thought we could legally form the Herndon-Shea Corporation. All of our assets would be transferred to the corporation. Our combined income would be funneled through the corporation without double taxation, with one corporate tax on our earnings. Moreover, we would have the numerous advantages of corporate deductions and provisions such as the pension plans permitted to corporations. "You have to understand this is a special type of partnership corporation. It's permitted under the laws as long as there are no more than ten stockholders." David laughed. "We're under the wire with nine of us; one to go!"

Tanya and I were slightly bewildered with the details. "Do we understand you right? All of us including the kids would be equal stockholders?"

"It's the only practical way, because it would minimize taxes. If we issued one thousand shares, each of us and each child would immediately be given one hundred shares while a hundred unissued shares would be left for contingencies.

"If you're grinning at me, forget it," I said. "No contingencies. I take my pills religiously. Nine under one roof is enough."

We tossed the idea around for several days. The potential for us as a united family was fascinating and intriguing to contemplate. Our corporation would have sufficient income and assets to swing a mortgage on a unique house designed for a unified family. The corporation could not only be planned for so that we would have ample financial security for the four of us, but it could become a continuing source of income for the children as they grew older. If we designed our new home correctly, it could become a living thing, expanding to meet the needs of the entire family. Later, if any or all of the kids wanted to live with us, our corporate home could become a truly family compound.

Tanya immediately got us involved in drawing plans for the kind of home we would need. Horace wanted to gamble. Could we immediately create what he called a "three-generation home"? He grinned at David. "You and I are without living parents, but Sea and Tanya each have a mother and father who are alive.

"You mean build a house large enough so that my mother and father could move in?" Tanya was stunned. "Jesus, NO!"

I agreed. "My mother and father would drive us insane. But you don't have to worry, the immorality of the whole business would give mother a fatal heart attack. She'd never come in with us."

Horace wanted to know what Tanya and I would do if our father or mother died. Put the survivor in a senior citizen center? I shrugged. It was something I didn't like to think about.

"I agree with Horace," David admitted. "After all, do we or don't we believe in what we're doing? If we don't, we should split up. If we do, then the purpose is to create stability for an entire family. If you think ahead, in thirty years, if we all live, we're going to be outcasts. The kids will have to decide what to do with us."

Tanya suggested we might begin to dislike each other after just a few years. What if we couldn't tolerate each other? Jokingly, Horace suggested that we design the house with hate-each-other apartments. David's in-triguing contribution was, if someone should die or we couldn't get along, to have a prior agreement to sell the individual shares in our corporation to an outsider of the same sex. "That way," he said, "if Horace and I got bored, we could sell out to some impotent old man who might get a charge out of having two young wives."

Tanya and I, hysterical with laughter, vetoed that idea. If Horace and David got bored servicing two women, the only alternative would be for them to sleep together.

"What if one of us dies?" I asked.

"That's just the point," Horace said. "Let's say I die first. You and Tanya and the kids would have the kind of security with David that he and I are both trying to achieve for you independently."

"David would be a bigamist." Tanya wiped the tears of laughter from her eyes. "That would be illegal."

"Somehow, I think we're illegal right now." I was convinced of it. "I wish one of us dared ask a lawyer. Could we be put in jail for immoral conduct?"

"The hell with the legality of our private, married lives." David frowned. "We aren't hurting anyone. What we do together is nobody's damned business but our own!"

Educational disorganization

10

SOCIALIZATION AND EDUCATION

Socialization is one of the most basic and persistent functions of society. If society is to maintain itself beyond a single generation, the cultural heritage must be transmitted to new members. Most animals are equipped for survival by built-in hereditary instincts and tendencies. Man, on the other hand, has few instincts. His values, beliefs, and basic views of the world are learned. The importance of socialization is accentuated not only by man's malleability but also by his dependence. The human infant is extraordinarily vulnerable, incapable of survival without the care and comfort provided by adults.

In most societies the socialization function is the primary responsibility of the family. Children are cared for, nurtured, and protected by parents. "In relatively undifferentiated societies, education is blended with other activities of the family and the larger social groupings of tribe, clan, estate, and community . . . and, hence, education is part of the socialization that takes place in these contexts" (Clark, 1964:736). Education emerged as a separate institution in more complex societies characterized by a greater division of labor. The family continues to play an important role in informal training and value transmission, but socialization is no longer its exclusive domain.

The educational institution is a structure of norms and values whose primary function is to prepare children and adolescents to assume adult roles. It is important to distinguish educational aims or goals from educational functions. Socialization, for instance, is one of the major functions of education. It is an objective consequence or effect of the educational institution, although it is not necessarily an aim or goal. Socialization is, of course, an ongoing process that continues throughout one's lifetime. Educational goals, on the other hand, are the avowed purposes of the educational institution. "Sociological" and "educational" analyses of the educational institution in particular tend to have different foci. Sociologists are usually concerned with the functions of education, educators with the aims or goals of education. In other words, sociologists look at what education *does*, and educators at what it *should do*. Both are worthwhile pursuits, but much confusion is generated by a lack of distinction between them. This does not mean that purposes and functions are unrelated. The aims or goals of education influence the socialization process, and socialization, in turn, affects educational aims.

THE CHANGING ROLE OF EDUCATION

Education is not a completely static or stable phenomenon; its goals and functions have varied both across and within societies. In simpler societies the aims of education were coterminous with the aims of the larger society. "The aim of education, therefore, was definitely conservative: it was to conserve and perpetuate the funded capital of social experience" (Brubacher, 1966:1–2). The culture or way of life of a group was passed on from elders to children. Most learning took place informally and was part of growing up. The basic value underlying socialization was group survival. Societies struggling to maintain themselves and facing a hostile environment educated children to accept conventional folk wisdom.

As societies became larger and more complex, education became differentiated from simple socialization, but educational aims remained conservative. Despite the vast achievements of ancient Chinese civilization, education in China was traditional. Its basic aim was the perpetuation of a relatively static culture (Brubacher, 1966:2). Education was the prerogative of the elite scholar class. The scholar class studied the classics but did not challenge the basic values of society. A similar pattern was found in the educational system of ancient India. Conservation was buttressed by a philosophy that subordinated the needs and desires of the individual to the collective good. "In the main the Hindu sought nirvana, a state of selflessness in which one's individuality is absorbed in the universal world spirit. . . . education aimed to cultivate patience, resignation, and docility" (Brubacher, 1966:2). Although formal education was the province of the upper castes, the social order was justified through a complex system of beliefs and values that taught men to accept their station in life and to hope for a better life in the next world (see Chapter 3).

Ancient Hebrew civilization and early Christianity were also conservative in their educational aims. The Old Testament taught one to "train up a child in the way he should go," so that "when he is old he will not depart from it" (Proverbs 22:6). The Ten Commandments also sought to bring about conformity to traditional values and to maintain parental control over children. The Fifth Commandment states that one should "Honor thy father and thy mother" (Exodus 20:12).

The influence of Eastern educational philosophies is evident in early Western cultures. Education in Sparta was basically conservative. In order to ensure survival and subordination of surrounding populations, high priority was given to the training of the military. "Consequently, the chief aims of her educational system were identical with the military virtues of courage, endurance, respect for and obedience to superiors, patriotism, and loyalty to the state" (Brubacher, 1966:3). One of the earliest seats of progressive education was the Greek city-state of Athens. While enjoying an element of political and economic security, it was able to shift the focus of education from conservation and survival to individual development (Brubacher, 1966:3). The aim of education was to prepare the individual for citizenship. Emphasis was placed on a well-rounded education so that physical, intellectual, moral, and aesthetic qualities were developed—the educational system guarded against undue specialization and overdevelopment of any one area (Brubacher, 1966:3). A citizen was to have a well-balanced and temperate education. Although the elite constituted the intellectual class, there was concern with the education of all citizens. Greek philosophers devoted much of their time and energy to discussing and debating educational aims. In *The Republic* Socrates isolated three classes of citizens: artisans, warriors, and philosophers or guardians (Plato, 1966:167). Since each class occupied a different place in society, its education differed accordingly. Socrates sought to create a utopian system in which individuals would assume those positions for which they were best suited (Ofshe, 1970:318). He assumed that men are inherently different and that their "nature" prepares them for different occupations. At the top of the hierarchy in *The Republic* were the guardians of the state. They were best qualified to lead and to hold power, but the power was to be used for the good of the governed (Ofshe, 1970:318). The rulers were to be selected from the best qualified of the guardians. Mechanisms were introduced to ensure that the guardians did not abuse their power or use it to advance personal or selfish goals. First, they were to be tested for courage, gentleness, and the capacity to resist temptation. "Then, the good guard for our society will be a lover of learning (a philosopher, that is), high-spirited, quick in his acts, and strong" (Plato, 1966:48). Another control was introduced by limiting the guardians' possessions and private property to the barest essentials. If they ever came to possess land of their own and houses and money, they would be required to surrender their guardianship (Plato, 1966:68). It was not expected that guardians of the commonwealth would be particularly happy. Their individual happiness was to be subordinate to the common good and to the happiness of the entire community. But in the last analysis social control came from within, not through legislation. "Why give directions on such points to good men, for it won't be hard for them to make all the rules needed themselves?" (Plato, 1966:73).

Despite Socrates' interest in individual differences and in a well-rounded education, the utopian system described in *The Republic* is based on an extreme genetic view (Ofshe, 1970:318). The function of education was to bring out or develop the natural qualities of the individual rather than to create these qualities. Environment and education played a relatively minor role in the development of natural qualities. Much emphasis was placed on "discovering" the natural tendencies of persons and on placing them in those positions for which they were best suited. Desired qualities were perpetuated through selective mating. While educational aims in ancient Greece and Rome were predominantly secular, educational aims in Europe during the Middle Ages were dominated by supernatural and other worldly concerns (Brubacher, 1966:6). Focus was shifted from preparation for the problems and issues of this world to preparation for the hereafter. The goal of education was moral or ethical development. This other worldly concern was epitomized by the idealization of monastic life during the Middle Ages (Brubacher, 1966:6). The salvation of souls was to be attained by discipline and devotion to a world of sacrifice, penance, and the rejection of worldly pleasures. However, "toward the end of the Middle Ages social as well as individual regeneration became an object of the monastic orders" (Brubacher, 1966:7). Scholars moved from simply copying manuscripts to careful examination and study of the classics and particularly the work of ancient Greek philosophers.

The Renaissance brought a revival and regeneration of secular education. "Humanist" philosophers were concerned with liberating the human "spirit" through a balanced liberal education. Education was still limited largely to the aristocracy or the courtier who was to be educated to rule wisely and judiciously. While the courtier was a man of letters, he was to be a well-rounded gentleman and not simply a scholar whose head is "stuffed with knowledge" (Brubacher, 1966:8). It was not until the latter part of the eighteenth century as an aftermath of the French and American Revolutions that emphasis was placed on educational aims for the masses and not simply for the privileged classes.

Education in colonial America was influenced by the movement toward universal education. Schools were established shortly after the founding of the colonies and lip service was paid to liberal educational philosophies that were current in Europe. Yet education was still limited mostly to the well-to-do and was permeated with religious values. Schooling was "viewed by the colonists as the most important bulwark after religion in their incessant struggle against the satanic barbarism of the wilderness" (Cremin, 1970:176–177). The school was a means of enforcing religious and political orthodoxy (Rippa, 1967:42). Learning to read was encouraged—not necessarily for intellectual or personal development—but so that citizens could study the Bible. The first step toward compulsory education was taken with passage of the Act of 1642, which was passed twenty-two years after the Massachusetts Bay Colony was established. The act did not require that schools be established, but it imposed fines on parents and apprentices' masters "who refused to account for their children's ability 'to read and understand the principles of religion and the capital laws of the country'" (Rippa, 1967:42). A second step was taken in 1647 with passage of the "Old Deluder, Satan" Act, which required that communities with 50 households establish and support schools (Cremin, 1970:181–182). It also required towns with 100 families to set up a Latin grammar school to prepare adolescents for Harvard College. By 1650 the educational institution was firmly established on the North American continent (Cremin, 1970:182). Thus despite the alleged separation of church and state, the justification for the first system of public education in the American colonies was found in religious values.

In the New England colonies there were two basic types of schools: primary schools and Latin grammar schools. Primary schools were designed for lower-class children, Latin grammar schools for children of the elite. Primary schools taught reading and writing, usually stressing reading, which was considered more essential for religious training (Rippa, 1967:35). All indications are that schools were authoritarian and dogmatic. Children were treated as miniature adults whose basic nature was evil. Discipline was strict, and disobedience was met with severe punishment (Rippa, 1967:35). All instruction was dominated by Puritan religious values. "Learning" consisted of rote memorization of religious sayings, poems, or hymns that described man's degeneracy and depravity. The New England primer warned that "the devil was lurking everywhere ready to seize the souls of children already predisposed to sin and eternal damnation" (Rippa, 1967:36). "The Day of Doom," a popular poem written by Michael Wigglesworth, describes the Last Judgment. The "fear of God" was instilled in children through the vivid description of man's depravity and of God as a punishing and avenging judge (Rippa, 1967:37).

The Latin grammar school was the forerunner of the contemporary secondary school. The Boston Latin School, established in 1635, is the oldest secondary school in the United States. The curriculum of the Latin grammar school, modeled after British Latin schools, concentrated on the study of the classics (Rippa, 1967:38). Special emphasis was placed on learning to read and write Latin, which was believed to be an integral part of a balanced education, but there was also an introduction to Greek and sometimes to Hebrew (Cremin, 1970:185). The educational goals of the Latin grammar school were conservative. Attendance was limited largely to sons of the upper class. One of its primary goals was to prepare students for the entrance exams at Harvard College (Rippa, 1967:39). A second goal was to provide religious instruction. A portion of each day was devoted to prayer and religious exercises (Cremin, 1970:186). Thus the school conserved basic moral and religious values and ensured that these values were transmitted to the next generation of elite.

In the postcolonial period (post-colonial to present) educational goals and functions have changed concurrently with changes in the larger society. As the society became larger and more complex, education became more secular in orientation and religious goals were eventually supplanted by political and economic goals. Rather than simply teaching people minimal reading skills so that they could understand the Bible, education was to prepare persons for citizenship and for participation in the economic sphere. A more complex division of labor required more specialized and prolonged occupational and vocational training. Compulsory education became the dominant standard. Increasingly, education was extended to more and more persons. A high school education, once the province of the elite, became a prerequisite for relatively low-skilled occupations. Even higher education became accessible to a large proportion of the population. These changes meant that the school was the "gatekeeper" to participation in the economic institution. Education was the key to social mobility and to economic and occupational success. Persons wanting to climb the ladder of success were required to conform to the norms of the educational institution.

THE CONTEMPORARY SCHOOL: AGENT OF STABILITY OR INSTRUMENT OF CHANGE

This section will present some of the dominant goals of American schools as espoused by educators and other adult members of society and examine critically the discrepancy between these avowed goals and the functions of the educational institution. One of the major goals of education is reportedly to prepare youth for citizenship in a democratic society. This goal, expounded by Thomas Jefferson and James Madison, has a long heritage dating to the Greco-Roman ideal of an intellectually well-rounded and informed citizen. While universal education in the American colonies was originally justified by religious tenets, today it is likely to be justified by political ideals. A democratic society, it is said, cannot function adequately without an informed citizenry to participate in decision making. Universal literacy, according to the pluralistic model, is a safeguard against autocratic or totalitarian control by a powerful elite. Education is believed to be the birthright of citizens in a democratic society. According to one educator:

Democracy makes the many of such paramount political and educational importance because it believes in the essential dignity of all persons. It enjoins that every person be treated always as an end. This injunction holds no matter to which sex a person belongs, no matter what his color or race, no matter whether he is highborn or low, and no matter what the economic condition. . . . Since every individual counts, it would be a cosmic miscarriage for his capacities to go undeveloped (Brubacher, 1969:57).

This view holds that the school is founded on basic democratic principles that uphold the basic dignity of the person and "the freedom to assert his unique individuality . . ." (Brubacher, 1969:64). The school affirms the belief that all men are created equal and should be provided with equal opportunity to develop individual capacities.

There is great discrepancy, however, between the ideals of education and its actual operation in contemporary society. Despite the liberal and equalitarian rhetoric, schools are controlled by middle- and upper-class persons and serve as agencies for perpetuating dominant political values. The concept of equal opportunity is largely mythical. Lower-class children are at a disadvantage from the moment they enter public school. Their early socialization does not usually prepare them for adequate participation in the school. Not only are they likely to be deficient in verbal capacity and other academic skills, but their value system conflicts with that of middle-class teachers and administrators (Friedenberg, 1967:19). The school emphasizes verbal fluency, deferred gratification, honesty, neatness, and cleanliness (Cohen, 1966:65–66). Ironically, the equalitarian ethic that holds that all children should be evaluated according to the same "universal standards" places lower-class children at an even greater disadvantage because it ignores the fact that such standards are based on values of the dominant group. A teacher can easily justify his or her bias on the grounds that all children are "treated equally."

While the pluralistic model asserts that compulsory school attendance is essential for maintaining democratic principles, compulsory education is in effect a gross violation of civil liberties. School attendance laws require that a child stay in school until he reaches a specified age, but such laws are *not* contractual in that they do not guarantee a minimum standard of education or attainment of a certain level of competence in return for attendance (Friedenberg, 1967:12). "Even if he can establish that the school is substandard and that he is personally mistreated there, he cannot legally withdraw . . ." (Friedenberg, 1967:12). Paul Goodman asserts, moreover, that the contemporary emphasis on universal literacy is motivated by a desire in our society to increase control over the masses. He suggests that regimentation of the population would be more difficult if large numbers were illiterate. Literacy is used to create and maintain an "artificial demand" for useless products in an infinitely expanding economy (Goodman, 1964:23–26).

A second basic goal of education in a democratic society is moral and ethical development. The emphasis given this goal is not surprising in light of the historical link between religion and education in the United States. Direct religious instruction, however, has been replaced gradually by more subtle, moral and ethical training. "Moral and ethical development" are euphemisms for dominant middle-class values. Thus "drug education" becomes drug abuse, and "sex education" is synonymous with sexual repression. Jules Henry has noted that at the same time that schools are for some things they are inevitably against others: "While the Old Testament extols without cease the glory of the One God, it speaks with equal emphasis against the gods of the Philistines . . . and while our children are taught to love our American democracy, they are taught contempt for totalitarian regimes" (1963:285–286).

Children learn to be neat, polite, and perhaps most important to subordinate their needs to those of the teacher (Silberman, 1970:151). "Nice" boys and girls are compliant and can be controlled with ease. They also learn through the emphasis on competition that individual success is attained at the expense of others who fail (Henry, 1963:295–302). An apparently innocent game like "spelling baseball" masks a fierce system of competition whereby some children win and others lose—losers of the game experience rejection by peers and the teacher.

"Character development" means that children are taught to control their natural impulses for the sake of order. Jonathan Kozol has noted how the Boston schools extol the virtue of obedience and instill fear in children through punitive measures. A "character education" booklet lists the following traits that teachers are encouraged to try to develop in children: " 'CHARACTER TRAITS TO BE DEVELOPED: OBEDIENCE TO DULY CONSTITUTED AUTHORITY . . . SELF-CONTROL . . . RESPONSIBILITY . . . GRATITUDE . . . KINDNESS . . . GOOD WORKMANSHIP AND PERSEVERANCE . . . LOYALTY . . . TEAMWORK . . . HONESTY . . . FAIR PLAY' " (Kozol, 1968: 179).

Peter Marin has similarly observed that the school "breeds obedience, frustration, dependence, and fear: a kind of gentle violence that is usually turned against oneself . . ." (1969:68).

A third avowed goal of education, consistent with the democratic ethic, is the development of individual capacities. The school is designed supposedly to help the individual to develop his or her potential and to encourage creative expression. While some individuals are able to develop their capacities in school, one wonders whether this occurs as a result of or in spite of the school. There is little doubt that the school has not met with much success in the attainment of these goals. The schools tend to discourage individuality and creativity. Children, especially in larger urban school systems, are "batch" processed and treated as a uniform and undifferentiated mass. School systems are large bureaucratic organizations that process children in a manner not too dissimilar to the processing of a product or a prison inmate. "Just as our American society as a whole is more and more tightly organized, so its school system is more and more regimented as a part of that organization, with little leeway of its own" (Goodman, 1967:27). The school is also a vested interest group whose primary goal seems to be to maintain itself. According to Goodman, the school "keeps thousands busy, wastes wealth, crushes life, and pre-empts the space in which something interesting could go on" (1967:27). The prominence of the control function is illustrated by the conditions surrounding the dismissal of Jonathan Kozol from his position as a fourth-grade teacher in a Boston ghetto school. He was discharged for teaching a poem, "Ballad of the Landlord," which was written by a black author. The poem was regarded as objectionable because "it could be interpreted as advocating defiance of authority." One of the members of the school committee gave the following justification for Kozol's dismissal:

. . . the curriculum of this particular school, which is saturated with compensatory programs in an effort to specially assist disadvantaged pupils, does allow for innovation and creative teaching. However, this flexibility does not and should not allow for a teacher to implant in the minds of young children any and all ideas. Obviously, a measure of control over the course of study is essential to protect the 94,000 Boston school children from ideologies and concepts not acceptable to our way of life (Kozol, 1968:230).

Marin has observed that students can respond to control by either dropping out of school or making "themselves smaller and smaller until they can act in ways their elders expect" (1969:67). Students become "smaller" in the sense that their individual needs and initiatives are increasingly subordinated to the demands and needs of adults. The system produces what we commonly call good citizens but who are more accurately "good soldiers," compliant and acceptant of authority without question (Marin, 1969:67).

The last avowed goal of American education to be discussed is occupational and vocational training. Previously, the justification for schools, particularly secondary schools and colleges, was that they provided a general liberal education for the children of the elite, who were to assume leadership positions as adults. Education today is increasingly justified on the grounds that it not only trains children in specific occupational skills but provides them with general, basic skills that are essential for any occupation. The school program has been expanded greatly so that the traditional three Rs are only a small part of the total curriculum. High school curriculums are geared to two types of students: those who are preparing for college and those who will assume jobs after high school. Vocational education has therefore assumed an important part in the high school curriculum.

Industrialization and technological expansion require that more and more workers acquire specialized skills and training (Schwartz, 1972:2). Rapid change, however, also means that certain skills become obsolete as rapidly as they are created. The general trend during the twentieth century has been toward greater specialization and differentiation (Green, 1969:226). This specialization has meant that the economic institution has had a profound impact on education (see Adams, 1972; Carnoy, 1972). Since industry holds the key to economic rewards, the goals of education are shaped to a considerable extent by its demands. Goodman aptly characterizes the relationship between education and the corporate state: "Jobs are scarce, and the corporations and state can dictate the terms. Thus, IBM, Westinghouse, etc., swoop down on the colleges and skim off the youth who have been given what amounts to an apprenticeship at public and private expense . . ." (1967:29). It is interesting that a college diploma is held as a prerequisite to many corporate jobs even though a college education is not really essential for carrying out most of these roles. The major function of education is probably not developing occupational skills but "weeding out" persons with undesirable personal characteristics who will not fit into the corporation. A college diploma guarantees that a person is "punctual, obedient, and [has] a smooth record" (Goodman, 1967:29–30).

While the American public school subscribes to a number of lofty goals such as preparation for citizenship in a democracy, moral and ethical development, and vocational training, in practice it forces children to stay in school without regard to their constitutional rights, stifles creativity, enforces conformity, and perpetuates structured social inequality. The school is basically an agent of stability rather than an instrument of change. Education, in fact, is "the central conserving force of the culture" (Henry, 1963:286). The major change in American education from colonial times to the present seems to lie in a shift of control in the schools from religion to government and industry. Education, from kindergarten to graduate school, has become a gatekeeper for the corporate state. It is not a process through which individual capacities and potential are developed, but rather a process of selection according to which those who are unruly and irreverent are separated from those who are malleable and compliant. The school is in the words of Goodman (1967:30) a "universal trap," and those who are out of school are out of the mainstream of society.

THE SEARCH FOR ALTERNATIVES

The current state of American education has been accurately described by Silberman (1970), as "the crisis in the classroom." This section reexamines the crisis of the schools and analyzes alternatives to contemporary education. We have seen that changes in education do not occur in a vacuum but are linked to changes in other institutions. Changes in the economic institution have placed demands on education. If the movement toward social differentiation, specialization, and cybernation continues, we can expect these demands to intensify rather than diminish.

What then is wrong with the schools? While schools vary considerably, they tend to share certain common characteristics. The Carnegie Commission Report is one of the clearest and most outspoken indictments of American schools (Silberman, 1970). It charges that by and large schools fail to educate. They are "oppressive," "grim," and "joyless" institutions that are more concerned with order and control than with learning or inquiry (Stevens, 1972:5–7). One consequence of the bureaucratic structure and rigidity of the schools is to "make it impossible for a youngster to take responsibility for his own education, for they are structured in such a way as to make students totally dependent upon the teachers" (Silberman, 1970:135). Teachers are not totally to blame for this situation. In fact, they are generally competent and well meaning, but they are trapped in a bureaucratic system that rewards them for having orderly classrooms and keeping children under control rather than for facilitating learning or fostering creativity (Silberman, 1970:142). The report specifically criticizes the emphasis on structure, which subordinates the needs or interests of the child to those of the teacher or the curriculum. The result is what the Carnegie Commission terms "the tyranny of the lesson plan" (Silberman, 1970:125).

Much of what teachers and schools do has little or nothing to do with education, and frequently jeopardizes learning:

In the tender grades, the schools are a baby-sitting service during a period of collapse of the old-type family and during a time of extreme urbanization and urban mobility. In the junior and senior high school grades, they are an arm of the police, providing cops and concentration camps paid for in the budget under the heading "Board of Education" (Goodman, 1964:22).

Criticisms of education are not new. Many persons dissatisfied with the traditional school have attempted to establish more informal and open classrooms. Contemporary proponents of "open" or "free" schools have been influenced profoundly by earlier movements. In the early part of the twentieth century John Dewey and other pragmatists proposed what was at that time a very radical educational philosophy. Pragmatism, or "progressive education," shifted the focus of education from the needs of the society to the needs of the child. It was concerned with change and novelty in learning, emphasizing a problem-solving and experimental attitude toward learning and the development of initiative and self-reliance (Brubacher, 1969:330). Educational aims were no longer fixed or static but subject to revision as a result of experience. Progressive education stressed "growth" in the student and the development of individual differences.

Progressive education was also influenced by the Swiss psychologist Jean Piaget. In his research on developmental stages in learning Piaget stressed "that the child is the principal agent in his own education and mental development" (Silberman, 1970:215). One of the oldest and most successful experiments in progressive education is Summerhill. The school was founded by A. S. Neill in 1921 and is located in the village of Leiston, in Suffolk, England, about 100 miles from London. The underlying philosophy of Summerhill is that the school should fit the child, not that the child should fit the school (Neill, 1960:4). For Neill, Summerhill is a place where children are granted freedom and independence without repression. It is based on the assumption of faith "in the goodness of the child" (Neill, 1960:4). However, freedom does not mean license. Mutual respect between both teacher and pupil and among students is emphasized. The school renounces discipline and the use of force, as well as all moral and religious instruction. Summerhill is run on the basis of self-government, that is, with children "disciplining" themselves. Lessons are optional, and children are free to come or go at their pleasure. Learning is spontaneous and based on the child's interests. In such an atmosphere being deprived of lessons is frequently viewed as punishment. This is an interesting reversal of the conventional classroom, where learning is generally regarded as punishment.

Summerhill is no longer an experiment. After more than fifty years of operation it has demonstrated beyond doubt that freedom works (Neill, 1960:4). The school, however, is not without difficulties, and it has aroused vehement criticism. According to Max Rafferty, California Superintendent of Public Instruction, "Summerhill is a dirty joke. It degrades true learning to the status of a disorganized orgy. It turns a teacher into a sniggering projectionist of a stag movie. It transforms a school into a cross between a beer garden and a boiler factory. It is a caricature of education" (Hart, 1970:24). Supporters of Summerhill counter by noting that freedom and the lack of structure do not inhibit learning. Summerhill students have done quite well on college entrance exams, and many have gone on to assume positions of leadership in government and business (Neill, 1960:84–87). The success of Summerhill graduates, however, cannot be attributed solely to their education. Since Summerhill is a private boarding school, there is much selectivity in attendance. From throughout the world, parents in search of radical alternatives, send their children to Summerhill. The school is, therefore, limited to middle- and upper-class children and is not available to the very poor (Neill, 1960:17). Given the radical approach to education at Summerhill it is surprising, if not almost incredible, that the school's graduates adjust so well to the outside world. One would expect children raised in an open and nonpunitive environment to have difficulty adjusting to a world that places a premium on conformity, rigidity, and corporal punishment. From this perspective the "success" of Summerhill may be its greatest failing.

Neill was a pioneer in what has blossomed into a full-scale social movement to reform the schools. For a long time the impact of Summerhill was felt mostly in Great Britain and Scandinavia, but today Neill's works have been translated into many languages and the influence of Summerhill is virtually world-wide. The free school movement in the United States has gained considerable impetus in recent years as educational reformers and social critics have sought to free the school from the bonds of tradition. Some of the better-known critics of contemporary education are Edgar Friedenberg (1965 and 1967), Paul Goodman (1960, 1964, and 1967), Jules Henry (1963 and 1972), Jonathan Kozol (1968 and 1972), Charles Silberman (1970), Carl Rogers (1969), Ivan Illich (1970 and 1971), George Dennison (1969), and Paulo Freire (1970). These critics vary widely in intellectual persuasion and in their proposals for change; they include liberal reformers, humanistic psychologists, and revolutionary anarchists. But they agree on certain basic problems that the schools have and on broad, general reforms. They agree that the schools are basically instruments of conservation rather than change and that they stifle creativity and encourage docility and dependence. Some critics seek to make liberal reforms within the educational institution so that children are able to learn in a more informal and unstructured milieu; others call for radical changes in the larger society itself. Goodman characterizes compulsory education as a system of compulsory mis-education that "is no longer designed for the maximum growth and future practical utility of the children into a changing world . . ." (1964:56). He, like Neill, believes that real universal education requires the elimination of compulsory schooling. In schools "there is little attention to individual pace, rhythm, or choice, and none whatever to the discovery of identity or devotion to intellectual goals" (Goodman, 1964:150). He suggests that we already have too much formal education and that the more formal schooling we have, the less education we receive (Goodman, 1964:7).

Illich takes an even more radical view of the school. He suggests "that enforced instruction deadens for most people the will for independent learning . . ." (Illich, 1971:44). The problems of the schools, however, cannot be separated from the larger movement toward "schooling" society. The schooling of society means that knowledge is legitimate and valid only when it is acquired in school and transmitted by experts. "It conveys indelibly the message that only through schooling can an individual prepare himself for adulthood in society, that what is not taught in school is of little value, and that what is learned outside of school is not worth knowing" (Illich, 1971:45). "True knowledge" is believed to be held by technocratic experts who guard it as a treasured commodity, whether they be educators, therapists, or social workers. Basic educational reform will come about only through "deschooling" society and through the creation of "institutions which serve personal, creative, and autonomous interaction and the emergence of values which cannot be substantially controlled by technocrats" (Illich, 1970:2). One of the great tragedies of contemporary society is that progressive education, despite its liberal and equalitarian ideology, benefits the well-to-do and the elite. Liberal reformers typically seek to alter the system from within by pouring more money into schools and furnishing compensatory education programs for the disadvantaged. Such proposals generally benefit the well-to-do and improve their relative advantage over the poor:

As a case in point, between 1965 and 1968 over three billion dollars were spent in U.S. schools to offset the disadvantages of about six million children. The program is known as Title One. It is the most expensive compensatory program ever attempted anywhere in education, yet no significant improvement can be detected in the learning of these "disadvantaged" children. Compared with their classmates from middle-income homes, they have fallen further behind (Illich, 1970:6).

Programs of this kind also provide more jobs for those "experts" who specialize in helping the disadvantaged.

More radical critics tend to establish independent free schools outside of the system. These schools are available largely only to middle-class children, who profit from a freer and more enriching environment. As adults many will assume positions as "experts" in a technocratic society and will, in turn, design other alternative schools that will produce more experts. Unfortunately, neither liberal reformers nor revolutionary critics challenge the "schooled society."

Some critics have been concerned with education of the disadvantaged. Illich believes that the relative position of the poor can be improved by disestablishing schools (see the first reading for this chapter). In *The Lives of Children* George Dennison (1969) provides an interesting description of the First Street School on New York's Lower East Side. The school, based on Summerhillian principles, attempted to provide a free and liberating environment for lower-income children. Paulo Freire (1970) has devoted much of his life to developing a "pedagogy of the oppressed." His theory is based on the assumption that any person, whether ignorant or illiterate, is capable of looking at his surroundings critically and meaningfully. It is necessary, he argues, that "the oppressed must not, in seeking to regain their humanity . . . , become in turn oppressors of the oppressors, but rather restorers of the humanity of both" (Freire, 1970:28). The participation of the oppressed is thus critical for their own liberation. Once the oppressed become aware of their oppression and of their capacity to liberate themselves, they can begin to transform their environment and transcend their oppression (Freire, 1970:33–36). They must liberate themselves: "This is why, as we affirmed earlier, the pedagogy of the oppressed cannot be developed or practiced by the oppressors. It would be a contradiction in terms if the oppressors not only defended but actually implemented a liberating education" (Freire, 1970:39). The process of liberation is ultimately educational in character as the oppressed become conscious of themselves and their environment and begin to deal critically with it (Freire, 1970:133). In the words of the oppressed: " 'I now realize I am a man, an educated man.' 'We were blind, now our eyes have been opened.' 'Before this, words meant nothing to me; now they speak to me and I can make them speak' " (Freire, 1970:14).

REFERENCES

Adams, Don
1972 Schooling and Social Change in Modern America. New York: McKay.
Brubacher, John S.
1966 A History of the Problems of Education. Second ed. New York: McGraw-Hill.
1969 Modern Philosophies of Education. Fourth ed. New York: McGraw-Hill.
Carnoy, Martin
1972 Schooling in a Corporate Society. New York: McKay.
Clark, Burton R.
1964 "Sociology of Education." Pp. 734–769 in Robert E. L. Faris (ed.), Handbook of Modern Sociology. Skokie, Ill.: Rand McNally.
Cohen, Albert K.
1966 Deviance and Control. Englewood Cliffs, N.J.: Prentice-Hall.
Cremin, Lawrence A.
1970 American Education: The Colonial Experience, 1607–1783. New York: Harper & Row.
Dennison, George
1969 The Lives of Children. New York: Random House.
Freire, Paulo
1970 Pedagogy of the Oppressed. New York: Herder and Herder.
Friedenberg, Edgar Z.
1965 Coming of Age in America. New York: Random House.
1967 "An Ideology of School Withdrawal." Pp. 11–25 in Daniel Schreiber (ed.), Profile of the School Dropout. New York: Random House.
Goodman, Paul
1960 Growing Up Absurd. New York: Vintage Books.
1964 Compulsory Mis-education and the Community of Scholars. New York: Horizon.
1967 "The Universal Trap." Pp. 26–39 in Daniel Schreiber (ed.), Profile of the School Dropout. New York: Random House.
Green, Thomas F.
1969 "Schools and Communities: A Look Forward." Harvard Educational Review 39 (Spring):221–252.
Hart, Harold H.
1970 Summerhill: For and Against. New York: Hart.

Henry, Jules
1963 Culture Against Man. New York: Random House.
1972 Jules Henry on Education. New York: Vintage Books.
Illich, Ivan
1970 Deschooling Society. New York: Harrow Books.
1971 "The Alternative to Schooling." Saturday Review (June 19):44–48, 59–60.
Kozol, Jonathan
1968 Death at an Early Age. New York: Bantam.
1972 Free Schools. Boston: Houghton Mifflin.
Marin, Peter
1969 "The Open Truth and Fiery Vehemence of Youth." The Center Magazine 2 (January):61–74.
Neill, A. S.
1960 Summerhill, A Radical Approach to Child Rearing. New York: Hart.
Ofshe, Richard
1970 The Sociology of the Possible. Englewood Cliffs, N.J.: Prentice-Hall.
Plato
1966 The Republic. (Edited and Translated by I. A. Richards). London: Cambridge University Press.
Rippa, S. Alexander
1967 Education in a Free Society: An American History. New York: McKay.
Rogers, Carl R.
1969 Freedom to Learn. Columbus, Ohio: Merrill.
Schwartz, Barry N.
1972 Affirmative Education. Englewood Cliffs, N.J.: Prentice-Hall.
Silberman, Charles E.
1970 Crisis in the Classroom. New York: Vintage Books.
Stevens, William K.
1972 "Review of the Carnegie Commission Report. Pp. 5–9 in Barry N. Schwartz (ed.), Affirmative Education. Englewood Cliffs, N.J.: Prentice-Hall.

INTRODUCTION TO THE READINGS

Ivan Illich is one of the most intense critics of contemporary education. In the article that is reprinted here, "The Alternative to Schooling," he argues for the "deschooling" of society. Education and learning in a technological society become commodities that are created, packaged, and sold by experts. The society is "schooled" in the sense that knowledge is legitimate only when it occurs in school and is certified by technocratic experts.

The second reading is a selection from science fiction. In "Profession" Isaac Asimov describes an educational system in a futuristic society. While the account is fictional, the parallels between it and Illich's article are frightening. Is the educational system depicted in "Profession" a logical extension of the technocratic society? Will qualities such as intelligence, motivation, initiative, and creativity become obsolete?

The alternative to schooling

IVAN ILLICH

For generations we have tried to make the world a better place by providing more and more schooling, but so far the endeavor has failed. What we have learned instead is that forcing all children to climb an open-ended education ladder cannot enhance equality but must favor the individual who starts out earlier, healthier, or better prepared; that enforced instruction deadens for most people the will for independent learning; and that knowledge treated as a commodity, delivered in packages, and accepted as private property once it is acquired, must always be scarce.

In response, critics of the educational system are now proposing strong and unorthodox remedies that range from the voucher plan, which would enable each person to buy the education of his choice on an open market, to shifting the responsibility for education from the school to the media and to apprenticeship on the job. Some individuals foresee that the school will have to be disestablished just as the church was disestablished all over the world during the last two centuries. Other reformers propose to replace the universal school with various new systems that would, they claim, better prepare everybody for life in modern society. These proposals for new educational institutions fall into three broad categories: the reformation of the classroom within the school system; the dispersal of free schools throughout society; and the transformation of all society into one huge classroom. But these three approaches —the reformed classroom, the free school, and the worldwide classroom —represent three stages in a proposed escalation of education in which each step threatens more subtle and more pervasive social control than the one it replaces.

I believe that the disestablishment of the school has become inevitable and that this end of an illusion should fill us with hope. But I also believe that the end of the "age of schooling" could usher in the epoch of the global schoolhouse that would be distinguishable only in name from a global madhouse or global prison in which education, correction, and adjustment become synonymous. I therefore believe that the breakdown of the school forces us to look beyond its imminent demise and to face fundamental alternatives in education. Either we can work for fearsome and potent new educational devices that teach about a world which progressively becomes more opaque and forbidding for man, or we can set the conditions for a new era in which technology would be used to make society more simple and transparent, so that all men can once again know the facts and use the tools that shape their lives. In short, we can disestablish schools or we can deschool culture.

In order to see clearly the alternatives we face, we must first distinguish education from schooling, which means separating the humanistic intent

From Ivan Illich, "The Alternative to Schooling," Copyright 1971 by Saturday Review Co. First appeared in Saturday Review, June 19, 1971. Used with permission. Ivan Illich is author of *Deschooling Society* (1971) and *Fools for Conviviality* (1973), both published by Harper & Row.

of the teacher from the impact of the invariant structure of the school. This hidden structure constitutes a course of instruction that stays forever beyond the control of the teacher or of his school board. It conveys indelibly the message that only through schooling can an individual prepare himself for adulthood in society, that what is not taught in school is of little value, and that what is learned outside of school is not worth knowing. I call it the hidden curriculum of schooling, because it constitutes the unalterable framework of the system, within which all changes in the curriculum are made.

The hidden curriculum is always the same regardless of school or place. It requires all children of a certain age to assemble in groups of about thirty, under the authority of a certified teacher, for some 500 to 1000 or more hours each year. It doesn't matter whether the curriculum is designed to teach the principles of fascism, liberalism, Catholicism, or socialism; or whether the purpose of the school is to produce Soviet or United States citizens, mechanics, or doctors. It makes no difference whether the teacher is authoritarian or permissive, whether he imposes his own creed or teaches students to think for themselves. What is important is that students learn that education is valuable when it is acquired in the school through a graded process of consumption; that the degree of success the individual will enjoy in society depends on the amount of learning he consumes; and that learning *about* the world is more valuable than learning *from* the world.

It must be clearly understood that the hidden curriculum translates learning from an activity into a commodity —for which the school monopolizes the market. In all countries knowledge is regarded as the first necessity for survival, but also as a form of currency more liquid than rubles or dollars. We have become accustomed, through Karl Marx's writings, to speak about the alienation of the worker from his work in a class society. We must now recognize the estrangement of man from his learning when it becomes the product of a service profession and he becomes the consumer.

The more learning an individual consumes, the more "knowledge stock" he acquires. The hidden curriculum therefore defines a new class structure for society within which the large consumers of knowledge—those who have acquired large quantities of knowledge stock—enjoy special privileges, high income, and access to the more powerful tools of production. This kind of knowledge capitalism has been accepted in all industrialized societies and establishes a rationale for the distribution of jobs and income. (This point is especially important in the light of the lack of correspondence between schooling and occupational competence established in studies such as Ivar Berg's *Education and Jobs: The Great Training Robbery.*)

The endeavor to put all men through successive stages of enlightenment is rooted deeply in alchemy, the Great Art of the waning Middle Ages. John Amos Comenius, a Moravian bishop, self-styled Pansophist, and pedagogue, is rightly considered one of the founders of the modern schools. He was among the first to propose seven or twelve grades of compulsory learning. In his *Magna Didactica*, he described schools as devices to "teach everybody everything" and outlined a blueprint for the assembly-line production of knowledge, which according to his method would make education cheaper and better and make growth into full humanity possible for all. But Comenius was not only an early efficiency expert, he was an alchemist who adopted the technical language of his craft to describe the art of rearing children. The alchemist sought to refine base elements by leading their distilled spirits through twelve stages of successive enlightenment, so that for their own and all the world's benefit they might be transmuted into gold. Of course, alchemists failed no matter how often they tried, but each time their "science" yielded new reasons for their failure, and they tried again.

Pedagogy opened a new chapter in the history of Ars Magna. Education became the search for an alchemic process that would bring forth a new type of man, who would fit into an environment created by scientific magic. But, no matter how much each generation spent on its schools, it always turned out that the majority of people were unfit for enlightenment by this process and had to be discarded as unprepared for life in a man-made world.

Educational reformers who accept the idea that schools have failed fall into three groups. The most respectable are certainly the great masters of alchemy who promise better schools. The most seductive are popular magicians, who promise to make every kitchen into an alchemic lab. The most sinister are the new Masons of the Universe, who want to transform the entire world into one huge temple of learning. Notable among today's masters of alchemy are certain research directors employed or sponsored by the large foundations who believe that schools, if they could somehow be improved, could also become economically more feasible than those that are now in trouble, and simultaneously could sell a larger package of services. Those who are concerned primarily with the curriculum claim that it is outdated or irrelevant. So the curriculum is filled with new packaged courses on African Culture, North American Imperialism, Women's Lib, Pollution, or the Consumer Society. Passive learning is wrong—it is indeed—so we graciously allow students to decide what and how they want to be taught. Schools are prison houses. Therefore, principals are authorized to approve teach-outs, moving the school desks to a roped-off Harlem street. Sensitivity training becomes fashionable. So, we import group therapy into the classroom. School, which was supposed to teach everybody everything, now becomes all things to all children.

Other critics emphasize that schools make inefficient use of modern science. Some would administer drugs to make it easier for the instructor to change the child's behavior. Others would transform school into a stadium for educational gaming. Still others would electrify the classroom. If they are simplistic disciples of McLuhan, they replace blackboards and textbooks with multimedia happenings; if they follow Skinner, they claim to be able to modify behavior more efficiently than old-fashioned classroom practitioners can.

Most of these changes have, of course, some good effects. The experimental schools have fewer truants. Parents do have a greater feeling of participation in a decentralized district. Pupils, assigned by their teacher to an apprenticeship, do often turn out more competent than those who stay in the classroom. Some children do improve their knowledge of Spanish in the language lab because they prefer playing with the knobs of a tape recorder to conversations with their Puerto Rican peers. Yet all these improvements operate within predictably narrow limits, since they leave the hidden curriculum of school intact.

Some reformers would like to shake

loose from the hidden curriculum, but they rarely succeed. Free schools that lead to further free schools produce a mirage of freedom, even though the chain of attendance is frequently interrupted by long stretches of loafing. Attendance through seduction inculcates the need for educational treatment more persuasively than the reluctant attendance enforced by a truant officer. Permissive teachers in a padded classroom can easily render their pupils impotent to survive once they leave.

Learning in these schools often remains nothing more than the acquisition of socially valued skills defined, in this instance, by the consensus of a commune rather than by the decree of a school board. New presbyter is but old priest writ large.

Free schools, to be truly free, must meet two conditions: First, they must be run in a way to prevent the reintroduction of the hidden curriculum of graded attendance and certified students studying at the feet of certified teachers. And, more importantly, they must provide a framework in which all participants—staff and pupils—can free themselves from the hidden foundations of a schooled society. The first condition is frequently incorporated in the stated aims of a free school. The second condition is only rarely recognized, and is difficult to state as the goal of a free school.

It is useful to distinguish between the hidden curriculum, which I have described, and the occult foundations of schooling. The hidden curriculum is a ritual that can be considered the official initiation into modern society, institutionally established through the school. It is the purpose of this ritual to hide from its participants the contradictions between the myth of an egalitarian society and the class-conscious reality it certifies. Once they are recognized as such, rituals lose their power, and this is what is now beginning to happen to schooling. But there are certain fundamental assumptions about growing up—the occult foundations—which now find their expression in the ceremonial of schooling, and which could easily be reinforced by what free schools do.

Among these assumptions is what Peter Schrag calls the "immigration syndrome," which impels us to treat all people as if they were newcomers who must go through a naturalization process. Only certified consumers of knowledge are admitted to citizenship. Men are not born equal, but are made equal through gestation by Alma Mater.

The rhetoric of all schools states that they form a man for the future, but they do not release him for his task before he has developed a high level of tolerance to the ways of his elders: education *for* life rather than *in* everyday life. Few free schools can avoid doing precisely this. Nevertheless they are among the most important centers from which a new lifestyle radiates, not because of the effect their graduates will have but, rather, because elders who choose to bring up their children without the benefit of properly ordained teachers frequently belong to a radical minority and because their preoccupation with the rearing of their children sustains them in their new style.

The most dangerous category of educational reformer is one who argues that knowledge can be produced and sold much more effectively on an open market than on one controlled by school. These people argue that most skills can be easily acquired from skill-models if the learner is truly interested in their acquisition; that individual entitlements can provide a more equal purchasing power for education.

They demand a careful separation of the process by which knowledge is acquired from the process by which it is measured and certified. These seem to me obvious statements. But it would be a fallacy to believe that the establishment of a free market for knowledge would constitute a radical alternative in education.

The establishment of a free market would indeed abolish what I have previously called the hidden curriculum of present schooling—its age-specific attendance at a graded curriculum. Equally, a free market would at first give the appearance of counteracting what I have called the occult foundations of a schooled society: the "immigration syndrome," the institutional monopoly of teaching, and the ritual of linear initiation. But at the same time a free market in education would provide the alchemist with innumerable hidden hands to fit each man into the multiple, tight little niches a more complex technocracy can provide.

Many decades of reliance on schooling has turned knowledge into a commodity, a marketable staple of a special kind. Knowledge is now regarded simultaneously as a first necessity and also as society's most precious currency. (The transformation of knowledge into a commodity is reflected in a corresponding transformation of language. Words that formerly functioned as verbs are becoming nouns that designate possessions. Until recently dwelling and learning and even healing designated activities. They are now usually conceived as commodities or services to be delivered. We talk about the manufacture of housing or the delivery of medical care. Men are no longer regarded fit to house or heal themselves. In such a society people come to believe that professional services are more valuable than personal care. Instead of learning how to nurse

grandmother, the teen-ager learns to picket the hospital that does not admit her.) This attitude could easily survive the disestablishment of school, just as affiliation with a church remained a condition for office long after the adoption of the First Amendment. It is even more evident that test batteries measuring complex knowledge-packages could easily survive the disestablishment of school—and with this would go the compulsion to obligate everybody to acquire a minimum package in the knowledge stock. The scientific measurement of each man's worth and the alchemic dream of each man's "educability to his full humanity" would finally coincide. Under the appearance of a "free" market, the global village would turn into an environmental womb where pedagogic therapists control the complex navel by which each man is nourished.

At present schools limit the teacher's competence to the classroom. They prevent him from claiming man's whole life as his domain. The demise of school will remove this restriction and give a semblance of legitimacy to the life-long pedagogical invasion of everybody's privacy. It will open the way for a scramble for "knowledge" on a free market, which would lead us toward the paradox of a vulgar, albeit seemingly egalitarian, meritocracy. Unless the concept of knowledge is transformed, the disestablishment of school will lead to a wedding between a growing meritocratic system that separates learning from certification and a society committed to provide therapy for each man until he is ripe for the gilded age.

For those who subscribe to the technocratic ethos, whatever is technically possible must be made available at least to a few whether they want it or not. Neither the privation nor the frustration of the majority counts. If cobalt treatment is possible, then the city of Tegucigalpa needs one apparatus in each of its two major hospitals, at a cost that would free an important part of the population of Honduras from parasites. If supersonic speeds are possible, then it must speed the travel of some. If the flight to Mars can be conceived, then a rationale must be found to make it appear a necessity. In the technocratic ethos poverty is modernized: Not only are old alternatives closed off by new monopolies, but the lack of necessities is also compounded by a growing spread between those services that are technologically feasible and those that are in fact available to the majority.

A teacher turns "educator" when he adopts this technocratic ethos. He then acts as if education were a technological enterprise designed to make man fit into whatever environment the "progress" of science creates. He seems blind to the evidence that constant obsolescence of all commodities comes at a high price: the mounting cost of training people to know about them. He seems to forget that the rising cost of tools is purchased at a high price in education: They decrease the labor intensity of the economy, make learning on the job impossible or, at best, a privilege for a few. All over the world the cost of educating men for society rises faster than the productivity of the entire economy, and fewer people have a sense of intelligent participation in the commonweal.

A revolution against those forms of privilege and power, which are based on claims to professional knowledge, must start with a transformation of consciousness about the nature of learning. This means, above all, a shift of responsibility for teaching and learning. Knowledge can be defined as a commodity only as long as it is viewed as the result of institutional enterprise or as the fulfillment of institutional objectives. Only when a man recovers the sense of personal responsibility for what he learns and teaches can this spell be broken and the alienation of learning from living be overcome.

The recovery of the power to learn or to teach means that the teacher who takes the risk of interfering in somebody else's private affairs also assumes responsibility for the results. Similarly, the student who exposes himself to the influence of a teacher must take responsibility for his own education. For such purposes educational institutions—if they are at all needed—ideally take the form of facility centers where one can get a roof of the right size over his head, access to a piano or a kiln, and to records, books, or slides. Schools, TV stations, theaters, and the like are designed primarily for use by professionals. Deschooling society means above all the denial of professional status for the second-oldest profession, namely teaching. The certification of teachers now constitutes an undue restriction of the right to free speech: the corporate structure and professional pretensions of journalism an undue restriction on the right to free press. Compulsory attendance rules interfere with free assembly. The deschooling of society is nothing less than a cultural mutation by which a people recovers the effective use of its Constitutional freedoms: learning and teaching by men who know that they are born free rather than treated to freedom. Most people learn most of the time when they do whatever they enjoy; most people are curious and want to give meaning to whatever they come in contact with; and most people are capable of personal intimate intercourse with others unless they are stupefied by inhuman work or turned off by schooling.

The fact that people in rich countries do not learn much on their own constitutes no proof to the contrary. Rather it is a consequence of life in an environment from which, paradoxically, they cannot learn much precisely because it is so highly programed. They are constantly frustrated by the structure of contemporary society in which the facts on which decisions can be made have become elusive. They live in an environment in which tools that can be used for creative purposes have become luxuries, an environment in which channels of communication serve a few to talk to many.

A modern myth would make us believe that the sense of impotence with which most men live today is a consequence of technology that cannot but create huge systems. But it is not technology that makes systems huge, tools immensely powerful, channels of communication one-directional. Quite the contrary: Properly controlled, technology could provide each man with the ability to understand his environment better, to shape it powerfully with his own hands, and to permit him full intercommunication to a degree never before possible. Such an alternative use of technology constitutes the central alternative in education.

If a person is to grow up he needs, first of all, access to things, to places and to processes, to events and to records. He needs to see, to touch, to tinker with, to grasp whatever there is in a meaningful setting. This access is now largely denied. When knowledge became a commodity, it acquired the protections of private property, and thus a principle designed to guard personal intimacy became a rationale for declaring facts off limits for people without the proper credentials. In schools teachers keep knowledge to themselves unless it fits into the day's program. The media inform, but exclude those things they regard as unfit to print. Information is locked into special languages, and specialized teachers live off its retranslation. Patents are protected by corporations, secrets are guarded by bureaucracies, and the power to keep others out of private preserves—be they cockpits, law offices, junkyards, or clinics—is jealously guarded by professions, institutions, and nations. Neither the political nor the professional structure of our societies, East and West, could withstand the elimination of the power to keep entire classes of people from facts that could serve them. The access to facts that I advocate goes far beyond truth in labeling. Access must be built into reality, while all we ask from advertising is a guarantee that it does not mislead. Access to reality constitutes a fundamental alternative in education to a system that only purports to teach *about* it.

Abolishing the right to corporate secrecy—even when professional opinion holds that this secrecy serves the common good—is, as shall presently appear, a much more radical political goal than the traditional demand for public ownership or control of the tools of production. The socialization of tools without the effective socialization of know-how in their use tends to put the knowledge-capitalist into the position formerly held by the financier. The technocrat's only claim to power is the stock he holds in some class of scarce and secret knowledge, and the best means to protect its value is a large and capital-intensive organization that renders access to know-how formidable and forbidding.

It does not take much time for the interested learner to acquire almost any skill that he wants to use. We tend to forget this in a society where professional teachers monopolize entrance into all fields, and thereby stamp teaching by uncertified individuals as quackery. There are few mechanical skills used in industry or research that are as demanding, complex, and dangerous as driving cars, a skill that most people quickly acquire from a peer. Not all people are suited for advanced logic, yet those who are make rapid progress if they are challenged to play mathematical games at an early age. One out of twenty kids in Cuernavaca can beat me at Wiff 'n' Proof after a couple of weeks' training. In four months all but a small percentage of motivated adults at our CIDOC center learn Spanish well enough to conduct academic business in the new language.

A first step toward opening up access to skills would be to provide various incentives for skilled individuals to share their knowledge. Inevitably, this would run counter to the interest of guilds and professions and unions. Yet, multiple apprenticeship is attractive: It provides everybody with an opportunity to learn something about almost anything. There is no reason why a person should not combine the ability to drive a car, repair telephones and toilets, act as a midwife, and function as an architectural draftsman. Special-interest groups and their disciplined consumers would, of course, claim that the public needs the protection of a professional guarantee. But this argument is now steadily being challenged by consumer protection associations. We have to take much more seriously the objection that economists raise to the radical socialization of skills: that "progress" will be impeded if knowledge—patents, skills, and all the rest —is democratized. Their argument can be faced only if we demonstrate to them the growth rate of futile diseconomies generated by any existing educational system.

Access to people willing to share their skills is no guarantee of learning. Such access is restricted not only by the monopoly of educational programs over learning and of unions over licensing but also by a technology of scarcity. The skills that count today are know-how in the use of highly specialized tools that were designed to be scarce. These tools produce goods or render services that everybody wants but only a few can enjoy, and which only a limited number of people know how to use. Only a few privileged individuals out of the total number of people who have a given disease ever benefit from the results of sophisticated medical technology, and even fewer doctors develop the skill to use it.

The same results of medical research have, however, also been employed to create a basic medical tool kit that permits Army and Navy medics, with only a few months of training, to obtain results, under battlefield conditions, that would have been beyond the expectations of full-fledged doctors during World War II. On an even simpler level any peasant girl could learn how to diagnose and treat most infections if medical scientists prepared dosages and instructions specifically for a given geographic area.

All these examples illustrate the fact that educational considerations alone suffice to demand a radical reduction of the professional structure that now impedes the mutual relationship between the scientist and the majority of people who want access to science. If this demand were heeded, all men could learn to use yesterday's tools, rendered more effective and durable by modern science, to create tomorrow's world.

Unfortunately, precisely the contrary trend prevails at present. I know a coastal area in South America where most people support themselves by fishing from small boats. The outboard motor is certainly the tool that has changed most dramatically the lives of these coastal fishermen. But in the area I have surveyed, half of all outboard motors that were purchased between 1945 and 1950 are still kept running by constant tinkering, while half the motors purchased in 1965 no longer run because they were not built to be repaired. Technological progress provides the majority of people with gadgets they cannot afford and deprives them of the simpler tools they need.

Metals, plastics, and ferro cement used in building have greatly improved since the 1940s and ought to provide more people the opportunity to create their own homes. But while in the United States, in 1948, more than 30 percent of all one-family homes were owner-built, by the end of the 1960s the percentage of those who acted as their own contractors had dropped to less than 20 percent.

The lowering of the skill level through so-called economic development becomes even more visible in Latin America. Here most people still build their own homes from floor to roof. Often they use mud, in the form of adobe, and thatchwork of unsurpassed utility in the moist, hot, and windy climate. In other places they make their dwellings out of cardboard, oildrums, and other industrial refuse. Instead of providing people with simple tools and highly standardized, durable, and easily repaired components, all governments have gone in for the mass production of low-cost buildings. It is clear that not one single country can afford to provide satisfactory modern dwelling units for the majority of its people. Yet, everywhere this policy makes it progressively more difficult for the majority to acquire the knowledge and skills they need to build better houses for themselves.

Educational considerations permit us to formulate a second fundamental characteristic that any post-industrial society must possess: a basic tool kit that by its very nature counteracts technocratic control. For educational reasons we must work toward a society in which scientific knowledge is incorporated in tools and components that can be used meaningfully in units small enough to be within the reach of all. Only such tools can socialize access to skills. Only such tools favor temporary associations among those who want to use them for a specific occasion. Only such tools allow specific goals to emerge in the process of their use, as any tinkerer knows. Only the combination of guaranteed access to facts and of limited power in most tools renders it possible to envisage a subsistence economy capable of incorporating the fruits of modern science.

The development of such a scientific subsistence economy is unquestionably to the advantage of the overwhelming majority of all people in poor countries. It is also the only alternative to progressive pollution, exploitation, and opaqueness in rich countries. But, as we have seen, the dethroning of the GNP cannot be achieved without simultaneously subverting GNE (Gross National Education—usually conceived as manpower capitalization). An egalitarian economy cannot exist in a society in which the right to produce is conferred by schools.

The feasibility of a modern subsistence economy does not depend on new scientific inventions. It depends primarily on the ability of a society to agree on fundamental, self-chosen anti-bureaucratic and anti-technocratic restraints.

These restraints can take many forms, but they will not work unless they touch the basic dimensions of life. (The decision of Congress against development of the supersonic transport plane is one of the most encouraging steps in the right direction.) The substance of these voluntary social restraints would be very simple matters that can be fully understood and judged by any prudent man. The issues at stake in the SST controversy provide a good example. All such restraints would be chosen to promote stable and equal enjoyment of scientific know-how. The French say that it takes a thousand years to educate a peasant to deal with a cow. It would not take two generations to help all people in Latin America or Africa to use and repair outboard motors, simple cars, pumps, medicine kits, and ferro cement machines if their design does not change every few years. And since a joyful life is one of constant meaningful intercourse with others in a meaningful environment, equal enjoyment does translate into equal education.

At present a consensus on austerity is difficult to imagine. The reason usually given for the impotence of the majority is stated in terms of political or economic class. What is not usually understood is that the new class structure of a schooled society is even more powerfully controlled by vested interests. No doubt an imperialist and capitalist organization of society provides the social structure within which a minority can have disproportionate influence over the effective opinion of the majority. But in a technocratic society the power of a minority of knowledge capitalists can prevent the formation of true public opinion through control of scientific know-how and the media of communication. Constitutional guarantees of free speech, free press, and free assembly were meant to ensure government by the people. Modern electronics, photo-offset presses, time-sharing computers, and telephones have in principle provided the hardware that could give an entirely new meaning to these freedoms. Unfortunately, these things are used in modern media to increase the power of knowledge-bankers to funnel their program-packages through international chains to more people, instead of being used to increase true networks that provide equal opportunity for encounter among the members of the majority.

Deschooling the culture and social structure requires the use of technology to make participatory politics possible. Only on the basis of a majority coalition can limits to secrecy and growing power be determined without dictatorship. We need a new environment in which growing up can be classless, or we will get a brave new world in which Big Brother educates us all.

From "Profession"

ISAAC ASIMOV

For most of the first eighteen years of his life, George Platen had headed firmly in one direction, that of Registered Computer Programmer. There were those in his crowd who spoke wisely of Spationautics, Refrigeration Technology, Transportation Control, and even Administration. But George held firm.

He argued relative merits as vigorously as any of them, and why not? Education Day loomed ahead of them and was the great fact of their existence. It approached steadily, as fixed and certain as the calendar—the first day of November of the year following one's eighteenth birthday.

After that day, there were other topics of conversation. One could discuss with others some detail of the profession, or the virtues of one's wife and children, or the fate of one's space-polo team, or one's experiences in the Olympics. Before Education Day, however, there was only one topic that unfailingly and unwearyingly held everyone's interest, and that was Education Day.

"What are you going for? Think you'll make it? Heck, that's no good. Look at the records; quota's been cut. Logistics now ———"

Or Hypermechanics now ——— Or Communications now ——— Or Gravitics now ———

Especially Gravitics at the moment. Everyone had been talking about Gravitics in the few years just before George's Education Day because of the development of the Gravitic power engine.

Any world within ten light-years of a dwarf star, everyone said, would give its eyeteeth for any kind of Registered Gravitics Engineer.

The thought of that never bothered George. Sure it would; all the eyeteeth it could scare up. But George had also heard what had happened before in a newly developed technique. Rationalization and simplification followed in a flood. New models each year; new types of gravitic engines; new principles. Then all those eyeteeth gentlemen would find themselves out of date and superseded by later models with later educations. The first group would then have to settle down to unskilled labor or ship out to some backwoods world that wasn't quite caught up yet.

Now Computer Programmers were in steady demand year after year, century after century. The demand never reached wild peaks; there was never a howling bull market for Programmers; but the demand climbed steadily as new worlds opened up and as older words grew more complex.

He had argued with Stubby Trevelyan about that constantly. As best friends, their arguments had to be constant and vitriolic and, of course, neither ever persuaded or was persuaded.

But then Trevelyan had had a father who was a Registered Metallurgist and had actually served on one of the Outworlds, and a grandfather who had also been a Registered Metallurgist. He himself was intent on becoming a Registered Metallurgist almost as a matter of family right and was firmly convinced that any other profession was a shade less than respectable.

"There'll always be metal," he said, "and there's an accomplishment in molding alloys to specification and watching structures grow. Now what's a Programmer going to be doing. Sitting at a coder all day long, feeding some fool mile-long machine."

Even at sixteen, George had learned to be practical. He said simply, "There'll be a million Metallurgists put out along with you."

"Because it's good. A good profession. The best."

"But you get crowded out, Stubby. You can be way back in line. Any world can tape out its own Metallurgists, and the market for advanced Earth models isn't so big. And it's mostly the small worlds that want them. You know what percent of the turn-out of Registered Metallurgists get tabbed for worlds with a Grade A rating. I looked it up. It's just 13.3 percent. That means you'll have seven chances in eight of being stuck in some world that just about has running water. You may even be stuck on Earth; 2.3 percent are."

Trevelyan said belligerently, "There's no disgrace in staying on Earth. Earth needs technicians, too. Good ones." His grandfather had been an Earthbound Metallurgist, and Trevelyan lifted his finger to his upper lip and dabbed at an as yet nonexistent mustache.

George knew about Trevelyan's grandfather and, considering the Earth-bound position of his own ancestry, was in no mood to sneer. He said diplomatically, "No intellectual disgrace. Of course not. But it's nice to get into a Grade A world, isn't it?

"Now you take Programmers. Only the Grade A worlds have the kind of computers that really need first-class Programmers so they're the only ones in the market. And Programmer tapes are complicated and hardly any one

fits. They need more Programmers than their own population can supply. It's just a matter of statistics. There's one first-class Programmer per million, say. A world needs twenty and has a population of ten million, they have to come to Earth for five to fifteen Programmers. Right?

"And you know how many Registered Computer Programmers went to Grade A planets last year? I'll tell you. Every last one. If you're a Programmer, you're a picked man. Yes, sir."

Trevelyan frowned. "If only one in a million makes it, what makes you think *you'll* make it?"

George said guardedly, "I'll make it."

He never dared tell anyone; not Trevelyan; not his parents; of exactly what he was doing that made him so confident. But he wasn't worried. He was simply confident (that was the worst of the memories he had in the hopeless days afterward). He was as blandly confident as the average eight-year-old kid approaching Reading Day—that childhood preview of Education Day.

Of course, Reading Day had been different. Partly, there was the simple fact of childhood. A boy of eight takes many extraordinary things in stride. One day you can't read and the next day you can. That's just the way things are. Like the sun shining.

And then not so much depended upon it. There were no recruiters just ahead, waiting and jostling for the lists and scores on the coming Olympics. A boy or girl who goes through the Reading Day is just someone who has ten more years of undifferentiated living upon Earth's crawling surface; just someone who returns to his family with one new ability.

By the time Education Day came, ten years later, George wasn't even sure of most of the details of his own Reading Day.

Most clearly of all, he remembered it to be a dismal September day with a mild rain falling. (September for Reading Day; November for Education Day; May for Olympics. They made nursery rhymes out of it.) George had dressed by the wall lights, with his parents far more excited than he himself was. His father was a Registered Pipe Fitter and had found his occupation on Earth. This fact had always been a humiliation to him, although, of course, as anyone could see plainly, most of each generation must stay on Earth in the nature of things.

There had to be farmers and miners and even technicians on Earth. It was only the late-model, high-specialty professions that were in demand on the Outworlds, and only a few millions a year out of Earth's eight billion population could be exported. Every man and woman on Earth couldn't be among that group.

But every man and woman could hope that at least one of his children could be one, and Platen, Senior, was certainly no exception. It was obvious to him (and, to be sure, to others as well) that George was notably intelligent and quick-minded. He would be bound to do well and he would have to, as he was an only child. If George didn't end on an Outworld, they would have to wait for grandchildren before a next chance would come along, and that was too far in the future to be much consolation.

Reading Day would not prove much, of course, but it would be the only indication they would have before the big day itself. Every parent on Earth would be listening to the quality of reading when his child came home with it; listening for any particularly

easy flow of words and building that into certain omens of the future. There were few families that didn't have at least one hopeful who, from Reading Day on, was the great hope because of the way he handled his trisyllabics.

Dimly, George was aware of the cause of his parents' tension, and if there was any anxiety in his young heart that drizzly morning, it was only the fear that his father's hopeful expression might fade out when he returned home with his reading.

The children met in the large assembly room of the town's Education hall. All over Earth, in millions of local halls, throughout that month, similar groups of children would be meeting. George felt depressed by the grayness of the room and by the other children, strained and stiff in unaccustomed finery.

Automatically, George did as all the rest of the children did. He found the small clique that represented the children on his floor of the apartment house and joined them.

Trevelyan, who lived immediately next door, still wore his hair childishly long and was years removed from the sideburns and thin, reddish mustache that he was to grow as soon as he was physiologically capable of it.

Trevelyan (to whom George was then known as Jawjee) said, "Bet you're scared."

"I am not," said George. Then, confidentially, "My folks got a hunk of printing up on the dresser in my room, and when I come home, I'm going to read it for them." (George's main suffering at the moment lay in the fact that he didn't quite know where to put his hands. He had been warned not to scratch his head or rub his ears or pick his nose or put his hands into his pockets. This eliminated almost every possibility.)

Trevelyan put *his* hands in his pockets and said, "My father isn't worried."

Trevelyan, Senior, had been a Metallurgist on Diporia for nearly seven years, which gave him a superior social status in his neighborhood even though he had retired and returned to Earth.

Earth discouraged these re-immigrants because of population problems, but a small trickle did return. For one thing the cost of living was lower on Earth, and what was a trifling annuity on Diporia, say, was a comfortable income on Earth. Besides, there were always men who found more satisfaction in displaying their success before the friends and scenes of their childhood than before all the rest of the Universe besides.

Trevelyan, Senior, further explained that if he stayed on Diporia, so would his children, and Diporia was a one-spaceship world. Back on Earth, his kids could end anywhere, even Novia.

Stubby Trevelyan had picked up that item early. Even before Reading Day, his conversation was based on the carelessly assumed fact that his ultimate home would be in Novia.

George, oppressed by thoughts of the other's future greatness and his own small-time contrast, was driven to belligerent defense at once.

"My father isn't worried either. He just wants to hear me read because he knows I'll be good. I suppose your father would just as soon not hear you because he knows you'll be all wrong."

"I will not be all wrong. Reading is *nothing*. On Novia, I'll *hire* people to read to me."

"Because *you* won't be able to read yourself, on account of you're *dumb!*"

"Then how come I'll be on Novia?"

And George, driven, made the great denial, "Who says you'll be on Novia? Bet you don't go anywhere."

Stubby Trevelyan reddened. "I won't be a Pipe Fitter like your old man."

"Take that back, your dumbhead."

"You take *that* back."

They stood nose to nose, not wanting to fight but relieved at having something familiar to do in this strange place. Furthermore, now that George had curled his hands into fists and lifted them before his face, the problem of what to do with his hands was, at least temporarily, solved. Other children gathered round excitedly.

But then it all ended when a woman's voice sounded loudly over the public address system. There was instant silence everywhere. George dropped his fists and forgot Trevelyan.

"Children," said the voice, "we are going to call out your names. As each child is called, he or she is to go to one of the men waiting along the side walls. Do you see them? They are wearing red uniforms so they will be easy to find. The girls will go to the right. The boys will go to the left. Now look about and see which man in red is nearest to you ———"

George found his man at a glance and waited for his name to be called off. He had not been introduced before this to the sophistications of the alphabet, and the length of time it took to reach his own name grew disturbing.

The crowd of children thinned; little rivulets made their way to each of the red-clad guides.

When the name "George Platen" was finally called, his sense of relief was exceeded only by the feeling of pure gladness at the fact that Stubby Trevelyan still stood in his place, uncalled.

George shouted back over his shoulder as he left, "Yay, Stubby, maybe they don't want you."

That moment of gaiety quickly left.

He was herded into a line and directed down corridors in the company of strange children. They all looked at one another, large-eyed and concerned, but beyond a snuffling, "Quitcher pushing" and "Hey, watch out" there was no conversation.

They were handed little slips of paper which they were told must remain with them. George stared at his curiously. Little black marks of different shapes. He knew it to be printing but how could anyone make words out of it? He couldn't imagine.

He was told to strip; he and four other boys who were all that now remained together. All the new clothes came shucking off and four eight-year-olds stood naked and small, shivering more out of embarrassment than cold. Medical technicians came past, probing them, testing them with odd instruments, pricking them for blood. Each took the little cards and made additional marks on them with little black rods that produced the marks, all neatly lined up, with great speed. George stared at the new marks, but they were no more comprehensible than the old. The children were ordered back into their clothes.

They sat on separate little chairs then and waited again. Names were called again and "George Platen" came third.

He moved into a large room, filled with frightening instruments with knobs and glassy panels in front. There was a desk in the very center, and behind it a man sat, his eyes on the papers piled before him.

He said, "George Platen?"

"Yes, sir," said George, in a shaky whisper. All this waiting and all this going here and there was making him nervous. He wished it were over.

The man behind the desk said, "I am Dr. Lloyd, George. How are you?"

The doctor didn't look up as he spoke. It was as though he had said those words over and over again and didn't have to look up any more.

"I'm all right."

"Are you afraid, George?"

"N—— no, sir," said George, sounding afraid even in his own ears.

"That's good," said the doctor, "because there's nothing to be afraid of, you know. Let's see, George. It says here on your card that your father is named Peter and that he's a Registered Pipe Fitter and your mother is named Amy and is a Registered Home Technician. Is that right?"

"Y—— yes, sir."

"And your birthday is February 13, and you had an ear infection about a year ago. Right?"

"Yes, sir."

"Do you know how I know all these things?"

"It's on the card, I think, sir."

"That's right." The doctor looked up at George for the first time and smiled. He showed even teeth and looked much younger than George's father. Some of George's nervousness vanished.

The doctor passed the card to George. "Do you know what all those things there mean, George?"

Although George knew he did not he was startled by the sudden request into looking at the card as though he might understand now through some sudden stroke of fate. But they were just marks as before and he passed the card back. "No, sir."

"Why not?"

George felt a sudden pang of suspicion concerning the sanity of this doctor. Didn't he know why not?

George said, "I can't read, sir."

"Would you like to read?"

"Yes, sir."

"Why, George?"

George stared, appalled. No one had ever asked him that. He had no answer. He said falteringly, "I don't know, sir."

"Printed information will direct you all through your life. There is so much you'll have to know even after Education Day. Cards like this one will tell you. Books will tell you. Television screens will tell you. Printing will tell you such useful things and such interesting things that not being able to read would be as bad as not being able to see. Do you understand?"

"Yes, sir."

"Are you afraid, George?"

"No, sir."

"Good. Now I'll tell you exactly what we'll do first. I'm going to put these wires on your forehead just over the corners of your eyes. They'll stick there but they won't hurt at all. Then, I'll turn on something that will make a buzz. It will sound funny and it may tickle you, but it won't hurt. Now if it does hurt, you tell me, and I'll turn it off right away, but it won't hurt. All right?"

George nodded and swallowed.

"Are you ready?"

George nodded. He closed his eyes while the doctor busied himself. His parents had explained this to him. They, too, had said it wouldn't hurt, but then there were always the older children. There were the ten- and twelve-year-olds who howled after the eight-year-olds waiting for Reading Day, "Watch out for the needle." There were the others who took you off in confidence and said, "They got to cut your head open. They use a sharp knife that big with a hook on it," and so on into horrifying details.

George had never believed them but he had had nightmares, and now he closed his eyes and felt pure terror.

He didn't feel the wires at his temple. The buzz was a distant thing, and there was the sound of his own blood in his ears, ringing hollowly as though

it and he were in a large cave. Slowly he chanced opening his eyes.

The doctor had his back to him. From one of the instruments a strip of paper unwound and was covered with a thin, wavy purple line. The doctor tore off pieces and put them into a slot in another machine. He did it over and over again. Each time a little piece of film came out, which the doctor looked at. Finally, he turned toward George with a queer frown between his eyes.

The buzzing stopped.

George said breathlessly, "Is it over?"

The doctor said, "Yes," but he was still frowning.

"Can I read now?" asked George. He felt no different.

The doctor said, "What?" then smiled very suddenly and briefly. He said, "It works fine, George. You'll be reading in fifteen minutes. Now we're going to use another machine this time and it will take longer. I'm going to cover your whole head, and when I turn it on you won't be able to see or hear anything for a while, but it won't hurt. Just to make sure I'm going to give you a little switch to hold in your hand. If anything hurts, you press the little button and everything shuts off. All right?"

In later years, George was told that the little switch was strictly a dummy; that it was introduced solely for confidence. He never did know for sure, however, since he never pushed the button.

A large smoothly curved helmet with a rubbery inner lining was placed over his head and left there. Three or four little knobs seemed to grab at him and bite into his skull, but there was only a little pressure that faded. No pain.

The doctor's voice sounded dimly. "Everything all right, George?"

And then, with no real warning, a

layer of thick felt closed down all about him. He was disembodied, there was no sensation, no universe, only himself and a distant murmur at the very ends of nothingness telling him something—telling him—telling him————

He strained to hear and understand but there was all that thick felt between.

Then the helmet was taken off his head, and the light was so bright that it hurt his eyes while the doctor's voice drummed at his ears.

The doctor said, "Here's your card, George. What does it say?"

George looked at his card again and gave out a strangled shout. The marks weren't just marks at all. They made up words. They were words just as clearly as though something were whispering them in his ears. He could *hear* them being whispered as he looked at them.

"What does it say, George?"

"It says—it says—'Platen, George. Born 13 February 6492 of Peter and Amy Platen in . . .' " He broke off.

"You can read, George," said the doctor. "It's all over."

"For good? I won't forget how?"

"Of course not." The doctor leaned over to shake hands gravely. "You will be taken home now."

It was days before George got over this new and great talent of his. He read for his father with such facility that Platen, Senior, wept and called relatives to tell the good news.

George walked about town, reading every scrap of printing he could find and wondering how it was that none of it had ever made sense to him before.

He tried to remember how it was not to be able to read and he couldn't. As far as his feeling about it was concerned, he had always been able to read. Always.

At eighteen, George was rather dark, of medium height, but thin enough to look taller. Trevelyan, who was scarcely an inch shorter, had a stockiness of build that made "Stubby" more than ever appropriate, but in this last year he had grown self-conscious. The nickname could no longer be used without reprisal. And since Trevelyan disapproved of his proper first name even more strongly, he was called Trevelyan or any decent variant of that. As though to prove his manhood further, he had most persistently grown a pair of sideburns and a bristly mustache.

He was sweating and nervous now, and George, who had himself grown out of "Jaw-jee" and into the curt monosyllabic gutturality of "George," was rather amused by that.

They were in the same large hall they had been in ten years before (and not since). It was as if a vague dream of the past had come to sudden reality. In the first few minutes George had been distinctly surprised at finding everything seem smaller and more cramped than his memory told him; then he made allowance for his own growth.

The crowd was smaller than it had been in childhood. It was exclusively male this time. The girls had another day assigned them.

Trevelyan leaned over to say, "Beats me the way they make you wait."

"Red tape," said George. "You can't avoid it."

Trevelyan said, "What makes *you* so damned tolerant about it?"

"I've got nothing to worry about."

"Oh, brother, you make me sick. I hope you end up Registered Manure Spreader just so I can see your face when you do." His somber eyes swept the crowd anxiously.

George looked about, too. It wasn't quite the system they used on the children. Matters went slower, and instructions had been given out at the start in print (an advantage over the pre-Readers). The names Platen and Trevelyan were well down the alphabet still, but this time the two knew it.

Young men came out of the education rooms, frowning and uncomfortable, picked up their clothes and belongings, then went off to analysis to learn the results.

Each, as he come out, would be surrounded by a clot of the thinning crowd. "How was it?" "How'd it feel?" "Whacha think ya made?" "Ya feel any different?"

Answers were vague and noncommittal.

George forced himself to remain out of those clots. You only raised your own blood pressure. Everyone said you stood the best chance if you remained calm. Even so, you could feel the palms of your hands grow cold. Funny that new tensions came with the years.

For instance, high-specialty professionals heading out for an Outworld were accompanied by a wife (or husband). It was important to keep the sex ratio in good balance on all worlds. And if you were going out to a Grade A world, what girl would refuse you? George had no specific girl in mind yet; he wanted none. Not now! Once he made Programmer; once he could add to his name, Registered Computer Programmer, he could take his pick, like a sultan in a harem. The thought excited him and he tried to put it away. Must stay calm.

Trevelyan muttered, "What's it all about anyway? First they say it works best if you're relaxed and at ease. Then they put you through this and make it impossible for you to be relaxed and at ease."

"Maybe that's the idea. They're separating the boys from the men to begin with. Take it easy, Trev."

"Shut up."

George's turn came. His name was not called. It appeared in glowing letters on the notice board.

He waved at Trevelyan. "Take it easy. Don't let it get you."

He was happy as he entered the testing chamber. Actually happy.

The man behind the desk said, "George Platen?"

For a fleeting instant there was a razor-sharp picture in George's mind of another man, ten years earlier, who had asked the same question, and it was almost as though this were the same man and he, George, had turned eight again as he had stepped across the threshold.

But the man looked up and, of course, the face matched that of the sudden memory not at all. The nose was bulbous, the hair thin and stringy, and the chin wattled as though its owner had once been grossly overweight and had reduced.

The man behind the desk looked annoyed. "Well?"

George came to Earth. "I'm George Platen, sir."

"Say so, then. I'm Dr. Zachary Antonelli, and we're going to be intimately acquainted in a moment."

He stared at small strips of film, holding them up to the light owlishly.

George winced inwardly. Very hazily, he remembered that other doctor (he had forgotten the name) staring at such film. Could these be the same? The other doctor had frowned and this one was looking at him now as though he were angry.

His happiness was already just about gone.

Dr. Antonelli spread the pages of a thickish file out before him now and put the films carefully to one side. "It says here you want to be a Computer Programmer."

"Yes, doctor."

"Still do?"

"Yes, sir."

"It's a responsible and exacting position. Do you feel up to it?"

"Yes, sir."

"Most pre-Educates don't put down any specific profession. I believe they are afraid of queering it."

"I think that's right, sir."

"Aren't you afraid of that?"

"I might as well be honest, sir."

Dr. Antonelli nodded, but without any noticeable lightening of his expression. "Why do you want to be a Programmer?"

"It's a responsible and exacting position as you said, sir. It's an important job and an exciting one. I like it and I think I can do it."

Dr. Antonelli put the papers away, and looked at George sourly. He said, "How do you know you like it? Because you think you'll be snapped up by some Grade A planet?"

George thought uneasily: He's trying to rattle you. Stay calm and stay frank.

He said, "I think a Programmer has a good chance, sir, but even if I were left on Earth, I know I'd like it." (That was true enough. I'm not lying, thought George.)

"All right, how do you know?"

He asked it as though he knew there was no decent answer and George almost smiled. He had one.

He said, "I've been reading about Programming, sir."

"You've been *what?*" Now the doctor looked genuinely astonished and George took pleasure in that.

"Reading about it, sir. I bought a book on the subject and I've been studying it."

"A book for Registered Programmers?"

"Yes, sir."

"But you couldn't understand it." ·

"Not at first. I got other books on mathematics and electronics. I made out all I could. I still don't know much, but I know enough to know I like it and to know I can make it." (Even his parents never found that secret cache of books or knew why he spent so much time in his own room or exactly what happened to the sleep he missed.)

The doctor pulled at the loose skin under his chin. "What was your idea in doing that, son?"

"I wanted to make sure I would be interested, sir."

"Surely you know that being interested means nothing. You could be devoured by a subject and if the physical make-up of your brain makes it more efficient for you to be something else, something else you will be. You know that, don't you?"

"I've been told that," said George cautiously.

"Well, believe it. It's true."

George said nothing.

Dr. Antonelli said, "Or do you believe that studying some subject will bend the brain cells in that direction, like that other theory that a pregnant woman need only listen to great music persistently to make a composer of her child. Do you believe that?"

George flushed. That had certainly been in his mind. By forcing his intellect constantly in the desired direction, he had felt sure that he would be getting a head start. Most of his confidence had rested on exactly that point.

"I never ———" he began, and found no way of finishing.

"Well, it isn't true. Good Lord, youngster, your brain pattern is fixed at birth. It can be altered by a blow hard enough to damage the cells or by a burst blood vessel or by a tumor or by a major infection ——— each time, of course, for the worse. But it certainly can't be affected by your thinking special thoughts." He stared at George thoughtfully, then said, "Who told you to do this?"

George, now thoroughly disturbed, swallowed and said, "No one, doctor. My own idea."

"Who knew you were doing it after you started?"

"No one. Doctor, I meant to do no wrong."

"Who said anything about wrong? Useless is what I would say. Why did you keep it to yourself?"

"I—I thought they'd laugh at me." (He thought abruptly of a recent exchange with Trevelyan. George had very cautiously broached the thought, as of something merely circulating distantly in the very outermost reaches of his mind, concerning the possibility of learning something by ladling it into the mind by hand, so to speak, in bits and pieces. Trevelyan had hooted, "George, you'll be tanning your own shoes next and weaving your own shirts." He had been thankful then for his policy of secrecy.)

Dr. Antonelli shoved the bits of film he had first looked at from position to position in morose thought. Then he said, "Let's get you analyzed. This is getting me nowhere."

The wires went to George's temples. There was the buzzing. Again there came a sharp memory of ten years ago.

George's hands were clammy; his heart pounded. He should never have told the doctor about his secret reading.

It was his damned vanity, he told himself. He had wanted to show how enterprising he was, how full of initiative. Instead, he had showed himself superstitious and ignorant and aroused the hostility of the doctor. (He could tell the doctor hated him for a wise guy on the make.)

And now he had brought himself to such a state of nervousness, he was sure the analyzer would show nothing that made sense.

He wasn't aware of the moment when the wires were removed from his temples. The sight of the doctor, staring at him thoughtfully, blinked into his consciousness and that was that; the wires were gone. George dragged himself together with a tearing effort. He had quite given up his ambition to be a Programmer. In the space of ten minutes, it had all gone.

He said dismally, "I suppose no?"

"No what?"

"No Programmer?"

The doctor rubbed his nose and said, "You get your clothes and whatever belongs to you and go to room 15-C. Your files will be waiting for you there. So will my report."

George said in complete surprise, "Have I been Educated already? I thought this was just to ———"

Dr. Antonelli stared down at his desk. "It will all be explained to you. You do as I say."

George felt something like panic. What was it they couldn't tell him? He wasn't fit for anything but Registered Laborer. They were going to prepare him for that; adjust him to it.

He was suddenly certain of it and he had to keep from screaming by main force.

He stumbled back to his place of waiting. Trevelyan was not there, a fact for which he would have been thankful if he had had enough self-possession to be meaningfully aware of his surroundings. Hardly anyone was left, in fact, and the few who were looked as though they might ask him questions were it not that they were too worn out by their tail-of-the-alphabet waiting to buck the fierce, hot look of anger and hate he cast at them.

What right had *they* to be technicians and he, himself, a Laborer? Laborer! He was *certain!*

He was led by a red-uniformed guide along the busy corridors lined with separate rooms each containing its groups, here two, there five: the Motor Mechanics, the Construction Engineers, the Agronomists —— There were hundreds of specialized Professions and most of them would be represented in this small town by one or two anyway.

He hated them all just then: the Statisticians, the Accountants, the lesser breeds and the higher. He hated them because they owned their smug knowledge now, knew their fate, while he himself, empty still, had to face some kind of further red tape.

He reached 15-C, was ushered in and left in an empty room. For one moment, his spirits bounded. Surely, if this were the Labor classification room, there would be dozens of youngsters present.

A door sucked into its recess on the other side of a waist-high partition and an elderly, white-haired man stepped out. He smiled and showed even teeth that were obviously false, but his face was still ruddy and unlined and his voice had vigor.

He said, "Good evening, George. Our own sector has only one of you this time, I see."

"Only one?" said George blankly.

"Thousands over the Earth, of course. Thousands. You're not alone."

George felt exasperated. He said, "I don't understand, sir. What's my classification? What's happening?"

"Easy, son. You're all right. It could happen to anyone." He held out his hand and George took it mechanically. It was warm and it pressed George's hand firmly. "Sit down, son. I'm Sam Ellenford."

George nodded impatiently. "I want to know what's going on, sir."

"Of course. To begin with, you can't be a Computer Programmer, George. You've guessed that, I think."

"Yes, I have," said George bitterly. "What will I be, then?"

"That's the hard part to explain, George." He paused, then said with careful distinctness, "Nothing."

"*What!*"

"Nothing!"

"But what does that mean? Why can't you assign me a profession?"

"We have no choice in the matter, George. It's the structure of your mind that decides that."

George went a sallow yellow. His eyes bulged. "There's something wrong with my mind?"

"There's *something* about it. As far as professional classification is concerned, I suppose you can call it wrong."

"But why?"

Ellenford shrugged. "I'm sure you know how Earth runs its Educational program, George. Practically any human being can absorb practically any body of knowledge, but each individual brain pattern is better suited to receiving some types of knowledge than others. We try to match mind to knowledge as well as we can within the limits of the quota requirements for each profession."

George nodded. "Yes, I know."

"Every once in a while, George, we come up against a young man whose mind is not suited to receiving a superimposed knowledge of any sort."

"You mean I can't be Educated?"

"That is what I mean."

"But that's crazy. I'm intelligent. I can understand ——" He looked helplessly about as though trying to find some way of proving that he had a functioning brain.

"Don't misunderstand me, please," said Ellenford gravely. "You're intelligent. There's no question about that. You're even above average in intelligence. Unfortunately that has nothing to do with whether the mind ought to be allowed to accept superimposed knowledge or not. In fact, it is almost always the intelligent person who comes here."

"You mean I can't even be a Registered Laborer?" babbled George. Suddenly even that was better than the blank that faced him. "What's there to know to be a Laborer?"

"Don't underestimate the Laborer, young man. There are dozens of sub-classifications and each variety has its own corpus of fairly detailed knowledge. Do you think there's no skill in knowing the proper manner of lifting a weight? Besides, for the Laborer, we must select not only minds suited to it, but bodies as well. You're not the type, George, to last long as a Laborer."

George was conscious of his slight build. He said, "But I've never heard of anyone without a profession."

"There aren't many," conceded Ellenford. "And we protect them."

"Protect them?" George felt confusion and fright grow higher inside him.

"You're a ward of the planet, George. From the time you walked through that door, we've been in charge of you." And he smiled.

It was a fond smile. To George it seemed the smile of ownership; the smile of a grown man for a helpless child.

He said, "You mean, I'm going to be in prison?"

"Of course not. You will simply be with others of your kind."

Your kind. The words made a kind of thunder in George's ear.

Ellenford said, "You need special treatment. We'll take care of you."

To George's own horror, he burst into tears. Ellenford walked to the other end of the room and faced away as though in thought.

George fought to reduce the agonized weeping to sobs and then to strangle those. He thought of his father and mother, of his friends, of Trevelyan, of his own shame ————

He said rebelliously, "I learned to read."

"Everyone with a whole mind can do that. We've never found exceptions. It is at this stage that we discover—exceptions. And when you learned to read, George, we were concerned about your mind pattern. Certain peculiarities were reported even then by the doctor in charge."

"Can't you trying Educating me? You haven't even tried. I'm willing to take the risk."

"The law forbids us to do that, George. But look, it will not be bad. We will explain matters to your family so they will not be hurt. At the place to which you'll be taken, you'll be allowed privileges. We'll get you books and you can learn what you will."

"Dab knowledge in by hand," said George bitterly. "Shred by shred. Then, when I die I'll know enough to be a Registered Junior Office Boy, Paper-Clip Division."

"Yet I understand you've already been studying books."

George froze. He was struck devastatingly by sudden understanding. "That's it . . ."

"What is?"

"That fellow Antonelli. He's knifing me."

"No, George. You're quite wrong."

"Don't tell me that." George was in an ecstasy of fury. "That lousy bastard is selling me out because he thought I was a little too wise for him. I read books and tried to get a head start toward programming. Well, what do you want to square things? Money? You won't get it. I'm getting out of here and when I finish broadcasting this ————"

He was screaming.

Ellenford shook his head and touched a contact.

Two men entered on catfeet and got on either side of George. They pinned his arms to his sides. One of them used an air-spray hypodermic in the hollow of his right elbow and the hypnotic entered his vein and had an almost immediate effect.

His screams cut off and his head fell forward. His knees buckled and only the men on either side kept him erect as he slept.

. . .

Religious disorganization

11

THE UNIVERSALITY OF RELIGION

One of the few things that can be said with much certainty in the social sciences is that there are few cultural universals. Cross-cultural comparisons reveal that diversity rather than uniformity is the rule. Given this diversity, it is not surprising that social scientists, especially those of a functionalist persuasion, should search for cultural universals. The family, as noted earlier, is universal or nearly universal. A second institution that seems to be universal is religion.

"Three things appear to distinguish man from all other living creatures: the systematic making of tools, the use of abstract language, and religion" (Kluckhohn, 1965:xi). This does not mean, of course, that religion in its present form, with churches, clergy, and formal theology, is universal. Religion is defined here simply "as a set of symbolic forms and acts which relate man to the ultimate conditions of his existence" (Bellah, 1964:359). All indications are that every society about which we have information, from written history or archaeology, has had such symbolic forms and acts.

RELIGIOUS EVOLUTION

Although religion is characteristic of society, its structure, function, and form have changed as society has changed. Robert Bellah has isolated five basic stages in the evolution of religion: primitive, archaic, historic, early modern, and modern (1964 and 1970:20–44). In very simple, "primitive" societies religion is not differentiated as an institution separate from the rest of society. "At the primitive level *religious organization* as a separate social structure does not exist. Church and society are one" (Bellah, 1964:363). One of the earliest religious forms is The Dreaming found among Australian aborigines ("the blacks"). It is difficult to comprehend The Dreaming, or "the dream time," for it does not correspond to our conception of time or reality: "A central meaning of The Dreaming *is* that of a sacred, heroic time long long ago when man and nature came to be as they are; but neither 'time' nor 'history' as we understand them is involved in this meaning" (Stanner, 1965:159). The concepts of time and history are alien to the blacks. The Dreaming is part of the past, but the "past" is part of the present. It is "a kind of narrative of things that once happened; a kind of charter of things that still happen; and a kind of *logos* or principle of order transcending everything significant for aboriginal man" (Stanner, 1965:159).

Our difficulty in understanding this religious system stems from the tendency of Western man to dichotomize past from present and future, the individual from the collective, and religion from objective reality. In The Dreaming "man, society, and nature and past, present, and future are at one together within a unitary system . . ." (Stanner, 1965:160). Facing an unfavorable and barren environment the blacks have developed an ontology based on stability and permanence (Stanner, 1965:160). Their tools and way of life are crude and primitive by our standards. They do not dominate nor seek to alter their environment, but rather are " 'at one' with nature" (Stanner, 1965:163). Religion, even at this primitive level, is an evolutionary advance in that it enables man to transcend his immediate environment. "Animals or pre-religious men could only 'passively endure' suffering or other limitations imposed by the conditions of their existence . . ." (Bellah, 1964:361).

The archaic stage of religious evolution subsumes much of what is usually termed "primitive" religion in anthropological literature. "The characteristic feature of archaic religion is the emergence of true cult with the complex of gods, priests, worship, sacrifice and in some cases divine or priestly kingship" (Bellah, 1964:364). Mythical beings become objectified, and they are viewed as having responsibility for controlling the physical and social environments. In other words, they move from being diffuse spirits to being gods. The basic view of the world is still monistic—there is only one world, and it is a world controlled by gods (Bellah, 1964:364). "But though the world is one it is far more differentiated, especially in a hierarchical way, than was the monistic world view of the primitives . . ." (Bellah, 1964:364). There is greater differentiation both in the religious order and in the social structure. A two-class system emerges, and the upper-status group, with greater political and military power, usually assumes a superior religious status (Bellah, 1964:365).

The next stage is called historic religion because it developed relatively recently and in societies that were fairly literate. Hence they are part of recorded history. "The criterion that distinguishes the historic religions from the archaic is that the historic religions are all in some sense trans-cendental" (Bellah, 1964:366). Whereas the earlier stages were monistic in their world view, historic religions are characterized by a rejection of the present world. Despite the vast differences among historic religions, they are alike in their dualistic view of reality. Hierarchical ordering con-tinues to be stressed as in archaic religions. "Not only is the supernatural realm 'above' this world in terms of both value and control but both the supernatural and earthly worlds are themselves organized in terms of a religiously legitimated hierarchy" (Bellah, 1964:366). The dualism involves a shift in religious emphasis from this life to the other world. ". . . the religious goal of salvation . . . is for the first time the central religious preoccupation" (Bellah, 1964:366). Historic religions are universalistic in the sense that a man is no longer evaluated in terms of class or group membership but in terms of his capacity for salvation. The goal of religious action is not to put man in harmony with the cosmos but to attain salva-tion. The dualism brings forth a sharper distinction of the self as a sepa-rate and responsible agent:

Devaluation of the empirical world and the empirical self highlights the con-ception of a responsible self, a core self or a true self, deeper than the flux of everyday experience, facing a reality over against itself. . . . Primitive man can only accept the world in its manifold givenness. Archaic man can through sacrifice fulfill his religious obligations and attain peace with the gods. But the historic religions promise man for the first time that he can understand the fundamental structure of reality and through salvation participate actively in it (Bellah, 1964:367).

This religious view presents man with immense opportunity, but the risk of failure is also great. "Perhaps partly because of the profound risks involved the ideal of the religious life in the historic religions tends to be one of separation from the world" (Bellah, 1964:367). Societies that have historic religions are more highly differentiated than those that have archaic religions. The single religious and political hierarchy found in archaic religions is split in historic religions into two relatively independent hierarchies—political and religious. There is greater differentiation within the religious order, and a religious elite emerges. The separation of the political institution from the religious creates the potential for tension and conflict between them. The political and religious orders become competing sources of power and authority in a more complex structure.

While the previous evolutionary stages are based on several empirical cases, the next stage is based on a single case—the Protestant Reformation. "The defining characteristic of early modern religion is the collapse of the hierarchical structuring of both this and the other world" (Bellah, 1964:368). The dualism between this and the other world continues, but there is a confrontation between them. Unlike the historic stage, salvation is attained not by withdrawal from this world but by active participation in it. The Reformation was able to "break through the whole mediated system of salvation and declare salvation potentially available to any man no matter what his station or calling might be" (Bellah, 1964:368–369). Emphasis was placed on the direct relationship between the person and the other world. The world was "the theater of God's glory," and good works were to be carried out on this earth. "*Religious action* was now conceived to be identical with the whole of life" (Bellah, 1964:369). The service of God was to be carried out in all activities. Much of the religious hierarchy was eliminated and replaced by a simple division between the "elect and reprobates." The elect were the chosen, but they were a religious rather than a bureaucratic elite.

Protestantism emerged during a period of increasing societal differentiation and complexity. Max Weber (1958) attempted to relate the rise of modern capitalism to the Protestant Ethic. He suggested that while it would be naïve to see Protestantism as the cause of capitalism, the basic tenets of Protestant thought are consistent with the demands of capitalism. According to Calvinism, for instance, man is predestined, but he does not know who is among the chosen. He can, however, receive external signs that he is among the saved. Work becomes a calling to glorify God rather than a means of making money. "Not leisure and enjoyment, but only activity serves to increase the glory of God, according to the definite manifestations of His will" (Weber, 1958:157). Unwillingness to work is seen as a sign that one lacks grace (Weber, 1958:159). More recently, Robert Merton (1963) has attempted to link Protestantism to the emergence of modern science.

Under Protestantism religion was no longer isolated from this world. Protestantism was associated with the secularization of society, as religion permeated other institutions. "The emphasis on the ascetic importance of a fixed calling provided an ethical justification of the modern specialized division of labour" (Weber, 1958:163). Thus "in the early modern stage for the first time pressures to social change in the direction of greater realization of religious values are actually institutionalized as part of the structure of the society itself" (Bellah, 1964:370).

The last evolutionary stage is modern religion. This stage does not differ radically from the early modern stage but simply accentuates and further develops some of the earlier tendencies. "The central feature of the change is the collapse of the dualism that was so crucial to all the historic religions" (Bellah, 1964:371). Modern religious symbolization rejects the dualistic system of the historic period, but it does not replace this with primitive monism. "It is not that life has become again a 'one possibility thing' but that it has become an infinite possibility thing" (Bellah, 1964: 371). Religious orthodoxy is rejected and replaced by a relativistic morality, which enables man to reconcile his faith and beliefs with the realities of the world. While it is difficult to generalize about a stage that is in our midst, a dominant feature of contemporary religious symbolization seems to be the realization that man is capable of shaping his destiny. There is a growing awareness that religious symbolism *is* symbolism and that man is accountable for the symbolism he elects (Bellah, 1964:372–373). Religious action is not confined to the church or to organized religion. All values and positions are open to question in the quest of making sense out of a complex world. The current trend probably involves a greater commitment to religious symbolization: "The historic religions discovered the self; the early modern religion found a doctrinal basis on which to accept the self in all its empirical ambiguity; modern religion is beginning to understand the laws of the self's own existence and so to help man take responsibility for his own fate" (Bellah, 1964:372).

The theory of religious evolution outlined here must be interpreted with caution in order to avoid the many pitfalls inherent in any abstract model that attempts to make sense out of a myriad of facts. The model is intended as a heuristic device for understanding complex phenomena and not as a description of specific historical events. The real world does not usually fit into neat categories. Furthermore, the evolutionary stages are not discrete categories but continuous ones—they overlap, and characteristics found in one stage may persist into the next. Early stages sometimes anticipate later developments, and a more complex stage may revert to a simpler stage. Each stage "builds on" the previous stage so that "all earlier stages continue to coexist with and often within later ones" (Bellah, 1964:361).

ORIGINS OF RELIGION

Although numerous theories have been advanced to explain the origins of religion, each is at best, an "educated guess" (Lessa and Vogt, 1965:8). Since we do not have adequate evidence to "prove" or "disprove" these explanations, they must be evaluated on logical rather than empirical grounds. In the last analysis one must ask: How plausible is this theory?

One of the earliest explanations of the origin of religion was provided by Sir Edward B. Tylor, a founder of contemporary anthropology. For Tylor a conception of the soul was critical in understanding the origin of religion. He defined religion, minimally, as "the belief in Spiritual Beings"

(Tylor, 1889:424). Such a belief is found universally even among the "low races." The belief in spiritual beings, or spiritualism, was termed "animism." Animism developed out of the elementary belief in the human soul or spirit. Belief in the soul emerged as primitive man sought answers to two persistent biological problems:

In the first place, what is it that makes the difference between a living body and a dead one; what causes walking, sleep, trance, disease, death? In the second place, what are those human shapes which appear in dreams and visions? Looking at these two groups of phenomena, the ancient savage philosophers probably made their first step by the obvious inference that every man has two things belonging to him, namely, a life and a phantom (Tylor, 1889: 428).

The next step was simply to combine the life and phantom into a single entity, the soul, or spirit. In order to understand Tylor's theory of the origin of souls it is necessary to recognize the ideological underpinnings of the theory. Tylor approached the study of religion from an extremely evolutionary perspective. He saw religion as evolving from the simple animism of "savages" to polytheism, and finally to monotheism (Lessa and Vogt, 1965:11). The ultimate evolutionary stage is the belief in one high god. Other religious forms are primitive or savage. Thus Tylor speaks with contempt of primitive practices such as human or animal sacrifice and the imposition of animism to inanimate objects such as trees, rivers, and stones (1889:477). While such practices and beliefs may appear irrational to us at first glance, they are rational when viewed from the perspective of the "childlike savage":

Our comprehension of the lower stages of mental culture depends much on the thoroughness with which we can appreciate this primitive, childlike conception, and in this our best guide may be the memory of our own childish days. He who recollects when there was still personality to him in posts and sticks, chairs and toys, may well understand how the infant philosophy of mankind could extend the notion of vitality to what modern science only recognises as lifeless things . . ." (Tylor, 1889:478).

A theory of religious origin that contrasts sharply with Tylor's was proposed by Father Wilhelm Schmidt (1931). In an ingenious though improbable theory Schmidt inverted Tylor's basic thesis and argued that monotheism was the original rather than the final stage in the evolutionary process. He took the presence of a high god among primitive tribes as evidence that monotheism was the original pattern that was later perverted and distorted by beliefs in magic and animism. Although the Supreme Being is referred to by different names such as "father," "creator," "Sky," and "the old one," he is generally identified by certain attributes. Among the more common attributes are eternity, omniscience, beneficence, morality (righteousness), omnipotence, and creative power. While Schmidt's view is less pejorative than Tylor's, it is no more palatable. Despite their apparent differences, both views treat monotheism as a more desirable or advanced religious form.

Another well-known theory of the origin of religion was expounded by Sigmund Freud in *Totem and Taboo*. Freud argues "that the beginnings of religion, morals, society and art converge in the Oedipus complex" (1950: 156). The origins of society and of religion are to be found in the acting out of the Oedipal conflict. Early man, according to this view, lived in small bands consisting of an adult male, several women, and their children. When the sons reached maturity and started competing for sexual favors, they were driven off by the father. The exiled brothers finally entered into collusion, killed and devoured the father, and took the females for themselves (Freud, 1950:141–142). However, the ambivalence toward the father, who is both loved and hated, induced feelings of guilt. "They undid their deed by declaring that the killing of the father substitute, the totem, was not allowed, and renounced the fruits of their deed by denying themselves the liberated women" (Kroeber, 1920:49). These are the oldest of all taboos, "not to kill the totem animal and to avoid sexual intercourse with members of the totem clan of the opposite sex" (Freud, 1950:32). The incest prohibition has practical origins in that competition over the women would reduce the solidarity of the brothers (Freud, 1950:144). "The new organization would have collapsed in a struggle of all against all, for none of them was of such overmastering strength as to be able to take on his father's part with success" (Freud, 1950:144). The totem feast and sacrifice is filled with symbolism, representing the original slaying of the father and a kind of reconciliation with the father substitute or totem (Freud, 1950:144).

Thus, Freud claimed to have accounted not only for the origin of religion but also for the beginning of civilization: "All later religions are seen to be attempts at solving the same problem. . . . all have the same end in view and are reactions to the same great event with which civilization began and which, since it occurred, has not allowed mankind a moment's rest" (Freud, 1950:145). Freud's theory has been the object of numerous criticisms that will not be elaborated on here.[1] It may be as Alfred Kroeber (1920:49) has suggested, that the "mere extrication and presentation of the framework of the Freudian hypothesis on the origin of socio-religious civilization is probably sufficient to prevent its acceptance. . . ." The Freudian thesis appears highly improbable, to say the least. Like the other theories of the origin of religion that have been presented, it is based on a very narrow and ethnocentric view of man. It assumes that psychoanalytic concepts such as the Oedipus complex, guilt, and displacement have universal validity. In fact, all of the foregoing attempts to explain the origin of religion suffer from a narrowness of perspective that tends either to see primitive religion as inferior or to

---

[1] For a detailed critique of *Totem and Taboo* see Kroeber (1920 and 1939).

impute contemporary symbolization to such religions. For Tylor elementary religious forms are crude antecedents to modern religion; for Schmidt they are corruptions or distortions of monotheism; and for Freud they represent neurotic symptomatology.

The last theory of the origin of religion to be presented is that of the nineteenth century sociologist Emile Durkheim, outlined in his classic work *The Elementary Forms of the Religious Life* (1961). It is difficult to find a direct statement on the origin of religion in Durkheim, since for him religion was ubiquitous to society. In a sense, then, questions of religious origins invariably involve questions about the basic nature of society. The distinction between the *sacred* and the *profane* is, according to Durkheim, essential for understanding religious phenomena. All religious beliefs follow from a division of the world into these two categories (Durkheim, 1961:52). "But by sacred things one must not understand simply those personal beings which are called gods or spirits; a rock, a tree . . . anything can be sacred" (Durkheim, 1961:52). Sacred things are superior to profane things, but the difference is qualitative or absolute rather than quantitative. The sacred and profane are distinct and separate classes. "The sacred thing is *par excellence* that which the profane should not touch, and cannot touch with impunity" (Durkheim, 1961:55). Thus sacred objects are viewed with awe and respect. From this conceptualization Durkheim arrives at the following definition of religion: "A religion is a unified system of beliefs and practices relative to sacred things, that is to say, things set apart and forbidden—beliefs and practices which unite into one single moral community . . ." (1961:62).

Durkheim's work represents a radical departure, for he does not resort to a special class of theory to explain the origin of religion. He would have difficulty conceiving of society without religion or religion without society. Wherever one finds human society, he will also find religion, that is, a division of the world into the sacred and the profane. The sacred is held in awe and treated with respect because it is a symbolic representation of society. Religion is "something eminently social" (Durkheim, 1961:22).

FUNCTIONS OF RELIGION

One can hardly talk about the origin of religion without also considering its functions. Durkheim, in fact, spurned the traditional approach to origins:

. . . if by origin we are to understand the very first beginning, the question has nothing scientific about it, and should be resolutely discarded. There was no given moment when religion began to exist. . . . Like every human institution religion did not commence anywhere. . . . But the problem which we raise is quite another one. What we want to do is to find a means of discerning the ever-present causes upon which the most essential forms of religious thought and practice depend (1961:20).

For Durkheim then, the study of origins is identical to the study of functions. His concern is not with how or why religion came into being but with how and why it is maintained.[2]

Religion has many functions, according to Durkheim, some specific and others general. However, things are not always as they appear. We must therefore go beyond the manifest reasons or explanations for social phenomena and search for deeper meanings:

The theorists who have undertaken to explain religion in rational terms have generally seen in it before all else a system of ideas, corresponding to some determined object. This object has been conceived in a multitude of ways: nature, the infinite, the unknowable, the ideal, etc.; but these differences matter but little (Durkheim, 1961:463).

The "believer" is also likely to object to a rational conception. "The believer who has communicated with his god is not merely a man who sees new truths of which the unbeliever is ignorant; he is a man who is *stronger*" (Durkheim, 1961:464). This inner strength comes from collective strength, for religion is the embodiment of the collective conscience: ". . . we have seen that this reality, which mythologies have represented under so many different forms, but which is the universal and eternal objective cause of these sensations *sui generis* out of which religious experience is made, is society" (Durkheim, 1961:465). Durkheim went a step further and argued that not only is society religious in origin but "that the fundamental categories of thought, and consequently of science, are of religious origin" (1961:466). All social institutions develop from religion. Religious life is eminent because it is the collective expression of all life. "If religion has given birth to all that is essential in society, it is because the idea of society is the soul of religion" (Durkheim, 1961:466).

Some maintain that religion ignores the reality of society, but in effect it is a reflection or mirror image of society, including all elements, even the most repulsive (Durkheim, 1961:468). Religion is an idealization or symbolic representation of reality: "Animals know only one world, the one which they perceive by experience. . . . Men alone have the faculty of conceiving the ideal, of adding something to the real" (Durkheim, 1961:469). Durkheim's *Elementary Forms* was a landmark work in the study of religion, representing a shift in focus from the causes to the functions of religion. During the twentieth century other scholars came to accept the existence of religion as universal and to inquire about what religion does for the individual and the society (Lessa and Vogt, 1965:88).

One of the earliest but unheralded functional theorists was the historian Fustel de Coulanges (1896). He was interested mainly in examining inter-

---

[2] It is not surprising, therefore, that many of Durkheim's critics have been primarily interested in the problem of the origin of religion rather than in its functions. See, for example, Goldenweiser (1917).

relations among institutions in Greek and Roman life and in the effects of religious beliefs on historical change (Lessa and Vogt, 1965:89). Durkheim was one of his students at the École Normal Supérieure in Paris and was profoundly influenced by the master (Lessa and Vogt, 1965:89). Durkheim, in turn, influenced many other scholars, including Radcliffe-Brown.

Bronislaw Malinowski's theory of magic and religion is a significant departure from earlier theories of primitive religions. Unlike Tylor, who saw primitive religion as infantile behavior, and Frazer, who saw magic as a "false science" that preceded the age of religion (Lessa and Vogt, 1965: 103), and Durkheim, who saw a sharp distinction and opposition between magic and religion (1961:58–60), Malinowski believed that magic was an extension of a rational scientific method. Every primitive culture has a fund of rational knowledge that, like modern science, is used to control the environment and enhance man's needs.[3] When rational methods fail, however, man turns to magic in order to reduce anxiety. Magic emerges only when there is a gap in knowledge, when rational solutions to practical problems fail (Malinowski, 1948:59). Magic is rational and goal oriented:

To most types of magical ritual, therefore, there corresponds a spontaneous ritual of emotional expression or of a forecast of the desired end. . . . Thus foundations of magical belief and practice are not taken from the air, but are due to a number of experiences actually lived through, in which man receives the revelation of his power to attain the desired end (Malinowski, 1948:62).

Since magic does not actually alter the environment, how are magical beliefs sustained in the face of contradictory evidence? First, there is the element of selective perception so that "a positive case always overshadows the negative one" (Malinowski, 1948:62). Second, the magician is generally a man of extraordinary and charismatic qualities. "This personal renown of the magician and its importance in enhancing the belief about the efficiency of magic are the cause of an interesting phenomenon: what may be called the *current mythology* of magic" (Malinowski, 1948: 63). Myth, however, is a living and constantly evolving force that produces new phenomena. The rational quality of magic is illustrated by its relation to science. Magic is like science in that it has a specific aim and is related to the pursuit of human needs and interests (Malinowski, 1948: 66). Both magic and science have as their goal the attainment of practical ends.

Magic and religion are similar in that they arise in situations of stress and are surrounded by rituals and taboos (Malinowski, 1948:67–68). The essential difference is that magic is defined "as a practical art consisting of

[3] In an interesting reversal of Malinowski, Judith Willer suggests that modern science is a form of magic (1971:134). For a general discussion of similarities and differences between magic and religion see Goode (1951:50–55). Jeffrey Russell distinguishes further among magic, religion, science, and witchcraft (1972:4).

acts which are only means to a definite end expected to follow later on; religion as a body of self-contained acts being themselves the fulfillment of their purpose" (Malinowski, 1948:68). Magical beliefs, being more practical in orientation, involve more direct and less complex techniques, rituals, and beliefs. The art of magic is also the domain of a select few (wizards and witches), whereas religion is available to all (Malinowski, 1948:68).

In "Taboo," the Frazer Lecture, Radcliffe-Brown took issue with Malinowski's conception of magic and religion.[4] In particular he questions the assertion that magic has a practical purpose while religion is an end in itself (Radcliffe-Brown, 1952:137–138). How does one determine the utility of an act? Radcliffe-Brown, influenced by Durkheim, was concerned with going beyond appearances or avowed purposes and isolating actual functions: "The reasons given by the members of a community for any custom they observe are important data for the anthropologist. But it is to fall into grievous error to suppose that they give a valid explanation of the custom" (1952:142). There is great danger that the anthropologist in analyzing customs will "attribute to them some purpose or reason on the basis of his own preconceptions about human motives" (Radcliffe-Brown, 1952:142). Instead of attempting to ascertain the purposes of action, the observer should determine their social and psychological functions. If we look at a rain-making ceremony from the standpoint of its ostensible goal, to bring rain, we must conclude that it fails to attain this goal (Radcliffe-Brown, 1952:144). But this is not to say that the ritual is without function. It has important symbolic meaning for the individual participants and for the collective. Radcliffe-Brown also differed with Malinowski's contention that magic and religion give men security and reduce anxiety. ". . . it could equally well be argued that they give men fears and anxieties from which they would otherwise be free . . ." (Radcliffe-Brown, 1952:149). Like Durkheim, Radcliffe-Brown was concerned with societal functions rather than origins. ". . . the social function of a religion is independent of its truth or falsity . . ." (Radcliffe-Brown, 1952:154). The function of religion is the contribution it makes to the formation and maintenance of the society (Radcliffe-Brown, 1952:154).

Clyde Kluckhohn (1944) has skillfully applied the functional perspective in the analysis of Navaho witchcraft.[5] He is concerned with the latent and manifest functions of witchcraft for both the individual and society. The most general manifest function of witchcraft for the individual is the acquisition of supernatural power, which enables one to attain wealth, gain access to women, get rid of enemies, and "be mean" (Kluckhohn, 1944: 81). It provides, moreover, an outlet for those persons who are unusually

[4] George Homans (1941) has attempted to reconcile these two positions.
[5] Carlos Castaneda (1968, 1971, and 1972a and b) has written a fascinating account of "Don Juan," a Yaqui sorcerer.

aggressive. Witchcraft also has important manifest functions for those who are not witches. One function is to provide dramatic and exciting stories; another is to answer perplexing questions (Kluckhohn, 1944:82–83). In addition to its manifest functions, witchcraft has latent functions that are not officially recognized. It is a means by which individuals can gain attention. A large proportion of the victims of witchcraft are persons who are neglected or occupy a low social rank (Kluckhohn, 1944:83–84). A second latent function is to provide a legitimate channel for expressing deviant or aberrant impulses and fantasies (Kluckhohn, 1944:85). A man can daydream about performing incest, for example, but not feel guilty if he believes that he is possessed. The third, and perhaps most important, latent function is that "witchcraft beliefs and practices allow the expression of direct and displaced antagonisms" (Kluckhohn, 1944:85). In a society in which overt aggression is negatively rewarded, witchcraft provides an important imaginary outlet for hostile and aggressive impulses. ". . . if myths and rituals provide the principal means of *sublimating* the Navaho individual's antisocial tendencies, witchcraft provides one of the principally socially understood means of *expressing* them" (Kluckhohn, 1944: 85).

To the outsider witchcraft may appear to be an irrational and capricious exercise, but within Navaho culture it is a very adaptive response. The Navaho live in a hostile and tension-filled environment. Much conflict and tension arises among members of a consumption group in the course of their daily activities. Yet direct expression of hostility represents a grave threat to survival and therefore is not tolerated. The net result is a state of "antagonistic cooperation" with few opportunities for overt expression of hostility and antagonisms. Witches then become scapegoats, culturally approved objects for repressed hostility. Illness, bad luck, and personal misfortune are blamed on them. It is not surprising that the rich or more fortunate are typically regarded as witches and the poor and unfortunate as their victims.

In a more recent analysis, Peter Berger (1967) posits two basic and universal functions of religion: world-construction and world-maintenance. He notes, as Durkheim did earlier, that man differs from other animals largely in that he lives in a world of his own creation (Berger, 1967:5). The world is necessarily unstable, continually "produced" or "created" by man's imputation of meaning. World-building is a collective activity; symbols and meanings must be validated consensually to be "real." Thus not only is objective, external reality defined by society, but subjective, personal reality is also defined. Religion is crucial in world-construction. "Religion is the human enterprise by which a sacred cosmos is established" (Berger, 1967:25). The division of the world into sacred and profane is part of man's never-ending attempt to build a meaningful and orderly world. The opposite of the sacred is not so much the profane as chaos: "The sacred cosmos emerges out of chaos and continues to confront the latter as its terrible contrary. . . . The sacred cosmos, which transcends and includes man in its ordering of reality, thus provides man's ultimate shield against the terror of anomy" (Berger, 1967:26). Religion is the ultimate in self-externalization whereby man's own meaning is merged with a total cosmic being (Berger, 1967:27–28). "Put differently, religion is the audacious attempt to conceive of the entire universe as being humanly significant" (Berger, 1967:28).

The world that man constructs, however, is a fragile order held together only by common beliefs. This order must be legitimated if it is to maintain itself. "By legitimation is meant socially objectivated 'knowledge' that serves to explain and justify the social order" (Berger, 1967:29). The why of things, particularly institutional orders, must be explained and justified. Legitimation may be either cognitive or normative, defining the way things *are* as well as how they *should be.* While legitimation may be attained by fiat, or by the threat of force, religious justification is much more effective: ". . . religion has been the historically most widespread and effective instrumentality of legitimation. . . . Religion legitimates so effectively because it relates the precarious reality constructions of empirical societies with ultimate reality" (Berger, 1967:32). Religious legitimation places individual acts and social institutions within a cosmic perspective. Institutions are viewed not as instruments of power or the creations of man but as the correct or only way. "They transcend the death of individuals and the decay of entire collectivities, because they are now grounded in a sacred time within which merely human history is but an episode . . . they become immortal" (Berger, 1967:37).

Closely related to the world-construction and world-maintenance functions of religion is the problem of theodicy. Since the socially constructed world is fragile, it must be reaffirmed continually. Anomic or potentially disruptive phenomena must be explained in terms of the order created by society. "An explanation of these phenomena in terms of religious legitimations, of whatever degree of theoretical sophistication, may be called a theodicy" (Berger, 1967:53). Theodicy helps to explain or justify anomic events, suffering, inequities, and personal or collective tragedies. It functions as legitimation for both the oppressed and the privileged. For the former it is an "opiate" that makes their lot tolerable, for the latter a justification of their special status (Berger, 1967:59). Theodicies also vary along a rationality-irrationality continuum. At the irrational end of the continuum is "the simple, theoretically unelaborated transcendence of self brought about by complete identification with the collectivity" (Berger, 1967:60). This occurs typically in simpler societies in which a sharp distinction is not made between the individual and the collective. In primitive religions there is a mergence of the individual, society, and nature. At the other extreme are rational theodocies that elaborate a complex theoretical system. In the *Karma-samsara* complex of India "every conceivable anomy is integrated within a thoroughly rational, all-embracing interpretation of the universe" (Berger, 1967:65). Since every action has a reaction and each reaction is, in turn, the consequence of a previous action, a person's life is only a link in a complex and infinite human chain (Berger, 1967: 65). A person is, accordingly, blamed for his misfortune and credited for his good fortune. "It legitimates the conditions of all social strata simultaneously and, in its linkage with the conception of *dharma* (social duty, particularly caste duty), constitutes the most thoroughly conservative religious system devised in history" (Berger, 1967:65).

RELIGION IN MASS SOCIETY

Religion in contemporary society is in a state of confusion and flux. Not only is it difficult to assess and interpret current trends but also to predict future directions. This section attempts to analyze the changing function of religion in mass society and to place such change within a meaningful perspective.

Analyses of religion in American society are complicated by the fact that no single, monolithic religion predominates. Although broadly speaking the society is monotheistic and Christianity prevails, there is much internal diversity with hundreds of churches, denominations, sects, and cults. There is also a growing interest in Eastern religions, mysticism, yoga, the "black arts," and transcendental meditation.[6] This pluralism makes the problem of religious legitimation extremely difficult. In simpler or more primitive societies in which a single religion predominates, religious beliefs are coterminous with socially created reality. "Whenever the socially established nomos attains the quality of being taken for granted, there occurs a merging of its meanings with what are considered to be the fundamental meanings inherent in the universe" (Berger, 1967:24–25). In a sense, nomos, socially created order, and cosmos are one. But in complex, sectarian societies the plausibility structure of religion is more tenuous, and complex legitimations evolve (Berger, 1967:47). It becomes difficult to accept a set of beliefs as the "right way" or the "only way" when one is surrounded by conflicting and competing ideological systems. The plausibility of a nomos is reduced further in a complex society by rapid social change, anomie, and instability. The secularization of society tends to introduce a "crisis of credibility" (Berger, 1967:127). Traditional religions must compete not only with one another and with secular definitions of reality for credibility but with other sociopolitical ideologies as well. In modern society science emerges as an alternative nomos. "The consequence of all this is that the importance of religion as a system of knowledge has declined" (Willer, 1971:134). How does one reconcile an archaic

---

[6] The literature on witchcraft and the "black arts" is growing so rapidly that it is only possible to mention a few of these works. See, for example, Robbins (1959), Haining (1972), Murray (1970), and Russell (1972).

religious nomos, developed in a prescientific era, with available scientific knowledge?

One of the consequences of increasing secularization and rationalization in industrial-technological society is that religion loses its monopoly on definitions of reality. In a pluralistic society religion is voluntary, essentially private matter (Berger, 1967:133). The religious nomos is no longer taken for granted but must be "sold" or "marketed" to a consumer. Religion itself becomes secularized and assumes a stance relative to its public—a stance analogous to that assumed by marketing agencies toward their public. It must sell a product to a consumer who can no longer be coerced into buying (Berger, 1967:138). Religious organizations adopt modern marketing techniques, including the soft sell, effective use of the media, advertising, and, perhaps most important, proper "packaging."

In its quest for legitimation religion has become more consumer oriented. Not only has lay influence increased, but most religions have joined the "relevance kick." Many de-emphasize supernatural elements and concentrate on filling psychological needs and providing social services. They are "less concerned with religion and more with social gospel . . ." (Willer, 1971:134). Ironically, though, relevancy further increases religious instability. Religion is merged with individual consciousness and loses its status as the legitimator of the world. Religion no longer defines reality for the individual, but rather the individual defines reality for religion. ". . . religion no longer refers to the cosmos or to history, but to individual *Existenz* or psychology" (Berger, 1967:152).

"THAT NEW-TIME RELIGION"

Throughout the history of man the primary function of religion has been world-building and world-maintenance. It has, in short, served as an opiate for the masses and a justificator for the powerful. Nonetheless, religion has at other times served as an instrument of change. At the same time that established religions supported the status quo, protest, reform, and revolutionary religious movements questioned tradition and opposed social inequities.[7] The Protestant Reformation altered the established position of the medieval church and had a profound effect on the course of human history. Ironically, Protestantism fostered the development of rational capitalism and science, two movements that have helped to bring about its own demise. While Protestantism was the product of a reform movement, it too became institutionalized and resistant to change. Through-

[7] Christianity, for example, was used to justify the institution of slavery, as slaves were indoctrinated with the scriptural passages that legitimized their subordination. But religion also served as a catalyst of civil rights militancy. Slave revolts were led by the clergy, and religious leaders have been actively involved in civil rights (Marx, 1967).

out the course of American history established churches have been challenged with varying degrees of intensity by protest and reform groups. The United States has a rich tradition of religious revivals dating to the Great Awakening of the 1730s and 1740s, which was led by the eloquent preacher Jonathan Edwards (Jorstad, 1972:17–27). Four other revival movements attained national prominence: the Second Awakening led by Charles Grandison Finney in the 1830s, Dwight L. Moody's revival of the 1870s and 1880s, Billy Sunday's famous crusade in the 1910s, and Billy Graham's post-World War II revival. Despite the prominence of these revivals, they were not radical in their ideology. They called for a rekindling of the Christian spirit and a return to traditional American values like laissez faire capitalism, patriotism, sexual puritanism, and more recently an attack on world communism. In short, the revivals were conservative, if not reactionary. Many less noted but more revolutionary revivals, however, led to the establishment of hundreds of utopian communities that sought to change traditional economic and familial values (see Chapter 9).

In contemporary American society we are currently in the midst of a revival that shares certain traditions with the great revivals of the past but also differs from them in important respects. This revival is variously labeled as the "Jesus people," "Jesus freaks," and "that new-time religion."[8] Many young members of the counter-culture have turned from drug use and radical politics to evangelism. These middle-class youth have, in a sense, "turned on" to Christ and fundamentalist religious beliefs that were previously the province of the disadvantaged. The new-time religion shares important features with previous revivals. "Its understanding of Christian teaching is evangelical rather than analytic; its source of authority is the Bible as the verbally inspired, inerrant word of God; it believes in the efficacy of instant conversion; and it emerged during a time of grave national crisis" (Jorstad, 1972:120). However, the differences between the new- and old-time religion are greater than the similarities (Jorstad, 1972:123). While the old-time revivals called for a return to the established churches, the new revival works outside of the established order and is critical of organized religion. It shuns the Madison Avenue tactics of mass revivalism in preference for small discussion groups and one-to-one evangelism. Unlike traditional revivals, there is no call for a rekindling of traditional political and religious values. Instead, the new revivalists reject materialism and advocate a return to communal sharing of goods and property. They have established half-way houses, urban cooperatives, and rural communes (Jorstad, 1972:64–70; Fairfield, 1972:101–162) for collective sharing as in the original Pentecostal Church.

---

[8] For a historical overview and analysis of revivalism see Jorstad (1972). More focused and personal accounts are found in Streiker (1971 and 1972) and in Harder, Richardson, and Simmonds (1972). A book that "preaches to" but is not about Jesus people is by Graham (1971).

The new revival has emerged out of frustration and alienation. Members of the counter-culture frustrated by the inability to alter basic institutions and by the irrelevancy of established religion have evolved a new nomos.[9] Since the new order has emerged out of *praxis* rather than theory, it is little wonder that established religions view the new revival with skepticism, if not contempt. It is a religion that is plausible to its adherents but one that questions the legitimation of institutionalized and bureaucratized religion. Established religion is critical of the new nomos because "little effort is made to lead the new converts into understanding the more substantial and challenging dimensions of the Christian faith" (Jorstad, 1972: 125). Paradoxically, the established orders, having internalized the secular and bureaucratic ethos, are unable to cope with a movement that seeks to revive traditional Christian beliefs.

Thus while the monopoly of religion has ended, man's need for religion is as intense as ever. As the world becomes more complex, uncertain, and anomic, man continues the endless search for a meaningful nomos. The alternative is chaos and the fear that man stands "on the edge of the abyss of meaninglessness" (Berger, 1967:27).

REFERENCES

Bellah, Robert N.
1964 "Religious Evolution." American Sociological Review 29 (June):358–374.
1970 Beyond Belief: Essays on Religion in a Post-Traditional World. New York: Harper & Row.

Berger, Peter L.
1967 The Sacred Canopy: Elements of a Sociological Theory of Religion. Garden City, N.Y.: Anchor Books.

Castaneda, Carlos
1968 The Teachings of Don Juan: A Yaqui Way of Knowledge. New York: Ballantine.
1971 A Separate Reality: Further Conversations with Don Juan. New York: Simon & Schuster.
1972a Journey to Ixtlan: *The Lessons of Don Juan.* New York: Simon & Schuster.
1972b "Excerpts From Journey to Ixtlan." Psychology Today 6 (December): 102–109.

Durkheim, Emile
1961 The Elementary Forms of the Religious Life. (Translated by Joseph Ward Swain). New York: Collier.

[9] The broader interest in the occult, witchcraft, the "black arts," and in mysticism is undoubtedly related to the same frustration. Judith Willer suggests that mysticism involves a greater escape or withdrawal from empirical reality than magic or religion (1971:91–92).

Fairfield, Richard
1972 Communes USA. Baltimore, Md.: Penguin.
Freud, Sigmund
1950 Totem and Taboo: Some Points of Agreement Between the Mental Lives of Savages and Neurotics. (Translated by James Strachey). London: Routledge & Kegan Paul.
Fustel de Coulanges, Numa-Denys
1896 The Ancient City. (Translated by Willard Small). Ninth ed. Boston: Lee and Shepard.
Goldenweiser, Alexander
1917 "Religion and Society: A Critique of Émile Durkheim's Theory of the Origin and Nature of Religion." The Journal of Philosophy, Psychology, and Scientific Methods 14 (March):113–124.
Goode, William J.
1951 Religion Among the Primitives. New York: The Free Press.
Graham, Billy
1971 The Jesus Generation. Grand Rapids, Mich.: Zondervan.
Haining, Peter
1972 The Anatomy of Witchcraft. New York: Taplinger.
Harder, Mary White, James T. Richardson, and Robert B. Simmonds
1972 "Jesus People." Psychology Today 6 (December):45–50, 110, 112–113.
Homans, George C.
1941 "Anxiety and Ritual: The Theories of Malinowski and Radcliffe-Brown." American Anthropologist 43 (April-June):164–172.
Jorstad, Erling
1972 That New-Time Religion: The Jesus Revival in America. Minneapolis, Minn.: Augsburg.
Kluckhohn, Clyde
1944 Navaho Witchcraft. Boston: Beacon.
1965 "Foreword." Pp. xi–xii in William A. Lessa and Evon Z. Vogt (eds.), Reader in Comparative Religion: An Anthropological Approach. Second ed. New York: Harper & Row.
Kroeber, Alfred L.
1920 "Totem and Taboo: An Ethnologic Psychoanalysis." American Anthropologist 22 (January-March):48–55.
1939 "Totem and Taboo in Retrospect." American Journal of Sociology 45 (November):446–451.
Lessa, William A., and Evan Z. Vogt
1965 Reader in Comparative Religion: An Anthropological Approach. Second ed. New York: Harper & Row.
Marx, Gary
1967 "Religion: Opiate or Inspiration of Civil Rights Militancy." American Sociological Review 32 (February):64–72.
Malinowski, Bronislaw
1948 Magic, Science and Religion and Other Essays. New York: The Free Press.
Merton, Robert K.
1963 "Puritanism, Pietism and Science." Pp. 574–606 in Social Theory and Social Structure. Revised ed. New York: Free Press.

Murray, Margaret A.
1970 The God of the Witches. New York: Oxford University Press.
Radcliffe-Brown, A. R.
1952 Structure and Function in Primitive Society. New York: Free Press.
Robbins, Rossell Hope
1959 The Encyclopedia of Witchcraft and Demonology. New York: Crown.
Russell, Jeffrey Burton
1972 Witchcraft in the Middle Ages. Ithaca, N.Y.: Cornell University Press.
Schmidt, Wilhelm
1931 The Origin and Growth of Religion: Facts and Theories. New York: Lincoln MacVeagh.
Stanner, W. E. H.
1965 "The Dreaming." Pp. 158–167 in William A. Lessa and Evon Z. Vogt (eds.), Reader in Comparative Religion: An Anthropological Approach. Second ed. New York: Harper & Row.
Streiker, Lowell D.
1971 The Jesus Trip: Advent of the Jesus Freaks. Nashville, Tenn.: Abingdon.
1972 "Advent of the Jesus Freaks." Dialog 11 (Spring):90–94.
Tylor, Edward B.
1889 Primitive Culture. Two vols. Second ed. New York: Holt, Rinehart & Winston.
Weber, Max
1958 The Protestant Ethic and the Spirit of Capitalism. (Translated by Talcott Parsons). New York: Scribner.
Willer, Judith
1971 The Social Determination of Knowledge. Englewood Cliffs, N.J.: Prentice-Hall.

INTRODUCTION TO THE READINGS

The two readngs in this chapter are concerned with the problem of religious legitimation. The first, "The Selling of the Lord 1973," illustrates the attempt by organized religion to gain legitimation in contemporary society. While earlier revivals relied heavily on live audiences and face-to-face contacts in attaining religious conversion, contemporary mass evangelism effectively employs the mass media and advertising techniques. The end result is that religion is marketed and sold like other products. Mass evangelism contrasts sharply not only with earlier revivals but with the evangelism of "that new-time religion."

The second selection also deals with an evangelism of sorts, although the setting is a fictional nonhuman society. "The Streets of Ashkelon" is concerned with competition for legitimation among conflicting nomos. Specifically, the selection shows the conflict experienced by members of a nonhuman species as a result of their exposure to religious and scientific systems of knowledge.

The selling of the Lord 1973

EUGENE L. MEYER

Billy Frank Graham was lucky to rise above Consciousness I. Fresh off a North Carolina farm, he made his way through ultrafundamentalist Bob Jones College, where evolution is still a dirty word. His greening, such as it was, came later, at less conservative Wheaton College near Chicago, and in the company of Presidents. But he never made it to Consciousness III. Like Billy Sunday, the early 20th century evangelist, Billy Graham believes soul-saving is society-saving. The main difference is that Graham wants to use modern marketing methods to do the job.

In a recent issue of Graham's *Decision* magazine, the kingdom of God is compared to a

vast modern complex whose purpose and function is to produce the Gospel of love. God our heavenly father is the Owner and President; the Lord Jesus Christ is General Manager; and the Holy Spirit is in charge of sales. . . . The Kingdom of God cannot operate the way it should unless you men and women bring in some orders and some customers. . . . We have the finest product on the market. Nothing can touch it. . . .

If God is the President, and Christ the General Manager, then Billy Graham and his friends are PR men, and this year they have come up with a new marketing gimmick. It is called Key 73, and its goal is to confront 100 million people "with the claims of Christ," to make 1973 "a year of optimum impact for Christ in North America." Key 73 enthusiasts refer to it as a "Christian blitz" and "evangelistic saturation."

It is part of a plan to replace rebellion with religion, social unrest with the Peace that Passeth All Understanding. The 1960's, said Graham in a recent TV speech, was "an age of revolt and rebellion on the part of young people." The 1970's, on the other hand, he saw as "a period of depression. We seem depressed about ourselves. There is a philosophical and religious vacuum. Into this vacuum could come any ideal or any thing." Key 73 and the Jesus-is-the-answer folks are trying mightily to fill the void, and in the course of their campaign they have stood the movement of the 1960's on its head. Even the slogans parody the old: "Hell? No, I won't go"; and "End the war; Vote for Jesus."

It is one movement which the Nixon Administration views with considerable benevolence, and the President himself might properly credit himself with a share of its success to date. For while the Warren Court took religion out of the public schools, Richard Nixon has established it in the White House, in the form of unprecedented Sunday worship services there. He also bestowed his blessings on Explo 72, last summer's mass pray-in at Dallas. In the recent pre-inaugural festivities, Pat Boone and family won warm applause when they sang "a personal pledge of allegiance to Jesus." And after the swearing-in, Billy Graham told White House worshippers that all school kids should have to recite the ten commandments daily. Chief Justice Warren Berger, responding to a reporter's question, conceded this would

---

cause some constitutional problems "at this time." But, you never know.

What, in God's name, is going on here? Merely the establishment of an official state religion—a single theology that is self-righteous and pious, uncompassionate and unbending. A theology that calls the end of a war marked by My Lai and saturation bombing "peace with honor," but papers over the nation's cracks, ratholes and sores with, as one critic put it, "a pious affirmation of faith."

It is the Protestant ethic, but it is neither protesting nor ethical. It holds that the poor get what they deserve— and that only the "deserving poor" should get. It is a neo-Social Darwinism that sanctifies and excuses the corporate giants. It is absolutely moralistic, but not particularly moral. It commends law and order and the work ethic to the poor but fails to apply the same standards to white collar crooks, corporate welfare cheaters or Watergate wiretappers. This established region is, for reasons of self-interest, the religion of the establishment. The flag and the cross have become so superimposed in the national psyche that most Americans no longer notice the double exposure. So it's onward Christian soldiers as America marches off to its destiny. At the head of the column are two standard bearers on horseback— Richard Nixon carrying the flag, and Billy Graham bearing the cross.

Graham and his evangelist friends are not, for the most part, your Bible Belt tent revival types, although many spring from that tradition. Nor are they the blatant God-and-country promoters, the Carl McIntires and Billy James Hargises, although many feel that way. They are superficially mod, if fundamentally un-modern. They are image-conscious and media-wise. These are the clerical counterparts of the people who sold Nixon for President in 1968. Their job: The Selling of the Lord, 1973.

THE GREAT COMMISSION

It all began with a June 1967 editorial in *Christianity Today*, a magazine established in the 1950's as a conservative answer to liberal church journals. Founders included Carl F. H. Henry, who wrote the editorial, and Billy Graham, who remains today on the Board of Directors. (To complete the trinity, the current executive editor, L. Nelson Bell, is Graham's father-in-law.) In his editorial, Henry called for all evangelicals to "somehow get together" for a united soul-winning effort.

Soon after the editorial appeared, the Billy Graham Evangelistic Association underwrote a special meeting at the Marriott Key Bridge Motor Hotel in Rosslyn, Va., across the Potomac from Washington. (The choice of the motel was symbolic. The organizers revere Key as a fervent 19th century evangelist, as well as the author of "The Star Spangled Banner.") To those 42 clergymen who convened at the Key Bridge Motel, it was the best of times and the worst of times. On the one hand, all hell was breaking loose, in the personification of hippies, yippies and other malcontents who couldn't abide war and racism. It was the best of times for two reasons. For one, according to Biblical prophecies, the worst of times is a prelude to the Second Coming. Then again, a united evangelical crusade seemed the next logical step after the 1966 World Conference on Evangelism in Berlin, sponsored by Billy Graham.

Hence Key Bridge One (there were a few more such "consultations" at the Marriott motel) adopted a proposal to undertake the Great Commission on a massive scale in 1973. And so Key 73 was born.

Initially, the target audience consisted of both separatist church leaders and mainline clergymen. Timing was, you might say, providential. The liberal churches, despite their efforts to be "relevant," were losing members and money, especially from their conservative wings. Superstitious and charismatic movements, the Jesus freaks and Pentacostals, were beginning to gather steam.

To the disheartened and discouraged liberal clergy, the Key 73 salesmen offered a form of institutional salvation. To sweeten the pill, they even added an ambiguous objective about "the issues shaping man and his society." The sales pitch worked, and six years and many meetings later, Key 73 has grown to include some 150 groups, from Brunk Revivals Corp. to the United Methodist Church. It has even been endorsed by the National Council of Churches (evangelism section) and the U.S. Conference of Catholic Bishops. It has, in short, become a kind of umbrella operation. As it happens, semantics are crucial to keeping the umbrella open. "Ecumenical, to some, is a dirty word," says the Rev. Theodore A. Raedeke, Key 73's executive director. "We say 'simultaneous evangelistic thrust.' " The literature stresses, "separately, simultaneously, cooperatively."

Raedeke is an experienced hand in this business. Before Key 73, he ran evangelism for the three million member Lutheran Church, Missouri Synod, where they still debate the infallibility of the Bible. As executive director, he supervises the day to day operation of the campaign. He is responsible to the general assembly, in which each of the 150 groups has one vote, and the executive committee. Chairman of both these bodies is Thomas F. Zim-

merman, the head of the Assemblies of God, a Pentecostal church. The vice-chairman of the executive group is Dr. Victor Nelson, vice-president of the Billy Graham Evangelical Association and a very important figure in the Graham operation. Bill Bright, spearhead of Explo 72, serves on the executive board of Key 73 and is chairman of Bible reading and soul-winning.

KEY 73 IS COMING

Key 73's main office is located on the 11th floor of the aging Commerce Building in downtown St. Louis. It is rented from the Missouri Synod and has carpets and furniture that look like they came straight off the shelves at Sears-Roebuck. As late as mid-December, half its rooms were unused. The staff is small, consisting of Raedeke, an administrative assistant, and two secretaries. Downstairs, on the fourth floor, there is the Key Seventy-Three Fund, actually a private firm, Ketchum, Inc., hired to raise for Key 73 the $2–5 million needed for promotion. There is also a "mass media office" in suburban Madison, N.J., located above a drug store in the headquarters of the National Religious Broadcasters.

Raedeke might pass for Lawrence Welk, though he is somewhat taller and heavier and exhibits a weakness for mod jackets and red flared-bottom pants. His office is wood-paneled. Above the TV set hangs a framed picture of Christ, which might have been found in a religious souvenir shop. On a bookcase sits a color photograph of the Rev. Billy and Ruth Graham. And above the couch is a four-by-six foot tapestry of the professionally-designed Key 73 logo: red flame encompassing a white dove, not soaring but pointing downward.

The aim of evangelism, says Raedeke, is "to make disciples, which automatically results in church membership." It encompasses "proclamation and demonstration"—though not the political kind. "If you want society to change you have to change people. You don't evangelize structures. If you change people, you're building the foundation for changing structures. . . ."

Key 73 has two budgets. One, for operating expenses, is only $150,000, but last year the finance committee could raise only half of it from the participating groups. "We had to cut back on promotion, publicity," Raedeke said. The second budget of $2–5 million is for media promotion, and must be raised entirely from private sources. Since Key 73 is a non-profit tax-exempt corporation, donations are tax deductible. Jim Shaffer ("spelled the way God intended it") is associate director of the Key 73 Fund. "It's not that we don't want the $5 and $10 contributions, but we're aiming our appeal at those giving between $10,000 and $100,000," he said. "The top gift will run around $200,000."

Shaffer said fund-raising efforts would be concentrated in 20 large cities. In Houston alone, he boasted, "we have 20 prospects who could write the $2 million goal among themselves." The fund-raising campaign was timed to begin in February 1973, instead of earlier, "so [donors] can bridge two income years." The chairman of the fund-raising committee is William Walton, president of Holiday Inns, International, and Explo's Dr. Bill Bright will be "very much involved" in soliciting money, Shaffer said.

According to its brochures, Key 73's primary purpose is "to share with every person in North America more fully and more forcefully the claims and messages of the Gospel of Jesus Christ . . . to employ every means

and method of communicating the Gospel. . . ."

Key 73's first "high-visibility event" was to begin the day after Christmas. Throughout the U.S., at noon, bells were to ring, horns sound, and people pause to pray. This "noon prayer call" was to take place every day from December 26 through the first week of January. The noon prayer calls were coordinated by the Rev. Robert Yawberg, founder of the Prayer-A-Gram foundation.

The overall media plan was focussed around three TV specials, starting with a "Launch Special" on January 6. Ultimately, 667 stations—in every state except Wyoming—aired the program, and the Armed Forces Network plans to run it throughout the year. By and large, Key 73 pays nothing for this exposure since the stations show the programs as "public service" to fulfill FCC requirements. (The second show, starring Pat Boone, is described as "Christian entertainment." Entitled "Come Together," it was produced at Southern California's Melodyland Christian Center for showing after Easter.) To promote the "Launch Special," the Key 73 mass media office sent out packages containing a 45 rpm record of radio spots, sample newspaper ads, a poster "for local promotion," fact sheets, a study guide, a catalog of materials for sale, and a comic book for kids, in which little Tommy tells playmate Ann: "Key 73 is coming. An' it's outasight."

Those who tuned into Key 73 on January 6 saw a semi-soft-sell half-hour documentary entitled "Faith in Action," depicting recently activated Christians from different walks of life —a Seattle judge, an American Indian, a black government executive, rock and roll artists, and a Jew for Jesus. There was a lot of Now Music, shots of people on beaches, and kids. It all carried the implication that these good vibes come from belief in Christ. This particular show was selected after Key 73 leaders decided against inviting President Nixon to appear ("lest there be political implications," says Raedeke).

The real test of Key 73, according to critic Gabriel Fackre, "is the McLuhan thesis: the medium is the message." Johnson/Nyquist Productions of California produced the Launch Special, and their "concept treatment" for the show conveys a message of slick, Madison Ave. marketing techniques, geared to sell the Christian message as if it were, say, a new vaginal deodorant.

A 30-minute format was chosen over 60 minutes, the producers say, because of "better placement during prime time, less chance of losing part of your audience because of channel-switching at half-hour slots . . . enough time to make an effective statement. . . ."

The "intended audience" is men and women 18 to 45, with "particular impact" on the 25 to 35 age bracket. "Our primary TARGET AUDIENCE can be described," according to the producers,

as those people who are trying to live a meaningful life in the midst of what often seems to be an urban-technological crossword puzzle. . . . They are worried about drugs and crime, war and racial problems, high taxes and overcrowded schools, lack of security. They feel caught in a materialistic value system. They have lost a sense of the supernatural. Many of them have a personal anguish over old beliefs that have collapsed. They sense that there must be a God, and they want some answers from, or about Him, that can have meaning within their own frustrated lives."

The "target audience" is "dubious of most conscious attempts to manipu-

late them." It is "indifferent toward the church but not hostile. . . . Our Target Audience is REACHABLE through television. . . ."

DO IT YOURSELF

Even before the airing of the Launch Special, Key 73 was geared up for a local organizing blitz. Piles of free "resource materials" were sent out to Key 73 participants. These include, for instance, the plan for "Operation Andrew," devised by the Missouri Synod (Michigan District). Each missionary carried a bunch of red cards bearing the Key 73 emblem, and having room for names of 10 souls won for Christ. There is also an "Assurance Survey" card with 40 questions, mainly statistical. "Should you find the family very receptive and anxious to visit," the card instructs, "you may flip this card and graciously continue the following expression of your faith." The first question then is: "Have you come to the place in your spiritual life where you know for certain that if you died today you would go to heaven?"

In addition to such free "resources," Key 73 also offers what might be called love for sale. These are general pamphlets, buttons and other paraphernalia for selling "the Lord's love." For cities under 50,000, there is a "small community planning packet" for $5.95, consisting of radio spots, glossies of the noon prayer and Key 73 logos, in one and two colors, six prayer call posters, table grace cards, bumper stickers, Prayer-a-Gram leaflets, etc. For big cities, there's more of the same for $34.50.

Beyond such grass-roots, door-to-door work, Key 73 planners push the need for exposure in local newspapers. Toward that end they prepared a 45-page booklet of canned "articles and news releases." The latter contain blank space for local date and places, and helpful hints like the following:

The above news article can be adapted for use at various times throughout Phase One. If the local newspaper does not use it in late November, rewrite it with emphasis on Section 2 (noon prayer activities) and resubmit it again. Likewise, an article might be appropriate for the Launch Weekend. Personalize the above material for your local situation.

But let there be no misunderstanding here. The press releases and "news stories" make it perfectly clear where Key 73 is coming from, and where it intends to take us as a nation. For example:

The cup of God's patience may finally be filled to the brim with rebellion, immorality, and disobedience of man. . . . If Christians will turn from apathy, indifference and the sin of self-satisfied pride, God will hear from heaven and "heal their land."

A huge portion of our continent has flagrantly repudiated the Word of God, choosing rather to feed on the impoverished ideas of humanism and relativism. . . .

The 40 million children in America without any formal church instruction, and the growing number of pagan adults are all subjects who need to be called to the word of God.

In addition, radio is recommended "to those interested in reaching large audiences, particularly teenagers and housewives." The book also tells how to make a good appearance on TV talk shows, by "occasionally looking from your host, straight into the camera. This brings you much nearer to your audiences because it gives the impression that you are including them in the conversation. . . ."

About press releases, the book warns,

Most times the editor will rewrite the release to suit himself. This is standard practice, and you should never feel miffed that he "tampered" with your prose. This rewritten material will tend to be of a more skeptical tone. This again is routine. . . . [In writing releases] stick to the things that the editor will accept as facts. This is called objectivity in the mass media. . . .

CHRISTIAN CRITICS

The message of this medium is clear: it is the message of corporate America. Run Jesus up the flagpole and see who salutes. It is a well-heeled, well-orchestrated campaign to sell Christ to the American people in hopes that He will fill the emptiness in their lives and provide them with a new sense of purpose. You are, as they say, as young as you feel. It is no backwoods, radical right, bible-thumping revival. In fact, the initiators of Key 73 have been far more solicitous of their liberal brethren than of the so-called separatists like Billy James Hargis and Bob Jones, Jr. As a result, they have succeeded in broadening their original, conservative base to include some liberal representation, notably the United Methodist Church and the American Baptist Convention.

The latter justify their participation in Key 73 by emphasizing different aspects of the overall theme, and urging local churches to "do their own thing." According to the Methodists, "Some churches will choose to distribute bibles, some will hold lay witness missions and revivals, and some will choose to witness through militant confrontation of the evils of society." Initially, the UMC suggests that local groups focus on "the particular issues that afflict the community."

The 1.3 million member American Baptist Convention is committed to social action under the Key 73 banner. In the words of Atha J. Bough, its representative on the Key 73 executive board, "The mission of the Church to-day is to live in the world in such a way as to be a constant deterrent to the misuse of our technology, our corporate strength, and as a constant witness against racism and war."

"Key 73," says Jitsuo Morikawa, the ABC's Key 73 director, "is the occasion to repeat the awful apostasy of the church whoring after . . . gods in the image of General Motors and Wall Street, Cape Canaveral and the Pentagon. . . ." In an interview, he added, "We feel our involvement with the various kinds of churches in Key 73 is a new and significant event. Previously, there was cooperation only with churches in the ecumenical movement. We think this large ecumenicity very significant."

Be that as it may, Morikawa's report to the ABC national staff council acknowledged Key 73's "low credibility, unimpressive credentials, lack in stature, with some marks here and there of the reappearance of 19th century revivalism, without its power and vitality." He also admitted, in the interview, some apprehension about the Key 73 leadership.

It is an apprehension he shares with the so-called Right opposition of separatists like Bob Jones, Jr., who runs Billy Graham's alma mater. Being in Key 73 with the liberals is like trucking with the Devil, Jones thinks. In a letter to *Christianity Today*, he wrote that Key 73 amounted to "compromise with infidelity, cultism, Roman Catholicism, and apostasy." What its promoters like to call the greatest evangelical "thrust" in history has, ironically, also failed to gain the endorsement of the National Association of Evangelicals.

More significant criticism has come from groups like the United Presbyterian Church of the U.S.A., whose Council of Evangelism found an

"autocratic style of decision-making" by the Key 73 executive committee "distressing and out of keeping with our tradition." It also expressed a "major concern" with Key 73's "use of all public media . . . at the national level . . . as representing American Protestantism." Finally, the Council said it was "gravely concerned over . . . a possibility of the national emphases of Key 73 equating the concerns and commitments of the Church with those of the state. . . ."

Summed up George Peters, chief executive of the Presbyterian Church's evangelism staff:

We thought there were just too many booby-traps in it. . . . The Key 73 people made the claim each denomination can do whatever it wants to do, but the emphases are on bible reading, prayer, study-groups—each fine in its own place, but it tends to be personalistic and pietistic instead of world-oriented. You withdraw from society: The end of the world is coming, everything is so bad that the only thing is for Jesus to come and end the whole thing. . . .

Along similar lines, the United Church of Christ Board of Home Missions (UCCBHM) refused to associate with Key 73. "An evangelism that calls our nation to repentance cannot ignore the monstrous problems of war, racial injustice, poverty or powerlessness, nor mute the word of judgment on forces that cause them," says the UCCBHM statement adopted last November. "Moreover, we are troubled by the eagerness of Key 73 to seek approval and support from the very powers that should be called to accountability."

To Gabriel Fackre, a theology professor at the Andover Newton School and a consultant to UCCBHM, Key 73 is a "real attempt to [carry off] a planned civil religion trip." Key 73, he says, began with a constituency basically conservative politically, upset by the visionary movement for social change and looking for ways to combat it. Subsequently, Key 73 became more broad-based, virtually accredited by the powers that be. . . . But the mainline responsible people in this are very leary. . . .

FLAG AND CROSS

In 19th century America, evangelists were in the forefront of movements for change. They preached the Social Gospel, and they practiced it. They ran social welfare agencies for new immigrant, also schools, industrial institutes, orphanages, employment bureaus. Their activity was heavily concentrated in the ghettos. But it was more than bandaid do-gooder stuff. Nineteenth century evangelism was also into political movements for the right to organize and strike, abolition of child labor, women's equality. In turn, populist politics borrowed heavily from religion (witness William Jennings Bryan's "Cross of Gold").

In what has since been tagged The Great Reversal, evangelists abandoned the Social Gospel in the early part of the 20th century. (Bryan, in a political version of this turnabout, wound up defending Prohibition, refusing to denounce the KKK, and participating in the Scopes monkey trial on behalf of the literal Bible.) Although Billy Graham and a few others now give lip service to the notion that "proclamation and demonstration" of the Gospel are inseparable—an important concept of 19th century evangelism—it is clear that they remain committed to the Great Reversal. They are in agreement with Key 73 founder Carl Henry, who wrote last September, "There are confused ecclesiastics who think evangelism is politics. . . . Those who rallied to Key 73 decided to keep the proclamation of the evangel at the center of the first nationwide effort. . . . There is but one way to blast open an obdurate social consciousness, and that is to permeate it with the Holy Spirit."

This political passivity, in the name of Christ, just happens to fit beautifully with Nixon's game plan. "The Protestant ethic has not produced a whole and humane society," says the United Church of Christ. But to Nixon, and the leaders of Key 73, there is no other way. There is only One Way.

On NBC's Today Show one morning, Nixon told Barbara Walters that the "fundamental cause" for the unrest and protest was not war, poverty or prejudice but "a sense of insecurity that comes from the old values being torn away." He attributed the ferment to the lessened influence of church and family. It was a page, again, from Billy Graham's remarks at the first inaugural that "a whirlwind of crime, division and rebellion" had resulted from America attempting to solve its problems without turning to God.

"If patriotism and piety are inseparable attitudes, as they seem to be for President Nixon," writes Charles P. Henderson, assistant chaplain at Princeton, "then religion can only be a bastion of establishment ideas."

"We can't have an 'established' religion in America. The Constitution explicitly forbids it," writes UPI religion reporter Louis Cassels. "But under President Nixon a certain type of evangelical Protestantism has gone about as far as it's possible to go toward achieving official establishment."

"I don't think everything in America is hopeless, as some people seem to believe," Billy Graham told White House worshippers in the spring of 1970. "Our moral and spiritual sickness can be cured. If we could have a revival of genuine faith in God and a return to moral principles, if we could say individually, 'The Lord is our shepherd,' I believe the American people could be brought together. I don't think there is any question that divides us that couldn't be vanquished in the heat of a great spiritual awakening, renewal and revival."

Four months later, Billy Graham was national co-chairman of Honor America Day.

In 1973, Protestant evangelism is still keeping the faith and Billy Graham is the President's minister now more than ever. Implored by liberal clergy to use his influence with Nixon and end the war sooner, Graham spoke for the new mod old-time religion, which is being cleverly packaged in Key 73. "While some interpret an evangelist to be primarily a social reformer or political activist, I do not," he said. "An evangelist is a proclaimer of the message of God's grace and love in Jesus Christ and the necessity of repentance and faith."

So, despite the cosmetics, the veneer of social concern and the ambiguous rhetoric of Key 73, the message is the same. Win one for the Big Gipper. It's The American Way.

"The streets of ashkelon"

HARRY HARRISON

Somewhere above, hidden by the eternal clouds of Wesker's World, a thunder rumbled and grew. Trader John Garth stopped when he heard it. . . .

"That noise is the same as the noise of your sky-ship," Itin said, with stolid Wesker logicality, slowly pulverizing the idea in his mind and turning over the bits one by one for closer examination. "But your ship is still sitting where you landed it. It must be, even though we cannot see it, because you are the only one who can operate it. And even if anyone else could operate it we would have heard it rising into the sky. Since we did not, and if this sound is a sky-ship sound, then it must mean . . ."

"Yes, another ship," Garth said, too absorbed in his own thoughts to wait for the laborious Weskerian chain of logic to clank their way through to the end. . . .

"You better go ahead, Itin," he said. "Use the water so you can get to the village quickly. Tell everyone to get back into the swamps, well clear of the hard ground. That ship is landing on instruments and anyone underneath at touchdown is going to be cooked."

This immediate threat was clear enough to the little Wesker amphibian. Before Garth finished speaking Itin's ribbed ears had folded like a bat's wing and he slipped silently into the nearby canal. Garth squelched on through the mud, making as good time as he could over the clinging surface. He had just reached the fringes of the village clearing when the rumbling grew to a head-splitting roar and the spacer broke through the low-hanging layer of clouds above. Garth shielded his eyes from the down-reaching tongue of flame and examined the growing form of the grey-black ship with mixed feelings.

After almost a standard year on Wesker's World he had to fight down a longing for human companionship of any kind. While this buried fragment of herd-spirit chattered for the rest of the monkey tribe, his trader's mind was busily drawing a line under a column of figures and adding up the total. This could very well be another trader's ship, and if it were his monopoly of the Wesker trade was at an end. Then again, this might not be a trader at all, which was the reason he stayed in the shelter of the giant fern and loosened his gun in its holster.

The ship baked dry a hundred square metres of mud, the roaring blast died, and the landing feet crunched down through the crackling crust. Metal creaked and settled into place while the cloud of smoke and steam slowly drifted lower in the humid air.

"Garth, where are you?" the ship's speaker boomed. The lines of the spacer had looked only slightly familiar, but there was no mistaking the rasping tones of that voice. Garth wore a smile when he stepped out into the open and whistled shrilly through two fingers. A directional microphone ground out of its casing on the ship's fin and turned in his direction.

"What are you doing here, Singh?" he shouted toward the mike. . . .

"I am on course to a more fairly atmosphered world where a fortune is waiting to be made. I only stopped here since an opportunity presented to turn an honest credit by running a taxi service. I bring you friendship, the perfect companionship, a man in a different line of business who might help you in yours. I'd come out and say hello myself, except I would have to decon for biologicals. I'm cycling the passenger through the lock so I hope you won't mind helping with his luggage."

At least there would be no other trader on the planet now, that worry was gone. But Garth still wondered what sort of passenger would be taking one-way passage to an uninhabited world. And what was behind that concealed hint of merriment in Singh's voice? He walked around to the far side of the spacer where the ramp had dropped, and looked up at the man in the cargo lock who was wrestling ineffectually with a large crate. The man turned towards him and Garth saw the clerical dog-collar and knew just what it was Singh had been chuckling about.

"What are you doing here?" Garth asked; in spite of his attempt at self control he snapped the words. If the man noticed this he ignored it, because he was still smiling and putting out his hand as he came down the ramp.

"Father Mark," he said. "Of the Missionary Society of Brothers. I'm very pleased to . . ."

"I said what are you doing here." Garth's voice was under control now, quiet and cold. He knew what had to be done, and it must be done quickly or not at all.

"That should be obvious," Father Mark said, his good nature still unruffled. "Our missionary society has raised funds to send spiritual emissaries to alien worlds for the first time. I was lucky enough . . ."

"Take your luggage and get back into the ship. You're not wanted here and have no permission to land. You'll be a liability and there is no one on Wesker to take care of you. Get back into the ship."

"I don't know who you are sir, or why you are lying to me," the priest said. He was still calm but the smile was gone. "But I have studied galactic law and the history of this planet very well. There are no diseases or beasts here that I should have any particular fear of. It is also an open planet, and until the Space Survey changes that status I have as much right to be here as you do."

The man was of course right, but Garth couldn't let him know that. He had been bluffing, hoping the priest didn't know his rights. But he did. There was only one distasteful course left for him, and he had better do it while there was still time.

"Get back in that ship," he shouted, not hiding his anger now. With a smooth motion his gun was out of the holster and the pitted black muzzle only inches from the priest's stomach. The man's face turned white, but he did not move.

"What the hell are you doing, Garth!" Singh's shocked voice grated from the speaker. "The guy paid his fare and you have no rights at all to throw him off the planet."

"I have this right," Garth said, raising his gun and sighting between the priest's eyes. "I give him thirty seconds to get back aboard the ship or I pull the trigger."

"Well I think you are either off your head or playing a joke," Singh's exasperated voice rasped down at them. "If a joke it is in bad taste, and either way you're not getting away with it. Two can play at that game, only I can play it better."

There was the rumble of heavy bearings and the remote-controlled four-gun turret on the ship's side rotated and pointed at Garth. "Now—down gun and give Father Mark a hand with the luggage," the speaker commanded, a trace of humour back in the voice now. "As much as I would like to help, Old Friend, I cannot. I feel it is time you had a chance to talk to the father; after all, I have had the opportunity of speaking with him all the way from Earth."

Garth jammed the gun back into the holster with an acute feeling of loss. Father Mark stepped forward, the winning smile back now and a bible taken from a pocket of his robe, in his raised hand. "My son," he said.

"I'm not your son," was all Garth could choke out as defeat welled up in him. His fist drew back as the anger rose, and the best he could do was open the fist so he struck only with the flat of his hand. Still the blow sent the priest crashing to the ground and fluttered the pages of the book splattering into the thick mud.

Itin and the other Weskers had watched everything with seemingly emotionless interest, and Garth made no attempt to answer their unspoken questions. He started towards his house, but turned back when he saw they were still unmoving.

"A new man has come," he told them. "He will need help with the things he has brought. If he doesn't have any place for them, you can put them in the big warehouse until he has a place of his own."

He watched them waddle across the clearing towards the ship, then went inside and gained a certain satisfaction from slamming the door hard enough to crack one of the panes. There was an equal amount of painful pleasure in breaking out one of the remaining bottles of Irish whiskey that he had been saving for a special occasion. Well this was special enough, though

not really what he had had in mind. The whiskey was good and burned away some of the bad taste in his mouth, but not all of it. If his tactics had worked, success would have justified everything. But he had failed and in addition to the pain of failure there was the acute feeling that he had made a horse's ass out of himself. Singh had blasted off without any good-byes. There was no telling what sense he had made of the whole matter, though he would surely carry some strange stories back to the trader's lodge. Well, that could be worried about the next time Garth signed in. Right now he had to go about setting things right with the missionary. Squinting out through the rain he saw the man struggling to erect a collapsible tent while the *entire* population of the village stood in ordered ranks and watched. Naturally none of them offered to help.

By the time the tent was up and the crates and boxes stowed inside it the rain had stopped. The level of fluid in the bottle was a good bit lower and Garth felt more like facing up to the unavoidable meeting. In truth, he was looking forward to talking to the man. This whole nasty business aside, after an entire solitary year any human companionship looked good. *Will you join me now for dinner. John Garth*, he wrote on the back of an old invoice. But maybe the guy was too frightened to come? Which was no way to start any kind of relationship. Rummaging under the bunk, he found a box that was big enough and put his pistol inside. Itin was of course waiting outside the door when he opened it, since this was his tour as Knowledge Collector. He handed him the note and the box.

"Would you take these to the new man," he said.

"Is the new man's name New Man?" Itin asked.

"No, it's not!" Garth snapped. "His name is Mark. But I'm only asking you to deliver this, not get involved in conversation."

As always when he lost his temper, the literal minded Weskers won the round. "You are not asking for conversation," Itin said slowly, "but Mark may ask for conversation. And others will ask me his name, if I do not know his na . . ." The voice cut off as Garth slammed the door. This didn't work in the long run either because next time he saw Itin—a day, a week, or even a month later—the monologue would be picked up on the very word it had ended and the thought rambled out to its last frayed end. Garth cursed under his breath and poured water over a pair of the tastier concentrates that he had left.

"Come in," he said when there was a quiet knock on the door. The priest entered and held out the box with the gun.

"Thank you for the loan, Mr. Garth, I appreciate the spirit that made you send it. I have no idea of what caused the unhappy affair when I landed, but I think it would be best forgotten if we are going to be on this planet together for any length of time."

"Drink?" Garth asked, taking the box and pointing to the bottle on the table. He poured two glasses full and handed one to the priest. "That's about what I had in mind, but I still owe you an explanation of what happened out there." He scowled into his glass for a second, then raised it to the other man. "It's a big universe and I guess we have to make out as best we can. Here's to Sanity."

"God be with you," Father Mark said, and raised his glass as well.

"Not with me or with this planet," Garth said firmly. "And that's the crux of the matter." He half-drained the glass and sighed.

"Do you say that to shock me?" the priest asked with a smile. "I assure you it doesn't."

"Not intended to shock. I meant it quite literally. I suppose I'm what you would call an atheist, so revealed religion is no concern of mine. While these natives, simple and unlettered stone-age types that they are, have managed to come this far with no superstitions or traces of deism whatsoever. I had hoped that they might continue that way."

"What are you saying?" the priest frowned. "Do you mean they have no gods, no belief in the hereafter? They must die. . . ?"

"Die they do, and to dust returneth like the rest of the animals. They have thunder, trees and water without having thunder-gods, tree sprites, or water nymphs. They have no ugly little gods, taboos, or spells to hag-ride and limit their lives. They are the only primitive people I have ever encountered that are completely free of superstition and appear to be much happier and sane because of it. I just wanted to keep them that way."

"You wanted to keep them from God—from salvation?" The priest's eyes widened and he recoiled slightly.

"No," Garth said. "I wanted to keep them from superstition until they knew more and could think about it realistically without being absorbed and perhaps destroyed by it."

"You're being insulting to the Church, sir, to equate it with superstition . . ."

"Please," Garth said, raising his hand. "No theological arguments. I don't think your society footed the bill for this trip just to attempt a conversion on me. Just accept the fact that my beliefs have been arrived at through careful thought over a period of years, and no amount of undergraduate metaphysics will change them. I'll promise not to try and convert you—if you will do the same for me."

"Agreed, Mr. Garth. As you have reminded me, my mission here is to save these souls, and that is what I must do. But why should my work disturb you so much that you try and keep me from landing? Even threaten me with your gun and . . ." the priest broke off and looked into his glass.

"And even slug you?" Garth asked, suddenly frowning. "There was no excuse for that, and I would like to say that I'm sorry. Plain bad manners and an even worse temper. Live alone long enough and you find yourself doing that kind of thing." He brooded down at his big hands where they lay on the table, reading memories into the scars and callouses patterned there. "Let's just call it frustration, for lack of a better word. In your business you must have had a lot of chance to peep into the darker places in men's minds and you should know a bit about motives and happiness. I have had too busy a life to ever consider settling down and raising a family, and right up until recently I never missed it. Maybe leakage radiation is softening up my brain, but I had begun to think of these furry and fishy Weskers as being a little like my own children, that I was somehow responsible to them."

"We are all His children," Father Mark said quietly.

"Well, here are some of His children that can't even imagine His existence," Garth said, suddenly angry at himself for allowing gentler emotions to show through. Yet he forgot himself at once, leaning forward with the intensity of his feelings. "Can't you realize the importance of this? Live with these Weskers awhile and you will discover a simple and happy life that matches the state of grace you people are always talking about. They

get *pleasure* from their lives—and cause no one pain. By circumstances they have evolved on an almost barren world, so have never had a chance to grow out of a physical stone age culture. But mentally they are our match —or perhaps better. They have all learned my language so I can easily explain the many things they want to know. Knowledge and the gaining of knowledge gives them real satisfaction. They tend to be exasperating at times because every new fact must be related to the structure of all other things, but the more they learn the faster this process becomes. Someday they are going to be man's equal in every way, perhaps surpass us. If— would you do me a favour?"

"Whatever I can."

"Leave them alone. Or teach them if you must—history and science, philosophy, law, anything that will help them face the realities of the greater universe they never even knew existed before. But don't confuse them with your hatreds and pain, guilt, sin, and punishment. Who knows the harm . . ."

"You are being insulting, sir!" the priest said, jumping to his feet. The top of his grey head barely came to the massive spaceman's chin, yet he showed no fear in defending what he believed. Garth, standing now himself, was no longer the penitent. They faced each other in anger, as men have always stood, unbending in the defence of that which they think right.

"Yours is the insult," Garth shouted. "The incredible egotism to feel that your derivative little mythology, differing only slightly from the thousands of others that still burden men, can do anything but confuse their still fresh minds! Don't you realize that they believe in truth—and have never heard of such a thing as a lie. They have not been trained yet to understand that other kinds of minds can think differently from theirs. Will you spare them this. . . ?"

"I will do my duty which is His will; Mr. Garth. These are God's creatures here, and they have souls. I cannot shirk my duty, which is to bring them His word, so that they may be saved and enter into the kingdom of heaven."

When the priest opened the door the wind caught it and blew it wide. He vanished into the stormswept darkness and the door swung back and forth and a platter of raindrops blew in. Garth's boots left muddy footprints when he closed the door, shutting out the sight of Itin sitting patiently and uncomplaining in the storm, hoping only that Garth might stop for a moment and leave with him some of the wonderful knowledge of which he had so much.

By unspoken consent that first night was never mentioned again. After a few days of loneliness, made worse because each knew of the other's proximity, they found themselves talking on carefully neutral grounds. Garth slowly packed and stowed away his stock and never admitted that his work was finished and he could leave at any time. He had a fair amount of interesting drugs and botanicals that would fetch a good price. And the Wesker Artifacts were sure to create a sensation in the sophisticated galactic market. Crafts on the planet here had been limited before his arrival, mostly pieces of carving painfully chipped into the hard wood with fragments of stone. He had supplied tools and a stock of raw metal from his own supplies, nothing more than that. In a few months the Weskers had not only learned to work with the new materials, but had translated their own designs and forms into the most alien— but most beautiful—artifacts that he had ever seen. All he had to do was release these on the market to create

a primary demand, then return for a new supply. The Weskers wanted only books and tools and knowledge in return, and through their own efforts he knew they would pull themselves into the galactic union.

This is what Garth had hoped. But a wind of change was blowing through the settlement that had grown up around his ship. No longer was he the centre of attention and focal point of the village life. He had to grin when he thought of his fall from power; yet there was very little humour in the smile. Serious and attentive Weskers still took turns of duty as Knowledge Collectors, but their recording of dry facts was in sharp contrast to the intellectual hurricane that surrounded the priest.

Where Garth had made them work for each book and machine, the priest gave freely. Garth had tried to be progressive in his supply of knowledge, treating them as bright but unlettered children. He had wanted them to walk before they could run, to master one step before going on the next.

Father Mark simply brought them the benefits of Christianity. The only physical work he required was the construction of a church, a place of worship and learning. More Weskers had appeared out of the limitless planetary swamps and within days the roof was up, supported on a framework of poles. Each morning the congregation worked a little while on the walls, then hurried inside to learn the all-promising, all-encompassing, all-important facts about the universe.

Garth never told the Weskers what he thought about their new interest, and this was mainly because they never asked him. Pride or honour stood in the way of his grabbing a willing listener and pouring out his grievances. Perhaps it would have been different if Itin was on Collecting duty; he was the brightest of the lot; but Itin had been rotated the day after the priest had arrived and Garth had not talked to him since.

It was a surprise then when after seventeen of the trebly-long Wesker days, he found a delegation at his doorstep when he emerged after breakfast. Itin was their spokesman, and his mouth was open slightly. Many of the other Weskers had their mouths open as well, one even appearing to be yawning, clearly revealing the double row of sharp teeth and the purple-black throat. The mouths impressed Garth as to the seriousness of the meeting: this was the one Wesker expression he had learned to recognize. An open mouth indicated some strong emotion; happiness, sadness, anger, he could never be really sure which. The Weskers were normally placid and he had never seen enough open mouths to tell what was causing them. But he was surrounded by them now.

"Will you help us, John Garth," Itin said. "We have a question."

"I'll answer any question you ask," Garth said, with more than a hint of misgiving. "What is it?"

"Is there a God?"

"What do you mean by 'God'?" Garth asked in turn. What should he tell them?

"God is our Father in Heaven, who made us all and protects us. Whom we pray to for aid, and if we are saved will find a place . . ."

"That's enough," Garth said. "There is no God."

All of them had their mouths open now, even Itin, as they looked at Garth and thought about his answer. The rows of pink teeth would have been frightening if he hadn't known these creatures so well. For one instant he wondered if perhaps they had been already indoctrinated and looked upon

him as a heretic, but he brushed the thought away.

"Thank you," Itin said, and they turned and left.

Though the morning was still cool, Garth noticed that he was sweating and wondered why.

The reaction was not long in coming. Itin returned that same afternoon. "Will you come to the church?" he asked. "Many of the things that we study are difficult to learn, but none as difficult as this. We need your help because we must hear you and Father talk together. This is because he says one thing is true and you say another is true and both cannot be true at the same time. We must find out what is true."

"I'll come, of course," Garth said, trying to hide the sudden feeling of elation. He had done nothing, but the Weskers had come to him anyway. There could still be grounds for hope that they might yet be free.

It was hot inside the church, and Garth was surprised at the number of Weskers who were there, more than he had seen gathered at any one time before. There were many open mouths. Father Mark sat at a table covered with books. He looked unhappy but didn't say anything when Garth came in. Garth spoke first.

"I hope you realize this is their idea—that they came to me of their own free will and asked me to come here?"

"I know that," the priest said resignedly. "At times they can be very difficult. But they are learning and want to believe, and that is what is important."

"Father Mark, Trader Garth, we need your help," Itin said. "You both know many things that we do not know. You must help us come to religion which is not an easy thing to do." Garth started to say something, then changed his mind. Itin went on. "We have read the bibles and all the books that Father Mark gave us, and one thing is clear. We have discussed this and we are all agreed. These books are very different from the ones that Trader Garth gave us. In Trader Garth's books there is the universe which we have not seen, and it goes on without God, for he is mentioned nowhere; we have searched very carefully. In Father Mark's books He is everywhere and nothing can go without Him. One of these must be right and the other must be wrong. We do not know how this can be, but after we find out which is right then perhaps we will know. If God does not exist . . ."

"Of course He exists, my children," Father Mark said in a voice of heartfelt intensity. "He is our Father in Heaven who has created us all . . ."

"Who created God?" Itin asked and the murmur ceased and everyone of the Weskers watched Father Mark intensely. He recoiled a bit under the impact of their eyes, then smiled.

"Nothing created God, since He is the Creator. He always was . . ."

"If He always was in existence—why cannot the universe have always been in existence? Without having had a creator?" Itin broke in with a rush of words. The importance of the question was obvious. The priest answered slowly, with infinite patience.

"Would that the answers were that simple, my children. But even the scientists do not agree about the creation of the universe. While they doubt —we who have seen the light *know*. We can see the miracle of creation all about us. And how can there be a creation without a Creator? That is He, our Father, our God in Heaven. I know you have doubts; that is be-

cause you have souls and free will. Still, the answer is so simple. Have faith, that is all you need. Just believe."

"How can we believe without proof?"

"If you cannot see that this world itself is proof of His existence, then I say to you that belief needs no proof —if you have faith!"

A babble of voices arose in the room and more of the Wesker mouths were open now as they tried to force their thoughts through the tangled skein of words and separate the thread of truth.

"Can you tell us, Garth?" Itin asked, and the sound of his voice quieted the hubbub.

"I can tell you to use the scientific method which can examine all things —including itself—and give you answers that can prove the truth or falsity of any statement."

"That is what we must do," Itin said, "we had reached the same conclusion." He held a thick book before him and a ripple of nods ran across the watchers. "We have been studying the bible as Father Mark told us to do, and we have found the answer. God will make a miracle for us, thereby proving that He is watching us. And by this sign we will know Him and go to Him."

"That is the sin of false pride," Father Mark said. "God needs no miracles to prove His existence."

"But *we* need a miracle!" Itin shouted, and though he wasn't human there was need in his voice. "We have read here of many smaller miracles, loaves, fishes, wine, snakes—many of them, for much smaller reasons. Now all He need do is make a miracle and He will bring us all to Him—the wonder of an entire new world worshipping at His throne as you have told us,

Father Mark. And you have told us how important this is. We have discussed this and find that there is only one miracle that is best for this kind of thing."

His boredom at the theological wrangling drained from Garth in an instant. He had not been really thinking or he would have realized where all this was leading. He could see the illustration in the bible where Itin held it open, and knew in advance what picture it was. He rose slowly from his chair, as if stretching, and turned to the priest behind him.

"Get ready!" he whispered. "Get out the back and get to the ship; I'll keep them busy here. I don't think they'll harm me."

"What do you mean. . . ?" Father Mark asked, blinking in surprise.

"Get out, you fool!" Garth hissed. "What miracle do you think they mean? What miracle is supposed to have converted the world to Christianity?"

"No!" Father Mark said. "It cannot be. It just cannot be. . . !"

"GET MOVING!" Garth shouted, dragging the priest from the chair and hurling him towards the rear wall. Father Mark stumbled to a halt, turned back. Garth leaped for him, but it was already too late. The amphibians were small, but there were so many of them. Garth lashed out and his fist struck Itin, hurling him back into the crowd. The others came on as he fought his way towards the priest. He beat at them but it was like struggling against waves. The furry, musky bodies washed over and engulfed him. He fought until they tied him, and he still struggled until they beat on his head until he stopped. Then they pulled him outside where he could lie in the rain and curse and watch.

Of course the Weskers were marvellous craftsmen, and everything had been constructed down to the last detail, following the illustration in the bible. There was the cross, planted firmly on the top of a small hill, the gleaming metal spikes, the hammer. Father Mark was stripped and draped in a carefully pleated loincloth. They led him out of the church.

At the sight of the cross he almost fainted. After that he held his head high and determined to die as he had lived, with faith.

Yet this was hard. It was unbearable even for Garth, who only watched. It is one thing to talk of crucifixion and look at the gentle carved bodies in the dim light of prayer. It is another to see a man naked, ropes cutting into his skin where he hangs from a bar of wood. And to see the needle-tipped spike raised and placed against the soft flesh of his palm, to see the hammer come back with the calm deliberation of an artisan's measured stroke. To hear the thick sound of metal penetrating flesh.

Then to hear the screams.

Few are born to be martyrs; Father Mark was not one of them. With the first blows, the blood ran from his lips where his clenched teeth met. Then his mouth was wide and his head strained back and the guttural horror of his screams sliced through the susurration of the falling rain. It resounded as a silent echo from the masses of watching Weskers, for whatever emotion opened their mouths was now tearing at their bodies with all its force, and row after row of gaping jaws reflected the crucified priest's agony.

Mercifully he fainted as the last nail was driven home. Blood ran from the raw wounds, mixing with the rain to drip faintly pink from his feet as the life ran out of him. At this time, somewhere at this time, sobbing and tearing at his own bonds, numbed from the blows on the head, Garth lost consciousness.

He awoke in his own warehouse and it was dark. Someone was cutting away the woven ropes they had bound him with. The rain still dripped and splashed outside.

"Itin," he said. It could be no one else.

"Yes," the alien voice whispered back. "The others are all talking in the church. Lin died after you struck his head, and Inon is very sick. There are some that say you should be crucified too, and I think that is what will happen. Or perhaps killed by stoning on the head. They have found in the bible where it says . . ."

"I know." With infinite weariness. "An eye for an eye. You'll find lots of things like that once you start looking. It's a wonderful book." His head ached terribly.

"You must go, you can get to your ship without anyone seeing you. There has been enough killing." Itin as well, spoke with a new-found weariness.

Garth experimented, pulling himself to his feet. He pressed his head to the rough wood of the wall until the nausea stopped. "He's dead." He said it as a statement, not a question.

"Yes, some time ago. Or I could not have come away to see you."

"And buried of course, or they wouldn't be thinking about starting on me next."

"And buried!" There was almost a ring of emotion in the alien's voice, an echo of the dead priest's. "He is buried and he will rise on High. It is written and that is the way it will happen. Father Mark will be so happy that it has happened like this." The voice ended in a sound like a human sob.

Garth painfully worked his way towards the door, leaning against the wall so he wouldn't fall.

"We did the right thing, didn't we?" Itin asked. There was no answer. "He will rise up, Garth, won't he rise?"

Garth was at the door and enough light came from the brightly lit church to show his torn and bloody hands clutching at the frame. Itin's face swam into sight close to his, and Garth felt the delicate, many fingered hands with the sharp nails catch at his clothes.

"He will rise, won't he, Garth?"

"No," Garth said, "he is going to stay buried right where you put him. Nothing is going to happen because he is dead and he is going to stay dead."

The rain runnelled through Itin's fur and his mouth was opened so wide that he seemed to be screaming into the night. Only with effort could he talk, squeezing out the alien thoughts in an alien language.

"Then we will not be saved? We will not become pure?"

"You were pure," Garth said; in a voice somewhere between a sob and a laugh. "That's the horrible ugly dirty part of it. You were pure. Now you are . . ."

"Murderers," Itin said, and the water ran down from his lowered head and streamed away into the darkness.

Index

75 76   9 8 7 6 5 4 3 2 1